A RHETORIC OF MOTIVES

OTHER BOOKS BY
KENNETH BURKE

Counter-Statement	1931
Revised Edition	1953
Revised Paperback Edition	1968
Towards a Better Life, A Series of Epistles, or Declamations	1932
Revised Edition	1966
Permanence and Change, An Anatomy of Purpose	1935
Revised Edition	1954
Paperback Edition	1965
Attitudes Toward History	1937
Revised Edition	1959
Paperback Edition	1961
Philosophy of Literary Form: Studies in Symbolic Action	1941
Paperback Edition (Abridged)	1957
Revised Edition	1967
A Grammar of Motives	1945
Paperback Edition	1962
A Rhetoric of Motives	1950
Paperback Edition	1962
Book of Moments, Poems 1915-1954	1955
The Rhetoric of Religion: Studies in Logology	1961
Language as Symbolic Action: Essays on Life, Literature, and Method	1966
Collected Poems, 1915-1967	1968
The Complete White Oxen: Collected Short Fiction	
First Version	1924
Augmented Version	1968
Perspectives by Incongruity,	
Edited by S. E. Hyman and B. Karmiller	1965
Terms for Order,	
Edited by S. E. Hyman and B. Karmiller	1965

A RHETORIC OF MOTIVES

by

KENNETH BURKE

UNIVERSITY OF CALIFORNIA PRESS
Berkeley and Los Angeles   1969

University of California Press
Berkeley and Los Angeles, California
University of California Press, Ltd.
London, England
Copyright 1950 by Prentice-Hall, Inc.
First paperback edition copyright © 1962 by The World Publishing Company

California edition © Kenneth Burke, 1969
Library of Congress Catalog Card Number: 69-16742
Manufactured in the United States of America

TO W. C. BLUM

ACKNOWLEDGMENTS

Portions of *A Grammar of Motives* have previously been published in *Accent, Chimera, The Kenyon Review, The Sewanee Review,* and *View.* And I wish to acknowledge here my indebtedness to the editors of these magazines. I also wish to state my indebtedness to various publishers, editors, and authors for permission to quote from certain copyrighted material; thus: International Publishers, V. I. Lenin's *What Is To Be Done?;* The Macmillan Company, Marianne Moore's *Selected Poems* and *What Are Years?,* and Herbert Read's *Poetry and Anarchism;* The University of Chicago Press, George Herbert Mead's *The Philosophy of the Act* and Otto Neurath's *Foundations of the Social Sciences;* Little, Brown and Company, Ralph Barton Perry's *The Thought and Character of William James;* the University of California Press, Josephine Miles's *Pathetic Fallacy in the Nineteenth Century;* Harcourt, Brace and Company, Inc., I. A. Richards' *Principles of Literary Criticism* and Matthew Josephson's *Jean-Jacques Rousseau;* Peter Smith, Publisher, *Baldwin's Dictionary of Philosophy and Psychology;* the Houghton Mifflin Company, *The Education of Henry Adams,* by Henry Adams; Randon House, Inc., Eugene O'Neill's *Mourning Becomes Electra;* Mr. Yvor Winters, *Primitivism and Decadence,* published by Arrow Editions; Mr. Allen Tate, *Reason in Madness,* published by G. P. Putnam's Sons; Mr. Edgar Johnson, *One Mighty Torrent: The Drama of Biography,* published by Stackpole Sons; *The New Republic,* Stark Young's review of Clifford Odets' *Night Music; Partisan Review,* the essay by John Dewey that appeared in the "Failure of Nerve" controversy; *Science & Society,* an article by Lewis S. Feuer on "logical empiricism" and one by K. Ostrovitianov on principles of the Russian economy; *View,* for permission to quote from Parker Tyler; *The New York Times* and Mr. Arthur Krock, for permission to quote a column by Mr. Krock entitled: "Is There a Way to Dispense with Elections?"; *The Virginia Quarterly Review* and M. Denis de Rougemont, for permission to quote from his essay, "The Idea of a Federation," appearing in the Autumn 1941 issue; *The University Review* and the authors, for permission to quote from a series of essays on the theory and practice of literary criticism by R. S. Crane, Norman Maclean, and Elder Olson.

The opening pages of *A Rhetoric of Motives* were previously published in *The Hudson Review,* and some remarks on science and magic are taken from my review of Ernst Cassirer's *The Myth of the State* that appeared in *The Nation*. Otherwise, to my recollection, no portions of the work have been previously published.

I wish to thank the members of my classes at Bennington College, who with charming patience participated in the working-out of the ideas here presented.

And I wish to thank Dr. J. Robert Oppenheimer for the opportunity to spend some very helpful months at the Institute for Advanced Study in Princeton, while making a final revision of the manuscript. Also, during this time, I was fortunate in being able to discuss many of these theories and analyses at the Princeton Seminars in Literary Criticism, then in process of formation.

I regret that I did not have an opportunity to incorporate additions suggested by a six-month sojourn at the University of Chicago where, under the auspices of the College, I presented some of this material.

Many authors of the past and present have contributed to the notions herein considered, in this project for "carving out a rhetoric," often from materials not generally thought to fall under the head. And I wish to make special acknowledgment for permission to quote from the following works still in copyright: Harcourt, Brace and Company, Inc., *Collected Poems* and *Four Quartets* by T. S. Eliot, and *The Meaning of Meaning* by C. K. Ogden and I. A. Richards; Charles Scribner's Sons, George Santayana's *Realms of Being*, and *The Prefaces of Henry James*, edited by Richard Blackmur; Dr. Clyde Kluckhohn, Director of the Russian Research Center, Harvard University, for permission to quote from his pamphlet, *Navaho Witchcraft*; Harvard University Press, the *Loeb Classical Library* translation (by H. Rackham) of Cicero's *De Oratore*; Princeton University Press, Walter Lowrie's translation of Kierkegaard's *Fear and Trembling*; The University of Chicago Press, Austin Warren's *Rage for Order; Modern Philology*, Richard McKeon's essay, "Poetry and Philosophy in the Twelfth Century," which appeared in the May 1946 issue. And to The Mediaeval Academy of America for permission to quote from an essay by the same author, "Rhetoric in the Middle Ages," published in the January 1942 issue of *Speculum*; Longmans, Green and Co., *The Varieties of Religious Experience*, by William James; Schocken Books, Inc., Franz Kafka's *The Castle*, copyright 1946, and Max Brod's *Kafka: A Biography*, copyright 1947; the Oxford University Press, a poem by Gerard Manley Hopkins; The Viking Press, Thorstein Veblen's *The Theory of the Leisure Class*; The Macmillan Company, W. B. Yeats' "Byzantium" in *Winding Stair*, copyright 1933.

K. B.

CONTENTS

I. THE RANGE OF RHETORIC

The "Use" of Milton's Samson	3
Qualifying the Suicidal Motive	5
Self-Immolation in Matthew Arnold	7
Quality of Arnold's Imagery	9
The Imaging of Transformation	10
Dramatic and Philosophic Terms for Essence	13
"Tragic" Terms for Personality Types	15
Recapitulation	16
Imagery at Face Value	17
Identification	19
Identification and "Consubstantiality"	20
The Identifying Nature of Property	23
Identification and the "Autonomous"	27
The "Autonomy" of Science	29
"Redemption" in Post-Christian Science	31
Dual Possibilities of Science	32
Ingenuous and Cunning Identifications	35
Rhetoric of "Address" (to the Individual Soul)	37
Rhetoric and Primitive Magic	40
Realistic Function of Rhetoric	43

II. TRADITIONAL PRINCIPLES OF RHETORIC

Persuasion	49
Identification	55
Other Variants of the Rhetorical Motive	59
Formal Appeal	65
Rhetorical Form in the Large	69

Imagination	78
Image and Idea	84
Rhetorical Analysis in Bentham	90
Marx on "Mystification"	101
Terministic Reservations (in View of Cromwell's Motives)	110
Carlyle on "Mystery"	114
Empson on "Pastoral" Identification	123
The "Invidious" as Imitation, in Veblen	127
Priority of the "Idea"	132
A Metaphorical View of Hierarchy	137
Diderot on "Pantomime"	142
Generic, Specific, and Individual Motives in Rochefoucauld	145
De Gourmont on Dissociation	149
Pascal on "Directing the Intention"	154
"Administrative" Rhetoric in Machiavelli	158
Dante's De Vulgari Eloquentia	167
Rhetoric in the Middle Ages	169
"Infancy," Mystery, and Persuasion	174

III. ORDER

Positive, Dialectical, and Ultimate Terms	183
Ultimate Elements in the Marxist Persuasion	189
"Sociology of Knowledge" vs. Platonic "Myth"	197
"Mythic" Ground and "Context of Situation"	203
Courtship	208
"Socioanagogic" Interpretation of Venus and Adonis	212
The Paradigm of Courtship: Castiglione	221
The Caricature of Courtship: Kafka (The Castle)	233
A "Dialectical Lyric" (Kierkegaard's Fear and Trembling)	244
The Kill and the Absurd	252
Order, the Secret, and the Kill	260
Pure Persuasion	267
Rhetorical Radiance of the "Divine"	294

CONTENTS

1. HENRY JAMES ON THE DEITY OF "THINGS" 294
2. "SOCIAL RATING" OF IMAGES IN JAMES 296
3. RHETORICAL NAMES FOR GOD 298
4. THE "RANGE OF MOUNTINGS" 301
5. ELATION AND ACCIDIE IN HOPKINS 313
6. YEATS: "BYZANTIUM" AND THE LAST POEMS 316
7. ELIOT: EARLY POEMS AND *"Quartets"* 318
8. PRINCIPLE OF THE OXYMORON 324
9. ULTIMATE IDENTIFICATION 328

INTRODUCTION

THE ONLY difficult portion of this book happens, unfortunately, to be at the start. There, selecting texts that are usually treated as pure poetry, we try to show why rhetorical and dialectical considerations are also called for. Since these texts involve an imagery of killing (as a typical text for today should) we note how, behind the surface, lies a quite different realm that has little to do with such motives. An imagery of killing is but one of many terminologies by which writers can represent the process of change. And while recognizing the sinister implications of a preference for homicidal and suicidal terms, we indicate that the principles of development or transformation ("rebirth") which they stand for are not strictly of such a nature at all.

We emerge from the analysis with the key term, "Identification." Hence, readers who would prefer to begin with it, rather than to worry a text until it is gradually extricated, might go lightly through the opening pages, with the intention of not taking hold in earnest until they come to the general topic of *Identification,* on page 19.

Thereafter, with this term as instrument, we seek to mark off the areas of rhetoric, by showing how a rhetorical motive is often present where it is not usually recognized, or thought to belong. In part, we would but rediscover rhetorical elements that had become obscured when rhetoric as a term fell into disuse, and other specialized disciplines such as esthetics, anthropology, psychoanalysis, and sociology came to the fore (so that esthetics sought to outlaw rhetoric, while the other sciences we have mentioned took over, each in its own terms, the rich rhetorical elements that esthetics would ban).

But besides this job of reclamation, we also seek to develop our subject beyond the traditional bounds of rhetoric. There is an intermediate area of expression that is not wholly deliberate, yet not wholly unconscious. It lies midway between aimless utterance and speech directly purposive. For instance, a man who identifies his private ambitions with the good of the community may be partly justified, partly unjustified. He may be using a mere pretext to gain individual advantage at the public expense; yet he may be quite sincere, or even may willingly make sacrifices in behalf of such identification. Here is a rhetorical area not analyzable either as sheer design or as sheer simplicity. And we would treat of it here.

Traditionally, the key term for rhetoric is not "identification," but "persuasion." Hence, to make sure that we do not maneuver ourselves unnecessarily into a weak position, we review several classic texts which track down all the major implications of that term. Our treatment, in terms of identification, is decidedly not meant as a substitute for the sound traditional approach. Rather, as we try to show, it is but an accessory to the standard lore. And our book aims to make itself at home in both emphases.

Particularly when we come upon such aspects of persuasion as are found in "mystification," courtship, and the "magic" of class relationships, the reader will see why the classical notion of clear persuasive intent is not an accurate fit, for describing the ways in which the members of a group promote social cohesion by acting rhetorically upon themselves and one another. As W. C. Blum has stated the case deftly, "In identification lies the source of dedications and enslavements, in fact of cooperation."

All told, persuasion ranges from the bluntest quest of advantage, as in sales promotion or propaganda, through courtship, social etiquette, education, and the sermon, to a "pure" form that delights in the process of appeal for itself alone, without ulterior purpose. And identification ranges from the politician who, addressing an audience of farmers, says, "I was a farm boy myself," through the mysteries of social status, to the mystic's devout identification with the source of all being.

That the reader might find it gratifying to observe the many variations on our two interrelated themes, at every step we have sought to proceed by examples. Since we did not aim to write a compendium, we have not tried to cover the field in the way that a comprehensive historical survey might do—and another volume will be needed to deal adequately with the polemic kinds of rhetoric (such as the verbal tactics now called "cold war").

But we have tried to show what portions of other works should be selected as parts of a "course in rhetoric," and how they should be considered for our particular purposes. We have tried to show how rhetorical analysis throws light on literary texts and human relations generally. And while interested always in rhetorical devices, we have sought above all else to write a "philosophy of rhetoric."

We do not flatter ourselves that any one book can contribute much to counteract the torrents of ill will into which so many of our contemporaries have so avidly and sanctimoniously plunged. But the more strident our journalists, politicians, and alas! even many of our churchmen become, the more convinced we are that books should be written for tolerance and contemplation.

Part I
THE RANGE OF RHETORIC

I
THE RANGE OF RHETORIC

The "Use" of Milton's Samson

An OLD POET, libertarian and regicide, blind, fallen on evil days, in sullen warlike verse celebrates Samson. On its face, his poem tells of Samson among the Philistines. A prisoner chained "eyeless in Gaza ... blind among enemies" because he could not keep "the secret of his strength" ... himself his "sepulchre" ... himself his own "dungeon" ... his sightlessness in captivity a "prison within prison" ... enraged with himself for having
>   divulged
> The secret gift of God to a deceitful
> Woman,

for having given up his "fort of silence to a woman," he hugely laments his "corporal servitude." He talks of patience, and mouths threats of revenge in the name of God. And finally, when brought to the pagan temple, standing between "those two massy pillars, That to the arched roof gave main support, by his own hands," in "self-violence" ("O lastly over-strong against thyself! ... Among thy slain self-killed ..."), he sufferingly acts:

> As with the force of winds and waters pent
> When mountains tremble, those two massy pillars
> With horrible convulsion to and fro
> He tugged, he shook, till down they came, and drew
> The whole roof after them with burst of thunder
> Upon the heads of all who sat beneath,
> Lords, ladies, captains, counsellors, or priests,
> Their choice nobility and flower, not only
> Of this, but each Philistian city round,
> Met from all parts to solemnize this feast.
> Samson, with these immixed, inevitably
> Pulled down the same destruction on himself;
> The vulgar only scaped, who stood without.

And at this act, or sufferance, a notable transformation has taken place. We learn that the enemy, "drunk with adolatry, drunk with wine," had been led by the wrath of Samson's God to bring on "their own destruction." For they were "with blindness internal struck." But Samson had been "with inward eyes illuminated." They are the sightless, he is the seer, and

> ... as an eagle
> His cloudless thunder bolted on their heads.

The vanquished enemy, by comparison, were but "tame villatic fowl."

More than twenty years before, in the *Areopagitica* ("A Speech for the Liberty of Unlicensed Printing, to the parliament of England"), his great verbal monument that gives dignity, resonance, and ultimate grounding to the doctrine of the free press, a related reference to the eagle appeared:

> Methinks I see in my mind's eye a noble and puissant nation rousing herself like a strong man after sleep, and shaking her invincible locks. Methinks I see her as an eagle mewing her mighty youth, and kindling her undazzled eyes at the full midday beam; purging and unscaling her long-abused sight at the fountain itself of heavenly radiance; while the whole noise of timorous and flocking birds, with those also that love the twilight, flutter about, amazed at what she means, and in their envious gabble would prognosticate a year of sects and schisms.

The prose reference is clearly rhetorical. It occurs in a work written with a definite audience in mind, and for a definite purpose. It was literature for *use*. Today, it would be called "propaganda."

But what of the poem? One can read it simply *in itself,* without even considering the fact that it was written by Milton. It can be studied and appreciated as a structure of internally related parts, without concern for the correspondence that almost inevitably suggests itself: the correspondence between Milton's blindness and Samson's, or between the poet's difficulties with his first wife and Delilah's betrayal of a divine "secret."

Besides this individual identification of the author with an aggressive, self-destructive hero who was in turn identified with God, there is also factional identification. Samson has said:

> All the contest is now
> 'Twixt God and Dagon. Dagon hath presumed,
> Me overthrown, to enter lists with God,
> His deity comparing and preferring
> Before the God of Abraham.

And this exalting of the issue, in terms of rival divinities at war, is allusive: the Philistines and Dagon implicitly standing for the Royalists, "drunk with wine," who have regained power in England, while the Israelites stand for the Puritan faction of Cromwell. The poem's righteous ferocity is no mere evidence of a virtuoso's craftsmanship; it is not sheer poetic exercise, as with a versatile playwright able to imagine whatever kind of role the exigencies of plot happened to require.

Rather, it is almost a kind of witchcraft, a wonder-working spell by a cantankerous old fighter-priest who would slay the enemy in effigy, and whose very translation of political controversy to high theologic terms helps, by such magnification, to sanction the ill-tempered obstinacy of his resistance. In saying, with fervor, that a blind Biblical hero *did* conquer, the poet is "substantially" saying that he in his blindness *will* conquer. This is moralistic prophecy, and is thus also a kind of "literature for use," use at one remove, though of a sort that the technologically-minded would consider the very opposite of use, since it is wholly in the order of ritual and magic.

Qualifying the Suicidal Motive

Note another result here: The recurring stress upon the *reflexive* nature of Samson's act (the element of self-destruction in his way of slaying the enemy) can be a roundabout device for sanctioning suicide; yet Milton's religion strongly forbade suicide. Compelled by his misfortunes to live with his rage, gnawed by resentments that he could no longer release fully in outward contest, Milton found in Samson a figure ambivalently fit to symbolize both aggressive and inturning trends. Here too, though still more remotely, would be "literature for use": the poetic reënactment of Samson's role could give pretexts for admitting a motive which, if not so clothed or complicated, if confronted in its simplicity, would have been inadmissible. By dramatic subterfuge Milton could include what he would have had to exclude, if reduced to a conceptually analytic statement.

The dramatic terms provide a rich context that greatly modifies whatever modicum of suicide may be present in the motivational formula as a whole. But all such important modifications, or qualifications, are dropped when we reduce the complexity to one essential strand, slant, or "gist," isolating this one reflexive element as the implicitly dominant motive, an all-pervasive generating principle. And these qualifications which the reduction would omit are strategic enough to make the motivations quite different from an out-and-out featuring of suicide as cause, in a poem stressing the theme directly, efficiently, without the modifiers of Milton's context. By comparison with such a poem, Milton's meaning would not be a recipe for suicide at all, having but a mere dash, or soupçon, of such an ingredient.

We do not mean to suggest that the figure of Samson in Milton's poem is to be interpreted purely as a "rationalization," in the psychoanalytic sense. We are taking the poem at its face value. If two statements, for instance, one humorous and the other humorless, are found to contain the same animus against someone, we are not thereby justified in treating them as the same in their motivational core. For the humorless statement may *foretell* homicide, and the humorous one may be the very thing that *forestalls* homicide. Thus *surrounded,* or modified by the total motivational context, the animus in one case may be as different from the other as yes from no. Indeed, the humorous motivation could lead to intentional homicide only insofar as it were reduced, with the qualifications of humor dropped from it. It could not, as *humor,* lead to this result, however "homicidal" might be the imagery in which it was expressed. For this imagery, *so long as it was humorous,* would contain a dimension which essentially qualified the animus. The imagery could "foretell" homicide only in the sense that it contained an ingredient which, if efficiently abstracted from its humorous modifiers, would in its new purity be homicidal. And such abstracting can take place, of course, whenever conditions place too much of a strain upon the capacity for humor.

Similarly, a motive introduced in one work, where the context greatly modifies it and keeps it from being drastically itself, may lack such important modifications in the context of another work. The *proportions* of these modifications themselves are essential in defining the total motivation, which cannot, without misinterpretation, be reduced merely to the one "gist," with all the rest viewed as mere concealment or "rationalization" of it. And in this sense, we would take the motivation of Milton's poem at face value, considering the aggressive and theocratic terms just as significant in the total recipe as the reflexive terms are. Whether there are gods or not, there is an *objective* difference in motivation between an act conceived in the name of God and an act conceived in the name of godless Nature.

Self-Immolation in Matthew Arnold

Contrast the imagery of self-immolation in Matthew Arnold's "Empedocles on Etna," for instance. Thinking of himself "as an orphan among prosperous boys"; complaining that "we feel, day and night,/ The burden of ourselves"; introspective ("Sink in thyself!"); renouncing ("thou hast no *right* to bliss,/No title from the gods to welfare and repose"); nonaggressively nostalgic ("Receive me, hide me, quench me, take me home!"); weary of both solitude and multitude ("thou fencest him from the multitude . . . Who will fence him from himself?"); yearning to descend "Down in our mother earth's miraculous womb . . ." Empedocles sees promise of freedom as he "plunges into the center," a self-immolation that unites him idealistically with mountain, sea, stars, and air, while the volcano, into which he had hurled himself, is also by legend the prison of a buried titan, a "self-helping son of earth" who had been "oppress'd" by the "well-counsell'd Zeus."

When matched with so clear an imagery of suicide, one could make out a good case for denying that Milton's identification with the "self-slain" Samson has any ingredient of suicide at all. Yet how do things look if we insert another step here? Though Arnold came to distrust his poem of Empedocles, and even suppressed its publication, much the same motives are discernible in his narrative of "Sohrab and Rustum," where the two warriors fight in single combat without knowing that they are father and son, and the son receives his death wound when paralyzed at the sound of his father's name, thus:

> When Rustum raised his head; his dreadful eyes
> Glared, and he shook on high his menacing spear,
> And shouted: *Rustum!*—Sohrab heard that shout,
> And shrank amazed; back he recoil'd one step,
> And scann'd with blinking eyes the advancing form;
> And then he stood bewilder'd; and he dropp'd
> His covering shield, and the spear pierced his side.
> He reel'd, and staggering back, sank to the ground,
> And then the gloom dispersed, and the wind fell,
> And the bright sun broke forth, and melted all
> The cloud; and the two armies saw the pair—
> Saw Rustum standing, safe upon his feet,
> And Sohrab, wounded, on the bloody sand.

Following the recognition, and the son's death, there is even the same cosmically unifying end as with Empedocles' self-immolating plunge into the crater. But here the action is transferred from the personae to sympathetic nature (from agents to similarly motivated scene, itself a new and transcendent order of action). As "Rustum and his son were left alone" by the river marge, "the majestic river floated on," a solemn course, charted by the poem through many lines,

> till at last
> The long'd for dash of waves is heard, and wide
> His luminous home of waters opens, bright
> And tranquil, from whose floor the new-bathed stars
> Emerge, and shine upon the Aral Sea.

Here, the son having been killed by the father, through the progress of the river to the sea he plunges by proxy into the universal home. And graced by the son's sacrifice, the armies are at peace.

Our knowledge of Matthew Arnold's relation to his father suggests an extra-literary "use" for the imagery of self-effacement in both these poems. Despite their many differences, both are acts of the same poetic agent, sharing the common substance of the one authorship. And both can be seen as aspects of the same attitude towards life. Indeed, when we put them together, we note this possibility: that Arnold could poetically identify himself with the figure of Empedocles because his pious deference to the authority of his father could be aptly expressed in such imagery of self-effacement as goes with Empedocles' cosmically motivated despair. And this self-abnegatory attitude, being in the same motivational cluster with his attitude towards his father, could find still more accurate expression in the imagery of a son "unconsciously" killed by his father, and *in the name of* his father.

Seen from this point of view, the "gist" of "Sohrab and Rustum" would be as "suicidal" as "Empedocles on Etna," where this theme is *explicitly* there. It would be "implicit" in "Sohrab and Rustum" because, for all the imagery of war surrounding the combat between father and son, it all "adds up" or "boils down" to a son's fatal admiration for his father. The poet, in both cases, imagines that the figure with whom he identifies himself is *being killed;* and in both cases the destruction terminates in imagery of a homecoming, a return to sources probably maternal.

Quality of Arnold's Imagery

Just what are we getting at here? We have tried to see how matters look if we put a transitional step between "Empedocles on Etna" and *Samson Agonistes*. Since Samson is self-killed in a warlike act that kills the enemy, we tried to match him against two figures by a later poet in the same "curve of history." The first figure (Empedocles) is killed by suicide; the second (Sohrab) is killed by war. But by putting Empedocles and Sohrab together, as variants of one attitude in the one poetic agent who had identified himself with both figures, we tried to establish the common character of both a suicide and a warlike death. Then, looking back at the poem by Milton, we find there, united in one poem, what Arnold has divided between two poems: the suicide and the warlike death are united in the same image.

See what our problem is. We seem to be going two ways at once. In some respects, we are trying to bring these poems together as instances of the *same* motivation; yet in other respects we are insisting that the unique context in which this motive appears in each poem makes the motive itself *different* in all three cases. Can we keep our line of thinking clear here for the reader? Milton's theocratic rage, for instance, is "warlike" in a much different way from the combats in "Sohrab and Rustum." Modifying this warrior, whose death was caused by the sound of his father's name, there are some significantly unwarlike images. Thus when Rustum, gazing in desolation at the wounded Sohrab,

> saw that Youth,
> Of age and looks to be his own dear son,
> Piteous and lovely, lying on the sand,
> Like some rich hyacinth which by the scythe
> Of an unskilful gardener has been cut,
> Mowing the garden grass-plots near its bed,
> And lies, a fragrant tower of purple bloom,
> On the mown, dying grass—so Sohrab lay,
> Lovely in death, upon the common sand.

And when Sohrab finally draws the spear, to ease "His wound's imperious anguish,"

> all down his cold, white side
> The crimson torrent ran, dim now and soil'd,
> Like the soil'd tissue of white violets

> Left, freshly gather'd, on the native bank,
> By children whom their nurses call with haste
> Indoors from the sun's eye ...

Such unwarlike modifiers radically modify the motive of war here, quite as the motive of self-destruction which we saw clearly stated in "Empedocles on Etna" is modified by the dramatic irony whereby the son is sacrificed in the name of the father. And as contrasted with the righteous fury of Milton, we see how Arnold's attitudes were more closely akin, rather, to the *next* step in the curve of literary history; we see how they led into the estheticism of Pater, and thence to father-problems as transformed perversely in the estheticism of Oscar Wilde.

The Imaging of Transformation

By adding one more confusion, we may add the element that can bring clarity. This time, from the same "curve of history," from Coleridge's "Religious Musings":

> ... in His vast family no Cain
> Injures uninjured (in her best-aimed blow
> Victorious Murder a blind Suicide).

This statement suggests a point at which murder and suicide can become convertible, each in its way an image for the same motive. The quotation is not quite analogous to the three other poems, since it is from a *doctrinal* poem (one of what Coleridge called his Conversation Pieces, *"sermoni propriora"*). But although it lacks the dramatic modifiers that complicate the motivation in the other poems, it avoids overefficient reduction to "gist," at least in the sense that it is dialectical, ironically making motives interchangeable which might usually be considered mutually exclusive. Indeed, the terms being equivalent, we might just as well read them backwards: "blind Suicide a Victorious Murder." Then we might think either of a poem which symbolized suicide by imagery of murder, or one which symbolized murder by imagery of suicide. And when you get to that point, you need one more step to complete your thinking: You need to look for a *motive that can serve as ground for both these choices,* a motive that, while not being exactly either one or the other, can ambiguously contain them both.

A term serving as ground for both these terms would, by the same token, "transcend" them. The battlefield, for instance, which permits rival contestants to join in battle, itself "transcends" their factionalism, being "superior" to it and "neutral" to their motives, though the conditions of the terrain may happen to favor one faction. The *principles* of war are not themselves warlike, and are ultimately reducible to universal principles of physics and dialectic. Similarly, a poet's identification with imagery of murder or suicide, either one or the other, is, from the "neutral" point of view, merely a concern with *terms for transformation in general.*

When we consider the resources of dialectic so broadly, of course, we necessarily disregard the animus of any particular image. This would be a very wrong thing to do, when some specific set of transformations is to be analyzed. But when considering transformation in general, we may stress the respects in which many different kinds of image can perform the same function. One may prefer imagery of the Upward Way and Downward Way, or of the Crossing and Return, or of Exile and Homecoming, or of a Winding-up and an Unwinding, or of Egressus and Regressus, or of a Movement Inward and a Movement Outward, or of seasonal developments, or of various antitheses, like Day and Night, Warmth and Frigidity, Yes and No, Losing and Finding, Loosing and Binding, etc., where the pairs are not merely to be placed statically against each other, but in given poetic contexts usually represent a development *from* one order of motives *to* another. Such terms, here selected at random, suggest different families of images in terms of which the processes of transformation in general might be localized, or particularized.

The Education of Henry Adams, for instance, exemplifies ritual transformation by a shift from personal images to impersonal ones. The student of life "in search of a father" (that is, looking for self-identification with a new motivating principle) would abandon his eighteenth-century identity as a member of the Adams family and adapt himself to the conditions of modern history, as he interprets them. Thus the ritual transformation is also, in its way, a kind of self-immolation. But instead of hurling himself, like Arnold's Empedocles, into the volcano as matrix, Adams contrives a methodic surrender to the sweep of history, which in turn is identified with impersonal force (his transformation by identification with it thus being a rite of depersonalization). That is, Adams' "law of the acceleration of history," considered from the symbolic point of view, is nothing other than the *imaging of a fall,* expressed roundabout in doctrinal or "educational" terms. Within the limitations imposed by the nature of the book, the final proclaiming of this "law," in strict analogy with the accelerated motion of falling bodies, in its way expresses but the same leap into the cosmic abyss that Matthew Arnold expresses through the suicide of Empedocles.

The range of images that can be used for concretizing the process of transformation is limited only by the imagination and ingenuity of poets. But the selective nature of existence favors some images above others—and high among them, naturally, is the imagery of Life and Death, with its variants of being born, being reborn, dying, killing, and being killed. Consider, now, the hypothetical case of a poet who would identify himself with some particular imagery of transformation selected from this order of terms, terms using the imagery of Life and Death. We can easily conceive of a poet who, wanting to symbolize the transformation of some evil trait within himself, writes a poem accordingly; and in this poem he might identify himself with a figure who, marked by this trait, takes his own life, thereby ritualistically transforming the trait. (That is, if the figure in the fiction possessed some outstanding vice, and slew himself as an act of judgment against this vice, such imagery of suicide could be a ritualistic means whereby the poet sought to purge his own self of this vice, or purified the vice by identifying it with the dignity of death.) Or another might symbolize this same transformation by imaginatively endowing some "outward enemy" with the trait, and then imaginatively slaying that enemy. Or a third poet might identify himself with a figure who possessed that trait, and then might imagine an enemy who slew his poetic counterpart. The trait, whatever its stylistic transformation (magnification, purification, martyrdom, etc.), may not even be "slain" by an "alien" principle at all, so far as the original poet was concerned; the contest may most likely symbolize the pitting of one motivational principle against another where *both* principles are strongly characteristic of the poet personally. (Think, for instance, of the "murderous" relation between the critical and poetic "selves" of T. S. Eliot, as symbolized in his *Murder in the Cathedral,* and previously discussed in our *Attitudes Toward History.*) Similarly, if a principle were located in the figure of mother, father, child, tyrant, or king, and were ritually transformed under these guises, we should have respectively: matricide, patricide, infanticide, tyrannicide, or regicide. The Nazis, locating the *transformandum* in the whole Jewish people as their chosen vessel, gave us a "scientific" variant: genocide. And the frequent psychoanalytic search for "unconscious" desires to kill some member of the family, either through rivalry or through love frustrated and expressed in reverse, puts the emphasis at the wrong place. For the so-called "desire to kill" a certain person is much more properly analyzable as a desire to *transform the principle* which that person *represents*.

Dramatic and Philosophic Terms for Essence

Since imagery built about the active, reflexive, and passive forms of death (killing, self-killing, and being killed) so obviously contributes to dramatic intensity, and since thoughts of death are so basic to human motivation, we usually look no farther to account for their use. But there is also an ultimate "Grammatical" incentive behind such imagery, since a history's *end* is a formal way of proclaiming its *essence* or *nature,* as with those who distinguish between a tragedy and a comedy by the outcome alone and who would transform "tragedy" into "comedy" merely by changing the last few moments of the last act.

Elsewhere (notably on "the temporizing of essence," *Grammar of Motives,* New York: Prentice-Hall, 1945, pp. 430-440) we have discussed the puns of logical and temporal priority whereby the *logical* idea of a thing's essence can be translated into a temporal or narrative equivalent by statement in terms of the thing's source or beginnings (as feudal thinking characterized a person's individual identity in terms that identified him with his family, the paradoxical ultimate of such definition being perhaps the use of "bastard" as epithet to describe a man's *character*). But if there is this ultimate of *beginnings,* whereby theological or metaphysical systems may state the essence of mankind in terms of a divine parenthood or an originating natural ground, there is also an ultimate of *endings,* whereby the essence of a thing can be defined narratively in terms of its *fulfillment* or *fruition*. Thus, you state a man's timeless essence in temporal terms if, instead of calling him "by nature a criminal," you say, "he will end on the gallows."

Metaphysically, this formal principle gets its best-rounded expression in the Aristotelian *entelechy,* which classifies a thing by conceiving of its kind according to the perfection (that is, finishedness) of which that kind is capable. Man is a "rational animal," for instance, not in the sense that he is immune to irrational motives, but in the sense that the perfection of humankind is in the order of rationality (an order or finishedness which one would not apply to things incapable of Logos, the Word).

Such thinking was probably itself a translation of narrative terms into "timeless" ones (as the Homeric ways of essentializing in terms of act and image eventually became transformed into the high generalizations of philosophy). But once we have a mature set of such abstract fixities (which are "fixities" in the sense that the "laws" or "principles" of motion do not themselves move, if they are stated abstractly enough), we can turn the matter around; and thus, whereas the philosophic expressions were later translations of the earlier narrative ones, we may look upon narrative expressions as translations of philosophic ones. By such heuristic reversal, we note how the imagery of death could be a narrative equivalent of the Aristotelian entelechy. For the poet could define the essence of a motive narratively or dramatically (in terms of a *history*) by showing how that motive *ended:* the maturity or fulfillment of a motive, its "perfection" or "finishedness," if translated into the terms of tragic outcome, would entail the identifying of that motive with a narrative figure whose acts led to some fitting form of *death.* By its fruition, we should judge it. In this respect, the Christian injunction to lead the "dying life" is itself a formula that translates the Aristotelian entelechy into its tragic equivalent; for in both the speculative and the tragic expressions, there is the same underlying Grammatical principle, the defining of an essence in terms of the *end* (the *perfection* being by the same token *death,* quite as the attaining of a given end marks the death of such efforts as went with the attaining of that end). The relations among our words "define," "determine," "termination," suggest the same ambiguities and possibilities of conversion. Taking a hint from the English translation of Richard Strauss's tone poem, *Death and Transfiguration,* we might say that the tragic dignifying of a motive is got by identifying it with death *as* transfiguration.

In sum: When considering "the temporizing of essence" in the *Grammar,* we were both put on the trail and misled somewhat by the suggestions in the word "prior." Following its leads, we saw how the search for "logical" priority can, when translated into temporal, or narrative terms, be expressed in the imagery of "regression to childhood," or in other imagery or ideas of things past. This concern with the statement of essence in terms of *origins* (ancestry) caused us to overlook the exactly opposite resource, the statement of essence in terms of *culminations* (where the narrative notion of "how it all ends up" does serve for the logically reductive notion of "what it all boils down to"). In either choice (the ancestral or the final) the narrative terminology provides for a *personalizing* of essence. Along similar lines we may note that the imagery of adult illness (*e.g.* Mann's use of the tuberculosis sanitarium in *Tristan* and *The Magic Mountain*) may serve particularly well as a narrative terminology of essence in that it combines both "regressive" and "culminative" principles of identification. For the adult patients, in being constantly nursed and cared for, are in a condition that harks back to the "priority" of childhood, and at the same time they are tragically under the culminative sign of death.

"Tragic" Terms for Personality Types

So universally felt is the Grammatical principle behind the defining of essence in terms of death, or tragic end, that in our pseudoscientific days, when the cult of questionnaires has developed its own peculiar unction, perhaps one might come closer to an accurate classifying of "personality types" if he worked out a system of "tragic" categories. Surely, for instance, the person who chooses to end his life by violence thereby distinguishes himself from those late Romans who preferred cutting their veins and bleeding to death in a warm bath. And the end of Milton's Samson differs from the end of Arnold's Empedocles quite as Milton differs from Arnold.

But perhaps to get the most generalized approach to such classification, while still keeping it in the *narrative* terminology of definition, our hypothetical neotragic categorist should greatly broaden the question of human endings. He should hire a batch of poets; and instead of putting them to work, as is usually the case now, on the avid imagining of reasons why our citizenry should intensely yearn for all sorts of manufactured and "processed" things (a narrow but unending succession of ends) he should commission them to fully realize, for the average middle-class audience, all the different ways in which, it is thought, the world itself might end. Surely, it would not take much to distinguish between the character of a person who foresaw a world ending "not with a bang but a whimper," and one who feared some mighty holocaust, as were the planets ripped into smithereens by explosions from within. Or contrast the medieval imagery of the mighty burning with many modern scientists' pale preference for the "heat death," according to the principle of inturning, or entropy, whereby the earlier potency of matter must finally dwindle into a universal, uniform impotence. Those who thought of a lethal gas that, wandering through space, stealthily enveloped the earth would be quite different from those obsessed by thoughts of huge astral collisions, or from those who worried lest our sun suddenly burst forth as a Nova, so intense in its new activity that even Neptune and Pluto would be scorched. People would here spontaneously classify themselves; for by reason of the "scene-agent ratio"[1] the individual can identify himself with the character of a surrounding situation, translating one into terms of the other; hence a shift to a grander order, the shift from thoughts of one's own individual end to thoughts of a universal end, would still contrive to portray the character of the individual, even while acquiring greater resonance and scope and enabling men to transcend too local a view of themselves.

Perhaps our plans here are too ambitious. We can at least claim, as remote members of our "neotragic" school of ethnic classification, certain modern biologists who propose to classify plant species according to differences in response to various kinds of mutilation (though such science perhaps has a trace of that purely *sadistic* motive which usually obscures our understanding of tragedy itself today).

Recapitulation

First, we noted Milton's identification with Samson, who was identified with God. Then we noted the identification of Royalists with Philistines and Puritans with Israelites. Next we noted the poet's opportunity to conquer ritualistically by writing a poem that used these identifications, whereas actually Milton as citizen was frustrate.

[1] See *A Grammar of Motives* (New York: Prentice-Hall, 1945), notably pages 7-9.

Next, while recognizing that the reflexive nature of Samson's act amounted to suicide, we noted how the dramatic identification of this motive contains other important strands. Such thoughts led us to consider the *proportions* of a motivational recipe: one cannot simply reduce the totality to the suicidal "gist" and feel that one has done justice to the motivation as a whole. The point was made clearer by contrasting *Samson Agonistes* with the imagery of self-immolation in Matthew Arnold. We noted modalities of holy war in Milton, as contrasted with modalities near to Pater and Wilde in Arnold.

Then, by quoting lines from Coleridge that make murder and suicide interchangeable, we went beyond imagery, to the subject of transformation in general. Thus we gave a list of other paired images, that might serve as well as Life and Death for localizing or dramatizing the principle of transformation. And we noted that killing, being killed, and the killing of the self might all localize the same principle of transformation.

However, there was one respect in which the imagery of killing was especially apt here. The depicting of a thing's *end* may be a dramatic way of identifying its *essence*. This Grammatical "Thanatopsis" would be a narrative equivalent of the identification in terms of a thing's "finishedness" we find in the Aristotelian "entelechy."

Then, in an aside, as an illustrative conceit, we proposed a project whereby personality types be defined in terms of the world's end, depending upon the type of such "eschatological" imagery with which a given person most readily identified himself.

All told, we would take care of two contrary purposes here. We would find ways of transcending the imagery of killing that pervades our opening anecdote. At the same time, we do not want to ignore the import of the imagery in its own right, first as needed for characterizing a given motivational recipe, and second for its rhetorical effect upon an audience.

Imagery at Face Value

Taken simply at its face value, imagery invites us to respond in accordance with its nature. Thus, an adolescent, eager to "grow up," is trained by our motion pictures to meditate much on the imagery of brutality and murder, as the most noteworthy signs of action in an ideal or imaginary adult world. By the time he is fifteen, he has "witnessed" more violence than most soldiers or gunmen experience in a lifetime. And he has "participated in" all this imagery, "empathically reënacting" it. Thus initiated, he might well think of "growing up" (that is, of "transformation") in such excessive terms. His awareness of himself as a developing person requires a vocabulary—and the images of brutality and violence provide such a vocabulary, with a simple recipe for the perfecting or empowering of the self by the punishing and slaying of troublesome motives as though they were wholly external. One can surely expect such imagery to have sinister effects, particularly in view of the fact that the excessive *naturalism* of modern photographic art presents the violence, as nearly as possible, without formal devices that bring out the purely *artistic* or *fictive* nature of such art. There is no difference, in photographic style, between the filming of a murder mystery and the filming of a "documentary." Nor should we forget the possible bad effect of the many devices whereby such brutality is made "virtuous," through dramatic pretexts that justify it in terms of retaliation and righteous indignation.

Our objections arise when certain kinds of speculation (often of psychoanalytic cast) unwittingly exemplify these same sinister trends. By itself stressing the primacy of vengeance and slaughter as motives (and looking upon friendly or ethical motives purely as a kind of benign fiction for harnessing these more nearly "essential" impulses), such thought is really more like the *forerunner* of modern militarism than its *critic*. And often the analysts will show such zeal, in behalf of "killing" as the essential motive, that they will seek many ingenious ways of showing that a work was motivated by the desire to slay some parental figure who suffered no such fate at all, in the imagery of the plot as interpreted on its face. They apparently assume that to show "unconscious" parricidal implications in a motive is by the same token to establish parricide as *the* motive. Where a play is explicitly about parricide, one might feel some justification in complaining if we would see behind it merely the choice of a parental symbol to represent some motivation not intrinsically parricidal at all, but using parental identifications as "imagined accidents" that personify it. But whatever may be the objections in such cases, they would not apply at all in cases where there is no explicit imagery of parricide, and one must by exegesis hunt out parricide as motive. Why, one may then ask, must an imagery of parricide be taken as essential, as primary, as the true designation of the ultimate motive? And we, of course, would similarly ask: why must *any* imagery of killing, even when explicit, be taken as ultimate, rather than as an "opportunistic" terminology for specifying or localizing a principle of motivation "prior" to *any imagery,* either scenic or personal?

That is, we can recognize that our anecdote is in the order of killing, of personal enmity, of factional strife, of invective, polemic, eristic, logomachy, all of them aspects of rhetoric that we are repeatedly and drastically encountering, since rhetoric is *par excellence* the region of the Scramble, of insult and injury, bickering, squabbling, malice and the lie, cloaked malice and the subsidized lie. Yet while admitting that the genius of our opening anecdote has malign inclinations, we can, without forcing, find benign elements there too. And we should find these; for rhetoric also includes resources of appeal ranging from sacrificial, evangelical love, through the kinds of persuasion figuring in sexual love, to sheer "neutral" *communication* (communication being the area where love has become so generalized, desexualized, "technologized," that only close critical or philosophic scrutiny can discern the vestiges of the original motive).

Identification

We considered, among those "uses" to which *Samson Agonistes* was put, the poet's identification with a blind giant who slew himself in slaying enemies of the Lord; and we saw identification between Puritans and Israelites, Royalists and Philistines, identification allowing for a ritualistic kind of historiography in which the poet could, by allusion to a Biblical story, "substantially" foretell the triumph of his vanquished faction. Then we came upon a more complicated kind of identification: here the poet presents a motive in an essentially magnified or perfected form, in some way tragically purified or transcended; the imagery of death reduces the motive to *ultimate* terms, dramatic equivalent for an "entelechial" pattern of thought whereby a thing's nature would be classed according to the fruition, maturing, or ideal fulfillment, proper to its kind.

As seen from this point of view, then, an imagery of slaying (slaying of either the self or another) is to be considered merely as a special case of identification in general. Or otherwise put: the imagery of slaying is a special case of transformation, and transformation involves the ideas and imagery of *identification*. That is: the *killing* of something is the *changing* of it, and the statement of the thing's nature before and after the change is an *identifying* of it.

Perhaps the quickest way to make clear what we are doing here is to show what difference it makes. Noting that tragic poets identify motives in terms of killing, one might deduce that "they are essentially killers." Or one might deduce that "they are essentially identifiers." Terms for identification in general are wider in scope than terms for killing. We are proposing that our rhetoric be reduced to this term of wider scope, with the term of narrower scope being treated as a species of it. We begin with an anecdote of killing, because invective, eristic, polemic, and logomachy are so pronounced an aspect of rhetoric. But we use a dialectical device (the shift to a higher level of generalization) that enables us to transcend the narrower implications of this imagery, even while keeping them clearly in view. We need never deny the presence of strife, enmity, faction as a characteristic motive of rhetorical expression. We need not close our eyes to their almost tyrannous ubiquity in human relations; we can be on the alert always to see how such temptations to strife are implicit in the institutions that condition human relationships; yet we can at the same time always look beyond this order, to the principle of identification in general, a teministic choice justified by the fact that the identifications in the order of love are also characteristic of rhetorical expression. We may as well be frank about it, since our frankness, if it doesn't convince, will at least serve another important purpose of this work: it will reveal a strategic resource of terminology. Being frank, then: Because of our choice, we can treat "war" as a *"special case of peace"* —not as a primary motive in itself, not as *essentially* real, but purely as a *derivative* condition, a *perversion*.

Identification and "Consubstantiality"

A is not identical with his colleague, B. But insofar as their interests are joined, A is *identified* with B. Or he may *identify himself* with B even when their interests are not joined, if he assumes that they are, or is persuaded to believe so.

Here are ambiguities of substance. In being identified with B, A is "substantially one" with a person other than himself. Yet at the same time he remains unique, an individual locus of motives. Thus he is both joined and separate, at once a distinct substance and consubstantial with another.

While consubstantial with its parents, with the "firsts" from which it is derived, the offspring is nonetheless apart from them. In this sense, there is nothing abstruse in the statement that the offspring both is and is not one with its parentage. Similarly, two persons may be identified in terms of some principle they share in common, an "identification" that does not deny their distinctness.

To identify A with B is to make A "consubstantial" with B. Accordingly, since our *Grammar of Motives* was constructed about "substance" as key term, the related rhetoric selects its nearest equivalent in the areas of persuasion and dissuasion, communication and polemic. And our third volume, *Symbolic of Motives,* should be built about *identity* as titular or ancestral term, the "first" to which all other terms could be reduced and from which they could then be derived or generated, as from a common spirit. The thing's *identity* would here be its uniqueness as an entity in itself and by itself, a demarcated unit having its own particular structure.

However, "substance" is an abstruse philosophic term, beset by a long history of quandaries and puzzlements. It names so paradoxical a function in men's systematic terminologies, that thinkers finally tried to abolish it altogether—and in recent years they have often persuaded themselves that they really did abolish it from their terminologies of motives. They abolished the *term,* but it is doubtful whether they can ever abolish the *function* of that term, or even whether they should *want* to. A doctrine of *consubstantiality,* either explicit or implicit, may be necessary to any way of life. For substance, in the old philosophies, was an *act;* and a way of life is an *acting-together;* and in acting together, men have common sensations, concepts, images, ideas, attitudes that make them *consubstantial*.

The *Grammar* dealt with the universal paradoxes of substance. It considered resources of placement and definition common to all thought. The *Symbolic* should deal with unique individuals, each its own peculiarly constructed act, or form. These unique "constitutions" being capable of treatment in isolation, the *Symbolic* should consider them primarily in their capacity as singulars, each a separate universe of discourse (though there are also respects in which they are consubstantial with others of their kind, since they can be classed with other unique individuals as joint participants in common principles, possessors of the same or similar properties).

The *Rhetoric* deals with the possibilities of classification in its *partisan* aspects; it considers the ways in which individuals are at odds with one another, or become identified with groups more or less at odds with one another.

Why "at odds," you may ask, when the titular term is "identification"? Because, to begin with "identification" is, by the same token, though roundabout, to confront the implications of *division*. And so, in the end, men are brought to that most tragically ironic of all divisions, or conflicts, wherein millions of cooperative acts go into the preparation for one single destructive act. We refer to that ultimate *disease* of cooperation: *war*. (You will understand war much better if you think of it, not simply as strife come to a head, but rather as a disease, or perversion of communion. Modern war characteristically requires a myriad of constructive acts for each destructive one; before each culminating blast there must be a vast network of interlocking operations, directed communally.)

Identification is affirmed with earnestness precisely because there is division. Identification is compensatory to division. If men were not apart from one another, there would be no need for the rhetorician to proclaim their unity. If men were wholly and truly of one substance, absolute communication would be of man's very essence. It would not be an ideal, as it now is, partly embodied in material conditions and partly frustrated by these same conditions; rather, it would be as natural, spontaneous, and total as with those ideal prototypes of communication, the theologian's angels, or "messengers."

The *Grammar* was at peace insofar as it contemplated the paradoxes common to all men, the universal resources of verbal placement. The *Symbolic* should be at peace, in that the individual substances, or entities, or constituted acts are there considered in their uniqueness, hence outside the realm of conflict. For individual universes, as such, do not compete. Each merely *is,* being its own self-sufficient realm of discourse. And the *Symbolic* thus considers each thing as a set of interrelated terms all conspiring to round out their identity as participants in a common substance of meaning. An individual does in actuality compete with other individuals. But within the rules of Symbolic, the individual is treated merely as a self-subsistent unit proclaiming its peculiar nature. It is "at peace," in that its terms *cooperate* in modifying one another. But insofar as the individual is involved in conflict with other individuals or groups, the study of this same individual would fall under the head of *Rhetoric*. Or considered rhetorically, the victim of a neurotic conflict is torn by parliamentary wrangling; he is heckled like Hitler within. (Hitler is said to have confronted a constant wrangle in his private deliberations, after having imposed upon his people a flat choice between conformity and silence.) Rhetorically, the neurotic's every attempt to legislate for his own conduct is disorganized by rival factions within his own dissociated self. Yet, considered Symbolically, the same victim is technically "at peace," in the sense that his identity is like a unified, mutually adjusted set of terms. For even antagonistic terms, confronting each other as parry and thrust, can be said to "cooperate" in the building of an over-all form.

The *Rhetoric* must lead us through the Scramble, the Wrangle of the Market Place, the flurries and flare-ups of the Human Barnyard, the Give and Take, the wavering line of pressure and counterpressure, the Logomachy, the onus of ownership, the Wars of Nerves, the War. It too has its peaceful moments: at times its endless competition can add up to the transcending of itself. In ways of its own, it can move from the factional to the universal. But its ideal culminations are more often beset by strife as the condition of their organized expression, or material embodiment. Their very universality becomes transformed into a partisan weapon. For one need not scrutinize the concept of "identification" very sharply to see, implied in it at every turn, its ironic counterpart: division. Rhetoric is concerned with the state of Babel after the Fall. Its contribution to a "sociology of knowledge" must often carry us far into the lugubrious regions of malice and the lie.

The Identifying Nature of Property

Metaphysically, a thing is identified by its *properties*. In the realm of Rhetoric, such identification is frequently by property in the most materialistic sense of the term, economic property, such property as Coleridge, in his "Religious Musings," calls a

>twy-streaming fount,
>Whence Vice and Virtue flow, honey and gall.

And later:

>From Avarice thus, from Luxury and War
>Sprang heavenly Science; and from Science, Freedom.

Coleridge, typically the literary idealist, goes one step further back, deriving "property" from the workings of "Imagination." But meditations upon the dual aspects of property as such are enough for our present purposes. In the surrounding of himself with properties that name his number or establish his identity, man is ethical. ("Avarice" is but the scenic word "property" translated into terms of an agent's attitude, or incipient act.) Man's moral growth is organized through properties, properties in goods, in services, in position or status, in citizenship, in reputation, in acquaintanceship and love. But however ethical such an array of identifications may be when considered in itself, its relation to other entities that are likewise forming their identity in terms of property can lead to turmoil and discord. Here is *par excellence* a topic to be considered in a rhetoric having "identification" as its key term. And we see why one should expect to get much insight from Marxism, as a study of capitalistic rhetoric. Veblen is also, from this point of view, to be considered a theorist of rhetoric. (And we know of no better way to quickly glimpse the range of rhetoric than to read, in succession, the articles on "Property" and "Propaganda" in *The Encyclopaedia of the Social Sciences*.)

Bentham's utilitarian analysis of language, treating of the ways in which men find "eulogistic coverings" for their "material interests," is thus seen to be essentially rhetorical, and to bear directly upon the motives of property as a rhetorical factor. Indeed, since it is so clearly a matter of rhetoric to persuade a man by identifying your cause with his interests, we note the ingredient of rhetoric in the animal experimenter's ways of conditioning, as animals that respond avidly at a food signal suggest, underlying even human motives, the inclination, like a house dog, to seek salvation in the Sign of the Scraped Plate. But the lessons of this "animal rhetoric" can mislead, as we learn from the United States' attempts to use food as an instrument of policy in Europe after the war. These efforts met with enough ill will to suggest that the careful "screening" of our representatives, to eliminate reformist tendencies as far as possible and to identify American aid only with conservative or even reactionary interests, practically *guaranteed* us a dismal rhetoric in our dealings with other nations. And when Henry Wallace, during a trip abroad, began earning for our country the genuine good will of Europe's common people and intellectual classes, the Genius of the Screening came into its own: our free press, as at one signal, began stoutly assuring the citizens of both the United States and Europe that Wallace did not truly represent us. What did represent us, presumably, was the policy of the Scraped Plate, which our officialdom now and then bestirred themselves to present publicly in terms of a dispirited "idealism," as heavy as a dead elephant. You see, we were not to be identified with very resonant things; our press assured our people that the outcome of the last election had been a "popular mandate" to this effect. (We leave this statement unrevised. For the conditions of Truman's reëlection, after a campaign in which he out-Wallaced Wallace, corroborated it "in principle.")

In pure identification there would be no strife. Likewise, there would be no strife in absolute separateness, since opponents can join battle only through a mediatory ground that makes their communication possible, thus providing the first condition necessary for their interchange of blows. But put identification and division ambiguously together, so that you cannot know for certain just where one ends and the other begins, and you have the characteristic invitation to rhetoric. Here is a major reason why rhetoric, according to Aristotle, "proves opposites." When two men collaborate in an enterprise to which they contribute different kinds of services and from which they derive different amounts and kinds of profit, who is to say, once and for all, just where "cooperation" ends and one partner's "exploitation" of the other begins? The wavering line between the two cannot be "scientifically" identified; rival rhetoricians can draw it at different places, and their persuasiveness varies with the resources each has at his command. (Where public issues are concerned, such resources are not confined to the intrinsic powers of the speaker and the speech, but depend also for their effectiveness upon the purely technical means of communication, which can either aid the utterance or hamper it. For a "good" rhetoric neglected by the press obviously cannot be so "communicative" as a poor rhetoric backed nation-wide by headlines. And often we must think of rhetoric not in terms of some one particular address, but as a general *body of identifications* that owe their convincingness much more to trivial repetition and dull daily reënforcement than to exceptional rhetorical skill.)

If you would praise God, and in terms that happen also to sanction one system of material property rather than another, you have forced Rhetorical considerations upon us. If you would praise science, however exaltedly, when that same science is at the service of imperialist-militarist expansion, here again you bring things within the orbit of Rhetoric. For just as God has been identified with a certain worldly structure of ownership, so science may be identified with the interests of certain groups or classes quite *unscientific* in their purposes. Hence, however "pure" one's motives may be actually, the impurities of identification lurking about the edges of such situations introduce a typical Rhetorical wrangle of the sort that can never be settled once and for all, but belongs in the field of moral controversy where men properly seek to "prove opposites."

Thus, when his friend, Preen, wrote of a meeting where like-minded colleagues would be present and would all be proclaiming their praise of science, Prone answered: "You fail to mention another colleague who is sure to be there too, unless you take care to rule him out. I mean John Q. Militarist-Imperialist." Whereat, Preen: "This John Q. Militarist-Imperialist must be quite venerable by now. I seem to have heard of him back in Biblical times, before Roger B. Science was born. Doesn't he get in everywhere, unless he is explicitly ruled out?" He does, thanks to the ways of identification, which are in accordance with the nature of property. And the rhetorician and the moralist become one at that point where the attempt is made to reveal the undetected presence of such an identification. Thus in the United States after the second World War, the temptations of such an identification became particularly strong because so much scientific research had fallen under the direction of the military. To speak merely in praise of science, without explicitly dissociating oneself from its reactionary implications, is to identify oneself with these reactionary implications by default. Many reputable educators could thus, in this roundabout way, *function* as "conspirators." In their zeal to get federal subsidies for the science department of their college or university, they could help to shape educational policies with the ideals of war as guiding principle.

Identification and the "Autonomous"

As regards "autonomous" activities, the principle of Rhetorical identification may be summed up thus: The fact that an activity is capable of reduction to intrinsic, autonomous principles does not argue that it is free from identification with other orders of motivation extrinsic to it. Such other orders are extrinsic to it, as considered from the standpoint of the specialized activity alone. But they are not extrinsic to the field of moral action as such, considered from the standpoint of human activity in general. The human agent, *qua* human agent, is not motivated solely by the principles of a specialized activity, however strongly this specialized power, in its suggestive role as imagery, may affect his character. Any specialized activity participates in a larger unit of action. "Identification" is a word for the autonomous activity's place in this wider context, a place with which the agent may be unconcerned. The shepherd, *qua* shepherd, acts for the good of the sheep, to protect them from discomfiture and harm. But he may be "identified" with a project that is raising the sheep for market.

Of course, the principles of the autonomous activity can be considered irrespective of such identifications. Indeed, two students, sitting side by side in a classroom where the principles of a specialized subject are being taught, can be expected to "identify" the subject differently, so far as its place in a total context is concerned. Many of the most important identifications for the specialty will not be established at all, until later in life, when the specialty has become integrally interwoven with the particulars of one's livelihood. The specialized activity itself becomes a different thing for one person, with whom it is a means of surrounding himself with family and amenities, than it would be for another who, unmarried, childless, loveless, might find in the specialty not so much a means to gratification as a substitute for lack of gratification.

Carried into unique cases, such concern with identifications leads to the sheer "identities" of Symbolic. That is, we are in pure Symbolic when we concentrate upon one particular integrated structure of motives. But we are clearly in the region of rhetoric when considering the identifications whereby a specialized activity makes one a participant in some social or economic class. "Belonging" in this sense is rhetorical. And, ironically, with much college education today in literature and the fine arts, the very stress upon the pure autonomy of such activities is a roundabout way of identification with a privileged class, as the doctrine may enroll the student stylistically under the banner of a privileged class, serving as a kind of social insignia promising preferment. (We are here obviously thinking along Veblenian lines.)

The stress upon the importance of autonomous principles does have its good aspects. In particular, as regards the teaching of literature, the insistence upon "autonomy" reflects a vigorous concern with the all-importance of the text that happens to be under scrutiny. This cult of patient textual analysis (though it has excesses of its own) is helpful as a reaction against the excesses of extreme historicism (a leftover of the nineteenth century) whereby a work became so subordinated to its background that the student's appreciation of first-rate texts was lost behind his involvement with the collateral documents of fifth-rate literary historians. Also, the stress upon the autonomy of fields is valuable methodologically; it has been justly praised because it gives clear insight into some particular set of principles; and such a way of thinking is particularly needed now, when pseudoscientific thinking has become "unprincipled" in its uncritical cult of "facts." But along with these sound reasons for a primary concern with the intrinsic, there are furtive temptations that can figure here too. For so much progressive and radical criticism in recent years has been concerned with the social implications of art, that affirmations of art's autonomy can often become, by antithesis, a roundabout way of identifying oneself with the interests of political conservatism. In accordance with the rhetorical principle of identification, whenever you find a doctrine of "nonpolitical" esthetics affirmed with fervor, look for its politics.

But the principle of autonomy does allow for historical shifts whereby the nature of an identification can change greatly. Thus in his book, *The Genesis of Plato's Thought,* David Winspear gives relevant insight into the aristocratic and conservative political trends with which Plato's philosophy was identified at the time of its inception. The Sophists, on the other hand, are shown to have been more closely allied with the rising business class, then relatively "progressive" from the Marxist point of view, though their position was fundamentally weakened by the fact that their enterprise was based on the acceptance of slavery. Yet at other periods in history the Platonist concern with an ideal state could itself be identified with wholly progressive trends.

During the second World War many good writers who had previously complained of the Marxist concern with propaganda in art, themselves wrote books in which they identified their esthetic with an anti-Fascist politics. At the very least such literature attributed to Hitlerite Germans and their collaborators the brutal and neurotic motives which in former years had been attributed to "Everyman." (Glenway Wescott's *Apartment in Athens,* for instance.) So the overgeneralized attempt to discredit *Marxist* Rhetoric by discrediting *all* Rhetoric was abandoned, at least by representative reviewers whose criticism was itself a rhetorical act designed to identify the public with anti-Fascist attitudes and help sell anti-Fascist books (as it later contributed to the forming of anti-Soviet attitudes and the sale of anti-Soviet books). In the light of such developments, many critics have become only too accommodating in their search for covert and overt identifications that link the "autonomous" field of the arts with political and economic orders of motivation. Head-on resistance to the questioning of "purity" in specialized activities usually comes now from another quarter: the liberal apologists of science.

The "Autonomy" of Science

Science, as mere instrument (agency), might be expected to take on the nature of the scenes, acts, agents, and purposes with which it is identified. And insofar as a faulty political structure perverts human relations, we might reasonably expect to find a correspondingly perverted science. Thus, even the apologists of the Church will grant that, in corrupt times, there is a corresponding corruption among churchmen; and it is relevant to recall those specialists whose technical training fitted them to become identified with mass killings and experimentally induced sufferings in the concentration camps of National Socialist Germany. Hence, insofar as there are similar temptations in our own society (as attested by the sinister imagery of its art), might we not expect similar motives to lurk about the edges of our sciences (though tempered in proportion as the sinister political motives themselves are tempered in our society, under our less exacting social and economic conditions)? But liberal apologetics indignantly resists any suggestion that sadistic motives may lurk behind unnecessary animal experiments that cause suffering. The same people who, with reference to the scientific horrors of Hitlerism, admonish against the ingredients of Hitlerite thinking in our own society, will be outraged if you follow out the implications of their own premises, and look for similar temptations among our specialists.

One can sympathize with this anxiety. The liberal is usually disinclined to consider such possibilities because applied science is for him not a mere set of instruments and methods, whatever he may assert; it is a *good* and *absolute,* and is thus circuitously endowed with the philosophic function of God as the grounding of values. His thinking thus vacillates indeterminately between his overt claims for science as sheer method, as sheer coefficient of power, and his covert claims for science as a substance which, like God, would be an intrinsically *good* power. Obviously, any purely secular power, such as the applications of technology, would not be simply "good," but could become identified with motives good, bad, or indifferent, depending upon the uses to which it was put, and upon the ethical attitudes that, as part of the context surrounding it, contributed to its meaning in the realm of motives and action.

The unavowed identification, whereby a theological *function* is smuggled into a term on its face wholly secular, can secretly reënforce the characteristically liberal principle of occupational autonomy, itself reënforced by the naïvely pragmatist notion that practical specialized work is a sufficient grounding of morality. If the technical expert, as such, is assigned the task of perfecting new powers of chemical, bacteriological, or atomic destruction, his morality *as technical expert* requires only that he apply himself to his task as effectively as possible. The question of what the new force might mean, as released into a social texture emotionally and intellectually unfit to control it, or as surrendered to men whose *specialty* is *professional killing*—well, that is simply "none of his business," as specialist, however great may be his misgivings as father of a family, or as citizen of his nation and of the world. The extreme division of labor under late capitalist liberalism having made dispersion the norm and having transformed the state of Babel into an ideal, the true liberal must view almost as an affront the Rhetorical concern with identifications whereby the principles of a specialty cannot be taken on their face, simply as the motives proper to that specialty. They *are* the motives proper to the specialty *as such,* but not to the specialty as *participant in a wider context of motives.*

In sum, as regards tests of "autonomy," the specialist need only consider, as a disciplinary factor, the objective resistances supplied by the materials with which he works. The liberal criterion was that propounded by Rousseau in *Émile:* the principle of constraint was to come from the nature of *things,* not from authorities and their precepts. Yet, willy nilly, a science takes on the moral qualities of the political or social movements with which it becomes identified. Hence, a new anguish, a crisis in the liberal theory of science. In his *Genealogy of Morals,* Nietzsche met the same problem keenly, but perversely, by praising "autonomy" as the *opposite* of the moral. Modern political authoritarianism, like the earlier theocratic kinds, would subordinate the autonomous specialty to over-all doctrinal considerations. The rhetorical concept of "identification" does not justify the excesses to which such doctrinaire tendencies can be carried. But it does make clear the fact that one's morality as a specialist cannot be allowed to do duty for one's morality as a citizen. Insofar as the two roles are at odds, a specialty at the service of sinister interests will itself become sinister.

"Redemption" in Post-Christian Science

With a culture formed about the idea of redemption by the sacrifice of a Crucified Christ, just what does happen in an era of post-Christian science, when the ways of socialization have been secularized? Does the need for the vicarage of this Sacrificial King merely dwindle away? Or must some other person or persons, individual or corporate, real or fictive, take over the redemptive role? Not all people, perhaps, seek out a Vessel to which will be ritualistically delegated a purgative function, in being symbolically laden with the burdens of individual and collective guilt. But we know, as a lesson of recent history, how anti-Semitism provided the secularized replica of the Divine Scapegoat in the post-Christian rationale of Hitler's National Socialist militarism; and we know how Jews and other minority groups are thus magically identified by many members of our society. And since we also know that there are at large in the modern world many militaristic and economic trends quite like those of Germany under the Hitlerite "science" of genocide, we should at least be admonished to expect, in some degree, similar cultural temptations. For the history of the Nazis has clearly shown that there are cultural situations in which scientists, whatever may be their claims to professional austerity, will contrive somehow to identify their specialty with modes of justification, or socialization, not discernible in the sheer motions of the material operations themselves. In its transcendence of natural living, its technical scruples, its special tests of purity, a clinic or laboratory can be a kind of secular temple, in which ritualistic devotions are taking place, however concealed by the terminology of the surface. Unless properly scrutinized for traces of witchcraft, these could furtively become devotions to a satanic order of motives. At least such was the case with the technological experts of Hitlerite Germany. The very scientific ideals of an "impersonal" terminology can contribute ironically to such disaster: for it is but a step from treating inanimate nature as mere "things" to treating animals, and then enemy peoples, as mere things. But they are not mere things, they are persons—and in the systematic denial of what one knows in his heart to be the truth, there is a perverse principle that can generate much anguish.

Dual Possibilities of Science

But one cannot be too careful here. Religion, politics, and economics are notoriously touchy subjects, and with many persons today, the cult of applied science has the animus of all three rolled into one. We should take pains to make this clear: we are most decidedly *not* saying that science *must* take on such malign identifications as it presumably has, for some scientists, when fitted into the motives of a Fascist state. In the United States, for instance, the Federation of American Scientists has been urgently seeking to dissociate the idea of atomic war power from the idea of national security. Thus, the Federation proclaimed, in a statement issued September 1, 1947, on the second anniversary of V-J Day:

Many persons have justified the support of science for its war potential, implying that national security will result. We hear this justification in Congress. We hear it even from the atomic mission. We assert that national security cannot result from military preparedness or the support of science for its war potential.

When men are of good will, we can always expect many such efforts to break such sinister identifications, which their knowledge of their special field enables them to recognize as false.

Unfortunately, good will as thus circumscribed is not enough. The same statement goes on to say: "Our Government has advocated a sound policy in the United Nations concerning atomic energy." Yet there seems much justice in the complaint of the Soviet delegates that the measures we propose would guarantee the United States perpetual superiority in this field, unless other nations deliberately violated the proposed treaty by finding ways to continue their experiments in secret.

In a speech made before the United Nations Atomic Energy Commission (Sept. 10, 1947), the Soviet representative, Gromyko, came upon some paradoxes in this connection. He was attacking United States' proposals for giving "the right of ownership" to an *international* organ of control. He contended that this arrangement would contradict the principle of state sovereignty. Thus the *socialist* delegate was arguing for the *restriction* of ownership to national boundaries, while the world's greatest *capitalist* country argued for ownership by a *universal* body. *On its face,* the capitalist proposal seems much nearer to the ideal socialist solution than the position of the Soviet Union is.

However, the history of corporate management in the United States, and of political parties everywhere, gives ample evidence of all the devices whereby *actual control* of a property differs from *nominal ownership* of it. And obviously the interests in *actual control* of the agency that allocated the rights and resources of atomic development could have all the advantages of *real* ownership, however international might be the *fictions* of ownership. Where the *control* resides, there resides the *function* of ownership, whatever the *fictions* of ownership may be. It would certainly be no new thing to rhetoric if highly *discriminatory* claims were here being protected in the name of *universal* rights. And the Soviet delegate was at least justified in calling for measures that *unmistakably* avoid such a possibility, which was not considered in the scientists' statement as published in the press. There was a hint of "maneuvering" in our proposals, maneuvering to put the Russians in the position of seeming to delay an adequate international control over the atomic bomb, when there were strong doubts whether our own Congress would itself have agreed to any such control.

Lying outside the orbit of the scientists' specialty, there are psychological considerations which are nearly always slighted, since they involve identifications manifestly extrinsic to atomic physics in itself. Possibilities of deception arise particularly with those ironies whereby the scientists' truly splendid terminology for the expert smashing of lifeless things can so catch a man's fancy that he would transfer it to the realm of human relations likewise. It is not a great step from the purely professional poisoning of harmful insects to the purely professional blasting and poisoning of human beings, as viewed in similarly "impersonal" terms. And such inducements are particularly there, so long as factional division (of class, race, nationality, and the like) make for the ironic mixture of identification and dissociation that marks the function of the scapegoat. Indeed, the very "global" conditions which call for the greater identification of all men with one another have at the same time increased the range of human conflict, the incentives to division. It would require sustained rhetorical effort, backed by the imagery of a richly humane and spontaneous poetry, to make us fully sympathize with people in circumstances greatly different from our own. Add now the international rivalries that goad to the opposite kind of effort, and that make it easy for some vocalizers to make their style "forceful" by simply playing up these divisive trends, and you see how perverted the austere scientific ideal may become, as released into a social texture unprepared for it.

The good will of scientists is not enough, however genuine it may be. There is the joke of the father who put his little son on the table and, holding out his arms protectively, said, "Jump." The trusting child jumped; but instead of catching him, the father drew back, and let him fall to the floor. The child was hurt, both physically and in this violation of its confidence. Whereupon the father drove home the moral: "Let that be a lesson to you. Never trust anyone, not even your own father." Now, when the apologists of science teach their subject thus, instead of merely exalting it, we can salute them for truly admonishing us, in being as "scientific" about the criticism of science as in the past they have been about the criticism of religion.

To sum up:

(1) We know, as a matter of record, that science under Fascism became sinister. (2) We are repeatedly being admonished that there is a high percentage of Fascist motivation in our own society. (3) Why, then, should there not be, in our society, a correspondingly high incentive to sinister science? Particularly inasmuch as sinister motives already show in much of our art, both popular and recondite, while the conditions of secrecy imposed upon many experimental scientists today add a "conspiratorial" motive to such "autonomous" activity. In the past, the great *frankness* of science has been its noblest attribute, as judged from the purely humanistic point of view. But any tendency to place scientific development primarily under the heading of "war potential" must endanger this essential moralistic element in science, replacing the norms of *universal clarity* with the divisive demands for *conspiracy*. Insofar as such conditions prevail, science loses the one ingredient that can keep it wholesome: its enrollment under the forces of *light*. To this extent, the scientist must reject and resist in ways that mean the end of "autonomy," or if he accepts, he risks becoming the friend of fiends. Scientific discoveries have always, of course, been used for the purposes of war. But the demand that scientific advance *per se* be guided by military considerations *changes the proportions* of such motivation tremendously. Scientists of good will must then become uneasy, in that the morality of their specialty is no longer enough. The liberal ideal of autonomy is denied them, except insofar as they can contrive to conceal from themselves the true implications of their role.

Ingenuous and Cunning Identifications

The thought of self-deception brings up another range of possibilities here. For there is a wide range of ways whereby the rhetorical motive, through the resources of identification, can operate without conscious direction by any particular agent. Classical rhetoric stresses the element of explicit design in rhetorical enterprise. But one can systematically extend the range of rhetoric, if one studies the persuasiveness of false or inadequate terms which may not be directly imposed upon us from without by some skillful speaker, but which we impose upon ourselves, in varying degrees of deliberateness and unawareness, through motives indeterminately self-protective and/or suicidal.

We shall consider these matters more fully later, when we study the rhetoric of *hierarchy* (or as it is less revealingly named, *bureaucracy*). And our later pages on Marx and Veblen would apply here. But for the present we might merely recall the psychologist's concept of "malingering," to designate the ways of neurotic persons who, though not actually ill, persuade themselves that they are, and so can claim the attentions and privileges of the ill (their feigned illness itself becoming, at one remove, genuine). Similarly, if a social or occupational class is not too exacting in the scrutiny of identifications that flatter its interests, its very philosophy of life is a profitable malingering (profitable at least until its inaccuracies catch up with it)—and as such, it is open to either attack or analysis, Rhetoric comprising both the *use* of persuasive resources (*rhetorica utens,* as with the philippics of Demosthenes) and the *study* of them (*rhetorica docens,* as with Aristotle's treatise on the "art" of Rhetoric).

This aspect of identification, whereby one can protect an interest merely by using terms not incisive enough to criticize it properly, often brings rhetoric to the edge of cunning. A misanthropic politician who dealt in mankind-loving imagery could still think of himself as rhetorically honest, if he meant to do well by his constituents yet thought that he could get their votes only by such display. Whatever the falsity in overplaying a role, there may be honesty in the assuming of that role itself; and the overplaying may be but a translation into a different medium of communication, a way of amplifying a statement so that it carries better to a large or distant audience. Hence, the persuasive identifications of Rhetoric, in being so directly designed for *use,* involve us in a special problem of *consciousness,* as exemplified in the Rhetorician's particular *purpose* for a given statement.

The thought gives a glimpse into rhetorical motives behind many characters in drama and fiction. Shakespeare's Iago and Molière's Tartuffe are demons of Rhetoric. Every word and act is addressed, being designed to build up false identifications in the minds of their victims. Similarly, there is a notable ingredient of Rhetoric in Stendhal's Julien Sorel, who combines "heightened consciousness" with "freedom" by a perversely frank decision to perfect his own kind of hypocrisy as a means of triumphing over the hypocrisy of others. All his actions thus become rhetorical, framed for their effect; his life is a spellbinding and spellbound address to an audience.

Did you ever do a friend an injury by accident, in all poetic simplicity? Then conceive of this same injury as done by sly design, and you are forthwith within the orbit of Rhetoric. If you, like the Stendhals and Gides, conceive a character by such sophistication, Rhetoric as the speaker's attempt to identify himself favorably with his audience then becomes so transformed that the work may seem to have been written under an esthetic of pure "expression," without regard for communicative appeal. Or it may appeal perversely, to warped motives within the audience. Or it may be but an internalizing of the rhetorical motive, as the very actions of such a representative figure take on a rhetorical cast. Hence, having woven a rhetorical motive so integrally into the very essence of his conception, the writer can seem to have ignored rhetorical considerations; yet, in the sheer effrontery of his protagonist there is embedded, however disguised or transformed, an *anguish* of communication (communication being, as we have said, a generalized form of love).

As regards the rhetorical ways of Stendhal's hero, moving in the perverse freedom of duplicity: After the disclosure of his cunning, Julien abandons his complex rhetorical morality of hypocrisy-to-outhypocritize-the-hypocrites, and regains a new, suicidally poetic level of simplicity. *"Jamais cette tête n'avait été aussi poétique qu'au moment où elle allait tomber."* The whole structure of the book could be explained as the account of a hero who, by the disclosure of his Rhetoric, was jolted into a tragically direct poetic. Within the terms of the novel, "hypocrisy" was the word for "rhetoric," such being the quality of the rhetoric that marked the public life of France under the reign of *Napoléon le Petit*.

Rhetoric of "Address" (to the Individual Soul)

By our arrangement, the individual in his uniqueness falls under the head of Symbolic. But one should not thereby assume that what is known as "individual psychology" wholly meets the same test. Particularly in the Freudian concern with the neuroses of individual patients, there is a strongly rhetorical ingredient. Indeed, what could be more profoundly rhetorical than Freud's notion of a dream that attains expression by stylistic subterfuges designed to evade the inhibitions of a moralistic censor? What is this but the exact analogue of the rhetorical devices of literature under political or theocratic censorship? The *ego* with its *id* confronts the *super-ego* much as an orator would confront a somewhat alien audience, whose susceptibilities he must flatter as a necessary step towards persuasion. The Freudian psyche is quite a parliament, with conflicting interests expressed in ways variously designed to take the claims of rival factions into account.

The best evidence of a strongly rhetorical ingredient in Freud's view of the psyche is in his analysis of *Wit and Its Relation to the Unconscious.* In particular, we think of Freud's concern with the role of an audience, or "third person," with whom the speaker establishes rapport, in their common enterprise directed against the butt of tendentious witticisms. Here is the purest rhetorical pattern: speaker and hearer as partners in partisan jokes made at the expense of another. If you "internalize" such a variety of motives, so that the same person can participate somewhat in all three positions, you get a complex individual of many voices. And though these may be treated, under the heading of Symbolic, as a concerto of principles mutually modifying one another, they may likewise be seen, from the standpoint of Rhetoric, as a parliamentary wrangle which the individual has put together somewhat as he puts together his fears and hopes, friendships and enmities, health and disease, or those tiny rebirths whereby, in being born to some new condition, he may be dying to a past condition, his development being dialectical, a series of terms in perpetual transformation.

Thus by a roundabout route we come upon another aspect of Rhetoric: its nature as *addressed,* since persuasion implies an audience. A man can be his own audience, insofar as he, even in his secret thoughts, cultivates certain ideas or images for the effect he hopes they may have upon him; he is here what Mead would call "an 'I' addressing its 'me' "; and in this respect he is being rhetorical quite as though he were using pleasant imagery to influence an outside audience rather than one within. In traditional Rhetoric, the relation to an external audience is stressed. Aristotle's *Art of Rhetoric,* for instance, deals with the appeal to audiences in this primary sense: It lists typical beliefs, so that the speaker may choose among them the ones with which he would favorably identify his cause or unfavorably identify the cause of an opponent; and it lists the traits of character with which the speaker should seek to identify himself, as a way of disposing an audience favorably towards him. But a modern "post-Christian" rhetoric must also concern itself with the thought that, under the heading of appeal to audiences, would also be included any ideas or images privately addressed to the individual self for moralistic or incantatory purposes. For you become your own audience, in some respects a very lax one, in some respects very exacting, when you become involved in psychologically stylistic subterfuges for presenting your own case to yourself in sympathetic terms (and even terms that seem harsh can often be found on closer scrutiny to be flattering, as with neurotics who visit sufferings upon themselves in the name of very high-powered motives which, whatever their discomfiture, feed pride).

Such considerations make us alert to the ingredient of rhetoric in all *socialization,* considered as a *moralizing* process. The individual person, striving to form himself in accordance with the communicative norms that match the cooperative ways of his society, is by the same token concerned with the rhetoric of identification. To act upon himself persuasively, he must variously resort to images and ideas that are formative. Education ("indoctrination") exerts such pressure upon him from without; he completes the process from within. If he does not somehow act to tell himself (as his own audience) what the various brands of rhetorician have told him, his persuasion is not complete. Only those voices from without are effective which can speak in the language of a voice within.

Among the Tanala of Madagascar, it is said, most of those tribesmen susceptible to *tromba* ("neurotic seizure indicated by an extreme desire to dance") were found to be among the least favored members of the tribe. Such seizures are said to be a device that makes the possessed person "the center of all the attention." And afterwards, the richest and most powerful members of the sufferer's family foot the bill, so that "the individual's ego is well satisfied and he can get along quite well until the next tromba seizure occurs." In sum, "like most hysterical seizures, tromba requires an audience."

The citations are from A. Kardiner, *The Individual and His Society* (New York: Columbia University Press). They would suggest that, when asking what all would fall within the scope of our topic, we could also include a "rhetoric of hysteria." For here too are expressions which are *addressed*—and we confront an ultimate irony, in glimpsing how even a catatonic lapse into sheer automatism, beyond the reach of all normally linguistic communication, is in its origins communicative, addressed, though it be a paralogical appeal-that-ends-all-appeals.

Rhetoric and Primitive Magic

The Kardiner citations are taken from a paper by C. Kluckhohn on "Navaho Witchcraft," containing observations that would also bring witchcraft within the range of rhetoric. Indeed, where witchcraft is imputed as a motive behind the individual search for wealth, power, or vengeance, can we not view it as a primitive vocabulary of *individualism* emerging in a culture where *tribal* thinking had been uppermost, so that the individualist motive would be admitted and suspect? And any breach of identification with the tribal norms being sinister, do we not glimpse rhetorical motives behind the fact that Macbeth's private ambitions were figured in terms of witches?

At first glance we may seem to be straining the conception of rhetoric to the breaking point, when including even a treatise on primitive witchcraft within its range. But look again. Precisely at a time when the *term* "rhetoric" had fallen into greatest neglect and disrepute, writers in the "social sciences" were, under many guises, making good contributions to the New Rhetoric. As usual with modern thought, the insights gained from *comparative culture* could throw light upon the classic approach to this subject; and again, as usual with modern thought, this light was interpreted in terms that concealed its true relation to earlier work. And though the present writer was strongly influenced by anthropological inquiries into primitive magic, he did not clearly discern the exact relation between the anthropologist's concern with magic and the literary critic's concern with communication until he had systematically worked on this *Rhetoric* for some years. Prior to this discovery, though he persisted in anthropological hankerings, he did so with a bad conscience; and he was half willing to agree with literary opponents who considered such concerns alien to the study of literature proper.

Now, in noting methodically how the anthropologist's account of magic can belong in a rhetoric, we are better equipped to see exactly wherein the two fields of inquiry diverge. Anthropology is a gain to literary criticism only if one knows how to "discount" it from the standpoint of rhetoric. And, ironically, anthropology can be a source of disturbance, not only to literary criticism in particular, but to the study of human relations in general, if one does not so discount it, but allows *its* terms to creep into one's thinking at points where issues *should* be studied explicitly in terms of rhetoric.

We saw both the respects in which the anthropologists' study of magic overlaps upon rhetoric and the respects in which they are distinct when we were working on a review of Ernst Cassirer's *Myth of the State*. The general proposition that exercised us can be stated as follows:

We must begin by confronting the typically scientist view of the relation between science and magic. Since so many apologists of modern science, following a dialectic of simple antithesis, have looked upon magic merely as an early form of bad science, one seems to be left only with a distinction between bad science and good science. Scientific knowledge is thus presented as a terminology that gives an accurate and critically tested description of reality; and magic is presented as antithetical to such science. Hence magic is treated as an early uncritical attempt to do what science does, but under conditions where judgment and perception were impaired by the naïvely anthropomorphic belief that the impersonal forces of nature were motivated by personal designs. One thus confronts a flat choice between a civilized vocabulary of scientific description and a savage vocabulary of magical incantation.

In this scheme, "rhetoric" has no systematic location. We recall noting the word but once in Cassirer's *Myth of the State,* and then it is used only in a random way; yet the book is really about nothing more nor less than a most characteristic concern of rhetoric: the manipulation of men's beliefs for political ends.

Now, the basic function of rhetoric, the use of words by human agents to form attitudes or to induce actions in other human agents, is certainly not "magical." If you are in trouble, and call for help, you are no practitioner of primitive magic. You are using the primary resource of human speech in a thoroughly realistic way. Nor, on the other hand, is your utterance "science," in the strict meaning of science today, as a "semantic" or "descriptive" terminology for charting the conditions of nature from an "impersonal" point of view, regardless of one's wishes or preferences. A call for help is quite "prejudiced"; it is the most arrant kind of "wishful thinking"; it is not merely descriptive, it is *hortatory*. It is not just trying to tell how things are, in strictly "scenic" terms; it is trying to *move people*. A call for help might, of course, include purely scientific statements, or preparations for action, as a person in need might give information about particular dangers to guard against or advantages to exploit in bringing help. But the call, in itself, as such, is not scientific; it is *rhetorical*. Whereas poetic language is a kind of symbolic action, for itself and in itself, and whereas scientific action is a preparation for action, rhetorical language is inducement to action (or to attitude, attitude being an incipient act).

If you have only a choice between magic and science, you simply have no bin in which to accurately place such a form of expression. Hence, since "the future" is not the sort of thing one can put under a microscope, or even test by a knowledge of *exactly equivalent conditions* in the past, when you turn to political exhortation, you are involved in decisions that necessarily lie beyond the strictly scientific vocabularies of description. And since the effective politician is a "spellbinder," it seems to follow by elimination that the hortatory use of speech for political ends can be called "magic," in the discredited sense of that term.

As a result, much analysis of political exhortation comes to look simply like a survival of primitive magic, whereas it should be handled in its own terms, as an aspect of what it really is: rhetoric. The approach to rhetoric in terms of "word magic" gets the whole subject turned backwards. Originally, the magical use of symbolism to affect natural processes by rituals and incantations was a mistaken transference of a proper linguistic function to an area for which it was not fit. The realistic use of addressed language to *induce action in people* became the magical use of addressed language to *induce motion in things* (things by nature alien to purely linguistic orders of motivation). If we then begin by treating this *erroneous* and *derived* magical use as *primary,* we are invited to treat a *proper* use of language (for instance, political persuasion) simply as a vestige of benightedly prescientific magic.

To be sure, the rhetorician has the tricks of his trade. But they are not mere "bad science"; they are an "art." And any overly scientist approach to them (treating them in terms of flat dialectical opposition to modern technology) must make our world look much more "neo-primitive" than is really the case. At the very least, we should note that primitive magic prevailed most strongly under social conditions where the rationalization of social effort in terms of money was negligible; but the rhetoric of modern politics would establish social identifications atop a way of life highly diversified by money, with the extreme division of labor and status which money served to rationalize.

Realistic Function of Rhetoric

Gaining courage as we proceed, we might even contend that we are not so much proposing to import anthropology into rhetoric as proposing that anthropologists recognize the factor of rhetoric in their own field. That is, if you look at recent studies of primitive magic from the standpoint of this discussion, you might rather want to distinguish between magic as "bad science" and magic as "primitive rhetoric." You then discover that anthropology does clearly recognize the rhetorical *function* in magic; and far from dismissing the rhetorical aspect of magic merely as bad science, anthropology recognizes in it a pragmatic device that greatly assisted the survival of cultures by promoting social cohesion. (Malinowski did much work along these lines, and the Kluckhohn essay makes similar observations about witchcraft.) But now that we have confronted the term "magic" with the term "rhetoric," we'd say that one comes closer to the true state of affairs if one treats the socializing aspects of magic as a "primitive rhetoric" than if one sees modern rhetoric simply as a "survival of primitive magic."

For rhetoric as such is not rooted in any past condition of human society. It is rooted in an essential function of language itself, a function that is wholly realistic, and is continually born anew; the use of language as a symbolic means of inducing cooperation in beings that by nature respond to symbols. Though rhetorical considerations may carry us far afield, leading us to violate the principle of autonomy separating the various disciplines, there is an intrinsically rhetorical motive, situated in the persuasive use of language. And this persuasive use of language is not derived from "bad science," or "magic." On the contrary, "magic" was a faulty derivation from it, "word magic" being an attempt to produce linguistic responses in kinds of beings not accessible to the linguistic motive. However, once you introduce this emendation, you can see beyond the accidents of language. You can recognize how much of value has been contributed to the New Rhetoric by these investigators, though their observations are made in terms that never explicitly confront the rhetorical ingredient in their field of study. We can place in terms of rhetoric all those statements by anthropologists, ethnologists, individual and social psychologists, and the like, that bear upon the *persuasive* aspects of language, the function of language as *addressed,* as direct or roundabout appeal to real or ideal audiences, without or within.

Are we but haggling over a term? In one sense, yes. We are offering a rationale intended to show how far one might systematically extend the term "rhetoric." In this respect, we are haggling over a term; for we must persist in tracking down the *function* of that term. But to note the ingredient of rhetoric lurking in such anthropologist's terms as "magic" and "witchcraft" is not to ask that the anthropologist replace his words with ours. We are certainly not haggling over terms in that sense. The term "rhetoric" is no substitute for "magic," "witchcraft," "socialization," "communication," and so on. But the term rhetoric designates a *function* which is present in the areas variously covered by those other terms. And we are asking only that this *function* be recognized for what it is: a linguistic function by nature as *realistic* as a proverb, though it may be quite far from the kind of realism found in strictly "scientific realism." For it is essentially a realism of the *act:* moral, persuasive—and acts are not "true" and "false" in the sense that the propositions of "scientific realism" are. And however "false" the "propositions" of primitive magic may be, considered from the standpoint of scientific realism, it is different with the peculiarly *rhetorical* ingredient in magic, involving ways of identification that contribute variously to social cohesion (either for the advantage of the community as a whole, or for the advantage of special groups whose interests are a burden on the community, or for the advantage of special groups whose rights and duties are indeterminately both a benefit and a tax on the community, as with some business enterprise in our society).

The "pragmatic sanction" for this function of magic lies outside the realm of strictly true-or-false propositions; it falls in an area of deliberation that itself draws upon the resources of rhetoric; it is itself a subject matter belonging to an art that can "prove opposites."

To illustrate what we mean by "proving opposites" here: we read an article, let us say, obviously designed to dispose the reading public favorably towards the "aggressive and expanding" development of American commercial interests in Saudi Arabia. It speaks admiringly of the tremendous changes which our policies of commerce and investment will introduce into a vestigially feudal culture, and of the great speed at which the rationale of finance and technology will accomplish these changes. When considering the obvious rhetorical intent of these "facts," we suddenly, in a perverse *non sequitur,* remember a passage in the Kluckhohn essay, involving what we would now venture to call "the rhetoric of witchcraft":

> In a society like the Navaho which is competitive and capitalistic, on the one hand, and still familistic on the other, any ideology which has the effect of slowing down economic mobility is decidedly adaptive. One of the most basic strains in Navaho society arises out of the incompatibility between the demands of familism and the emulation of European patterns in the accumulating of capital.

And in conclusion we are told that the "survival of the society" is assisted by "any pattern, such as witchcraft, which tends to discourage the rapid accumulation of wealth" (witchcraft, as an "ideology," contributing to this end by identifying new wealth with malign witchery). Now, when you begin talking about the optimum rate of speed at which cultural changes should take place, or the optimum proportion between tribal and individualistic motives that should prevail under a particular set of economic conditions, you are talking about something very important indeed, but you will find yourself deep in matters of rhetoric: for nothing is more rhetorical in nature than a deliberation as to what is too much or too little, too early or too late; in such controversies, rhetoricians are forever "proving opposites."

Where are we now? We have considered two main aspects of rhetoric: its use of *identification* and its nature as *addressed*. Since identification implies division, we found rhetoric involving us in matters of socialization and faction. Here was a wavering line between peace and conflict, since identification is got by property, which is ambivalently a motive of both morality and strife. And inasmuch as the ultimate of conflict is war or murder, we considered how such imagery can figure as a terminology of reidentification ("transformation" or "rebirth"). For in considering the wavering line between identification and division, we shall always be coming upon manifestations of the logomachy, avowed as in invective, unavowed as in stylistic subterfuges for presenting real divisions in terms that deny division.

We found that this wavering line between identification and division was forever bringing rhetoric against the possibility of malice and the lie; for if an identification favorable to the speaker or his cause is made to seem favorable to the audience, there enters the possibility of such "heightened consciousness" as goes with deliberate cunning. Thus, roundabout, we confronted the nature of rhetoric as *addressed* to audiences of the first, second, or third person. Socialization itself was, in the widest sense, found to be addressed. And by reason of such simultaneous identification-with and division-from as mark the choice of a scapegoat, we found that rhetoric involves us in problems related to witchcraft, magic, spellbinding, ethical promptings, and the like. And in the course of discussing these subjects, we found ourselves running into another term: persuasion. Rhetoric is the art of persuasion, or a study of the means of persuasion available for any given situation. We have thus, deviously, come to the point at which Aristotle begins his treatise on rhetoric.

So we shall change our purpose somewhat. Up to now, we have been trying to indicate what kinds of subject matter not traditionally labeled "rhetoric" should, in our opinion, also fall under this head. We would now consider varying views of rhetoric that have already prevailed; and we would try to "generate" them from the same basic terms of our discussion.

As for the relation between "identification" and "persuasion": we might well keep it in mind that a speaker persuades an audience by the use of stylistic identifications; his act of persuasion may be for the purpose of causing the audience to identify itself with the speaker's interests; and the speaker draws on identification of interests to establish rapport between himself and his audience. So, there is no chance of our keeping apart the meanings of persuasion, identification ("consubstantiality") and communication (the nature of rhetoric as "addressed"). But, in given instances, one or another of these elements may serve best for extending a line of analysis in some particular direction.

And finally: The use of symbols, by one symbol-using entity to induce action in another (persuasion properly addressed) is in essence not magical but *realistic*. However, the resources of identification whereby a sense of consubstantiality is symbolically established between beings of unequal status may extend far into the realm of the *idealistic*. And as we shall see later, when on the subject of order, out of this idealistic element there may arise a kind of magic or mystery that sets its mark upon all human relations.

Part II
TRADITIONAL PRINCIPLES OF RHETORIC

II

TRADITIONAL PRINCIPLES OF RHETORIC

Persuasion

"SPEECH designed to persuade" (*dicere ad persuadendum accommodate*): this is the basic definition for rhetoric (and its synonym, "eloquence,") given in Cicero's dialogue *De Oratore*. Crassus, who is spokesman for Cicero himself, cites it as something taken for granted, as the first thing the student of rhetoric is taught. Three hundred years before him, Aristotle's *Art of Rhetoric* had similarly named "persuasion" as the essence and end of rhetoric, which he defined as "the faculty of discovering the persuasive means available in a given case." Likewise, in a lost treatise, Aristotle's great competitor, Isocrates, called rhetoric "the craftsman of persuasion" (*peithous demiourgos*). Thus, at this level of generalization, even rivals could agree, though as De Quincey has remarked, "persuasion" itself can be differently interpreted.

Somewhat more than a century after Cicero, Quintilian, in his *Institutio Oratoria* changed the stress, choosing to define rhetoric as the "science of speaking well" (*bene dicendi scientia*).* But his system is clearly directed towards one particular kind of persuasion: the education of the Roman gentleman. Thus, in a chapter where he cites about two dozen definitions (two-thirds of which refer to "persuasion" as the essence of rhetoric), though he finally chooses a definition of his own which omits reference to persuasion, he has kept the *function* of the term. For he equates the perfect orator with the good man, and says that the good man should be exceptional in both eloquence and moral attributes. Rhetoric, he says, is both "useful" and a "virtue." Hence his notion of "speaking well" implies the moralistically hortatory, not just pragmatic skill at the service of any cause.

Add now the first great Christian rhetoric, the fourth book of St.

---

*He used the word "science" loosely. This definition is in Book II, Chapter XV. At the beginning of Book III he says he has shown rhetoric to be an "art."

Augustine's *De Doctrina Christiana* (written near the beginning of the fifth century) and you have ample material, in these four great peaks stretched across 750 years, to observe the major principles derivable from the notion of rhetoric as persuasion, as inducement to action, *ad agendum,* in the phrase of Augustine, who elsewhere, in the same book, states that a man is persuaded if

> he likes what you promise, fears what you say is imminent, hates what you censure, embraces what you commend, regrets whatever you built up as regrettable, rejoices at what you say is cause for rejoicing, sympathizes with those whose wretchedness your words bring before his very eyes, shuns those whom you admonish him to shun . . . and in whatever other ways your high eloquence can affect the minds of your hearers, bringing them not merely to know what should be done, but to do what they know should be done.

Yet often we could with more accuracy speak of persuasion "to attitude," rather than persuasion to out-and-out action. Persuasion involves choice, will; it is directed to a man only insofar as he is *free*. This is good to remember, in these days of dictatorship and near-dictatorship. Only insofar as men are potentially free, must the spellbinder seek to persuade them. Insofar as they *must* do something, rhetoric is unnecessary, its work being done by the nature of things, though often these necessities are not of a natural origin, but come from necessities imposed by man-made conditions, as with the kind of *peithananke* (or "compulsion under the guise of persuasion") that sometimes flows from the nature of the "free market."

Insofar as a choice of *action* is restricted, rhetoric seeks rather to have a formative effect upon *attitude* (as a criminal condemned to death might by priestly rhetoric be brought to an attitude of repentance and resignation). Thus, in Cicero and Augustine there is a shift between the words "move" (*movere*) and "bend" (*flectere*) to name the ultimate function of rhetoric. This shift corresponds to a distinction between act and attitude (attitude being an incipient act, a leaning or inclination). Thus the notion of persuasion to *attitude* would permit the application of rhetorical terms to purely *poetic* structures; the study of lyrical devices might be classed under the head of rhetoric, when these devices are considered for their power to induce or communicate states of mind to readers, even though the kinds of assent evoked have no overt, practical outcome.

All told, traditionally there is the range of rhetoric from an "Art of

Cheating" (as systematically "perfected" by some of the Greek Sophists) to Quintilian's view of rhetoric as a power, art or science that identifies right doing with right speaking. Similarly Isocrates in his *Antidosis* reminds the Athenians that they make annual sacrifices to the Goddess of Persuasion (Peitho), and he refers to speech as the source of most good things. The desire to speak well, he says, makes for great moral improvement. "True, just, and well-ordered discourse is the outward image (*eidolon*) of a good and faithful soul."

Or, since "rhetoric," "oratory," and "eloquence" all come from roots meaning "to speak," you can have the Aristotelian stress upon rhetoric as *sheer words*. In this respect, by his scheme, it is the "counterpart" of dialectic (though "dialectic" itself, in such a usage, is to be distinguished from the modern "dialectic of Nature"). Some theorists may choose to look upon the rhetorician as a very narrow specialist. On the other hand, since one can be "eloquent" about anything and everything, there are Quintilian's grounds for widening the scope of rhetoric to make it the center of an entire educational system. He was here but extending an emphasis strong in Cicero, who equated the ideal orator with the ideal citizen, the man of universal aptitude, sympathies, and experience. And though Aristotle rigorously divided knowledge into compartments whenever possible, his *Art of Rhetoric* includes much that falls under the separate headings of psychology, ethics, politics, poetics, logic, and history. Indeed, according to him, the characteristically rhetorical statement involves "commonplaces" that lie outside any scientific specialty; and in proportion as the rhetorician deals with special subject matter, his proofs move away from the rhetorical and towards the scientific. (For instance, a typical rhetorical "commonplace," in the Aristotelian sense, would be Churchill's slogan, "Too little and too late," which could hardly be said to fall under any special science of quantity or time.)

As for "persuasion" itself: one can imagine including purely logical demonstration as a part of it; or one might distinguish between appeals to reason and appeals to emotion, sentiment, ignorance, prejudice, and the like, reserving the notion of "persuasion" for these less orderly kinds of "proof." (Here again we encroach upon the term "dialectic." Augustine seems to follow the Stoic usage, in treating dialectic as the logical groundwork underlying rhetoric; dialectic would thus treat of the ultimate scenic reality that sets the criteria for rhetorical persuasion.)

The Greek word, *peitho*, comes from the same root as the Latin word for "faith." Accordingly, Aristotle's term for rhetorical "proof" is the related word, *pistis*. In his vocabulary, it names an *inferior* kind of proof, as compared with scientific demonstration (*apodeixis*). (See *Institutio Oratoria*, Book V, Chapter X.) But it is, ironically, the word which, in Greek ecclesiastical literature, came to designate the *highest* order of Christian knowledge, "faith" or "belief" as contrasted with "reason." While the active form of *peitho* means "to persuade," its middle and passive forms mean "to obey."

But the corresponding Latin word, *suadere,* comes from the same roots as "suavity," "assuage," and "sweet." And following these leads, one may want to narrow the scope of persuasion to such meanings as "ingratiation" and "delight." Thus Augustine often uses the term in this very restricted sense, preferring words like "move" and "bend" (*movere, flectere*) when he has the ultimate purpose of rhetorical utterance in mind. (In Sidney's statement that the end of speech is "the uttering sweetly and properly the conceits of the minde," one can discern the lineaments of "persuasion" behind "sweet utterance" when one appreciates the relation between English "sweet" and Cicero's stress upon the *suavitas* of oratory.)

More often, however, the ability of rhetoric to ingratiate is considered secondary, as a mere device for gaining good will, holding the attention, or deflecting the attention in preparation for more urgent purposes. Since persuasion so often implies the presence or threat of an adversary, there is the "agonistic" or competitive stress. Thus Aristotle, who looks upon rhetoric as a medium that "proves opposites," gives what amounts to a handbook on a manly art of self-defense. He describes the holds and the counter-holds, the blows and the ways of blocking them, for every means of persuasion the corresponding means of dissuasion, for every proof the disproof, for every praise the vituperation that matches it. While *in general* the truer and better cause has the advantage, he observes, no cause can be adequately defended without skill in the tricks of the trade. So he studies these tricks from the purely technical point of view, without reference to any one fixed position such as marks Augustine's analysis of the Christian persuasion. Even as Aristotle is teaching one man how most effectively to make people say "yes," he is teaching an opponent how to make them say just as forceful a "no."

This "agonistic" emphasis is naturally strong in Cicero, much of whose treatise is written out of his experiences in the Senate and the law courts. It is weaker in Quintilian with his educational emphasis; yet his account of eloquence frequently relies on military and gladiatorial images. (Which reminds us that Cicero's dialogue *De Oratore,* is represented as taking place among several prominent public figures who *have left Rome* for the far suburbs *during the season of the Games.*)

Whatever his polemic zeal in other works, in the *De Doctrina Christiana* Augustine is concerned rather with the *cajoling* of an audience than with the routing of opponents. Despite the disrepute into which pagan rhetoric had fallen in Augustine's day, he recognized the persuasiveness implicit in its forms. And though some Christians looked upon rhetoric as by nature pagan, Augustine (himself trained in rhetoric before his conversion) held that every last embellishment should be brought to the service of God, for the glory and power of the new doctrine.

The notion of rhetoric as a means of "proving opposites" again brings us to the relation between rhetoric and dialectic. Perhaps, as a first rough approximate, we might think of the matter thus: Bring several *rhetoricians* together, let their speeches contribute to the maturing of one another by the give and take of question and answer, and you have the *dialectic* of a Platonic dialogue. But ideally the dialogue seeks to attain a higher order of truth, as the speakers, in competing with one another, cooperate towards an end transcending their individual positions. Here is the paradigm of the dialectical process for "reconciling opposites" in a "higher synthesis."

But note that, in the Platonic scheme, such dialectic enterprise starts from *opinion.* The Socratic "midwifery" (maieutic) was thus designed to discover truth, by beginning with opinion and subjecting it to systematic criticism. Also, the process was purely verbal; hence in Aristotle's view it would be an art, not a science, since each science has its own particular extraverbal subject matter. The Socratic method was better suited for such linguistic enterprises as the dialectical search for "ideas" of justice, truth, beauty, and so on, than for the accumulating of knowledge derived from empirical observation and laboratory experiment. Dialectic of this sort was concerned with "ideology" in the primary sense of the term: the study of ideas and of their relation to one another. But above all, note that, in its very search for "truth," it began with "opinion," and thus in a sense was *grounded* in opinion.

The point is worth remembering because the verbal "counterpart" of dialectic, rhetoric, was likewise said to deal with "opinion," though without the systematic attempt to transcend this level.

The competitive and public ingredient in persuasion makes it particularly urgent that the rhetoric work at the level of opinion. Thus, in a situation where an appeal to prejudice might be more effective than an appeal to reason, the rhetorician who would have his cause prevail may need to use such means, regardless of his preferences. Cicero says that one should answer argument with argument and emotional appeal by a stirring of the opposite emotions (goading to hate where the opponent had established good will, and countering compassion by incitement to envy). And Aristotle refers with approval to Gorgias' notion that one should counter an opponent's jest with earnest and his earnest with jest. To persuade under such conditions, truth is at best a secondary device. Hence, rhetoric is properly said to be grounded in opinion. But we think that the relation between "truth" and the kind of opinion with which rhetoric operates is often misunderstood. And the classical texts do not seem to bring out the point we have in mind, namely:

The kind of opinion with which rhetoric deals, in its role of inducement to action, is not opinion *as contrasted with truth*. There is the invitation to look at the matter thus antithetically, once we have put the two terms (opinion and truth) together as a dialectical pair. But actually, many of the "opinions" upon which persuasion relies fall outside the test of truth in the strictly scientific, T-F, yes-or-no sense. Thus, if a given audience has a strong opinion that a certain kind of conduct is admirable, the orator can commend a person by using signs that identify him with such conduct. "Opinion" in this ethical sense clearly falls on the bias across the matter of "truth" in the strictly scientific sense. Of course, a speaker may be true or false in identifying a person by some particular sign of virtuous conduct. You may say that a person so acted when the person did not so act—and if you succeed in making your audience believe you, you could be said to be trafficking in sheer opinion *as contrasted with* the truth. But we are here concerned with motives a step farther back than such mere deception. We are discussing the underlying ethical assumptions on which the entire tactics of persuasion are based. Here the important factor is opinion (opinion in the moral order of *action,* rather than in the "scenic" order of truth). The rhetorician, as such, need operate only on this principle. If, in the opinion of a given audience, a certain kind of conduct is admirable, then a speaker might persuade the audience by using ideas and images that identify his cause with that kind of conduct.

Identification

"It is not hard," says Aristotle, in his *Rhetoric,* quoting Socrates, "to praise Athenians among Athenians." He has been cataloguing those traits which an audience generally considers the components of virtue. They are justice, courage, self-control, poise or presence (magnificence, *megaloprepeia*), broad-mindedness, liberality, gentleness, prudence and wisdom. And he has been saying: For purposes of praise or blame, the rhetorician will assume that qualities closely resembling any of these qualities are identical with them. For instance, to arouse dislike for a cautious man, one should present him as cold and designing. Or to make a simpleton lovable, play up his good nature. Or speak of quarrelsomeness as frankness, or of arrogance as poise and dignity, or of foolhardiness as courage, and of squandering as generosity. Also, he says, we should consider the audience before whom we are thus passing judgment: for it's hard to praise Athenians when you are talking to Lacedaemonians.

Part of the quotation appears in Book I. It is quoted again, entire, in Book III, where he has been discussing the speaker's appeal to friendship or compassion. And he continues: When winding up a speech in praise of someone, we "must make the hearer believe that he shares in the praise, either personally, or through his family or profession, or somehow." When you are with Athenians, it's easy to praise Athenians, but not when you are with Lacedaemonians.

Here is perhaps the simplest case of persuasion. You persuade a man only insofar as you can talk his language by speech, gesture, tonality, order, image, attitude, idea, *identifying* your ways with his. Persuasion by flattery is but a special case of persuasion in general. But flattery can safely serve as our paradigm if we systematically widen its meaning, to see behind it the conditions of identification or consubstantiality in general. And you give the "signs" of such consubstantiality by deference to an audience's "opinions." For the orator, following Aristotle and Cicero, will seek to display the appropriate "signs" of character needed to earn the audience's good will. True, the rhetorician may have to change an audience's opinion in one respect; but he can succeed only insofar as he yields to that audience's opinions in other respects. Some of their opinions are needed to support the fulcrum by which he would move other opinions. (Preferably he shares the fixed opinions himself since, "all other things being equal," the identifying of himself with his audience will be more effective if it is genuine.)

The so-called "commonplaces" or "topics" in Aristotle's *Art of Rhetoric* (and the corresponding *loci communes* in Latin manuals) are a quick survey of "opinion" in this sense. Aristotle reviews the purposes, acts, things, conditions, states of mind, personal characteristics, and the like, which people consider promising or formidable, good or evil, useful or dangerous, admirable or loathsome, and so on. All these opinions or assumptions (perhaps today they would be treated under the head of "attitudes" or "values") are catalogued as available means of persuasion. But the important thing, for our purposes, is to note that such types are derived from the principle of persuasion, in that they are but a survey of the things that people generally consider persuasive, and of methods that have persuasive effects.

Thus, Aristotle lists the kind of opinions you should draw upon if you wanted to recommend a policy or to turn people against it; the kind of motives which in people's opinion lead to just or unjust actions; what personal traits people admire or dislike (opinions the speaker should exploit to present himself favorably and his adversary unfavorably); and what opinions can be used as means for stirring men to rage, friendliness, fear, compassion, shame, indignation, envy, rivalry, charity, and so on. Reasoning based on opinion he calls "enthymemes," which are the rhetorical equivalent of the syllogism. And arguments from example (which is the rhetorical equivalent for induction) are likewise to be framed in accordance with his various lists of opinions. (Incidentally, those who talk of "ethical relativity" must be impressed by the "permanence" of such "places" or topics, when stated at Aristotle's level of generalization. As *ideas,* they all seem no less compelling now than they ever were, though in our society a speaker might often have to individuate them in a different *image* than the Greeks would have chosen, if he would convey a maximum sense of actuality.)

Aristotle also considers another kind of "topic," got by the manipulation of tactical procedures, by following certain rules of thumb for inventing, developing, or transforming an expression, by pun-logic, even by specious and sophistical arguments. The materials of opinion will be embodied in such devices, but their characterization as "topics" is got by abstracting some formal or procedural element as their distinguishing mark. Aristotle here includes such "places" as: ways of turning an adversary's words against himself, and of transforming an argument by opposites ("if war did it, repair it by peace"). Some other terms of this sort are: recalling what an adversary advocated in one situation when recommending a policy for a new situation ("you wanted it then, you should want it now"); using definitions to advantage (Socrates using his previous mention of his *daimonion* as evidence that he was not an atheist); dividing up an assertion ("there were three motives for the offense; two were impossible, not even the accusers have asserted the third"); tendentious selection of results (since a cause may have both good and bad effects, one can play up whichever set favors his position); exaggeration (the accused can weaken the strength of the accusation against him by himself overstating it); the use of signs (arguing that the man is a thief because he is disreputable); and so on. Among these tactics, he calls particular attention to the use of a shift between public and private orders of motivation. In public, one praises the just and the beautiful; but in private one prefers the test of expediency; hence the orator can use whichever of these orders better suits his purposes. Here is the paradigm for the modern rhetorician's shuttling between "idealistic" and "materialistic" motives, as when one imputes "idealistic" motives to one's own faction and "materialistic" motives to the adversary; or the adversary can be accused of "idealistic" motives when they imply ineffectiveness and impracticability.

Though the translation of one's wishes into terms of an audience's opinions would clearly be an instance of identification, this last list of purely formal devices for rhetorical invention takes us farther afield. However, it seems to be a fact that, the more urgent the oratory, the greater the profusion and vitality of the formal devices. So they must be *functional,* and not mere "embellishments." And processes of "identification" would seem to figure here, as follows:

Longinus refers to that kind of elation wherein the audience feels as though it were not merely receiving, but were itself creatively participating in the poet's or speaker's assertion. Could we not say that, in such cases, the audience is exalted by the assertion because it has the feel of collaborating in the assertion?

At least, we know that many purely formal patterns can readily awaken an attitude of collaborative expectancy in us. For instance, imagine a passage built about a set of oppositions (*"we* do *this,* but *they* on the other hand do *that; we* stay *here,* but *they* go *there; we* look *up,* but *they* look *down,"* etc.). Once you grasp the trend of the form, it invites participation regardless of the subject matter. Formally, you will find yourself swinging along with the succession of antitheses, even though you may not agree with the proposition that is being presented in this form. Or it may even be an opponent's proposition which you resent—yet for the duration of the statement itself you might "help him out" to the extent of yielding to the formal development, surrendering to its symmetry as such. Of course, the more violent your original resistance to the proposition, the weaker will be your degree of "surrender" by "collaborating" with the form. But in cases where a decision is still to be reached, a yielding to the form prepares for assent to the matter identified with it. Thus, you are drawn to the form, not in your capacity as a partisan, but because of some "universal" appeal in it. And this attitude of assent may then be transferred to the matter which happens to be associated with the form.

Or think thus of another strongly formal device like climax (*gradatio*). The editor of Demetrius' *On Style,* in the Loeb edition, cites this example from *As You Like It,* where even the name of the figure appears in the figure:

> Your brother and my sister no sooner met but they looked, no sooner looked but they loved, no sooner loved but they sighed, no sooner sighed but they asked one another the reason, no sooner knew the reason but they sought the remedy; and in these *degrees* they have made a *pair of stairs* to marriage.

Here the form requires no assent to a moot issue. But recall a *gradatio* of political import, much in the news during the "Berlin crisis" of 1948: "Who controls Berlin, controls Germany; who controls Germany controls Europe; who controls Europe controls the world." As a proposition, it may or may not be true. And even if it is true, unless people are thoroughly imperialistic, they may not want to control the world. But regardless of these doubts about it as a proposition, by the time you arrive at the second of its three stages, you feel how it is destined to develop—and on the level of purely formal assent you would collaborate to round out its symmetry by spontaneously willing its completion and perfection as an utterance. Add, now, the psychosis of nationalism, and assent on the formal level invites assent to the proposition as doctrine.

Demetrius also cites an example from Aeschines: "Against yourself you call; against the laws you call; against the entire democracy you call." (We have tinkered with the translation somewhat, to bring out the purely linguistic structure as greatly as possible, including an element that Demetrius does not discuss, the *swelling* effect at the third stage. In the original the three stages comprise six, seven, and ten syllables respectively.) To illustrate the effect, Demetrius gives the same *idea* without the cumulative form, thus: "Against yourself and the laws and the democracy you call." In this version it lacks the three formal elements he is discussing: repetition of the same word at the beginning of each clause (epanaphora), sameness of sound at the close of each clause (homoeoteleuton), and absence of conjunctions (asyndeton). Hence there is no pronouncedly formal feature to which one might give assent. (As a noncontroversial instance of cumulative form we recall a sentence cited approvingly in one of Flaubert's letters: "They proceeded some on foot, some on horse, some on the backs of elephants." Here the gradation of the visual imagery reënforces the effect of the syllabic elongation.)

Of the many "tropes" and "figures" discussed in the eighth and ninth books of Quintilian's *Institutio Oratoria,* the invitation to purely formal assent (regardless of content) is much greater in some cases than others. It is not our purpose here to analyze the lot in detail. We need but say enough to establish the principle, and to indicate why the expressing of a proposition in one or another of these rhetorical forms would involve "identification," first by inducing the auditor to participate in the form, as a "universal" locus of appeal, and next by trying to include a partisan statement within this same pale of assent.

Other Variants of the Rhetorical Motive

When making his claims for the universality of rhetoric (in the first book of the *De Oratore*) Cicero begins at a somewhat mythic stage when right acting and right speaking were considered one (he cites Homer on the training of Achilles). Next he notes regretfully the sharp dissociating of action and speech whereby the Sophists would eventually confine rhetoric to the verbal in a sheerly ornamental sense. And following this, he notes further detractions from the dignity of rhetoric caused by the dissociating of rhetoric and philosophy. (Cicero blames Socrates for this division. Thus, ironically, the Socratic attempt to make systematic allowance for the gradual increase of cultural heterogeneity and scientific specialization was blamed for the very situation which had called it forth and which it was designed to handle.) Rhetoric suffers by the division, Cicero notes, because there arises a distinction between "wisdom" and "eloquence" which would justify the Sophists' reduction of rhetoric to sheer verbal blandishments.

Later, philosophy and wisdom could be grouped under "dialectic," dialectic treated *as distinct from* the ingratiations of rhetoric (a distinction which the Stoics transformed into a flat opposition between dialectic and rhetoric, choosing the first and rejecting the second). Or dialectic could be treated as the ground of rhetoric, hence as not merely verbal, but in the realm of things, the realm of the universal order, guiding the rhetorician in his choice of purposes (as we noted with respect to Augustine). Cicero himself stressed the notion that, since the rhetorician must also be adept in logic and worldly knowledge, such universal aptitude is *intrinsic* to his eloquence.

Also (continuing our review) there is rhetoric as an art of "proving opposites"; as appeal to emotions and prejudices; as "agonistic," shaped by a strongly competitive purpose.

On this last score, we might note that Isocrates, responding to the element of unfairness in the war of words, chose to spiritualize the notion of "advantage" (*pleonexia*). While recognizing the frequent rhetorical aim to take advantage of an opportunity or to gain advantage for oneself, he located the "true advantage" of the rhetorician in *moral* superiority. He was thinking of an ideal rhetoric, of course, rather than describing the struggle for advantage as it ordinarily does take place in human affairs. But he here adds a very important term to our list: Among the marks of rhetoric is its use to *gain advantage,* of one sort or another.

Indeed, all the sources of "happiness" listed in Aristotle's "eudaimonist" rhetoric, as topics to be exploited for persuasion and dissuasion, could be lumped under the one general heading of "advantage," as could the nineteenth-century Utilitarians' doctrine of "interest," or that batch of motives which La Rochefoucauld, in his 213th maxim, gave as "the causes of that valor so celebrated among men": love of glory with its corollaries (fear of disgrace and envy of others), desire for money (and its corollary, comfortable and agreeable living) (*l'amour de la gloire, la crainte de la honte, le dessein de faire fortune, le désir de rendre notre vie commode et agréable, et l'envie d'abaisser les autres*).

We think this term, "advantage," quite useful for rhetorical theory, in that it can also subsume, before we meet them, all posssible "drives" and "urges" for the existence of which various brands of psychology and sociology may claim to find empirical evidence (terminologies with rhetorical implications of their own, as you can readily see by contrasting them, for instance, with the rhetorical implications of the Marxist terminology). Surely all doctrines can at least begin by agreeing that human effort aims at "advantage" of one sort or another, though there is room for later disputes as to whether advantage in general, or particular advantages are to be conceived idealistically, materialistically, or even cynically. Advantage can be individual, or the aim of a partisan group, or even universal. And that men should seek advantage of some sort is reasonable and ethical enough—hence the term need not confine one's terminology of rhetorical design to purely individualist cunning or aggrandizement, as with the rhetorical implications lurking in those "scientific" terminologies that reduce human motives to a few primitive appetites, resistances, and modes of acquisition ("post-Christian" terminologies in the sense that you could arrive at motivational orders of this sort, as La Rochefoucauld in his *Maxims* on the operations of self-love is said to have done, by merely deducting from the orthodox Christian version of human motives, until human behavior is but *"celle de la lumière naturelle et de la raison sans grâce"*).

Perhaps we should make clear: We do not offer this list as a set of ingredients all or most of which must be present at once, as the test for the presence of the rhetorical motive. Rather, we are considering a wide range of meanings already associated with rhetoric, in ancient texts; and we are saying that one or another of these meanings may be uppermost in some particular usage. But though these meanings are often not consistent with one another, or are even flatly at odds, we do believe that they can all be derived from "persuasion" as the "Edenic" term from which they have all "Babylonically" split, while "persuasion" in turn involves communication by the signs of consubstantiality, the appeal of *identification.* Even *extrinsic* consideration can thus be derived in an orderly manner from persuasion as generating principle: for an act of persuasion is affected by the character of the scene in which it takes place and of the agents to whom it is addressed. The same rhetorical act could vary in its effectiveness, according to shifts in the situation or in the attitude of audiences. Hence, the rhetorician's exploiting of opinion leads into the analysis of non-verbal factors wholly extrinsic to the rhetorical expression considered purely as a verbal structure.

Thus, if the Aristotelian concern with topics were adapted to the conditions of modern journalism, we should perhaps need to catalogue a kind of *timely topic,* such as that of the satirical cartoon, which exploits commonplaces of a transitory nature. The transitoriness is due not to the fact that the expressions are wholly alien to people living under other conditions, but to the fact that they are *more persuasive* with people living under one particular set of circumstances. Thus, even an exceptionally good cartoon exploiting the subject of unemployment (as with satire on federal "leaf-raking" and "boondoggling" projects during the "made work" period of the Franklin Roosevelt administration) would have a hard time getting published during a period of maximum employment, when a timelier topic might be the shortage of workers in general and of domestic help in particular (and when an editor would consider even a poor cartoon on labor shortage preferable to an exceptional one on unemployment).

When reduced to the level of *ideas,* timely cartoons will be found to exploit much the same list of universal commonplaces that Aristotle assembles. But topical shifts make certain *images* more persuasive in one situation than another. Quintilian touches upon such a narrowing down of the commonplaces when he notes how a general topic is made specific not merely by being attached to some individual figure, but also by a coupling with other particularizing marks, as "we make our adulterer blind, our gambler poor, and our profligate old." And Cicero, when discussing the function of *memory* in the orator, refers to a lost contemporary work on the systematic associating of topics and images (*simulacra*). Thus, a statement about "timely topics" would seem to be, not an extension of the rhetorical motive to fields not traditionally considered part of it, but merely as the application of classical theory to a special cultural condition set by the modern press. We pass over it hastily here, as we plan to consider the two major aspects of it in later sections of this project (when we shall consider the new level of "reality" which journalistic timeliness establishes, and shall study the relation between transient and permanent factors of appeal by taking the cartoons in *The New Yorker* as test case).

Meanwhile, again, the thought of the timely topic reminds us that sociological works reviewing the rise and fall of slogans, clichés, stock figures of folk consciousness, and the like, impinge upon the rhetorical motive. Indeed, unless this is material for rhetoric, an aspect of *rhetorica docens,* a body of knowledge about audiences, pragmatically available for use when planning appeals to audiences, then such material lacks pragmatic sanction and must be justified on purely "liberal" grounds, in terms of literary or philosophic "appreciation," as knowledge assembled, classified, and contemplated not for use, but for its own sake. There is most decidedly no objection to such a motive, when it is recognized for what it is; but it is usually concealed by the fact that much "pure" science, cultivated without concern for utility, was later found to be of pragmatic value. The fact that anything *might* be of use has allowed for a new unction whereby an investigation can be justified, not for what it is, but for what it might possibly lead to. Nature is so "full of gods" (powers) that a systematic directing of the attention anywhere is quite likely to disclose a new one, some genius local to the particular subject matter. Hence, a cult of "fact-finding," with no order of facts considered too lowly for the collector. In itself, the attitude has much to recommend it. It is scientific humility in the best sense. But it should not be allowed to give specious justification for inquiries where the sheer *absence of intrinsic value* is assumed to imply the *presence of pragmatic value.*

Equivalent to the narrowing and intensifying of appeal by the featuring of timely topics, there is another aspect of address more characteristic of modern conditions, particularly the kind of canvassing shaped primarily by postal communication. Both Aristotle and Cicero laid stress upon the differences among audiences. Indeed, Aristotle's recipes that distinguish between the commonplaces as appealing to a young audience and those appealing to an old one could serve as a playwright's formulas for the contrasted stock characters of "fiery youth" and timid age. For however strong Aristotle's bias towards science may have been, it was always modified by a highly dramatistic context. His rhetoric is thoroughly dramatist in its insights.

But Aristotle does not discuss varieties of audience with the systematic thoroughness which he brings to the classification of opinion in general. And both Aristotle and Cicero consider audiences purely as something *given*. The extreme heterogeneity of modern life, however, combined with the nature of modern postal agencies, brings up another kind of possibility: the systematic attempt to *carve out* an audience, as the commercial rhetorician looks not merely for persuasive devices in general, but for the topics that will appeal to the particular "income group" most likely to be interested in his product, or able to buy it. If immediacy or intensity of appeal is got by narrowing the topics and images to the group likely to be his best audience, he will seek to prod only these to action (if we could call it "active," rather than "passive," when a prospective customer is bent towards one brand of a commodity rather than another, though the brand he passes up may be a better buy than the one he purchases, a kind of conduct that may not be informed enough to be "rational" and "free," hence not rational and free enough to be truly an act, at least in the full philosophic sense of the term). In any case, here too would be a consideration of audiences; hence even by the tests of the classic tradition it would fall under the head of rhetoric, though it necessarily extended the range of the term to cover a situation essentially new.

Thus, all told, besides the *extension* of rhetoric through the concept of identification, we have noted these purely traditional evidences of the rhetorical motive: persuasion, exploitation of opinion (the "timely" topic is a variant), a work's nature as addressed, literature for use (applied art, inducing to an act beyond the area of verbal expression considered in and for itself), verbal deception (hence, rhetoric as instrument in the war of words), the "agonistic" generally, words used "sweetly" (eloquence, ingratiation, for its own sake), formal devices, the art of proving opposites (as "counterpart" of dialectic). We have also suggested that the "carving out" of audiences is new to the extent that there are new mediums of communication, but there is nothing here *essentially* outside the traditional concerns of rhetoric. As for the recognition of nonverbal, situational factors that can participate in a work's effectiveness, the neatest statement we know of, for establishing this principle, is by the late Bronislas Malinowski. We refer to his article on primitive languages (published as a supplement in Ogden and Richards' *The Meaning of Meaning*). His concept of "context of situation" establishes a principle which can, we believe, be applied in many ways for the New Rhetoric, most notably when considering the semiverbal, semiorganizational kinds of tactics one might classify as a "rhetoric of bureaucracy."

Formal Appeal

As for the purely formal kinds of appeal which we previously mentioned when trying to show how they involve the principle of identification, their universal nature makes it particularly easy to shift them from rhetoric to poetic. Thus, viewing even tendentious oratory from the standpoint of literary appreciation rather than in terms of its use, Longinus analyzes "sublimity" of effect in and for itself. Where Demosthenes would transport his auditors the better to persuade them, Longinus treats the state of transport as the aim. Hence he seeks to convey the quality of the excitement, and to disclose the means by which it is produced. Indeed, might not his key term, that is usually translated "sublime," come close to what we mean by "moving," not in the rhetorical sense, of moving an audience to a decision, but as when we say of a poem, "How moving!"

Admittedly, the cataloguing of rhetorical devices was carried to extreme lengths. You can't possibly make a statement without its falling into some sort of pattern. Its formality can then be abstracted and named, without reference to any particular subject matter, hence can be looked upon as capable of "reindividuation" in a great variety of subject matters. Given enough industry in observation, abstraction, and classification, you can reduce any expression (even inconsequential or incomplete ones) to some underlying skeletal structure. Teachers of Greek and Latin rhetoric had such industry; and they amassed so many such terms that they had a name for the formal design in practically any expression possible to words. Thus, if a statement proceeds by the repeating of a conjunction ("this *and* that *and* the other"), it will be a *polysyndeton*. Drop the connectives ("this, that, the other") and it becomes *asyndeton*. Build up, by expatiation or intensification, and you have amplification (*auxesis*); treat the more dignified in terms of the less dignified, and you have *meiosis;* amplify a build-up until you have it established as expectation, then break the symmetry of your series with a sudden let-down, and you have *bathos*. Allow a fleeting music of words with the same ending, and you have *homoioteleuton*. (Remember, incidentally, that the Greeks could not say "homoioteleuton"; they had to say, rather, "similarly ended.") Repeat the same word at the beginning of successive phrases, and you have *epanaphora*. And so on. Croce seems to have taken this terminology of piecemeal effects as the very essence of rhetoric. And though, in accordance with Croce's attitude, the modern replacing of logic, rhetoric, and poetic by "esthetics" relegated such forms to the class of "mere rhetoric," he could have quoted from Cicero and Quintilian passages that derived "artifice from eloquence, not eloquence from artifice."

The rhetorical devices can become obtrusive, sheer decadent decoration (as during the era of the "second sophistic" in Rome); but we have offered reasons for believing that even the most ostentatious of them arose out of great functional urgency. When pagan rhetoric grew weak, such verbal exercising could be sought for itself alone, for its appeal as a display of virtuosity. Thus, ironically, the splendidly enthusiastic analyses of Longinus ("enthusiasm" is one of his words) marked a step towards this very decay. But Augustine, who had been trained in pagan rhetoric prior to his conversion, reinfused many of the decaying forms with the zeal of the Christian persuasion.

A list of the more characteristic devices used by Augustine will be found in the volume, *S. Aureli Augusti De Doctrina Christiana Liber Quartus, A Commentary With a Revised Text, Introduction, and Translation,* by Sister Thérèse Sullivan. (For a quite comprehensive study of their vigorous use in English, see *Shakespeare's Use of the Arts of Language,* by Sister Miriam Joseph.) And the third book of Cicero's *De Oratore* gives a quick survey of such resources for varying an address "with the lights of thought and language" (*luminibus sententiarum atque verborum*). Here are selections from Cicero's list:

Dwelling on a subject, driving it home (*commemoratio*), bringing it before one's very eyes (*explanatio*), both of them devices valuable for stating a case, illustrating and amplifying it; review (*praecisio*);

disparagement (*extenuatio*), accompanied by raillery (*illusio*); digression (*digressio*), with neatly contrived return to the subject; statement of what one proposes to say; distinguishing it from what has already been said; return to a point already established; repetition, reduction to sharply syllogistic form (*apta conclusio*); overstatement and understatement; rhetorical question; irony, saying one thing and meaning another (*dissimulatio*), a device which, he says, is particularly effective with audiences if it is used in a conversational tone, not rantingly; stopping to ponder (*dubitatio*); dividing a subject into components (*distributio*), so that you can effectively dispose of them in one-two-three order; finding fault with a statement (*correctio*) which has been made by the opponent, or which one himself has said or is about to say; preparing the audience for what one is about to say (*praemunitio*); shifting of responsibility (*traiectio in alium*); taking the audience into partnership, having a kind of consultation with them (*communicatio*); imitation; impersonation (which he calls an especially weighty *lumen* of amplification); putting on the wrong scent; raising a laugh; forestalling (*anteoccupatio*); comparison (*similitudo*) and example (*exemplum*), "both of them most moving"; interruption (*interpellatio*); alignment of contrasting positions, antithesis (*contentio*); raising of the voice even to the point of frenzy, for purposes of amplificacation (*augendi causa*); anger; invective, imprecation, deprecation, ingratiation, entreaty, vowing "O would that . . ." (*optatio*)—and, yes, also, lapses into meaningful silence.

Regarding this last point, we recall a lecturer on music who interspersed his talk with songs accompanied on old instruments. Every now and then he paused, took a handkerchief from his breast pocket, carefully unfolded it, touched his hands with it ever so lightly, then slowly, painstakingly folded it again and replaced it in his pocket. In time the audience got to watching this silent ritual as attentively as though he were a magician about to do a trick.

We saw another speaker, a theologian, who periodically interrupted his sermonlike lecture while he gazed into space. The audience waited for a marvel—and slowly, as was made apparent by the changing expression on the speaker's face, there became manifest the signs of the next idea which he was about to fetch from these distant depths. Sometimes, when thus seeking to descry the next message, he turned his eyes intently upward, and to the right. At other times, he bent, and looked down, intently, to the left. Presumably he alternated these postures for the sake of variety; but we began to speculate: If, by looking upward, and to the right, he can bring forth ideas from heaven, then by the same token, when he has looked downward, and to the left, does he also have other things brought steaming hot from hell?

Cicero likens his lists of devices to weapons, which can be used for threat and attack, or can be brandished purely for show. He also mentions several kinds of repetition with variation (the highly inflected nature of Latin, with its corresponding freedom of word order, allows readily for many such effects which English can approximate only with difficulty). And he continues (we quote the *Loeb Classical Library* translation by H. Rackham, from which we adapted the previous citation):

> There is also advance step by step (*gradatio*), and inversion (transposition, metathesis, *conversio*), and harmonious interchange of words, and antithesis (*contrarium*), and omission of particles (*dissolutum*), and change of subject (*declinatio*), and self-correction (*reprehensio*), and exclamation (*exclamatio*), and abbreviation (*imminutio*), and the use of a noun in several cases [an English equivalent would be Mead's sloganlike formula, "An 'I' contemplating its 'me' "].

He goes on to mention such things as deliberate hesitation over the choice of a word, conceding of a point, surprise, continuity and discontinuity (*continuatum et interruptum*), the use of images (*imago*), metonymy (*immutatio*), "and distinguishing terms, and order, and reference back, and digression, and periphrasis" (*disiunctio et ordo et relatio et digressio et circumscriptio*), asking questions which one answers oneself.

Incidentally, when an issue is highly controversial, this last device can have disastrous results, unless one is an expert orator. Thus, shortly after the Allied armies had occupied Italy in the last war, the philosopher Croce was speaking in favor of monarchy. It was a good opportunity, since the gathering had been called to do him honor, as an old liberal. At one point, he asked himself, "Do we want the restoration of the King?" But before he had a chance to answer himself by saying, "We do," the audience shouted back a thunderous "No!" (Coleridge tells of an instance, on the other hand, where Demosthenes deliberately provoked an unruly answer from his audience. In his speech "On the Crown," when attacking his opponent Aeschines, he asked the audience: "Do you think Aeschines is Alexander's hireling, or his friend?" But he slightly mispronounced the word for "hireling," putting the accent on the wrong syllable. The audience, as connoisseurs of speech, shouted back at him the correct pronunciation for "hireling." Whereupon he concluded with an air of satisfaction: "You hear what they say.")

Of all rhetorical devices, the most thoroughgoing is amplification (Greek, *auxesis*). It seems to cover a wide range of meanings, since one can amplify by extension, by intensification, and by dignification. The last two kinds have an opposite: diminution (*meiosis*). But as extension, expatiation, the saying of something in various ways until it increases in persuasiveness by the sheer accumulation, amplification can come to name a purely poetic process of development, such systematic exploitation of a theme as we find in lyrics built about a refrain. In this sense, we could designate as "rhetorical" the characteristic method of a popular song, though the persuasive aspects of rhetoric in the sense of an ulterior purpose are wholly lacking. Perhaps a work efficiently exploiting the tactics of *meiosis* (the satire of *Gulliver's Travels,* for instance) could be treated paradoxically as an amplification of diminution.

Rhetorical Form in the Large

There is also persuasive form in the larger sense, formulated as a progression of steps that begins with an exordium designed to secure the good will of one's audience, next states one's own position, then points up the nature of the dispute, then builds up one's own case at length, then refutes the claims of the adversary, and in a final peroration expands and reinforces all points in one's favor, while seeking to discredit whatever had favored the adversary (vituperation, irony, and appeal to the emotions also being drawn upon here). The great concern with the classifying and analyzing of minute incidental effects has caused writers on ancient rhetoric to say that these larger principles of form were slighted. Yet they are recognized as set stages in the strucure of an oration, almost as formal as the movements of a symphony. (Aristotle's third book treats of them energetically, without running against the law of diminishing returns that does damage to

Quintilian. The steps listed above are a rough paraphrase of a passage in Cicero, where Crassus is briefly reviewing the standard education of an orator.) But literary theory is traditionally weak in the analysis of structure in the larger sense, if only because isolated stylistic effects lend themselves readily to quotation, whereas the discussion of formal development in the large is unwieldy. (Even Coleridge, with his stress upon the *unifying* function of the imagination, does not analyze structural unity in the over-all sense, but becomes involved in a kind of methodological oxymoron, illustrating total unity by fragmentary examples.)

But there were ways in which the art of persuasion could be conveniently discussed in the large; this was by generalizations about kinds of rhetoric, kinds of style, and the functions or duties of the rhetorician (Cicero's *officia oratoris*).

Considered broadly, in terms of *address,* an audience can have three primary purposes in listening: to hear advice about the future, or to pass judgment on some action in the past, or merely for the sake of interest in a speech or subject as such. Use these distinctions as a basis for classifying *kinds* of rhetoric, and you get the traditional three formulated in Aristotle's *Rhetoric:* (1) deliberative, directed towards the future, as with communication designed to sway an audience on matters of public policy; (2) forensic or judicial, involving the past, as with speeches designed to establish in a jury's mind the guilt or innocence of an accused person; and (3) demonstrative (epideictic, "display" oratory, sometimes also called panegyric). This third kind readily becomes a catch-all. Aristotle says that it aims at praise or blame. And he says that it is concerned primarily with the present. Even at the height of Greek rhetoric, its range included: funeral orations; tributes to some public character (or diatribes against such figures); patriotic addresses lauding one's city or one's countrymen; playful, often punning encomiums on animals and things (or playful invectives against them).

Perhaps the sturdiest modern variant of epideictic rhetoric is in "human interest" stories depicting the sacrificial life of war heroes in war times, or Soviet works (including propaganda motion pictures) that celebrate the accomplishments of individuals and groups who triumph over adversity in carrying out the government's plans for exploitation of the nation's resources. For Cicero says that epideictic (panegyric, *laudatio*) should deal especially in those virtues thought beneficial "not so much to their possessors as to mankind in general." Thus, the praise most welcome "is for deeds that seem to have been done without profit and reward." Toil and personal danger are good subjects, since the mark of an outstanding citizen is "virtue profitable to others" (*virtus . . . fructuosa aliis*).

Aristotle probably assigned this third kind to the present because, having defined the others with reference to the future (the deliberative concern with expedients) and the past (the forensic concern with the justice or injustice of things already done), by elimination he needed a kind aiming primarily at the present. Then he goes on to say that "epideictic" or demonstrative speakers, in their concern with praise and blame (the honorable and dishonorable) also frequently recall the past or look to the future—which would seem to take back all that had been given. But the selecting of the present as the most appropriate time for this kind is justified by another consideration. Often this third kind, as a rhetoric of "display," was aimed at praise, not as an attempt to win an audience's praise for the subject discussed, but as an attempt to win praise for the oratory itself. The appropriate time for such oratory could then be called the present in the sense that the appeal was directed to the very presence of the words and speaker themselves, not for some ulterior purpose, as with convincing a jury about a past act or moving an assembly to make a decision about the future, but purely because it aimed to give delight in the exercise of eloquence as such. We can see the appeal of subject matter merging with the appeal of diction in and for itself when Cicero selected toil and personal danger as good themes for panegyric on the ground that they get the readiest reception, since they offer "the richest opportunities for praise" and can be discussed "most ornately" (*ornatissime*).

Obviously, this third form would become uppermost in periods of rhetorical decay, as when the democratic functions of public debate were curtailed in Rome after the fall of the Republic. At such time, the sturdiest rhetoric with ulterior motive would be found, not in public utterance, but in the unrecorded cabals of courtiers. And public rhetoric, with only the forms of persuasion left, came eventually, as in school exercises, to deal with arbitrarily chosen subjects, which were then developed with all the resources of amplification, displayed for their own sake. But this was merely an extreme expression of a tendency present in epideictic at the start. For this kind contained the most essential motive of all: persuasion by words, rather than by force, on the part of those who loved eloquence for itself alone (those born verbalizers, so close to the very center of human motives, as distinct from the motives of other animals, those humane word-slingers who would rather fail in seeking to persuade by words than succeed in persuading by other means). Critics must have epideictic in mind who say that eloquence begins in the love of words for their own sake.

The "presentness" of epideictic, which brought it closest to appeal by sheer delight, also explains why it is, according to Aristotle, the kind that lends itself best to the written word. For its effects can be savored, hence may profit by a closer, more sustained scrutiny. Also, since pure display rhetoric comes closest to the appeal of poetic in and for itself, it readily permits the arbitrary selection of topics halfway between rhetoric and poetic. And here even methods originally forensic may be used as artifice. Thus, in the English tradition of love poems written in praise of one's mistress or as mock invective against love, etc., or where the lover pleads the "cause" of his mistress or brings indictments against her, the poet's tactics are not read as he would have them read unless the reader watches their playful adaptation of rhetorical forms to poetic purposes. (See Rosemond Tuve, *Elizabethan and Metaphysical Imagery,* for a good discussion of the rhetorical tradition implicit in such lyrical conceits.)

This application touches upon an aspect of rhetoric which, besides allowing for such playful or esthetic usages as we have been just considering, also figured in the rhetoric of ulterior purposes. Both Cicero and Quintilian make much of a traditional distinction between general theses (*quaestiones*) and particular cases (*causae*). The *quaestiones* were often of a sort wholly outside the scope of the flatly true-or-false (as were one to debate whether truth was greater than justice). The *causae* (as with debates whether such-and-such a man had been guilty of such-and-such an offense meriting such-and-such punishment) brought rhetoric within the orbit of *casuistry* (thereby suggesting that an extension of the rhetorical range to cover all cases in their *uniqueness* would be in order, Cicero saying that there are as many *causae* as there are people). The general and the particular directions of rhetoric overlap insofar as all unique cases will necessarily involve the application of the universal topics to the particular matter at hand, and

TRADITIONAL PRINCIPLES OF RHETORIC

insofar as even situations considered very broadly may possess uniqueness. (Since any one particular era in history, for instance, will be unlike any other in its exact combination of cultural factors, historiography seems naturally vowed to a measure of rhetorical casuistry, however scientific may be the pretensions of historians, economists, sociologists, etc., though the scientific pretensions themselves might be less effective rhetorically if such enterprise were formally recognized as involved in the rhetoric of casuistry.)

The forensic or judicial kind (as with speeches by prosecuting or defense attorneys in a law suit) seems clear enough. And so with deliberative, though by listing its main concerns, as stated in Aristotle, we might better realize how ubiquitous such "oratory" is today, particularly in written forms that often pass for sheer "information," "knowledge," "science." They are: ways and means, war and peace, national defense, imports and exports, legislation.

If we confine the third kind of rhetoric to praise and blame, just where, Quintilian asks, are we to place the rhetorical function of a speaker who would "complain, console, pacify, incite, frighten, encourage, instruct, interpret, narrate, plead for mercy, give thanks, congratulate, reproach, curse, describe, command, retract, state views and preferences," etc.? Such questions led to other ways of classification: by style and function (Cicero's three *officia oratoris*). In his *Orator,* an earlier work than the *De Oratore,* when defending his verbal opulence against a rising "Attic" school in Rome which called for simpler diction, Cicero distinguishes three styles (*genera dicendi, genera scribendi*): the grandiloquent, plain, and tempered. And he names as the three "offices" of the orator: (1) to teach, inform, instruct (*docere*); (2) to please (*delectare*); (3) to move or "bend" (*movere, flectere*).

He also refers to styles in a more personal or individual sense, when observing that orators are next of kin to poets, and that each poet has his own way of writing (and in a critical digression he gives a catalogue of formulas for succinctly characterizing and savoring the distinctive qualities in the personal style of various writers well known to antiquity). However, the three over-all styles of oratory are not thought of thus, as personal expression, but as a means for carrying out the three "offices." That is, the plain style is best for teaching, the tempered style for pleasing, and the ornate (grandiloquent) style for moving. Though human weakness makes an orator more able in one or another of these styles, the ideal orator should be master of all three, since an oration aims at all three functions. For though it aims ultimately to *move* the audience by a sweeping appeal to the emotions, it can do so only if it holds their interest (hence, using all the resources of verbal delight); and it can't either hold their interest or move them unless it has a groundwork of clarity. (Cicero says that the orator should call as much attention to his use of instruction as possible, but should thoroughly though unnoticeably infuse his speech with the other two functions.)

This way of dividing in terms of styles and offices cuts at an angle across the Aristotelian theory of kinds. But the tempered style, with its aim to delight, does closely parallel the motive of eloquence for its own sake that centers in epideictic (the *genus demonstrativum*). Cicero puts it to use; but it becomes the *end* of eloquence insofar as ulterior rhetorical purpose drops away.

Longinus' treatise *On the Sublime* is thought to have been written in the first century or the third, A.D. But with Aristotle's *Art of Rhetoric* dated at 330 B.C., Cicero's *De Oratore* at 55 B.C., Quintilian's *Institutio Oratoria* in the latter half of the first century A.D., and the fourth book of Augustine's *De Doctrina Christiana* in 426–7 A.D., it would make a very neat "curve" if Longinus could be placed as a transition between Quintilian and Augustine. For while its stress upon the sheer delight of literature (with even purposive oratory discussions from this "esthetic" point of view) would assign it to a period of decadence, and Longinus himself regrets the triviality of the times, so far as new writing is concerned, the quality of the exaltation in his love of literature seems like a matching, in pagan terms, for the Augustinian fervor in Christian persuasion. Longinus' treatise would seem to qualify perfectly as an estheticizing of the Christian motive *before* its institutional triumph, quite as much modern love of literature is a *relique* of Christianity, the reduction of its persuasion and passion to a cult of purely esthetic "grace."

In any case, when we turn to Augustine, we find the Ciceronian stress upon ulterior purpose restored in all its vigor. Also, the rhetoric with which Augustine is exclusively concerned, a rhetoric for persuading audiences to a Christian way of life, does not aim at systematic observations about the art of "proving opposites." His treatment is at once both narrowed and widened: narrowed in the sense that it is concerned only with the use of words for one purpose, the teaching of Christianity; widened in the sense that the persuasion it would establish was a doctrine of universal motivation. Thus, his discussion of persuasion in general is built about a close analysis of Biblical texts, which he selects and studies for their *craftsmanship*. His sense of purely literary appreciation is as vigorous and acute as with Longinus, but the appreciation is always subordinated to his ulterior purpose as propagandist of the Faith. He is particularly convincing in his treatment of St. Paul, like him a master of apologetics, and like him one of the twice-born whose sensitiveness to communicative problems was sharpened by the memory of harsh conflict within, of inner voices at one time opposing each other like rivals in debate.

Applying the three Ciceronian offices, he characteristically names the plain style (that is, the style for teaching, *docere*), the "subdued" (*genus submissum*), thereby spontaneously indicating perhaps, that both as a Christian and as an individual, he *had to impose restraint upon himself* in the use of a manner which many would practice merely through having nothing to restrain. Next comes the "tempered" or moderated style. (He is obviously affected by the category of the epideictic here, as he says that the temperate style is best suited for criticism and praise, even the praise of God being named as a fit subject for this style.) But one must speak grandly (*granditer*) when there is something to be done and "minds are to be swayed" (*ad flectendos animos*). Here again we see a replica of the Longinus esthetic in terms of Christian persuasion: for just as the concern with the "sublime" in Longinus culminates in ideas and images of the fearsome, so the ardor and vehemence of the grand style in Augustine is said to be particularly fit for admonishing against the neglect of God.

But the *totality* of motivation propounded by Christian doctrine provided a new poignancy to the relation between the rhetoric of particular cases and the rhetoric of generalization For though each of the three styles is appropriate for certain purposes, Augustine says there is a sense in which all topics of Christian rhetoric deserve treatment in the grand style, since there is nothing in life that does not somehow bear upon God. Thus, though money matters may be trivial from an ordinary point of view, no sum, however small, can be trivial to the true Christian. Wherefore St. Paul spoke of money in the grand style, since justice, charity, and righteousness are involved, "and no sane man can doubt that these are great, even in things exceptionally slight." The resonance of such a rhetoric is obvious. Since all was of God, for God, through God, the step from the lowly to the lofty was everywhere at hand. And just as, in the *Grammar of Motives,* we saw that "God" is the Term of Terms, the Title of Titles, the X of X's (Aristotle's definition of God as "thought of thought" can be the paradigm), so in the *Rhetoric of Motives* (using "commonplace" in the sense assigned it in classical theory) we see that "God" is the Commonplace of Commonplaces, the Topic of Topics, the universal *Quaestio* behind each local *Causa,* the Ultimate to which any particular matter of controversy might be grandly reduced.

Ironically, though Augustine was restoring the dignity of rhetoric, after the decay into which it had fallen during the pagan "second sophistic," he expressly denies the Ciceronian and Quintilian attempts to equate eloquence with moral excellence. Augustine was pleading for a "truth" greater than any purely human kind of moral grandeur. Hence, while saying that a good life on the part of the preacher was the most persuasive ingredient of all in commending Christian doctrine, he placed the power of this doctrine outside and beyond any merely human or natural vessels. A preacher might preach Christian doctrine purely for purposes of self-aggrandizement, or even as a lie, but if he preached it correctly his preaching could do good, because of its intrinsic worth, despite the viciousness of his motives.

This notion that the power of truth transcends the limitations of the personal agent who propounds it (or, as Augustine puts it, that the chair, *cathedra,* forces him to say what is good), finds its ironic counterpart in a situation today, when the "truth" of the Christian terminology has found its materialistic counterpart in the terminologies of science. For here again, the truth can transcend the vices of those who communicate it. Indeed, unfortunately, there is the risk that it can by the same token transcend their virtues also, as when earnest, hard-working men, whose efforts are guided by discipline and devotion, perfect powers which, in their pragmatic validity, can be used by men of different cast, in ways that threaten the very existence of mankind.

In the *De Oratore,* Cicero had said that "the faculty of speech flows from the deepest founts of wisdom" (*ex intimis sapientiae fontibus*). With the same distinctions in mind, Augustine refers to St. Paul as "a follower of wisdom, a leader of eloquence" (*comes sapientiae, dux eloquentiae*). But there is a notable difference: for Cicero is equating rhetoric with wisdom, whereas Augustine is relating them in a preferential order. In his scheme, wisdom (philosophy, "dialectic") is a "source of eloquence," not because it is one with eloquence (since the "truth" of Christian doctrine can be stated without eloquence), but because it is the *ground* of eloquence. Thus, whereas Aristotle grouped rhetoric with dialectic by reason of the fact that both were purely verbal instruments, in Augustine (as with the Stoics) dialectic is more than words: for when it is correct, it deals with the ultimate nature of *things,* hence has a kind of extraverbal reference to guide the use of ornament (eloquence, rhetoric). The end of rhetoric was "to persuade with words" (*persuadere dicendo*); but the principle of Logos behind such purely human language was "the Word" in another sense, a kind of Word that was *identical with* reality. Such seem to be the assumptions underlying Augustine's theories of rhetoric. And they seem to follow from the stress upon *teaching* as an "office" of rhetoric.

Cicero had made much of the distinction between words and things (*verba* and *res*). Aristotle was thinking along the same lines when he distinguished rhetoric, as an art of words, from the sciences, each having a special extraverbal subject matter. A passage in Aristotle's *Rhetoric* making a distinction between natural incentives, such as hunger, and those arising "through reason" (*para logou*) is often rendered in English as a distinction between "logical" and "illogical" motives; but *logos* means both "reason" and "word," hence we might assume that Aristotle was seeking to distinguish between nonverbal motives (*alogoi*—appetites that would arise even if there were no such thing as language) and "verbal" motives (*para logou*—appetitions depending upon language for their development, as with the "new needs" that go with the change of human purpose from mere "living" to "living well").

In any case, note that once you treat instruction as an aim of rhetoric you introduce a principle that can widen the scope of rhetoric beyond persuasion. It is on the way to include also works on the theory and practice of exposition, description, *communication* in general. Thus, finally, out of this principle, you can derive contemporary "semantics" as an aspect of rhetoric.

We thus see how each of the three "offices" comes to the end of a line, each in its way transcending the motive of persuasion (ulterior purpose) by becoming an end in itself. An ideal descriptive language *can be* aligned *in contrast with* hortatory languages. But one can also derive it *out of* the rhetorical. For one can get to this ideal by dwelling exclusively upon the first of the three rhetorical "offices." And, in so doing, one will be at the point where, in the Augustinian scheme, rhetoric overlaps upon dialectic, which in turn is taken to be one with the nature of *things* (the nonverbal ground of all verbalizing).

Imagination

Perhaps because theories of imagination, as a kind of *knowledge*, work best in those areas where poetic and scientist thought overlap, the concern with "imagination" as a suasive device does not reach full expression until the modern era. Also, such concern in the classical rhetorics was often treated in terms of "actualization" (*energeia*, the use of words that suggest purposive movement) and "vividness" (*enargeia*). And Aristotle's classing of "actualization" along with "antithesis" and "metaphor" as the three most effective devices of speech, would include much other matter which might in modern theory be treated from the standpoint of imagination.

According to Aristotle's scheme, and even in a philosopher so on the edge of modern scientific naturalism as Spinoza, "imagination" is quite low in the scale of mental functions, being next to brute sensation, and the highest faculty of which brutes were thought capable. In human beings, according to this hierarchy, it stood midway between sensation and intellect.*

But whereas, in this terminology, sensation requires the actual presence of the thing sensed, imagination does not require the presence of the thing imagined. Hence, though the imagination's necessary use of images testifies to its beginnings in sense, it can deal in images independently of sense (as in both dreams and willed imaginings).

This consideration opens another set of possibilities whereby imagina-

* It so appears in the *Ethics*. In the *Tractatus Theologico-Politicus* it is treated as a medium of prophetic vision for communicating the revelations of religion. Here is the kind of imagination which could later be secularized in romantic theories of artistic vision.

tion can be thought of as reordering the objects of sense, or taking them apart and imagining them in new combinations (such as centaurs) that do not themselves derive from sensory experience. It can thus become "creative," and even visionary of things forever closed to sense, as with the language of the mystic, who would express his intuitions in images meant to transcend imagery. Coleridge's "desynonymizing" of "fancy" and "imagination" was in part an attempt to dissociate these two meanings, leaving for "fancy" (from the Greek *phantasia*) the purely "mechanical" recombinations of sensory experience, and giving to "imagination" (from the Latin *imaginatio* that had been usually used to translate the Greek word) creative and supersensory meanings.

Longinus tells us that in his day, imagination (*phantasia*, which contributes to *enargeia*) had "come to be used of passages where, inspired by enthusiasm and passion, you seem to see what you describe and bring it vividly before the eyes of your audience." After citing examples in *poetry* which "show a strongly mythic exaggeration, far beyond the limits of literal belief," he says that the "best use of imagination" in *rhetoric* is to convince the audience of the "reality and truth" of the speaker's assertions. He also cites passages from Demosthenes where, according to him, imagination persuades by going beyond mere argument. ("When combined with argument, it not only convinces the audience, it positively masters them.") And he ends by equating imagination with genius (*megalophrosyne*, high-mindedness) and with imitation.

This is probably the highest tribute to "imagination" in all Greek and Roman literature (significantly, it appeared in a work not known to have been mentioned by any writer in antiquity, a work which did not come into its own until the currents of modern romanticism were well under way). But though he considers the aim of poetry "to strike with astonishment," and introduces talk of "ecstasy" into literary criticism, he attributes a different role to imagination in rhetoric, where it presumably serves to make the real seem doubly real rather than to make us, within the conditions of a fiction, believe in the "reality" of things which we may not otherwise believe at all. (Rosemond Tuve cites a relevant formula in Mazzoni: "The credible as credible is the subject of rhetoric, and the credible as marvelous is the subject of poetry.")

See Pico Della Mirandola's *On the Imagination* (the Latin text, with an introduction, an English translation, and notes; by Harry Caplan: footnote, p. 36) for references showing that medieval writers had often distinguished between productive and reproductive kinds of imagination, thus anticipating Coleridge's systematic dissociation, though not with his emphases. But Pico did not share this "desynonymizing" (in his tract written at the end of the fifteenth century). Aristotle had said, in the third book of his *Psychology:* "To the mind, images serve as if they were contents of perception. If it judges them to be good, it pursues them. If it judges them to be bad, it avoids them. That is why the mind never thinks without an image." According to his scheme, both imagination and reason can originate movement, the movements originated by imagination being dangerous except insofar as they are controlled by reason (which should in turn be guided by religion). Similarly Pico, when objecting to Avicenna's distinction between the phantastic and the imaginative, wrote: Man is moved to action (*ad operandum*) for the sake of either real or apparent good; but desire depends on perception: perception in turn depends on the senses (which require images). Hence, since even one who reasons and understands must observe images, "we must admit that our actions depend greatly on the nature of this power" (*actiones nostras de eius potestatis ingenio plurimum dependere*).

But while, in Pico's scheme, man shares imagination with the lower animals, human imagination extends farther, and includes motives of decoration, ambition, and honor to which animals are but slightly susceptible. Children are mostly motivated by the brutish kind of imagination. Hence, and because of their weak intellects, one best guides them in the ways of virtue by bringing them to imagine in detail the tortures of hell and the delights of Paradise.

The rhetorical implications of such thinking are brought out clearly by Francis Bacon's formula, in *The Advancement of Learning:* "The duty and office of Rhetoric is to apply Reason to Imagination for the better moving of the Will." According to Bacon, Rhetoric should "fill the imagination, to second Reason, and not to oppress it." And "it is the office of Rhetoric to make pictures of virtue and goodness, so that they may be seen." Or, in a fuller statement: "Rhetoric is subservient to the imagination, as logic is to the understanding; and the duty and office of rhetoric . . . is no other than to apply and recommend the dictates of reason to imagination, in order to excite the appetite and will."

Will itself, according to Bacon, is altered by religion, opinion, and apprehension—and obviously imagination could be brought to the reënforcement of all three. And in the remarks we have cited, he is considering the good uses of a power which will deserve distrust, once you stress rather the negative possibilities that imagination may reënforce prejudiced opinion, false apprehensions, and lapses from religion. Like Augustine, he here considers rhetorical inducement to action from the standpoint of sermonizing, and he judges imagination as a means of persuasion to this end.

Aristotle had said that, particularly in the arousing of pity, the rhetorician is most effective if he can bring before the audience the actual evidence of hardship and injustice suffered. Thus, in proportion as "imagination" went up in the scale of motivational values, one might come to speak of an appeal to the *imagination* in many instances which classical theory might have treated as persuasion by the appeals of *pathos* and *ethos* (appeals to "emotion" and by "character" or personality). In literary theories of romanticism, poetic appeal to the imagination could even be considered the very antithesis of logical appeals to reason, quite as appeal to passion and emotion had often been. There was also an opportunity here to think of imagination dualistically, advocating its use, as higher than reason, in the esthetic realm, while calling for vocabularies that completely outlawed it (in its emotional aspects) from the realm of practical administration (a dualism whereby the same person can now subscribe to both poetic estheticism and scientific positivism).

In sum, today any representation of passions, emotions, actions, and even mood and personality, is likely to be treated as falling under the heading of "images," which in turn explicitly or implicitly involve "imagination." Often "imagination" seems to sum up the "lyric motive," as distinct from the "dramatic motive" (whereupon it may also take unto itself the area of overlap between the two terms). It is a miscellany ranging all the way from the visible, tangible, here-and-now to the mystically transcendent, from the purely sensory and empirical, even the scientifically exact observation, to the dramatically empathic and sympathetic, from the literal to the fantastic, including all shades of sentiment and refinements of taste and judgment. It may also be taken to include the "unconscious," as the critic "unconsciously" feels that his term subsumes a batch of other terms variously at odds with one another; and often by the "imagination" today, as by the "unconscious," we mean simply the awareness of distinctions and discriminations not yet reduced to the systematic order of a filing system.

A good place to look, if you would see how imagination can come to take over areas once occupied by a more directly dramatist vocabulary of action, is George Santayana's *Realms of Being*. For Santayana's work is particularly designed to merge the realistic Latin stress upon the dramatic with the subjective-epistemological-psychological-scientist-lyrist stress of German transcendental idealism. Most notably one should examine his alignments in what he calls the "realm of Spirit," since "the only possible way for spirit to create is to imagine." (*Realms of Being*, p. 575.) Here we are told that spirit endures all passions (715), transmutes sympathy and pity into charity (783), and is liberated through suffering and death (761). Again:

> The potential sympathy that spirit has with all life is not purely perceptive but dramatic. . . . In the act of surveying and understanding action, spirit raises that action into an image; and the imagination, though likewise a living process, moves at another level (715).

Here the philosopher is considering the point at which imagery can cease to be a sensory representation of things in the practical realm, and can through imagination come to transcend that realm. But though holding that spirit naturally loves knowledge, he disagrees with Bacon's pragmatist equating of such knowledge with power (725). Rather, he says, spirit's love of knowledge is a "love of imagination"—and imagination relies on real knowledge, rather than confining itself to sheer fantasy, only because "it needs to be fed by contact with external things and by widening vital rhythms."

Also, when considering contemporary theory (which often, under the auspices of Blake and Coleridge, would make imagination and poetry identical, so that the study of poetry becomes the study of images), it is good to remember that in its beginnings, the term belongs in *psychology*. Then, in Western thought, it next seems to have been treated in rhetoric (because of the persuasive effect that a speaker's images may have upon the audience's acts and attitudes). And only much later, when critics were thinking less of expressions that move to responses beyond words and more of expressions that were "moving" in themselves, it began to take on the almost exclusively esthetic meaning so often imputed to it by some literary schools today. One may legitimately remember that the word is not "essentially poetic," as it now seems to be, but was originally a term applied to the general psychology of mankind, and even to animals; and except perhaps for the prophetic references in Longinus, it was not wholly poetized until the philosophic and literary theories that flowered in nineteenth-century romanticism. The fact is worth recalling when a critic resents the use of new psychological terms, objecting on the grounds that they introduce principles alien to poetry as such. There may be valid objections to such terms. But whatever the objections may be, the merely categorical one that the terms are, by their very nature, extraliterary, seems dubious, unless one is willing at the same time to surrender the term "imagination," as being overly psychologistic and extraliterary in its origins.

Even so "literary" a writer as William Hazlitt could treat of "imagination" more from the ethical than the esthetic point of view. In his *Essays on the Principles of Human Action,* he writes:

> The direct or primary motive, or impulse which determines the mind to the volition of anything must . . . in all cases depend on the idea of that thing as conceived by the imagination, and on the idea solely.

He also explains in terms of imagination both "the motives by which I am impelled to the pursuit of my own good, and those by which I am impelled to pursue the good of others." But whereas Pico and Bacon would subordinate imagination to the control of reason, Hazlitt prepares the way for its modern emancipation from reason when he says that imagination itself "must be the immediate spring and guide of action." He assumes that imagination can control "the blind impulses of associated mechanical feelings . . . making them subservient to the accomplishment of some particular purpose." While deriving from imagination both our ideas of self-interest and our sympathy for others, he uses relative ease of *identification* to account for instances where the motive of self-interest is the stronger:

> The only reason for my preferring my future interest to that of others must arise from my anticipating it with greater warmth of present imagination. It is this greater liveliness and force with

which I can enter into my future feelings, that in a manner identifies them with my present being: and this notion of identity being once formed, the mind makes use of it to strengthen its habitual propensity, by giving to personal motives a reality and absolute truth which they can never have. Hence it has been inferred that my real substantial interest in anything must be derived from the impression of the object itself, as if that could have any sort of communication with my present feelings, or excite any interest in my mind, but by means of the imagination, which is naturally affected in a certain manner by the prospect of future good or evil.

Image and Idea

The stress upon image involves a corresponding counterstress upon idea. Edmund Burke would doubtless have wanted to treat idea and image simply as reënforcements of each other, since by his prescription every important statement should have a thought, an image, and a sentiment. William Hazlitt bridged the distinction at one stroke by referring to "ideas of the imagination."

In Kant, "ideas" belonged to *reason;* and thus they were "dialectical," in the realm of "principle," as contrasted with empirical or positive experiences comprising intuitions of sensibility and concepts of the understanding. By "house," for instance, we refer to a vast manifold of sensations which we bring together, in one meaning, insofar as we can sum up the whole batch of sensations by the concept, "house."

Obviously, if we looked at such a house, the "image" that we saw would not correspond with the images of modern poetic theory. Rather, "image" in Kant's sense would be quite close to Aristotle's kind: it would be perceived through the senses, and remembered or anticipated in the imagination. The "poetic" image, on the other hand, can *stand for* things that never were or never will be. Hazlitt's usage is well worth considering here. The "poetic" image of a house is also an "idea" of a house, insofar as it has purely dialectical significance, allowing for verbal manipulations that transcend the empirical or positive. You can't *point to* the house that appears in a poem; even if the poet may have had a particular house in mind. For his word "house" will also *stand for* relationships alien to the *concept* of house as such. The *conceptual* house is a dwelling of such-and-such structure, material, dimensions, etc. The *poetic* house is built of *identifications*. (Thus it may equal sufferings in childhood, or sense of great security in childhood; a retreat from combat, or a place from which one sallies forth to combat; a "maternal" house as contrasted with some alternative location "paternal" in motive, etc.).

If these other, invisible meanings surrounding the poetic image are not exactly "ideas" in the purely intellectualistic sense of the term, they are certainly not empirical in the purely positivistic sense. And such connotations or overtones of the poetic image are at least "confused ideas," both in the sense that critical analysis can often discern some of them with sufficient clarity to name their "ideational" equivalents, and in the sense that such "imaginary" meanings are *fused together* in the image (as it functions in the poem).

The old rhetoricians used to be much concerned about a distinction between "infinite" (or "general") and "definite" (or "specific") questions. (Or, from the Greek, "theses" and "hypotheses.") Thus, to quote from Thomas Wilson's *Art of Rhetoric,* where he is practically paraphrasing a passage in Quintilian:

> Those questions are called infinite which generally are propounded, without the comprehension of time, place, and person, or any such like: that is to say, when no certain thing is named, but only words are generally spoken. As thus, whether it be best to marry, or to live single. Which is better, a courtier's life, or a scholar's life.
>
> Those questions are called definite, which set forth a matter, with the appointment and naming of place, time, and person. As thus, Whether it now be best here in England for a Priest to marry, or to live single. Whether it were mete for the King's Majesty that now is, to marry with a stranger, or to marry with one of his own Subjects. Now the definite question (as the which concerneth some one person) is most agreeing to the purpose of an Orator, considering particular matters in the law ... etc.

The more we puzzle over the relation between idea and image, the more we come to feel that it should be considered in accordance with the pattern of the old distinction between "infinite" and "definite" questions. One may write of "security" in general ("infinitely," without reference to conditions), while having about the edges of his consciousness the image of some particular place or condition that means security to him. Or one's writing may assemble the imagery of some particular place or condition which represents for him the "idea" of security, an organizing principle that may guide his selection and treatment of images, even though he never "consciously" refers to the general topic of security at all.

That is, behind productive *poetic* imagery, as contrasted with the reproductive imagery of raw sensation, there are *organizational principles*. And given acute enough means and terms of analysis, such organizational principles can be named in terms that express their equivalent in the vocabulary of *ideas*. This is the realm of reason (the "dialectical" realm of "principles" and "ideas"). And it is shared by poetic imagination (hence the justice of Coleridge's equations, which assign to "imagination" in the poetic sphere the place corresponding with that assigned to "reason" in the sphere of philosophy and ethics).

In sum: Insofar as a poet's images are organically related, there is a formal principle behind them. The images could be said to *body forth* this principle. The principle itself could, by a properly discerning critic, be named in terms of *ideas* (or one basic idea with modifiers). Thus, the imagery could be said to convey an invisible, intangible idea in terms of visible, tangible things. In this respect, the *pattern* of Platonism would seem to provide an accurate technical description of poetic structure.

In keeping with the genius of Hazlitt's expression, "ideas of the imagination," we began thinking that there should be a term for ideas and images both. "Titles" (or "epithets") seemed to meet the requirement. For the rhetorician uses "titles" (either imaginal or ideological) to identify a person or a cause with whatever kinds of things will, in his judgment, call forth the desired response. He will select such "titles" in accordance with the bias of his intention and the opinions of his audience. But what are such "titles" (or "entitlings," or "identifications") but another term for the Aristotelian "topics," which shift so easily and imperceptibly between ideas and images that you wonder how the two realms could ever come to be at odds?

Yet there is a difference between an abstract term naming the "idea" of, say, security, and a concrete image designed to stand for this idea, and to "place it before our very eyes." For one thing, if the image employs the full resources of imagination, it will not represent merely one idea, but will contain a whole bundle of principles, even ones that would be mutually contradictory if reduced to their purely ideational equivalents. Ideationally, a speaker might have to go through much reasoning if he wanted to equate a certain measure with public security. But if he could translate it imaginally into terms of, say, the mother, he might profit not only from this one identification, but from many kindred principles or ideas which, when approached in this spirit, are associated with the mother-image (or mother principle, or idea of the mother). Yet, whereas these further meanings might serve as implicit "arguments" if the speaker's thesis were translated into an *image,* they would not figure in the explicit *ideological* statement at all. Assume, for instance, that there are five major principles of appeal in a mother-image (security, affection, tradition, "naturalness," communion). Then assume an ideological argument identifying a cause in terms of security, but not explicitly pleading for it in terms of these four other principles. Now, if the speaker, in winding up his argument for his cause as an aid to security, translates it into a mother-image, might he not thereby get the "unearned increment" from the other four principles vibrant in this same image? (It would be "unearned," that is, from the standpoint of the purely ideological argument.)

Also, like the Leibnizian *petites perceptions,* images may anticipate clear ideas in history, or in a man's personal development, as he may *imagine* some character or act before clearly diagnosing the motivational *ideas* which it stands for. Or he may imagine dramatic or narrative figures or events which stand for *combinations of motives* not ideationally named. (Hobbes and Spinoza, for instance, give recipes for the complexity of motives underlying the various passions and emotions already named in their culture; but dramatic poets can offer imaginal equivalents for these, or for other combinations of motives not thus reduced to abstract philosophic formulation.)

Once you have a distinction so clear as that between image and idea at their extremes, you can expect to find some vocabularies treating them as almost diametrical opposites. Hence, the distinction could be taken as grounds for the feeling that, despite Aristotle's remarks about the close kinship between poetry and philosophy, and Cicero's remarks about the close kinship between poetry and rhetoric, there has arisen, along with the stress upon imagination as the very essence of poetry, a tendency to treat of ideas as though they were antithetical to poetry, until finally we come to the proportion: imagination is to poetry as ideology is to rhetoric. By this alignment, insofar as the rhetorician gains effects by the use of imagery, he would be said to have a "poetic strain" in him. In line with such thinking as it figures in much modern esthetics, you often find imagination and logic treated as *essentially antithetical* (though a more pliant attitude would, at the very least, call for a terminology which treated them as consistent in some respects and at variance in others).

The sensationalist position also fits well with the widespread resistance to "didactic" poetry, a resistance which reaches its fullest expression in the esthetic of Symbolism, Imagism, and Surrealism (though medieval thinkers who looked upon the "enigma" as natural to poetry would probably have found plenty of didactic, or even moralistic, motives in the work of such modern schools). Even an extremely imagistic poem is organized only insofar as it abides by integrating principles; and because they are principles, if criticism were discerning enough it could detect their counterparts in the realm of ideas; thus the sensory images could be said to embody ideas that transcend the sensory. In any case, the tendency to view image and idea as antithetical has given us today a frequent distinction between imagery (a cluster of interrelated images) and ideology (a structure of interrelated ideas). And though "ideology" originally meant but the study of ideas in themselves (as with Socrates' systematic concern with the problems involved in defining the idea of justice), it usually refers now to a system of political or social ideas, framed and propounded for an ulterior purpose. In this new usage, "ideology" is obviously but a kind of rhetoric (since the ideas are so related that they have in them, either explicitly or implicitly, inducements to some social and political choices rather than others). Yet, though rhetorical ideology thus comes to be contrasted with poetic imagery, Jeremy Bentham warned us to look for the images that, overtly or covertly, serve as models for ideas.

Where are we now? We have been saying that, since ideas and images are capable of being distinguished at least in their extremes, it follows that, from certain points of view, they may be treated as opposites. But we have also been considering how images are so related to ideas that an idea can be treated as the *principle* behind the systematic development of an image.

Another way of stating this would be by taking as a paradigm the relation between spirit and matter proclaimed in idealistic metaphysics. (See our remarks on Hegel's *Philosophy of History,* for instance, in the *Grammar.*) Since in such schemes, the principle of unification or relationship binding a cluster of related natural phenomena can be looked upon as an invisible, intangible spirit represented by the imagery, so a cluster of images organized in accordance with some principle of artistic order would correspond to the temporal or historical conditions by which the Universal Idea makes itself manifest at a given time and place. Whatever you may think of this pattern, as a *metaphysics of history,* such a view of nature as the representative embodiment of Universal Purpose is a good way in which to consider the relationship between some *limited artistic purpose* and its embodiment, or representation, in the imagery of nature and experience. The imagery is thus treated as the "natural incarnation" of the idea or organizing principle that guided the choice and development of it. (We should here have a secular esthetic equivalent of the Pauline formula for the word made flesh.)

As the imagery would be a translation of the idea into sensory terms, criticism might conversely propose to retranslate this sensory version back into purely dialectical or ideological terms, abstractions transcending sheer sensory experience. And it would look upon an image, not as the merely "positive" thing our senses take it to be, but as "negative," in the sense that the image existed by *exclusion,* by differentiation from other images, each of which would, in its way, be one particular, unique embodiment of the over-all principle organizing or generating the lot. This is like Hegel's doctrine of the "concrete universal," according to which any one "moment," any one thing, in its particularity or divisiveness, is not "positive" but "negative," when considered from the standpoint of the general principles represented by its thinghood.

Metaphysically this may be dubious. But the esthetic equivalent amounts to little more than the statement that, where a shifting body of imagery is considered in a unified work of art, the "spirit" of each individual image is to be found, not in itself, but in the artistic purpose behind the whole body of imagery. Of course, even if critics agreed on this statement of the case, there would still be room for much haggling as to just what may be behind a given artistic structure, and inspiriting it. We should also note that the distinction between "positive" and "negative" again allows an opening for those who would treat image and idea as in opposition, rather than in apposition. But that tendency can be "pantheistically" reversed by applying the thought of a correspondence between symbol and symbolized, as with Carlyle's formula, in *Sartor Resartus:* "Matter [i.e., image], being the manifestation of Spirit [i.e., idea], is Spirit."

But the point is: Seen from this angle, the antithetical relation between image and idea is replaced by a partial stress upon the bond of kinship between them. Add the fact that all abstractions themselves are necessarily expressed in terms of weakened and confused images, a consideration which doubtless explains why Aristotle said that we cannot think without images. It also figures in Jeremy Bentham's "theory of fictions," a method for disclosing the *imagery* that lurks behind purely *ideological* expressions.

Rhetorical Analysis in Bentham

Bentham's great contributions to the study of persuasion were made almost in spite of himself. In trying to promote ways of discussion that could truly transcend the suggestiveness of imagery, he revealed how thoroughly imaginal our thinking is. Scrutinizing the most abstract of legalistic terms, asking himself just what it meant to plead and pass judgment in terms of "legal fictions," he proposed a methodic search for "archetypes." By "archetypes" he meant the images that underly the use of abstractions. (To quote one of his favorite examples: Consider the irrelevant but suggestive and provocative images of *binding* that lurk in the term, "obligation.")

Bentham here discovered a kind of poetry concealed beneath legal jargon usually considered the very opposite of poetry. It was *applied poetry,* or rhetoric, since it was the use of poetic resources to affect judgments, decisions, hence attitudes and actions. As we noted when discussing Richards and Mead in the *Grammar,* the notion of an attitude or incipient act is ambiguous; an attitude of sympathy, for instance, may either lead into an overt act of kindness, or it may serve "liberally" as the *substitute* for an act of kindness. And since Richards stresses in the "imaginal" action of poetry its role as an alternative to the overt act, we can see how he "repoetized" Bentham's essentially rhetorical concerns. For when one thinks of poetry as the exercise of imaginal suggestiveness in areas that transcend the practical, one has again made the step from Cicero to Longinus: one admires an expression, not for its power to move a hearer towards this or that decision, but for its use of images that are "moving" in and for themselves. Once you think of the imaginal, not as inducement to action, but as the sensitive suspension of action, invitations that you might *fear* in rhetoric can be *enjoyed* in poetry.

In keeping with his search for "archetypes," or latent images, Bentham was also resentful of the linguistic device whereby, when the king is meant, we say instead the Crown or the Throne; instead of a churchman, the Church or Altar; instead of lawyers, the Law; instead of a judge, the Court; instead of rich men, Property. As he puts it, in his typically crabbed style:

> Of this device, the object and effect is, that any unpleasant idea that in the mind of the hearer or reader might happen to stand associated with the idea of the person or the class, is disengaged from it: and in the stead of the more or less obnoxious individual or individuals, the object present is a creature of the fancy, by the idea of which, as in poetry, the imagination is tickled—a phantom which, by means of the power with which the individual or class is clothed is constituted an object of respect and veneration.

He was here attacking from one angle an idealistic resource of language which Coleridge uses to great rhetorical advantage in his tract on *The Constitution of Church and State, According to the Idea of Each*. For by treating of institutions and social classes "according to the *idea* of each," Coleridge could, as it were, discover a perfect archetypal design lying behind the imperfections of his contemporary society, hence could lay more weight upon such perfect spirit than upon actual conditions. Bentham also calls such kinds of amplification "allegorical idols," and diagnoses them as appeal *ad imaginationem*.

Bentham's work has long been out of print. But his main concerns with "archetypation" have been reprinted in C. K. Ogden's *Bentham's Theory of Fictions*. Two other important contributions of Bentham's to rhetoric were his *Table of the Springs of Action* and his *Book of Fallacies* (the *Fallacies* as incisive as Schopenhauer's *Art of Controversy*, the *Table* probably the source of modern efforts to develop a vocabulary of purely descriptive, or "neutral" terms for the treatment of human relations).

The discussion of "question-begging appellatives" in the *Book of*

Fallacies states the principle of the triplicate vocabulary developed at length in the *Springs of Action*. Since the point he is considering is unquestionably the primary weapon in the war of words, we should dwell on it here. The "question-begging appellative," he says, is a "fallacy of confusion" that is used "for the designation of objects belonging to the field of moral science." If we include the "political" in his term "moral," we have here a name for a basic rhetorical device of modern journalism.

> Begging the question is one of the fallacies enumerated by Aristotle; but Aristotle has not pointed out (what it will be the object of this chapter to expose) the mode of using the fallacy with the greatest effect, and least risk of detection—namely, by the employment of a single appellative.

Thus, whereas we might speak of desire, labor, disposition, character, or habit (all of which, in his scheme, would be "neutral" terms), we might on the other hand use either laudatory ("eulogistic") words like industry, honor, generosity, gratitude, or vituperative ("dyslogistic") words like lust, avarice, luxury, covetousness, prodigality. Bentham believes that originally all words for "pains, pleasures, desires, emotions, motives, affections, propensities, dispositions, and other moral entities" were "neutral." But "by degrees they acquired, some of them an eulogistic, some a dyslogistic, cast. This change extended itself, as the *moral sense* (if so loose and delusive a term may on this occasion be employed) advanced in growth."

The project of a "neutral" vocabulary midway between the two "censorious" extremes of "eulogistic" and "dyslogistic" terms presents a notable contrast with the analysis of the virtues in Aristotle's *Ethics*. In Aristotle, a virtue is the happy medium between two extremes (which are vices). Thus, "courage" is a virtue midway between the vicious extremes, cowardice and rashness; liberality midway between squandering and meanness; good temper midway between irascibility and sluggishness; friendliness midway between obsequiousness and churlishness; truthfulness, midway between boastfulness and false modesty, etc. Here the middle terms are themselves "eulogistic," striking a balance between extremes that would be "dyslogistic." There are no "neutral" terms in the Benthamite sense.

The Benthamite project, as outlined in the Table, is constructed by a different principle. Thus: for the "pecuniary interest," there would be such "neutral" expressions as "desire of subsistence, plenty, profit, acquisition." And its two "censorial" counterparts would be: "economy, frugality, thrift" (eulogistic) and "parsimony, niggardliness, cupidity, avarice, venality, lust for gain" (dyslogistic). Or such "neutral" appellatives as "curiosity, inquisitiveness, desire of information" would have, as their rhetorically weighted counterparts: "love of knowledge, passion for literature, science," etc. (eulogistic) or "pryingness, impertinence, meddlesomeness," etc. (dyslogistic). The (neutral) expressions to name the desire of obtaining public good will, or the fear of ill-repute, would be matched eulogistically by honor, conscience, principle, probity, and dyslogistically by vanity, ostentation, pride, vainglory, arrogance. Fear of God or hope from God could be eulogized as piety, devotion, holiness, sanctity; dyslogized as superstition, bigotry, fanaticism, sanctimoniousness, hypocrisy. And so on, through fourteen different "interests" in all.

Aristotle does discuss a similar device. (See his *Art of Rhetoric*, I, IX, 28-29.) But Bentham analyzes it in much greater detail. Whereupon we realize that Nietzsche's entire work on *The Genealogy of Morals* is a picturesque interpretation of all Christian virtues as a rhetoric of this sort. Thus, in section 14, "how *ideals* are *manufactured* in this world," he lists substitutions whereby impotence is called goodness, cravenness is called meekness, a cowardly waiting, hat in hand, is called patience, submission to hated authority is called obedience to God, inability to avenge oneself is called forgiveness, and hope for revenge eventually is called the triumph of righteousness. A bit later, to make his perverse translations more plausible, he quotes from the Angelic Doctor: "The blessed in the heavenly kingdom shall look upon the tortures of the damned, that their blessedness please them the more."

Usage has already so changed that the Benthamite list has somewhat lost its symmetry. Thus, he is hard put to name a eulogistic expression for the "self-regarding interest" for which the subsequent spread of his own utilitarian thinking has since given us "enlightened self-interest." And he can find no eulogistic appellatives for sexual desire, which seems an austere limitation even for the England of those days. (Elsewhere at least he observes that "gallantry" can be used as a flattering word for "adultery.") But the list is much more valuable "in principle" than for its particulars. And as he says in his *Book of*

Fallacies, when considering the choice of censorial terms that reflect "interest-begotten prejudice":

> It neither requires nor so much as admits of being taught: a man falls into it but too naturally of himself; and the more naturally and freely, the less he finds himself under the constraint of any such sense as that of shame. The great difficulty is to unlearn it: in the case of this, as of so many other fallacies, by teaching it, the humble endeavour here is, to unteach it.

The persuasive function of this most spontaneous and ubiquitous rhetorical practice (this use of weighted words that makes all men rhetoricians because they are all poets) is analyzed thus:

> Having, without the *form,* the *force* of an assumption,—and having for its object, and but too commonly for its effect, a like assumption on the part of the hearer or reader,—the sort of allegation in question, how ill-grounded soever, is, when thus masked, apt to be more persuasive than when expressed simply and in its own proper form: especially where, to the character of a *censorial* adding the quality and tendency of an *impassioned* allegation, it tends to propagate, as it were by contagion, the passion by which it was suggested. On this occasion, it seeks and finds support in that *general* opinion, of the existence of which the eulogistic or dyslogistic sense, which thus, as it were by adhesion, has connected itself with the import of the appellative, operates as proof.

This is an unlovely paragraph, and not very viable. But it is well worth dwelling on. And dwelling on it, we find that it is the analysis of the appeal to "imagination" in terms of a *logical* fallacy (or deception), the *petitio principii.* Here, we might say, by the use of tonalities, one begins by positing the very thing that is to be proved. That is what Bentham means by saying that the censorial term has the *force* of an assumption, without its *form.* It would have the *form* of an assumption only if the speaker said explicitly, "I am here assuming the judgment which is to be proved." Obviously, in such a form, the suggestiveness of the censorial tonality would be lost. But by basing one's statement on a censorial assumption without labeling it as such, the speaker has an opportunity to *establish this very assumption* in the mind of his hearer.

Of course, where the interests of an audience are strongly bound to the contrary assumption, too obvious a use of such *tonality* (we inject a term not used by Bentham) would cause the audience rather to recoil. Thus, in *Julius Caesar,* Mark Antony cautiously begins his speech to the mob by using the expression "honourable men" as a "eulogistic appellative" for the murderers of Caesar. And only gradually, by the ambiguities of irony to bridge the transition, does he dare convert it into the dyslogistic. Had he begun by using dyslogistic tonalities, he would have turned the mob fatally against himself.

Would we be excessive in glimpsing, beneath the Benthamite project, an almost mystical way of thinking? For the dialectic of mysticism aims at a systematic withdrawal from the world of appearances, a crossing into a realm that transcends everyday judgments—after which there may be a return: the Upward Way is matched by a Downward Way; or the period of exile, withdrawal, and negation terminates in a new vision, whereupon the visionary can once again resume his commerce with the world, which he now sees in a new light, in terms of the vision earned during his stage of exile. But in his homecoming to the world of appearances, he sees things quite differently, so that what he had formerly contemned he seeks, and what he had formerly sought, he contemns. Eulogistic and dyslogistic have changed places, with a *neutral period of transition* between them.

We thus seem to see lurking behind the Benthamite triplicate vocabulary, a kind of attenuated and secularized dialectic of the *via negativa*. And we believe that we can similarly see, in the peripety scene of Shakespeare's play, a playwright's equivalent, as Antony employs the devices of irony to replace the realm of pure neutrality (ironic ambiguity being the dramatic equivalent of a dialectic movement towards neutrality which, in its purity, would be the transcending of drama).

But perhaps we are here taking on more burdens than we need to. In any case, we should also note that, whatever his contribution to the ideal of a scientifically neutral vocabulary, Bentham did not by any means attempt to deny himself weighted terms. Indeed, insofar as a motive met his standard (in contributing to what he considered "the greatest good of the greatest number"), he was quite frank in applying a eulogistic appellative to it. He would doubtless have explained that he was not merely exploiting an assumption, since he was always willing to show why, in his opinion, a given act should be named eulogistically or dyslogistically. That is, though a given appellative might, considered *in itself,* have the force without the form of an assumption, in its *context* he justified it by explicit argument. Thus, on reasoned assumptions that monarchy is a power inimical to the greatest good of the greatest number, he unhesitatingly asserts that we should not say "the influence of the crown" (an expression either neutral or eulogistic) but "the corruption of the crown." And the term "innovation" being generally used in his day as a "dyslogistic appellative" for legislative change, the measures which he favored in the name of the greatest good of the greatest number were named by him, not neutrally but eulogistically: "improvements."

Where inducement to action is concerned, a genuinely neutral vocabulary would defeat its own ends: for there would be no act in it. It would give full instructions for conditioning—but it could not say to what one should condition. But since purposes indigenous to the monetary rationale are so thoroughly built into the productive and distributive system as in ours, a relatively high proportion of interest in purely "neutral" terminologies of motives can be consistent with equally intense ambition. For however "neutral" a terminology may be, it can function as rhetorical inducement to action insofar as it can in any way be used for monetary advantage.

In fact, "neutralization" may often serve but to eliminate, as far as is humanly possible, the various censorial weightings that go with the many different philosophic, religious, social, political, and personal outlooks extrinsic to the monetary motive. Thus, the terminology of investment is "neutral," but the mortgagee, personally, may want to employ a heavily weighted term as "appellative" for the mortgagor who would foreclose. And if the mortgagor could foreclose at a profit, but is deterred by other scruples, then he abides by censorial weightings alien to the pure "neutrality" of the financial logic alone.

We do not mean that the Benthamite concern with a neutral terminology was "nothing but" a reflex of the monetary motive. Obviously, the utilitarian principle of "the greatest good of the greatest number" itself surpassed purely individualistic theories of profit. But just as orthodox capitalism could be said to have institutionalized, in one particular set of historical conditions, a competitive-cooperative process true of dialectic in general, so the tests of strictly monetary utility could be considered as a reduction of Bentham's broader utilitarian formula. Despite Bentham's distrust of idealizations, his principle of social utility could serve as a rhetorical cloak for purely monetary utility. The close connection between them (in that the profits were earned by business men aiming eventually at mass markets) made it possible for the two orders of motives to become interwoven. Hence any proposals to neutralize nonutilitarian motives would be influenced by the extent to which the monetary motive had already transcended other motivational weightings.

While such neutralization of vocabulary is not confined to monetary incentives, it could fit well with the monetary rationale precisely because the original insight *did* owe much to the "emancipatory" workings of money. For the strengthening of the monetary rationale of action had favored motives alien to more primitive ethical vocabularies, thereby making it easier for men to adopt a relativistic attitude towards the censorial appellatives rooted in other motives.

True, as we have noted, there can also be purely dialectical ways (akin to the mystical search for the *via negativa*) whereby the censorial weightings of rhetoric can be transcended. Though, in a money economy, we can expect such purely dialectical processes to be *institutionalized* in terms of monetary organization, the mystical process of transcendence is traditionally stated in nonmonetary terms, and the dialectic underlying it has nothing to do with money. Yet, if an *organized priestly technique* for the mystical neutralization and transcending of opinion has ever arisen outside a monetary economy, we should have to conclude that a wide diversity of social classes can arise without money to mediate among the corresponding diversity of occupations. And we strongly doubt such a possibility. However, a little money might go a long way in providing the insight of a money-grounded diversity: the illumination would not require such full development as with modern finance. A society would need only enough monetary development to support a priestly class which, in meditating by profession, and in mediating between classes, could "get the idea" of a neutral stage alien to any single class.

Of all fables, surely the best for characterizing the discomfitures of rhetoric is the one of the father and son leading an ass to market. Whether the father walks and the son rides, or the son walks and the father rides, or they both walk, or they both ride, there is someone to find fault. Eventually, in their eagerness to meet all possible objections, they try to carry the ass—and that is no solution either. As Aristotle showed systematically, there are objections to any position. You can even attack a thing on the grounds that it is exactly what it claims to be, as were you to "refute" a philosophy by saying, "The trouble with this is, it is a philosophy."

Such is particularly the case because the rhetorical striving for advantage is usually conducted in a very piecemeal way, with refutations of a purely opportunistic and catch-as-catch-can sort. "It's smart to be shifty in a new country"—and the equivalent in an old country would be the rhetorical smartness that shifts with the news. Given the world as it is, with its jangling variety of imputed motives, most often one merely assumes that there is a well-rounded philosophic, scientific, or theological rationale to justify the censorial weighting of his terms.

You meet a new person, and the *first* sentence he utters on some controversial subject is spoken in such tonalities as though he were speaking *in conclusion*. To be sure, his tonalities are not in the stentorian accents of a Demosthenes, topping off his arguments by an appeal to the emotions. Rather they are a barely detectable inflection, which you must strain to catch, but which unmistakably implies, "This is the slant you have too, if you have the proper slant." It is a device used especially by teachers: as the adolescent, uneasy and puzzled at best, keeps watching furtively for leads into the "right things," conditions are favorable for the teacher, by subtle tonalities, to *suggest* a set of judgments which establish and protect his position; but if he explicitly mustered the arguments for that position, he would risk *freeing* the students of his limitations, by enabling them to become critically aware of those limitations.

It is by such tonalities, more than by reasoned arguments, that our newspapers persuade. The arguments are on the editorial page, which relatively few readers ever see. The tonalities are in the headlines, which no reader can possibly avoid. These headlines are the "single appellatives," which we call "tonalities" because they imply a certain tone of voice, and this is the tone of voice proper to a certain kind of conclusion. We might as justly call them "gestures," "postures," "attitudes." Subtly, they act by the principle of empathy (for, as Cicero reminds us, in the mere representation of emotion there is something which invites the beholder to participate in it). And they are "question-begging" terms in that they are *suggestive* ("suggestiveness" being perhaps one word for Bentham's formula: "having, without the *form,* the *force* of an assumption"—or as we might put it, *beginning* with the tonality that would suit the desired *conclusion*).

Hence, the importance of the Benthamite principles, not only for analyzing rhetoric, but also for use by rhetoricians. Bentham but offers systematic terms for linguistic procedures that are spontaneous, even inevitable. Thus he may induce us to ask ourselves in each instance just what resource should be exploited. (This is not, we grant, exactly the purpose Bentham had in mind. Hence his linguistic analysis can be a kind of rhetoric-in-spite-of-itself.)

Subsequently, in the use of rhetoric to attack rhetoric, there has been much talk of "unmasking," as rival ideologies are said to compete by "unmasking" one another. The groundwork of this approach is laid in Bentham, with his methodical search for *tegumen* and *res tegenda,* the *tegumen* being a linguistic covering for an interest that itself lies outside the linguistic. (For though his mode of analysis was centered upon the linguistic, he likewise sought to characterize the extralinguistic elements in rhetorical situations.) In the *Table,* he explains that there are usually several motives involved in any particular act. But where there is such "conjunct action of motives," the speaker may represent the lot by selecting one motive as significant and neglecting the others. Such a procedure is inevitable, since any decision usually sums up a complexity of motives. Rhetorically, this fact invites to censorial appellatives since, if the speaker is identifying an act of his own, or of an ally, he can gain an easy advantage by picking out the most favorable motive and presenting it as either predominant or exclusive (or as the one that sets the tone for the lot). And conversely, he can select the least favorable to name the essence of an enemy's motives. But sometimes "no such sufficiently respected motive can be found"—and then, Bentham observes, instead of the actual motive, a speaker may select some other which "shall, by the nearness of its connexion with the actual one, have been rendered most difficultly distinguishable from it." He calls such changes "substituted" or "covering" motives. Or, as he explains:

> In political contention, no line of conduct can be pursued by either of two parties, but what, by persons of the *same* party, is ascribed to *good* motives; by persons of the *opposite* party, to *bad* motives:—and so in every case of *competition,* which (as most cases have) has anything in it of enmity. On any such occasion, the motive which, though but one out of several actual and cooperating motives, or though it be but . . . a *substituted* motive; is thus put forward, may be designated by the appellation of the *covering motive* being em-

ployed to serve as a covering, to whatever actually operating motives would not have been so well adapted as itself to the purpose in view.

Thus, he notes that the "desire corresponding to the *pleasures of the palate*" can have, as "eulogistic covering," the motive of "sympathy," stressing the elements of sociability and companionship that may go with eating and drinking. Or "sexual desire" can have *love* as its eulogistic covering. The desire for gain can be eulogistically covered by *industry; love of power* can be eulogized as *love of country; fear of punishment* or *of bad reputation* can be called *love* or *sense of duty;* desire to get the good offices of friends can have *sympathy* or *gratitude* as coverings; and *antipathy* or *ill will* can be eulogistically covered in the name of *public spirit* or *love of justice*. Since such desires and motives, in their unadorned form, "may be considered as *the unseemly parts of the human mind,*" he has here offered specimens "of the fig-leaves, commonly employed for the covering of them."

Similarly, in the *Book of Fallacies* Bentham calls attention to ways whereby "Vague Generalities" can also be used as covering devices. Thus, since "order" is a more inclusive word than the term for any particular order, it may include both good order and bad, whereby a call for order can cloak a call for *tyranny,* tyranny also being a species of order. (Perhaps we could class, as a contemporary variant of such devices, De Gaulle's Rally of the French People, a project for *political* unification presented in the name of *no politics*.) In Bentham's case, since men were, to his way of thinking, using the British Constitution in ways that gave them many antisocial advantages, they could leave the advantages unmentioned, while becoming edified in their zeal for the Constitution itself, the "matchless Constitution." Thus, at the peak of his attack upon "Vague Generalities," he writes:

> Rally round the constitution: that is, rally round waste, rally round depredation, rally round oppression, rally round corruption, rally round imposture—imposture in the hustings, imposture in the Honourable House, imposture in every judicatory.

At the end of his *Book of Fallacies,* this great methodologist of debunking (the Greeks might have called him *Rhetoromastix,* The Scourge of Spellbinders) permits himself a vision. Having analyzed the various standard devices whereby men are induced to fight their battles at the wrong place, so that, while they aim and fire to the left, the enemy advances undetected and unharmed from the right, Bentham foresees the day when it would be risky indeed if anyone were "so far off his guard, as through craft or simplicity to let drop any of these irrelevant, or at one time deceptious arguments." But if any speaker does speak thus, in an unguarded moment, "instead of Order! Order! a voice shall be heard, followed, if need be, by voices in scores, crying aloud, 'Stale! Stale! Fallacy of authority! Fallacy of Distrust!' Etc., etc."

But that, he says, "will form an epoch in the history of civilization." So much for his vision, at once simple and sophisticate.

Marx on "Mystification"

Discussing rhetorical theory in the early middle ages (*Speculum,* January, 1942), Richard McKeon writes: "According to Cassiodorus, 'The art of rhetoric is, as the masters of secular letters teach, the science of speaking well in civil questions,' and that definition is repeated in almost the same words by Isidore, Alcuin, and Rhabanus Maurus." Both Bentham's and Marx's contributions to the analysis of rhetoric would fall under this same head, except that their polemic emphasis might rather have led them to define rhetoric (or those aspects of it upon which they centered their attention) as: the knack of speaking ill in civil matters.

Whatever may be the claims of Marxism as a "science," its terminology is not a neutral "preparation for action" but "inducement to action." In this sense, it is unsleepingly rhetorical, though much of its persuasiveness has derived from insistence that it is purely a science, with "rhetoric" confined to the deliberate or unconscious deceptions of non-Marxist apologetics. Thus, we once saw a Marxist (he has since left the Communist Party) get soundly rebuked by his comrades for the suggestion that leftist critics collaborate in a study of "Red Rhetoric." Despite their constant efforts to find the slogans, catchwords, and formulas that will most effectively influence action in given situations, and their friendliness to "propaganda" or "social significance" in art, they would not allow talk of a "Red Rhetoric." For them, "Rhetoric" applied solely to the persuasiveness of capitalist, fascist, and other non-Marxist terminologies (or "ideologies").

Yet in actual practice their position seems (*mutatis mutandis!*) to be pretty much that of Augustine. That is: the Marxists have a rhetoric, a persuasion, which in turn is grounded in a dialectic. The rhetoric is words; the dialectic, being concerned with the non-verbal order of motives, could be equated with "science." And an art in keeping would be grounded in "science" (or "dialectic") insofar as it took its start from the experiences of natural reality, while being rhetorical in proportion as its persuasiveness helped form judgments, choices, attitudes deemed favorable to Communist purposes. All this seems obvious enough; but rhetoric having become identified with non-Marxist rhetoric, the Marxist persuasion is usually advanced in the name of no-rhetoric.

In his *Book of Fallacies*, Bentham had recognized both factional and universal interests. Factionally, he treated parliamentary wrangles in terms of the ins vs. the outs. And since, "whatsoever the *ins* have in possession, the *outs* have in expectancy," to this extent he saw no difference in their "sinister interests," nor in the fallacies by which they sought to protect or further these interests. But in addition to such factional splits, he observed, "these rivals have their share in the universal interest which belongs to them in their quality of members of the community at large. In this quality, they are sometimes occupied in such measures as in their eyes are necessary for the maintenance of the universal interest."

For a comprehensive statement of human motives, this distinction of Bentham's seems very necessary. An ideal of cooperation, for instance, can certainly be applied for sinister *factional* advantage, as when conspirators cooperate against a common victim. Yet cooperation is also an ideal serving the interest of *mankind in general*.

It might be said that the Marxist analysis of rhetoric is primarily designed to throw new light on Bentham's "Fallacy of Vague Generalities." Otherwise put: As a critique of capitalist rhetoric, it is designed to disclose (unmask) sinister *factional* interests concealed in the bourgeois terms for benign *universal* interests. Though Marx twitted Bentham for his stress upon "interests," Marxism gives grand lineaments to the Benthamite notion of "interest-begotten prejudice." In its analysis of property, it puts an almost architecturally firm foundation beneath Bentham's somewhat flimsy distinction between ins and outs (indeed, as Bentham himself would probably have agreed, Marxism shows that often the shifts between ins and outs is but the most trivial of palace revolutions, where an apparently cleansing change of agents has left the morbidities of the scene itself substantially unchanged). And where Bentham had looked into extraverbal, situational factors behind rhetorical expressions, recognizing "the influence of time and place in matters of legislation," and holding that a law good for one situation was not thereby to be considered categorically good, Marx imposingly formalized such "conditional" thinking by linking it with his revisions of the Hegelian dialectic. All told, Marx thus forged a formidable machine; and he could apply it to shatter, as deceptive "ideology," traditions which had been the pride of mankind, but which in being upheld by economic and social classes that got special advantage from them, and in being put forward as universally valid, thus protected factional interests in the wider, more general name of universal interests.

To expose the workings of such "ideologies," it was necessary to give an exhaustive analysis of the "objective situation" in which they figured. Insofar as the terms describing this extraverbal situation were correct, they would apparently be a "dialectic" (in the sense that equates "dialectic" with "science"—i.e., with a subject matter of nonverbal things and relationships). They could be called a rhetoric, however, in several important senses: (1) The account of extralinguistic factors in a rhetorical expression (as when disclosing how economic interests influence modes of expression that, considered "in themselves," seem wholly to transcend the economic) is itself an aspect of *rhetorica docens,* though perhaps on the outer edges; (2) insofar as the Marxist vocabulary itself is partial, or partisan, it is rhetorical, and we could not have a dialectic in the fullest sense unless we gave equally sympathetic expression to competing principles (though we shall later see that this objection must be modified); (3) it is concerned with advantage, not only in analyzing the hidden advantage in other terminologies (or "ideologies"), but also in itself inducing to advantages of a special sort. (Here it becomes a kind of *rhetorica utens.*)

The main principles of Marxism, as a theory of rhetoric, are most directly stated, perhaps, in an early work by Marx and Engels, *The German Ideology.* But though Marxist writings probably contributed much to the current prestige of the word, "ideology," it is seldom used in exactly the sense that Marx gave it. So we might begin by noting the several meanings it now seems to have, meanings which, while not necessarily antagonistic to one another, are quite different in insight and emphasis:

1. The study, development, criticism of ideas, considered in themselves. (As in a Socratic dialogue.)

2. A system of ideas, aiming at social or political action. (Pareto's sociology, or Hitler's *Mein Kampf*.)

3. Any set of interrelated terms, having practical civic consequences, directly or indirectly. (A business men's code of fair practices might be a good instance.)

4. "Myth" designed for purposes of governmental control. ("Ideology" would here be an exact synonym for "myth of the state.")

5. A partial, hence to a degree deceptive, view of reality, particularly when the limitations can be attributed to "interest-begotten prejudice." (For instance, a white Southern intellectual's "ironic resignation" to a *status quo* built on "white supremacy.")

6. Purposefully manipulated overemphasis or underemphasis in the discussion of controversial political and social issues. (For instance, the kind of verbalizing done by a statesman, home from a discordant conference with foreign diplomats. In a "confidential" radio talk he gives the people a "frank and simple report of the facts." But the report is scrupulously designed to allow them no inkling of how the matter looks from the other side.)

7. An inverted genealogy of culture, that makes for "illusion" and "mystification" by treating ideas as *primary* where they should have been treated as *derivative*.

This last meaning is the most difficult. But because Marxism is a materialist revision of Hegel's idealism, not only do the authors of *The German Ideology* take their start from this seventh definition, they continually circle back to it. If we understand this special usage, we can see why a Marxist might legitimately object when, after he has attacked his political opponents as "ideologists," they retort by calling Marxism an "ideology" too. In the special sense of the word, as used in *The German Ideology,* it is quite true that the schools and movements there selected for attack are "ideologies," while Marxism is not.

Of course, in the War of Words, there is nothing to prevent contestants from hitting one another with anything they can lay hands on. So you could be sure that, once the Marxists had given the word a strong dyslogistic weighting, they too would be resoundingly dyslogized by it (as, having zealously helped make "fascism" a dyslogistic word, they end by being called "Red Fascists"). But for our present purposes, we should try to see the word exactly as Marx used it. For only by trying to get the matter straight can we understand the Marxist contribution to rhetoric, and thereby isolate a principle which can even be applied beyond the purposes of Marxism.

We consider it a sign of flimsy thinking, indeed, to let anti-Communist hysteria bulldoze one into neglect of Marx. (We say "bulldoze," but we are aware that the typical pedagogue today is not "bulldozed" into such speculative crudity; he welcomes it, and even feels positively edified by it. If he cannot grace his country with any bright thoughts of his own, he can at least persuade himself that he is being a patriot in closing his mind to the bright thoughts of his opponents. No wonder the tendency is so widespread. It is a negative kind of accomplishment for which many can qualify.)

With the division of labor, Marx says, and the corresponding cleavage of society into different social and economic classes, there arises a ruling class; likewise, from the distinction between manual and intellectual work, there arise specialists in words (or "ideas"), such as priests, philosophers, theoreticians, jurists, in general, "ideologists," who see things too exclusively in terms of their specialty, and thereby misinterpret the role played by "consciousness," "spirit," "idea," in human history. The whole relationship between "matter" and "spirit" thus seems to be exactly the reverse of what it really is. Property and the division of labor give rise to a ruling class with its peculiar set of ideas; each economic change calls forth a corresponding change in the nature of the ruling class (or at moments of revolutionary crisis a new ruling class takes over)—and each such alteration in the conditions of the ruling class is reflected as a corresponding change of "ideas."

The "ideologists" of the ruling class, in keeping with the nature of their specialty, perfect and systematize the ideas of the ruling class. And, since the ruling class controls the main channels of expression, the ideas of the ruling class become the "ruling ideas."

But, such is the nature of documents, after the economic basis of society has changed, and the class structure has changed accordingly, the ideas that had prevailed seem to remain unchanged. That is, once the verbal or esthetic expressions are recorded, they retain substantially the form that they had when they arose.

Imagine, now, an "ideologist" who, with the documents of many centuries to work from, inspects a whole developmental series of such successive "ruling" ideas, and who, considering these ideas "in themselves," attempts to work out an explanation for their development. If he proceeds in accordance with the Hegelian dialectic, he will get the kind of reversed genealogy which Marxism is attacking. He can treat these particular sets of ideas in terms of some over-all title, a word for ideas in general, such as Spirit, or Consciousness, or *die Idee*. Hence he can look upon the succession of "ruling" ideas (like "honor," "loyalty," "liberty") as though each were an expression of the one Universal Idea (his title for the lot, which he uses not just as a summarizing word, but as a "sub-ject" in the strict philosophic sense, that is, an underlying basis, a sub-stance, of which any step along the entire series can be considered as a property, or expression). He can next assign some direction to the entire series, such as the gradual increase of freedom or self-consciousness. Then he can treat this ultimate direction as the essence of the whole series, the end towards which the entire series strives, whereby it can be considered latent in even the first step of the series. Then this Purpose, or Universal Idea, can be viewed as the creative principle operating within the entire series. Each step along the way would be a limited expression of this universal principle; its nature would be determined by its particular place in the series; yet within the limitations of its nature, each stage would represent the principle of the total development (as bud, flower, and seed could each, at different stages in a plant's growth, be called successive momentary expressions of a single biologic continuity).

"The Idea" thus becomes a universal self-developing organism. Its successive stages make a dialectical series, as shifts in the nature of property, production, and rule make for shifts in the ruling ideas; but these ruling ideas are considered "purely" (as manifestations, not of particular ruling classes, but of the "Absolute Idea"). The Absolute Idea thus becomes the creator of nature and history, which are but concrete expressions of it. Hence, all the *material* relations in history are interpreted as the products of this Universal Spirit, manifesting itself in the empirical world. The study of this empirical world, of course, would include such matters as conflicts over property. But instead of considering ideas as weapons shaped by their use in such conflicts, the kind of "ideologist" Marx is attacking would treat the conflicts as themselves but "moments" in the expression of the Universal Idea underlying all historical development.

In this strictly Hegelian form, Marx may here seem to be attacking a doctrine to which few practical-minded persons would subscribe. Quite true, yet once you begin to follow the logic of Marx's critique, you see that most people differ from Hegel, not in being immune to such thinking, but in being immune to its *thoroughness*. Marx shows how this position generates a whole *set* of beliefs. And what you usually encounter, in the piecemeal thinking of the non-philosophic mind, is a view comprising various detached fragments of such "ideology." Since these fragments prevail on important issues, such as our views of nationalism, a rhetorical critique of such patterns, as they lurk in our thinking, is of tremendous importance.

The authors list three telltale tricks of such "theodicy," whereby the "hegemony" or "hierarchy" of spirit in history is "proved": (1) The thinker separates the ruling ideas from the ruling class, and by thus dealing with the ideas in their "pure" form, concludes that the ruling force of history is "ideas" or "illusions"; (2) the ideas are arranged in a developmental series, with a "mystical" connection among them (this is done by treating the successive ideas as though they were "acts of self-determination" on the part of the divine, absolute, or pure Idea); (3) the "mystical appearance" can be removed by putting progressively increasing "self-consciousness" in place of "the self-determining concept"; or it can be made to *look* thoroughly materialistic (despite its underlying principle of "mystification") if it is transformed into a developmental series of persons, thinkers, philosophers, "ideologists," who are said to be the historical representatives of the "concept."

From the standpoint of rhetoric, the picture that emerges from *The German Ideology* looks somewhat like this:

Private property and the division of labor are identical. This is an important *situational* fact, since it leads to "illusions" or "mystifications" in the realm of ideas. The ideologist's inclination to consider ideas in their "purity" makes for an approach to human relations in terms of such over-all god-terms as "consciousness" or "the human essence," whereas the typical conflicts of society are rooted in *property*. If, when there is a quarrel over property, instead of confronting it squarely you begin considering abstruse problems of universal consciousness or looking for remote kinds of metaphysical or theological anguish and alienation embedded in the very essence of humanity, you are blinded by a principle of "mystification." At every significant point where there is an economic factor to be faced, your "ideology" introduces an "illusion," a purely spiritual "appearance." Where empires are striving for *world markets,* you are "ideologically" inclined to ponder the ways of "universal spirit." Where classes within a nation are struggling for dominance, you are likely to confuse the issue by ideals that give a semblance of national unity.

The same newspapers that are run for money, that get their income by advertising goods sold for money, that are read by people on their way to and from the place where they work for money, and that distribute accounts of political, economic, and social events bearing upon money (high among them, news of the crimes against property)— these same papers, in their more edified moments, will talk rather of "liberty," "dignity of the individual," "Western man," "Christian civilization," "democracy," and the like, as the motives impelling at least *our* people and *our* government, and to a lesser extent the "nations" that "we" want as allies, but not the small ruling class, or clique, that dominates countries with which "we" are at odds.

It takes abstruse metaphysics to use such "ideological mystifications" (or what Bentham would have called "eulogistic coverings"). An uncriticized idea of "the nation" is as thoroughly an ideology, in the specifically Marxist sense, as any Hegelian talk of the Absolute. A nationalist "we" is at least as dubious as an editorial "we," which generously includes writers, readers, and owners under the same term (*up to a certain point,* at which point readers and writers will be *excluded*).

Dialectically, the Marxist analysis would apparently begin with a principle of division where idealism begins with a principle of merger. And, as regards the purposes of rhetoric, it admonishes us to look for "mystification" at any point where the social divisiveness caused by property and the division of labor is obscured by unitary terms (as with terms whereby a state, designed to protect a certain structure of ownership, is made to seem equally representative of both propertied and propertyless classes). Indeed, we find the stress upon private property as a rhetorical motive so convincing, that we question whether communism is possible under the conditions of extreme specialization (division of labor) required by modern industry. *The German Ideology* explicitly pictures man under communism, shifting from job to job like a Jack-of-all-trades, as the mood strikes him (hunting in the morning, fishing in the afternoon, rearing cattle in the evening, and criticizing after dinner, "without ever becoming hunter, fisherman, shepherd, or critic"). Given the highly specialized nature of modern technology, which requires of its operators an almost Puritanic severity of application, if so dilettantelike a way of life as Marx describes is the sign of a true communist society, then every step in the evolution of Soviet Russian industry would seem likely to take it farther from a world free of the cleavage that arises with the division of labor (and with the separation of property that goes with it, and the disparate states of consciousness that go with that).

But we do not have to believe the Marxist promises to apply the Marxist diagnosis for rhetorical purposes. We might question whether, by Marx's own theory, private property could possibly be abolished in a technological society marked by extreme division of labor; we might expect no more than changes which produce a structure of **ownership** better suited to the conditions of modern industrial production. With the means of production "owned" by the state, private property might arise secondarily, through the diversity of ways in which different individuals and classes of workers participated in the economic process and derived rewards from it. But such ownership, or structure of private expectancies and rights, might not look at all like private property as tested by the criteria of orthodox capitalism. Maybe yes, maybe no. That's not what we have to settle for our present purposes. It is enough for our purposes to note the value of the admonition that private property makes for a rhetoric of mystification, as the "ideological" approach to social relations sets up a fog of merger-terms where the clarity of division-terms is needed.

We do not pretend to have given here a complete summary of *The German Ideology*. For our present purposes we are concerned only with the ways in which its analysis of "ideology" becomes a contribution to rhetoric. Formally, we might say that, whereas one can talk of generic, specific, or individual human motives, the treatment of "ideas" in terms of class conflicts would place the stress upon specific motives. That is, instead of some generally human motive, such as "the essence of mankind," Marx stresses the specifically *class* nature of ideologies. And the imputing of universal or generic motives is then analyzed as a concealment of the specific motives (hence, as "mystification"). Then, according to Marx, only by the abolition of property relationships that make for such specific, or class motives, might we hope to get truly universal motivation. And such universal or generic motivation would, by the same token, mean the freeing of the individual. Hence, dialectically, all three levels of motivation are involved (generic, specific, and individual). One may argue that social classification is inevitable in a state of high occupational diversity, even under communism. But we need not settle that argument here. We need only note that the materialist critique of Spirit is the analysis of it as a rhetorical device, and that the dialectical symmetry behind the Marxist terms of analysis seems to involve the approach to generic and individual motives through the specific.

All told, "ideology" is equatable with illusion, mystification, discussion of human relations in terms like absolute consciousness, honor, loyalty, justice, freedom, substance, essence of man—in short, that "inversion" whereby material history is derived from "spirit" (in contrast with the method of dialectical materialism whereby the changing nature of consciousness would be derived from changes in material conditions).

Terministic Reservations (in View of Cromwell's Motives)

Might the Marxist critique of ideology be partly misled by the fact that only the "ideas" survive in the literary or esthetic reliques of the past? Any over-all term for motivation, such as honor, loyalty, liberty, equality, fraternity, is a *summing up* of many motivational strands. And though *on its face* it reduces a whole complexity of terms to one apparently simple term, the people who used it may have been quite aware of many other meanings subsumed in it, but not explicitly proclaimed.

Thus, if a tangle of relationships (including a clear recognition of the material privileges and deprivations that went with a given social structure) was epitomized in the god-term *honor,* but if all that survived for us was the "spirituality" of the term, then it might be the materialist who was duped. For he might accuse the term of much more reticence and deception than it actually possessed, for persons who once summed up their *material* conditions in its name.

In the *Grammar* we noted: If a tribe is living by a river, and has adapted its entire way of life to the conditions of that river, it might sum up its motives in the name of what we would call a "river god." Yet such a title would not be a mere animistic superstition; there would be much realistic and materialistic justification for it (to say nothing of its purely dialectical advantages, as a term for summing up the tribe's ways and recognizing the material conditions mainly responsible for these ways). "Animism" is too much the mark of a nineteenth-century idealistic philosopher trying to be a materialistic anthropologist (at least as regards somebody else's gods, or summarized terms for motives).

In brief, a summarizing term like "honor" might be much more "illusory" and "mystifying" to us, in the abstract and "spiritual" form it has for us, than it was for those who used it as a counter in their everyday life, and so found plenty of cause to discount it. The very term, which looks absolute and unconditional to us, was but the *title for all the conditions.* In this sense, even the most theological of terms can be implicitly modified by very accurate nontheological meanings which, though they may not show through the expression itself, were clearly felt by the persons using it.

A meaning can be omitted from an expression either because those who used it were unaware of the meaning, or because they were aware of it but wanted to conceal it, or because it was so obvious to them that it did not need mention. If the expressions surviving from a given past era were sufficiently ample, we could eventually extract from these themselves all the meanings that were known but concealed, and the meanings that were too obvious to be mentioned. (Even the wholly unperceived meanings might be detected by studying what-goes-with-what and what-follows-what in the images and ideas overtly expressed.) But the expression of past eras survives in fragments, and often without explicit reference to the situations in which it arose (but of which people were wholly conscious at the time). So the "mystifications" are in part merely a by-product of the written record, and in this sense mystify us as they did not mystify their contemporaries. Marx seems quite correct in his discovery that idealistic history built a whole life's work out of such misinterpreted abstractions. But the same error would affect us too, if we assumed that the people who used such god-terms as counters in their daily lives had been equally mystified by them. Insofar as a "context of situation" had participated, for them, as a part of the term's meaning, the documentary survival of the term after the death of its historical context might make it seem to have been much more "spiritual" than it actually was. In the books, it is but a spirit; yet those who used it when it flourished may have recognized it rather by its body.

For instance, consider Cromwell's speech, delivered before the House of Commons, January 22, 1655. He here looks upon the Revolution as "God manifesting Himself"; he justifies it on the grounds that its success is *per se* the evidence of God's will; he sees in it the "necessity" imposed by Providence. Judged by Marxist criteria, such expressions would be a perfect instance of the "mystifying."

Now, he might conceivably have stopped at such statements. But he is addressing a legislative body; there is business to be done. So he himself provides the qualifications which might have been missing:

> Religion was not the thing at first contested for "at all": but God brought it to that issue at last; and gave it unto us by way of redundancy; and at last it proved to be that which was most dear to us.

Not an opponent, but Cromwell himself, says that the conflict did not begin with religious motives. He is saying what his contemporaries knew, but what a *later* mystification might deny (as Carlyle actually did, when asserting that, although Cromwell's remark was "true in form," it was not true "in essence").

Again, after asserting that "they do vilify and lessen the works of God" who accuse him of "having, in these great Revolutions, 'made Necessities,'" he says:

> There is another Necessity, which you have put upon us, and we have not sought. I appeal to God, Angels and Men,—if I shall now raise money according to the Article in the Government, whether I am not compelled to do it!

Indeed, if you would inspect this speech as a theory of revolutionary motives, but a slight emendation is necessary to make it a perfect fit for Marxist thinking. You need but think of "God" or "Providence" in a "neutral" or "technical" sense, merely as a term for the universal scene, for the sum total of conditions (scholastic theology itself having provided the bridge, in defining God as "the ground of all possibility").

Thus Cromwell ridicules the charge that the Revolution depended upon his special skill as a conspirator:

> "It was," say some, "the cunning of the Lord Protector,"—I take it to myself,—"it was the craft of such a man, and his plot, that hath brought it about!" And, as they say in other countries, "There are five or six cunning men in England that have skill; they do all these things." Oh, what blasphemy is this! Because men that are without God in the world, and walk not with Him, know not what it is to pray or believe, and to receive returns from God.

This reference to "five or six cunning men in England" may have been the source of Churchill's remark about the "handful of very able men who now hold 180 million Soviet citizens in their grasp." But in any case, the reference to "God in the world" gives us our hint as to how this statement would be translated into Marxism. The reference to "blasphemy" would become a reference to "enemy propaganda." Instead of the partnership with God (as word for universal ground) there would be a knowledge of dialectical materialism (as word for universal ground). Praying and believing in God would become planning according to belief in the materialist interpretation of history. The "returns from God" would have, as their analogue, the success that comes of acting in accordance with the nature of the "objective situation." Both would agree that the situation cannot be forced, that one cannot rule in violation of "necessity." If the régime in Russia is but the work of a handful of cunning men, then it cannot succeed, as the most devout Stalinist would assure you. The course of history must be behind it. Or, in Cromwell's terms:

> If this be of human structure and invention, and if it be an old Plotting and Contriving to bring things to this Issue, and that they are not the Births of Providence,—then they will tumble.

We are not trying to deny the obvious differences in motivation between the English protectorate and the Russian dictatorship. We are trying to indicate that, even the most "mystifying" of terms may subsume much materialistic relevancy. And, conversely, there is a very close parallel between both Cromwellian and Marxist appeal to "necessity"; for any ultimate terms of motivation must, by their very nature as "high abstractions," omit important ingredients of motivation. The *general* statement of historical motives in terms of dialectical materialism is as "mystifying" as any such statement in terms of "Providence"—for in both, all reference to minute administrative situations is omitted. In either language, the bureaucratic, administrative details are "spiritualized." As regards the pragmatic operations of production and government, the treatment of conditions in terms of "necessity" is as "mystifying" when the necessity is identified with the inevitable laws of history as when it is identified with the will of Providence manifesting itself through such laws. Yet on the other hand, neither statement may be as "mystifying" or "general" as it seems, since it is used by people in specific social contexts, and in various unspecified ways derives meaning from such material conditions.

Indeed, even where people choose to present their motives in terms of a "eulogistic covering," La Rochefoucauld has suggested reasons for treating such usage, not as self-deception, but as roundabout evidence of self-criticism. For when people are talking of their own conduct, he says, the self-love that usually blinds them gives them so accurate a view that they suppress or disguise the slightest unfavorable details. And he takes such tactics as evidence that they know their faults better than you'd think:

> Ce qui fait voir que les hommes connaissent mieux leurs fautes qu'on ne pense, c'est qu'ils n'ont jamais tort quand on les entend parler de leur conduite; le même amour-propre qui les aveugle d'ordinaire les éclaire alors et leur donne des vues si justes qu'il leur fait supprimer ou déguiser les moindres choses qui peuvent être condamnées.

Where a class, or company, prefers words that similarly disguise (La Rochefoucauld's remark would suggest), there is not so much "illusion" as *conspiracy*. But he is considering only individual cases, his concern being *amour-propre* as manifested by the individuals of his class. And perhaps when disguise has attained the proportions of a social conspiracy, it really is on the way to becoming an out-and-out illusion.

Carlyle on "Mystery"

Marx's insight into the mystification of class can get corroboration from an unexpected quarter, an equally urgent nineteenth-century writer, but one who, treating "mystery" as a eulogistic term, would have looked upon the rejection of it as an atheistic abomination. We refer to Carlyle and his "philosophy of clothes" in *Sartor Resartus*.

Carlyle says in terms of stomach trouble what the Promethean Marx says in terms of a gnawed liver.

Reading *The German Ideology* and *Sartor Resartus* together, with the perhaps somewhat perverse pleasure of seeing how they can be brought to share the light that each throws upon the other, we might begin with the proposition that mystery arises at that point where different *kinds* of beings are in communication. In mystery there must be *strangeness;* but the estranged must also be thought of as in some way capable of communion. There is mystery in an animal's eyes at those moments when a man feels that he and the animal understand each other in some inexpressible fashion.

While the mystery of sex relations, which leads to the rhetoric of courtship, is grounded in the communication of beings *biologically* estranged, it is greatly accentuated by the purely *social* differentiations which, under the division of human labor, can come to distinguish the "typically masculine" from the "typically feminine."

Similarly, the conditions for "mystery" are set by *any* pronounced social distinctions, as between nobility and commoners, courtiers and king, leader and people, rich and poor, judge and prisoner at the bar, "superior race" and underprivileged "races" or minorities. Thus even the story of relations between the petty clerk and the office manager, however realistically told, draws upon the wells of mystery for its appeal, since the social distinction between clerk and manager makes them subtly mysterious to each other, not merely two different people, but representing two different *classes* (or "kinds") of people. The clerk and the manager are identified with and by different social *principles*.

And all such "mystery" calls for a corresponding rhetoric, in form quite analogous to sexual expression: for the relations between classes are like the ways of courtship, rape, seduction, jilting, prostitution, promiscuity, with variants of sadistic torture or masochistic invitation to mistreatment. Similarly, there are strong homosexual analogies in "courtly" relations between persons of the same sex but of contrasting social status. This tendency is a marked attribute of youth at college age when, with sexual experience still vague and tentative, adolescents related to each other as bully and toady can carry their mutual fascination quite to the borders of the mystical, particularly if they come of different social classes, or if a sense of social discrimination so pervades the school that it puts its mark even on the relation between persons of the same class (as each is afraid of appearing outclassed in the other's eyes).

The consummate literary expression of social courtship translated into homosexual terms is found in the sonnets of Shakespeare. There seems little point in trying to decide whether the poet "really was homosexual." For our purposes, whether he was or wasn't, in his role as a literary expert looking for the kind of imagery that would best convey his courtly theme he could be expected to find that the situation where a man of lower class addresses flattering appeals to a man of higher class can be readily dramatized by the use of terms homosexual in their implications. And the imagery that marked the precious and perverse author of *The Soul of Man Under Socialism* would disclose but a fraction of its meaning, if we saw in it only Wilde's sexual quandaries, while we overlooked its relations to his motives as a social climber. By the same token, the strong intermixture of mysticism and homosexuality among some of our best contemporary English writers (at one time or another, they have shown Leftist leanings) might well be examined, not so much for signs of "unconscious" fixations upon the parents, as for "unconscious" fixations on *substitutes* which might represent, in parental imagery, the principle of a "superior" class. Hence, the suggestions of awe, guilt, incest, parricide, and the like, might derive most from the pudencies of intercourse between social classes.

But in mentioning the pudencies of social intercourse, we are reminded that, in making a tentative analysis of the key words in some works by the snob-conscious Henry James, we noted his special fondness for the ambiguities of that word, "intercourse." In the case of so conscious a writer, we hesitated to assume that he completely overlooked the sexual connotations of the word. Yet we hesitated also to assume that so subtle and scrupulous a writer was aiming merely to exploit its mildly pornographic suggestions. But our thoughts on the sexual and homosexual analogies in courtship between classes seem to provide the missing qualification.

In particular they would seem to indicate the full significance of the word in *The Turn of the Screw,* where the vaguely and morbidly sexual implications of the plot involve an ambiguous relation between the master's children and the servants (a governess and her sinister predecessors), who are struggling for the possession of the children. The struggle is "preternaturally" (his word) infused with malign attributes (the conventions of the ghost story enabling the author to deal with *unnatural* attachments in terms of the "preternatural," though the word "unnatural" is also used). The governess' struggle with the ghosts of her predecessors for the possession of the children is not sexual, as judged by literal tests of sexual appetite. But it is ambiguously sexual, a sexuality surrounded at every point by *mystification*—and we believe that this mystification can be largely explained if seen in terms of one class struggling to possess the soul of another class. The fact that the other class is symbolized in terms of children may, of course, indicate still other possible orders, neither precisely social nor sexual, but rather personal or familial, as were the prototypes of this story, in the author's own life, to derive from the "mysteries" of childhood. (For there is also, at the roots of everyone's experience, a sense of classification solely by age: parents and offspring, generalized as the sense of a qualitative distinction between adults and children—a classification "prior" to sex, and leading into the mysteries of ancestor worship, and thence into the strong feeling for social differentiation that goes with ancestor worship.)

Sexual analogies are clearly enough revealed in the white man's fantasies or apprehensions that regularly accompany the doctrine of "white supremacy." And we find them expressed, from the Negro's side, in the interweaving of social and sexual tension that runs through the plot of Richard Wright's *Native Son* (where the wealthy white girl, though she had befriended the Negro, is killed in a context of imagery connoting coitus, and becomes the vicarious bearer of Bigger's heavy social load).

Dostoevski, writing in Czarist Russia at a time when the distinction between nobles and peasants was so pronounced that the physical beating of peasants by the upper class or their representatives was the norm, gives us a mysticism of many strands, but among these strands are such ambiguous associations as we are now considering. The cult of abjectness, the strangely mystical dream (in *Crime and Punishment*) of the horse being beaten to death, by a peasant who afflicts upon this still more abject creature the signs of his own socially abject status, the masochistic cult of suffering—there is an endless labyrinth of possibilities here, which we can never exhaust: social, sexual, and personal or familial. The familial order of motives (grounded in the relation between elders and children as "classe"), presumably impinges upon the reverence for the "Little Father" on the side of social distinctions, while its sexual implications are revealed in the theme of paedophilia that runs throughout Dostoevski's works. The mystic reverence for the saintly prostitute seems to symbolize the very essence of the hierarchic order. This figure combines both maternal and erotic woman (she is in essence virginal, but in the accidents of her social status a whore); in this duality she is as exalted as Christ the King and as abject as Christ the Crucified. (There is a Bengalese proverb: "He who gives blows is a master, he who gives none is a dog.")

Kafka's novels are fanciful delving into the mystery of bureaucracy and the rhetoric that goes with it. Indeed, if we were to propose, for readers of Kafka, a work that matches him in the same perversely illuminating way that Carlyle matches Marx, we would select the writings of Dionysius the Areopagite, on the Celestial Hierarchy and the Ecclesiastical Hierarchy. "Hierarchy" is the old, eulogistic word for "bureaucracy," with each stage employing a rhetoric of obeisance to the stage above it, and a rhetoric of charitable condescension to the stage beneath it, in sum, a rhetoric of courtship, while all the stages are infused with the spirit of the Ultimate Stage, which sums up the essence implicit in the hierarchic mode of thought itself, and can thus be "ideologically" interpreted as its "cause." In Kafka this same mystery of class distinctions is all-pervasive, while the Ultimate Bureaucrat, ever Above and Beyond and Behind, is a vaguely dyslogistic but always mysterious mixture of God and Mr. Big.

But let us return to Carlyle, and his particular way of handling the element of "mystification" in the social order: "Is it not to Clothes that most men do reverence?" Carlyle asks, or rather the ironically conceived representative of himself, Teufelsdröckh, asks in his chapter on "Old Clothes." And in this same chapter he says, "Trust not the heart of that man for whom old Clothes are not venerable." But Carlyle is not writing a book on the clothing industry. He is writing a book about symbols, which demand reverence because, in the last analysis, the images of nature are the Symbols of God. He uses Clothes as a surrogate for the symbolic in general. Examining his book to see what they are symbolic of, you find how Carlyle resembles Marx: Both are talking about the kind of hierarchy that arose in the world with the division of labor. Marx says that the modern division of labor began in earnest with the manufacture of Cloth. Carlyle approaches the same subject in his figurative way by saying that Tools are Clothes.

In his chapter on "The World in Clothes," where he proposes to write on "The Spirit of Clothes" as Montesquieu had written on the Spirit of Laws, Carlyle says: "The first purpose of clothes . . . was not warmth or decency, but ornament." For "the first spiritual want of a barbarous man is Decoration." Next, you find him talking about Money, how Money transformed Barter into Sale; whereupon, now

> whoso has sixpence is Sovereign (to the length of sixpence) over all men; commands Cooks to feed him, Philosophers to teach him, Kings to mount guard over him,—to the length of sixpence.— Clothes too, which began in foolishest love of Ornament, what have they not become! Increased Security, and pleasurable Heat soon followed: but what of these? Shame, divine Shame (Schaam, Modesty), as yet a stranger to the Anthropophagous bosom, arose there mysteriously under Clothes; a mystic grove-encircled shrine for the Holy in man. Clothes gave us *individuality, distinctions, social polity;* Clothes have made Men of us; they are threatening to make Clothes-screens of us. [The four italicized words in the last sentence are our emphasis.]

Then he turns abruptly to say that man is a "Tool-using animal," and concludes: "of which truth Clothes are but one example." The chapter ends by mentioning ultimate instances of the division of labor: modern transportation ("Steam-carriages" at that time), and political representation ("the British House of Commons," whose members "toil for us, bleed for us, hunger, and sorrow, and sin for us"). Elsewhere he refers to "the moral, political, and even religious Influences of Clothes," since "Man's earthly interests are all hooked and buttoned together, and held up, by Clothes," and "Society is founded upon Cloth . . . sails through the Infinitude on Cloth." Much to our purposes is his remark on the propriety of saying that men are "clothed with Authority." Without clothes, not "the smallest Politeness, Polity, or even Police, could exist." And "how, without Clothes, could we possess the master-organ, soul's seat, and true pineal gland of the Body Social: I mean, a Purse?"

There are two other primary steps in Carlyle's thinking. First, there is his application of the Pauline doctrine, proclaiming the body to be as Clothes of the Mind, all Nature as the visible garment of invisible Spirit, and any "imagined" thing as but "a Clothing of the higher, celestial Invisible, 'unimaginable, formless dark with excess of bright,'" since Nature is a "Flesh-Garment" which Imagination wove with "Metaphors as her stuff," and Fantasy (that is, Imagination) is "the organ of the Godlike."

This doctrine brings him to the ultimate mystery, the Symbol as Enigma, as both clarification and obfuscation, speech and silence, publicity and secrecy. For it simultaneously expresses and conceals the thing symbolized:

> Of kin to the so incalculable influences of Concealment, and connected with still greater things, is the wondrous agency of *Symbols*. In a symbol there is concealment yet revelation: here, therefore, by Silence and by Speech acting together, comes a doubled significance.

Hence, while attacking "Thought without Reverence," "profess'd Enemies to Wonder," and those who would "have no Mystery and Mysticism," he is after a profounder vision that permits him to say of purely social reverence:

> Happy he who can look through the Clothes of a Man ... into the Man himself; and discern, it may be, in this or the other Dread Potentate, a more or less incompetent Digestive-apparatus; yet also an inscrutable venerable Mystery, in the meanest Tinker that sees with eyes!

For round a man's "mysterious ME,"

> there lies, under all those wool rags, a Garment of Flesh (or of Senses), contextured in the Loom of Heaven; whereby he is revealed to his like, and dwells with them in UNION and DIVISION.

But though he would thus seem to complete his journey by arriving at a "mother-idea, Society in a state of Nakedness," we must never overlook the spontaneous judgment in such an expression as, "Clothes, from the King's mantle downwards, are Emblematic." True, he admonishes:

> Perhaps not once in a lifetime does it occur to your ordinary biped, of any country or generation, be he gold-mantled Prince or russet-jerkined Peasant, that his Vestments and his Self are not one and indivisible; that *he* is naked, without vestments, till he buy or steal such ...

But his doctrines of reverence for the mysterious ground that unifies all men come to a head, so far as history is concerned, in the worship of heroes who represent the principle of divinity in the world. (This is the "identification" principle.) Thus, in *Heroes and Hero-Worship*, he tells us that the king "may be reckoned the most important of great men." For

> He is practically the summary for us of *all* the various figures of heroism; priest, teacher, whatsoever of earthly or of spiritual dignity we can fancy to reside in a man, embodies itself here, to *command* over us, to furnish us with constant practical teaching, to tell us for the day and hour what we are to *do*.

Perhaps the whole matter is summed up in his chapter on "Adamitism," where he sees through the "clothes" of class distinction to the naked universal man beneath, but restores with one hand the very hierarchic reverence he would take away with the other. Carlyle has just brought together the Judge "in fine Red" and the shuddering prisoner, "in coarse threadbare Blue," whom the judge has sentenced to be hanged. Carlyle meditates:

> How is this; or what make ye of your *Nothing can act but where it is?* Red has no physical hold of Blue, no *clutch* of him, is nowise in *contact* with him: neither are those ministerial Sheriffs and Lord Lieutenants and Hangmen and Tipstaves so related to commanding Red, that he can tug them hither and thither; but each stands distinct within his own skin. Nevertheless, as it is spoken, so it is done: the articulated Word sets all hands in Action; and Rope and Improved-drop perform their work.
>
> Thinking reader, the reason seems to me twofold: First, that *Man is a Spirit,* and bound by invisible bonds to *All Men:* Secondly, that *he wears Clothes,* which are the visible emblems of that fact. Has not your Red hanging-individual a horsehair wig, squirrel-skins, and a plush gown; whereby all mortals know that he is a JUDGE?—Society, which the more I think of it astonishes me the more, is founded upon Cloth.

Carlyle then goes on to say how, when reading of "pompous ceremonials," Coronations, Levees, Couchees, and the talk is of Dukes, Archdukes, Colonels, Bishops, Admirals, and "miscellaneous Functionaries," all "advancing to the Anointed Presence," in his "atrabiliar moods" he imagines that the clothes "fly off the whole dramatic corps." It is a good reduction. *But in its very fantasy of irreverence, it but once more reveals that in clothes, as thus symbolic of distinguished office, there is mystery.*

In sum, the stages of his doctrine are these:

1. Clothes symbolize a social order that, while it elicits men's reverence, does not represent man's true nature.

2. There should be reverence, but it should be more deeply directed. Seeing behind the pageantry of social distinctions ("Clothes"), we find that all nature and history are symbolic of a profounder reality. Here is the Mystery at once revealed and concealed by "Clothes" (the "garments" of the visible world). To this our reverence is due.

3. But because the world's "Clothes" symbolize this profounder, divine order, we must reverence them too, insofar as they are representative of it. In ultimate reality, all men are united—and it is by reason of this ultimate union that the different classes of men can communicate with one another. Hence, at stage 3 we can restore with a difference the reverence for "Clothes" (i.e., the "garments" of nature and the social order both) that we had withdrawn at stage 2. In particular, we can restore reverence for that major class distinction, between ruler and ruled (a pattern of thinking which could then, presumably, be reproduced in miniature, where lesser hierarchic differences were concerned). We should revere a true king ("hero") because he really does rule by divine right.

If the course of the argument still escapes you, we might make another try. In fact, perhaps our point can be made most clearly by deliberately letting the argument escape us, and noting merely what it "all adds up to," from the standpoint of "identifications." As thus telescoped, what you get is this: Over and above all the qualifications, *mystery* is equated with *class distinctions*.

We have not been trying to abolish, or debunk, or refute, or even to "approve with reservations." Above all, we are not trying to decide whether mystery should be considered dyslogistically, as with Marx, or eulogistically, as with Carlyle. For we need not decide here whether there should or should not be reverence and mystery (hence "mystification").

Perhaps there would be no mystery, of any appreciable resonance, if distinctions of class were abolished (as they do not seem to have been abolished in Soviet Russia, with regard to the courtly, Carlylean relations between the dictator and the people). Or perhaps there would be a truer kind of mystery, now hidden behind the fog of social inequality. Maybe, if there were no hierarchy of privilege, the imagination would not be led to conceive of divine dignity in such trivial forms, as with the feudal imaging of Man and God in terms of liege and lord, or servitude (like a theologically-minded dog conceiving of God in terms of his pudgy and puffy master). Perhaps reality would not look mysterious at all to our literary mystics, if it did not also include the reverence due their professional careerism; perhaps without such impunities, it would disclose a more urgent wonder.

Maybe there would be no mystery. Maybe there should be none. For present purposes, it does not matter. As regards rhetoric, our point is: Marx and Carlyle, taken together, indicate the presence of a "mystifying condition" in social inequality; and this condition can elicit "God-fearing" attitudes towards agents and agencies that are not "divine." The two doctrines, taken together, can put us on the lookout for expressions that both reveal and conceal such an aspect of "consciousness," as is the way with symbols (for the dictionaries tell us that "mystery" is related to *muein* which, accented on the second syllable, means "to initiate into the mysteries," and, accented on the first syllable, means "to shut the eyes"). But we believe that, if you will read *Sartor Resartus* with *The German Ideology* in mind, and without a blinding prejudice for or against either, Carlyle's enigmatic symbol may contribute as much as Marx towards indicating a relation between mystification and class relationships. This is a very important consideration for rhetoric, since it puts rhetorical analysis on the track of much courtship that might otherwise remain undetected. And courtship, however roundabout, is a form of persuasion.

Empson on "Pastoral" Identification

We previously spoke of "courtship, however roundabout." William Empson's ingenious work, *English Pastoral Poetry* (English edition entitled: *Some Versions of Pastoral*), can for our purposes be treated as an investigation into this recondite rhetoric. His book, which is his rare response to a vogue for "proletarian" literature, is profoundly concerned with the rhetoric of courtship between contrasted social classes. For pastoral, as a literary *genre,* was, in its essence, "felt to imply a beautiful relation between rich and poor."

True, whereas the "proletarian" critic's emphasis upon "class consciousness" would bring out the elements of class *conflict,* Empson is concerned with a kind of expression which, while thoroughly conscious of class differences, aims rather at a stylistic transcending of conflict. We might say that he examines typical social-stylistic devices whereby spokesmen for different classes aim at an over-all dialectic designed to see beyond the limitations of status. To this extent, the orthodox Marxist might want to accuse him of contributing to the "mystifications" of class, since the ruling class presumably profits more than any other by the maintenance of the *status quo*. And certainly an orthodox critic writing in Russia today would object because the approach to "proletarian" literature in terms of "pastoral" makes the relation between the common people of Russia and their representatives in the Kremlin seem much like the "pastoral" relation between nobleman and shepherd.

But the important consideration, for our purposes, is the concern with a politeness, or humility, stemming simultaneously from the conventions of love poetry and the mimetics of social inferiority. Empson analyzes variants of literary simplicity, irony, and mock-simplicity, as developed out of social pudencies (Carlyle's *"Schaam,* Modesty"). That is, the "mystery" is still present in such expression, but it is transformed into subtle embarrassments that cover a range extending from outright flattery to ironically veiled challenge. Or we might say that the "reverence" of social privilege has been attenuated into respect, the respect itself sometimes being qualified until it has moved as far in the direction of disrespect as one might go without unmistakably showing his hand. In the literary strategies Empson is examining, ideas and images under the sign of cajolery, however strained, are never abandoned for ideas and images under the sign of outright insult and injury. And we are led to feel that the impulse behind such compromises is not merely an underling's fear of a superior, but rather the magic of the hierarchic order itself, which imposes itself upon superior and inferior both, and leads them both to aim at a dialectic transcending their discordancy of status. Looking at matters thus, you find that many attitudes quite different from outright approval can serve such ends. Relations between classes, even where the aim is to make both sides feel themselves part of a larger unity, may be treated "as well by mockery as admiration."

Perhaps the clearest instance of Empson's book, considered as a contribution to the rhetorical analysis of "mystification," is with his comments on four lines from Gray's *Elegy:*

> Full many a gem of purest ray serene
> The dark, unfathomed caves of ocean bear;
> Full many a flower is born to blush unseen
> And waste its sweetness on the desert air.

While granting that it would be hard to say just how much "bourgeois ideology" there is in these lines, he analyzes them for their "latent political ideas." And his observations might be summed up under four heads:

1. The lines allude to society's neglect of such scholarly talents as this poet's.

2. Such neglected talents are presented in terms of virginal modesty (as of the blushing but unplucked flower).

3. The note of melancholy suggests that, while understanding "the conditions opposed to aristocracy," the poet will not protest, but will resign himself.

4. The churchyard setting, the universality and impersonality of the reflections, "claim as if by comparison that we ought to accept the injustice of society as we do the inevitability of death."

Perhaps we might add a fifth step here, when considering the "poetic" lines rhetorically, as a *social* strategy. For we have the feeling that the poem is not wholly resigned. Isn't there a possibility that the virginal flower might be plucked after all? Can't the bowed posture of ingredients 3 and 4 be an unassuming appeal (of a nature that befits ingredient 2) for someone to correct the condition of ingredient 1? For here is a kind of resignation that might also, in "mystifying" terms, serve as a bid for preferment. The sentiments expressed are thus a character reference, describing a person doubly reliable, since he doesn't protest even when neglected. In an imaginative way the poem answers such questions as a personnel director would record in his files, if interviews and questionnaires were capable of such subtle disclosures, rather than supplying merely such entries as would fit a punch card.

As we have seen, when considering Carlyle, the "mystery" of social relations can become identified with the mystery of first and last things. But as attenuated, in the forms of social embarrassment, it can perhaps be reduced to this: Where there is wealth and poverty, there is awkwardness in any one of these four situations:

> a rich man speaking in praise of wealth
> a rich man speaking in praise of poverty
> a poor man speaking in praise of wealth
> a poor man speaking in praise of poverty

Attenuate this in turn, and you get, as a rhetorical situation, the proposition that in any social inequality there is awkwardness, making for the kinds of squeamishness which Empson is studying in their most imaginative manifestations.

Among these pudencies, for instance, is what Empson calls "comic primness." Comic primness, or "prim irony," is an attitude characterizing a member of a privileged class who somewhat questions the state of affairs whereby he enjoys his privileges; but after all, he does enjoy them, and so in the last analysis he resigns himself to the dubious conditions, in a state of ironic complexity that is apologetic, but not abnegatory.

The analysis of such attitudes, as expressed in literary tactics, we would class under the head of rhetorical identification. Hence we would assign Empson's book an important place in the New Rhetoric. Above all, we can derive from his account of pastoral and its variants good hints as to the way in which irony may simultaneously reflect and transcend class motives. Such considerations have important bearing on the cult of irony among our Southern intellectuals, a commingling of irony and irrationality which, whatever its "cosmic" pretensions, is also qualified by its relation to the conditions of "white supremacy."

The literary criticism in Empson's *Seven Types of Ambiguity* is rhetorical in that it analyzes obscure savors having to do with poetic effects as such. It is a study of "eloquence." But perhaps we should recall that De Quincey *distinguished between* rhetoric and eloquence. Under rhetoric he classed all effects having to do with purely literary ingenuity (love of rhetorical tactics for their own sake: the "epideictic" interest, that gravitates towards sheer technical display). And he assigned to eloquence all urgencies of emotion and passion. (Thus Ovid's playful ostentation is his ideal instance of rhetoric, whereas Demosthenes is disqualified by the high degree of eloquence in his orations.) The book on "pastoral" is rhetorical in a different sense: in its bearing upon matters of advantage.

Having matched Marx and Carlyle, Kafka and the pseudo-Dionysius, we suggested that the concerns in Empson's book might serve as a bridge between the two kinds. But we might propose a match for it too: Veblen's *Theory of the Leisure Class*. Though its strongly sociological stress places it rather in our earlier chapter, where we tried to disclose the rhetorical motive in works not usually so considered, Veblen's book applies to rhetoric in the strictly literary sense because it centers upon the purely *symbolic expression* of advantage. All told, we might say that where Empson deals with the courtship of classes, Carlyle with their marriage, and Marx with their divorce, Veblen deals with one class and its fascinated appeal to itself.

The "Invidious" as Imitation, in Veblen

We consider Thorstein Veblen's *Theory of the Leisure Class* better "in principle" than in the particular. Where Empson is fine to the point of evanescence, Veblen treads cumbrously. And his terminology of motives is far too limited in scope; hence, at every step in his explanation, important modifiers would be needed, before we could have a version of human motives equal to the depths at which the ways of persuasion (appeal, communication, "justification") must really operate. His primary distinction (between the "invidious" or "pecuniary" motive and the "instinct of workmanship") is neither comprehensive nor pliant enough. For instance, when discussing "honorific" and "humilific" words like noble, base, higher, lower, he says that "they are in substance an expression of sportsmanship—of the predatory and animistic habit of mind." Or again: "The canons of pecuniary decency are reducible for the present purposes to the principles of waste, futility, and ferocity." But we would question whether any motive ample enough to rationalize wide areas of human relationship can be so reduced without misrepresentation. Allow, if you will, that there may be a high percentage of such ingredients in it. Yet there is nothing essentially "predatory" in the symbolic nature of money. Its nature is in its *dialectical* or *linguistic* function as a "spiritual" entity, a purely symbolic thing, a mode of abstraction that "transcends" the materially real.

Veblen's psychology is not so much dramatistic, as dramatized. Consider his choice of the "invidious" as the term in which to treat of the "competitive," "sportsmanlike," and "pecuniary." (For in

Veblen these four terms are equated with one another.) Presumably in keeping with the genius of Bentham's search for scientifically neutral "appellatives," he writes:

> In making use of the term "invidious," it may perhaps be unnecessary to remark, there is no intention to extol or depreciate, or to commend or deplore any of the phenomena which the word is used to characterize. The term is used in a technical sense as describing a comparison of persons with a view to rating and grading them in respect of relative worth or value—in an aesthetic or moral sense—and so awarding and defining the relative degrees of complacency with which they may legitimately be contemplated by themselves and by others. An invidious comparison is a process of valuation of persons in respect of worth.

Similarly, having identified the "invidious" with a cult of "conspicuous waste," he writes:

> The use of the term "waste" is in one respect an unfortunate one. As used in the speech of everyday life the word carries an undertone of deprecation. It is here used for want of a better term that will adequately describe the same range of motives and of phenomena, and it is not to be taken in an odious sense, as implying an illegitimate expenditure of human products or of human life. In the view of economic theory the expenditure in question is no more and no less legitimate than any other expenditure. It is here called "waste" because this expenditure does not serve human life or human well-being on the whole, not because it is waste or misdirection of effort or expenditure as viewed from the standpoint of the individual consumer who chooses it.

To use key terms as censorially charged as "invidious" and "waste," while at the same time assuring one's reader that one is being merely technical, and does not want the reader to read any unfavorable implications into them—well, it is a good stylistic device, and may be enjoyed for its blandness (rhetorically dramatizing in the name of the non-dramatic). Yet it reminds us of the wag who, having called his enemy a son of a bitch, went on to explain: "I want it understood that I employ the expression, not as an oath, but in the strictly scientific sense."

We have elsewhere complained that anthropological terminologies of motives often mislead, when applied to the contemporary world, because they slight the role of money in human relations. This objection seems particularly important, as regards the contemporary rhetoric of advantage, since the divisive aspects of money pervade the modern rhetorical situation with an especially urgent need for "mystifying" terms that proclaim the ideal unity of people thus set apart. Accordingly, one might think that Veblen's overwhelming stress upon the "pecuniary" motive would be just what we are asking for. However, his approach to money as motive is in terms of a "predatory instinct" which is even more "primitive" than the behavior studied by anthropologists, and which at best analyzes modern society in terms of a dyslogistically simplified version of the motives for ostentation in savages and the medieval nobility. Modern life itself becomes a kind of epideictic oratory, wherein social display itself, rather than the malaise behind it, is taken as a basic motive.

The "pecuniary" motive, we contend, should be analyzed as a special case of the linguistic motive. And the linguistic motive eventually involves kinds of persuasion guided not by appeal to any one local audience, but by the *logic of appeal in general* (treated in secular terms as "socialization," in theology as "justification"). The reductive, abstractive, metaphorical, analytic, and synthesizing powers of all language find their correspondences in the monetary idiom. Whatever fantastic appetites may finally arise under the goading of the pecuniary motive (particularly when it is not functioning adequately), Veblen's reductions are misleading unless they are enjoyed as a kind of deadpan satire. As so read and discounted, they are extremely illuminating. When taken at their face value, their very revelation of a superficial rhetoric in human relations but conceals a profounder rhetoric that Veblen leaves unanalyzed.

The book is valuable as an illustration of the ways in which identification (and a primary function of it, the vicarious) can operate. The notion of "vicarious leisure" whereby a man may work himself to death earning the money to help his wife be useless for the both of them, is good irony, good satiric reduction. At its best his book is a systematic exploiting of this solemn absurdity, until we see the reflections of it throughout society's assumptions about the good, the true, and the beautiful (respectability, the "higher learning," the esthetic).

When discussing "The American Way" we shall indicate why we think that this economist is not economist enough, in his account of the motives for "conspicuous consumption" and "vicarious consumption." The forms of ostentation which he eruditely ridicules may be treated as ways of "bearing witness"—a low order of such persuasion, perhaps, but with an ingredient of genuine piety, however ironically perverted its manifestations may be.

"The motive that lies at the root of ownership," Veblen writes, "is emulation; and the same motive of emulation continues active in the further development of the institution to which it has given rise." But wherein reside the "roots of ownership"? Do they not reside in the *individual centrality of the nervous system,* in the *divisiveness* of the individual human organism, from birth to death? What the body eats and drinks becomes its special private property; the body's pleasures and pains are exclusively its own pleasures and pains. True, there is the vicarious sharing by empathy, by sympathy, the "imaginative" identification with one another's states of mind. And there is the mutuality of cooperation and language whereby human society becomes, not an aggregate of isolated individuals, but a superentity, involving principles of interdependence that have in the past gone by such names as rationality, consciousness, conscience, and "God." Bring together a number of individual nervous systems, each with its own unique centrality, and from this indeterminate mixture of cooperation and division there emerge the conditions for the "basic rhetorical situation": an underlying biological incentive towards private property, plus the fact that the high development of production and language owes so much to its public or communal nature. And once a high development of public property has accumulated, private property is rather a function of that accumulation than an expression of the original biologic goading that is located in the divisive centrality of the nervous system. The cult of property comes to reflect public norms, norms identified with social classes which are differentiated by property. And emulation seems to derive from the imitation of class ways considered in some respect superior.

We previously spoke of Isocrates' device for "spiritualizing" the idea of "advantage." Similarly, "emulation" can be spiritualized (as in the Plutarchian theory of biography, where emulation means the ethical desire to pattern one's life after "noble" models). Veblen would warn us to be wary of such "nobility," or to see in it symbolic claims to more exclusive kinds of preferment. But when we get so far, we ask ourselves: Emulation being but a special case of imitation, what of imitation itself as motive?

We recall but one place in Veblen's book where the "competitive," "predatory," "pecuniary," "invidious" nature of emulation shows signs of giving way to this wider notion, of imitation in general. Thus, he writes:

> A still more characteristic and more pervasive alien element in the motives which have gone to formally uphold the scheme of the devout life is that non-reverent sense of aesthetic congruity with the environment, which is left as a residue of the latter-day act of worship after elimination of its anthropomorphic content. . . . This sense or impulse of aesthetic congruity is not primarily of an economic character, but it has considerable indirect effect in shaping the habit of mind of the individual for economic purposes in the later stages of industrial development.

Is not "non-reverent sense of aesthetic congruity with the environment" but a special case of imitation? But perhaps before pressing for an answer to this question, we should make clear just what we are after.

In considering the whole subject of competition, as the term is used either in capitalist apologetics or in critiques of capitalism, we began to see that competition itself is but a special case of imitation. For when you discuss competition as it has actually operated in our society, you discover that the so-called ways of competition have been almost fanatically zealous ways of *conformity*. And considering how men in their businesses, and how the families of business men in their social relations attempt to amass and display all the insignia felt proper to their status, we conclude: From the standpoint of "identification" what we call "competition" is better described as men's attempt to *out-imitate* one another.

Imitation is an essentially dramatistic concept. It makes for consubstantiality by community of ways ("identification"), since men can either crudely imitate one another's actions as revealed on the surface, or subtly imitate the *underlying principles* of such actions. (And in calling the motive "dramatistic" rather than "anthropomorphic," we can avoid the false promises too often lurking in the discarded word, which suggests that people can be "human" in some other way than by being "anthropomorphic.")

With imitation as the most generalized term, competition would be treated as a special case of it. The "invidious" would be at one further remove. We might characterize in another way the rhetorical blandness of Veblen's satire-masked-as-science by saying: He substitutes a censorially partisan word for a more generalized word, then asks us to discount the partisan connotations.

Emulation, as used by earlier writers, would be the word for imitation in the moral vocabulary, though its ethical pretensions might well be quizzically examined for traces of more mundane ambitions, and even for "magical" attempts to coerce material reality by ritual means. (Consider, for instance, the lurking hope that moral goodness will draw rewards from nature, as in *Comus,* where chastity is a protection against wild beasts.) However, whereas such ways may be latently "magical" where some of man's relations with nonverbal nature are concerned, they may be correctly rhetorical as regards human relations. Thus, as the rhetorically minded moralist, Rochefoucauld, put it: To establish yourself in the world, you do all you can to look established (*"Pour s'établir dans le monde, on fait tout ce que l'on peut pour y paraître établi"*). Another variant would be "admiration," as used in the dramatic theory of Corneille, where it is a special term linking esthetic criteria with the pageantry of privilege.

In sum, when Veblen reduces to the "invidious," we believe that this expression in turn should be reduced to imitation (except of course insofar as the purpose of his tract is not literally scientific, but satirical). If his statement of motives were reduced to a term of this scope, he might next consider the special "invidious" stress which certain conditions favor. In showing how this "invidious" stress, in conjunction with identification and the vicarious, makes for roundabout manifestations, he would give us the valuable insights into rhetoric which he now gives. But such modified procedure would of itself provide the correctives which otherwise must be introduced from without. The same remark applies, in varying degrees, to any discussion of imitation exclusively in terms of competition, where one has to stumble upon factors which he should have explicitly begun with, or where one leaves them in the offing, but pressing for acknowledgment.

Priority of the "Idea"

The "rhetoric of class" involves kinds of identification distinguishable somewhat like Coleridge's fancy, "primary" imagination and "secondary" imagination.

There are mechanical associations of the sort that Pavlov studied in his experiments with the "conditioned reflex." Thus, the mere associating of an idea with an image, or of a cause with a topic, could be called "mechanical." There is such association in the act of a child who, by the mere *noise* of hammering, imitates a carpenter driving nails.

A more organic kind would arise when the principles of one order are transferred to another order. We here have in mind the Marxist statement that the ideologist's view of history is derived from his nature as a specialist in ideas. And Bacon had said much the same, though in an almost reverse application, to account for the imaginings he called "Idols of the Cave." As he put it: When the scientific specialist takes "to philosophy and contemplations of a general character," he is likely to "distort and color them in obedience to" his "former fancies." Thus:

> The race of chemists . . . out of a few experiments of the furnace have built up a fantastic philosophy, framed with reference to a few things; and Gilbert also, after he had employed himself most laboriously in the study and observation of the lodestone, proceeded at once to construct an entire system in accordance with his favorite subject.

John Dewey has favored the term "occupational psychosis" to designate the same "imaginative" transference of principles from one field to another.

There is a most engaging example of such reversal in George Bernard Shaw's preface for his *Back to Methuselah*. He comes upon the principles of dialectic, which he discovers by speculating about the principles of his profession as playwright. Then, looking at nature, he conceives the dialectic of nature after the analogy of his dialectic as playwright. That is: He rejects Darwinian evolution for a view of "creative" evolution which he has developed after the analogy of his experiences as a playwright. Then he claims to derive his views of the playwright's art from this version of nature. Nature having been interpreted dramatistically, he can "deduce" drama from it. The "firsts" or principles of drama have thus been stated twice, once in their own terms and once in terms of a mythic ground or "past," an ideological "prehistory" that looks scientific in its pretense to be a discussion of natural evolution. Then, whereas his terms for nature are derived from his calling as dramatist, he can appear to be proceeding the other way round, and deriving drama from nature.

But how would Veblen's *Theory of the Leisure Class* fit into such a distinction? Sometimes the identifications he reveals seem of the first, more accidental sort. People seem to be bent on doing and acquiring certain things simply because these things happen to have become the signs of an admired status. And one can imagine these same people doing exactly the opposite, if the opposite happened to be the sign of the same status.

At other times the identification seems to be more deeply imaginative. Bacon had said that the Idols of the Cave "take their rise in the peculiar constitution, mental or bodily, of each individual; and also in education, habit, and accident." And the "predatory" instinct which Veblen imputed as the basic motive of the "leisure class" would seem to be such an idol, grounded in the natural constitution, but inured through "education, habit, and accident." "Accident," of course, would refer to linkages of the first sort, the almost automatic response to signs, as to the stop-and-go of traffic lights. But the notion of a natural trait, selected, developed, and trained by the conditions of living, implies rather a central core or principle from which all sorts of expressions could radiate. A "predatory" art, for instance, would not be formed merely by imitation of "predatory" business; rather, art would be "predatory" in ways proper to art while business would be "predatory" in ways proper to business, etc. The "predatory principle" would be generic; but the expression of it would be shaped by the principles specific to each kind of cultural activity.

In trying thus to decide wherein different fields seem to borrow from one another, and wherein they seem to be but different specialized radiations from a common center, you would find yourself involved in issues that would soon carry you far from Veblen. But now we see at least the possibility of three orders here: (1) There is the realm of accident, mechanical association, response to signs as signs, "magical" in the sense that it begins in infancy; it is related to Carlyle's pageantry of "Clothes," as the child gets a "mysterious" sense of class distinction through such appearances long before understanding their occupational logic. (2) There are *analogizing* associations, where terms are transferred from one order to another. Thus, a business culture may become much exercised over a work's "value" as an estheticized equivalent of "price." Or the classic criterion of fitness (decorum, *to prepon*), while referring to a purely technical adaptation of *artistic* means to *artistic* end, can be invoked against a work which violates dominant criteria of *social* propriety. That is, though the adaptation of means to end may be quite adequate, the fitness of the end itself may be questioned under the guise of questioning the means, a canon of artistic expression thereby acting as a canon of social suppression. (3) There are distinct, specialized expressions, *all derived from the same generating principle, hence all embodying it, without the need of direct "interactive" borrowing* (the sort of cultural essences that Spengler was always seeking to codify).

The third kind might bring us again, by another route, to the "ideological." For, given sufficient discernment and expressiveness on the part of the critic, such a unitary principle should lend itself to statement in terms of an *idea*. And it would be "prior" to the economic in the sense that it would be more general, so that the economic behavior, like all other modes of expression, would in its peculiar way manifest this same character.

Consider the bourgeois-Bohemian antithesis (the treatment of the esthetic as directly opposed to the practical, backed by the tendency to equate artistic imagination with unreason, since reason itself is conceived strictly in terms of financial or technological utility). The first step in this direction is probably taken at the beginning of intertribal trade, which breaks art from primitive magic. By the time the monetary rationale has emancipated men from a belief in any spiritual power but money itself and its psychoses, art is viewed not directly, but as refracted through the medium of money.

However, money itself is symbolic of general dialectical processes themselves not monetary. It is an aspect of reductive, abstractive, and substitutive resources inborn to symbolism. There is its nature as an imagery interwoven with other images (Freud, for instance, notes how the miser can be "anally" motivated, Gide in *The Counterfeiters* parallels monetary and personal relations, and we have frequently considered money as a burlesque of "spirit"). But beyond its relation to imagery, there lie its roots in dialectic, so that its origins are as mysterious as the word, with which it is identical, and as the Word, with which it is often identified. Ultimately, like moral striving and scientific or philosophic ordering, it is under the sign of the Ladder, hence its rhetorical convertibility with the patterns of "celestial hierarchy."

The typical nineteenth-century doctrines of esthetics seem to have been monetary in all three of the senses we have here tried to distinguish. Thus, in part, the cult of beauty can be analyzed merely as a symbolic claim to social distinction, in Veblen's term an "invidious" motive. In part, as where "aesthetic values" are a "spiritualized" equivalent of "monetary price," beauty was conceived analogously to money. (This would seem to fit our second category.) The third level seems to manifest itself in writers as different as Shelley and Freud. Shelley's anarchistic idealism is the "perfection" of monetary freedom, transcending it, but *from within*. Similarly, the Marxist critique of capitalism is intrinsic to capitalism, and could only be evolved by a man conversant with the very essence of capitalist motives. And both the Shelleyan and the Marxist departures from the orthodoxy of capitalist motives lead into a wider area of dialectic, where money is but a limiting image. Man, *qua* man, is a symbol user. In this respect, every aspect of his "reality" is likely to be seen through a fog of symbols. And not even the hard reality of basic economic facts is sufficient to pierce this symbolic veil (which is intrinsic to the human mind). One man may seek to organize a set of images, another may strive for order among his ideas, a third may feel goaded to make himself head of some political or commercial empire, but however different the situations resulting from these various modes of action, there are purely symbolic motives behind them all, for in all of them there is "overproduction."

Would it then be possible to make a distinction that allowed for "ideology" within limits? That is, could we consider the Marxist critique as usefully limiting the application of the ideological, but not as wholly discrediting it? For the human mind, as the organ of a symbol-using animal, is "prior" to any *particular* property structure—and in this sense the laws of symbols are prior to economic laws. Out of his symbols, man has developed all his inventions. Hence, why should not their symbolic origin remain concealed in them? Why should they not be not just *things*, but *images* of "ideas"?

So why could we not allow for a certain cooperation between "ideology" (in the sense distrusted by Marx) and the Marxist reversal of it ("in all ideology men and their circumstances appear upside down as in a *camera obscura*")? We are not merely trying to strike a compromise between irreconcilable opponents, or treating the two positions as ideal opposites, with the truth somewhere in between. Rather, we are assigning a definite function to each of the positions—and we are saying that, insofar as each performs its function, they are no more at odds than the stomach and liver of a healthy organism.

Given an economic situation, there are ways of thinking that arise in response to it. But these ways of living and thinking, in complex relationship with both specific and generic motives, can go deep, to the level of *principles*. For a way of living and thinking is reducible to terms of an "idea"—and that "idea" will be "creative" in the sense that anyone who grasps it will embody it or represent it in any mode of action he may choose. The idea, or underlying principle, must be approached by him through the sensory images of his cultural scene. But until he intuitively grasps the principle of such an imaginal clutter, he cannot be profoundly creative, so far as the genius of that "idea" is concerned. For to be profoundly representative of a culture, he will imitate not its mere insignia, but the principle behind the *ordering* of those insignia.

A Metaphorical View of Hierarchy

Let us try again. (A direct hit is not likely here. The best one can do is to try different approaches towards the same center, whenever the opportunity offers.)

Imagine a myth of this sort, built around the hierarchic principle of "higher" and "lower" beings, a principle found in both the Darwinian doctrine of natural evolution and the Marxist doctrine of social evolution. According to this myth, since all living kinds came out of the sea, the sea is their natural home. And they are, let us say, nostalgic for the sea. Physiologically, this state of longing manifests itself as "undernourishment." That is, only foods in and of the sea can wholly nourish forms of life descended from the sea. Hence, in birds and land animals, particularly those living far inland, there can never be complete "biological satiety." Accordingly there is a sect which holds that we should live as much as possible on raw sea food; should bathe often in the sea, for the pores of the body to absorb the sea environment; and as partial compensation for the fact that land organisms have lost the more radical mode of assimilating sea air through gills, we should try always to breathe spindrift, should experiment with the injection of natural sea water into the blood stream, and should try to heal wounds with emulsions and salves made from sea creatures.

Our myth is doubly "regressive." According to it, the offspring's yearning for a return to the womb is but a replica of a prior motive, the womb's yearning for a return to the sea. Though the womb can make a kind of internal sea environment for the foetus, it cannot enjoy this same relation in reverse. It must make a sea, without itself having a sea. Here again is frustration, a biological interference with the body's attempt to "live on the level of principle." For the hierarchic principle is complete only insofar as it works both ways at once. It is not merely the relation of higher to lower, or lower to higher, or before to after, or after to before. The hierarchic principle is not complete in the social realm, for instance, in the mere arrangement whereby each rank is overlord to its underlings and underling to its overlords. It is complete only when each rank accepts the *principle of gradation itself,* and in thus "universalizing" the principle, makes a spiritual *reversal* of the ranks just as meaningful as their actual material arrangement.

The Christian doctrine that the first shall be last and the last shall be first is often interpreted as a pattern of social revolution couched in theological terms. But looking at it from the present standpoint, we should interpret its rhetorical appeal as a dialectic more roundabout, thus: The state of first and last things, the heavenly state, is the realm of *principle*. In this state (a mythical term for the *logically prior*) the reversal of social status makes as much sense as its actual mundane order. For on this level, all that counts is the principle of hierarchy, or levels, or developments, or unfoldings, *per se* (the dialectic principle in general, which is "prior" to any particular kind of development, a kind of priority that can be stated mythically either in terms of a heavenly society before the world began, or one after the world has ended, or one outside of time). The reduction of such reversibility to the world of property can add up to political or social revolution, as the "Edenic" world of universal principle is ironically broken down into the divisions of property, confronting one with a choice between the frozen order of the *status quo* and the reversal of that order, through its "liquidation." We are then in the state of the "fall," the communicative disorder that goes with the building of the technological Tower of Babel.

So, out of the sea came the womb, out of the womb came the child, out of the child came the enlightened division of labor, out of the division of labor came the hierarchy, and out of the hierarchy came the new goadings of social property. And out of this came the variety of attitudes: first, ideally, love, charity, the attempt of the divided beings to overcome division; then, when the tension increased, the various departures from love, beginning with the slight ironic embarrassments, the modified tributes of courtship (as regards the relations between either social or sexual classes); then the tragic attempt to transform hate into love "on a higher level"; and finally, the organization of hate and war, the farthest stage of division, though out of it in turn arises a new compensatory union, the *conspiratorial* unity of faction, where "spies" go by the name of "intelligence." (There is a satanic caricature of the Trinity here. God being the source of power, the Son the bringer of light, the Holy Ghost the Gift of Love, in the conspiratorial unity of faction the war machine is power, espionage is the bringer of light, and the breathing-together of the warrior-conspirators is love.)

But would not our myth have started in the middle of things? Is not the sea itself a jungle of divisiveness? And were not its first denizens already marked by "original sin," as participants in the sea's division from a sea-behind-the-sea? And in the pride of their singularity, when they chose to risk nostalgia by living on the land, did they not do so because their sea-home had already become a wrangle, and the new hunger that would arise in time with their departure and evolution from the sea seemed at that stage more like a promise? How could they know that, in moving from the sea-jungle towards enlightenment, they had but begun a progress towards the speed-up of a Detroit factory, and thence towards atomic and bacteriological war? They had not yet encountered the "rhetorical situation," wherein division may be idealistically buried beneath a terminology of love, or ironically revealed in combination with varying grades of compensatory deference, or where the continuity is snapped, and there is war, hate, conspiracy, with a new terminology of "love" to mask the divisions among the conspirators.

So, the myth of society's return to the child, or the child's return to the womb, or the womb's return to the sea, can all but point towards a myth still farther back, the myth of a power prior to all parturition. Then divided things were not yet proud in the private property of their divisiveness. Division was still but "enlightenment."

The notion of the Son as bringer of light seems in its essence to suggest that the division of the part from the whole is enlightening, a principle that might be stated dialectically thus: Partition provides *terms;* thereby it allows the parts to comment upon one another. But this "loving" relation allows also for the "fall" into terms antagonistic in their partiality, until dialectically resolved by reduction to "higher" terms. (The reversibility possible when hierarchic or opposed orders are reduced to their common ground usually makes at best for a slovenly kind of dispute where the opponents switch sides, as each is tricked into taking over the other's arguments in the attempt to buttress his own.)

Where are we, then? Are we proposing that men cannot resolve their local fights over property until they have undergone the most radical revolution of all, a return to their source? Are we saying that because the warlike divisiveness of property is inherent in our very nature, such mythic design justifies the *status quo* or can properly serve as an argument for the "inevitability" of some particular war? We are not—but we do take our myth seriously to this extent: It reminds us how far back the unrest of *Homo Dialecticus* really goes, and suggests how thorough our shrewdness about property and hierarchy must be, before we could build a whole human society about the critique of ambition.

From the standpoint of pattern, for instance, the Marxist view of social evolution is no less hierarchic than the Areopagite's version of the heavenly and earthly orders. And as the principle of *any* hierarchy involves the possibility of reversing highest and lowest, so the moralizing of status makes for a revolutionary kind of expression, the scapegoat. The scapegoat is dialectically appealing, since it combines in one figure contrary principles of identification and alienation. And by splitting the hierarchic principle into factions, it becomes ritually gratifying; for each faction can then use the other as *katharma,* the unclean vessel upon which can be loaded the dyslogistic burdens of vocabulary (a procedure made all the more zealous by the secret awareness that, if not thus morally "protected," each faction might "court" the other). When this state of affairs prevails, it is not merely men's differences that drive them apart, it is also the *elements they share,* "vices" and "virtues" alike, since the same motives are capable of both eulogistic and dyslogistic naming.

The hierarchic principle itself is inevitable in systematic thought. It is embodied in the mere process of growth, which is synonymous with the class divisions of youth and age, stronger and weaker, male and female, or the stages of learning, from apprentice to journeyman to master. But this last hierarchy is as good an indication as any of the way in which the "naturalness" of grades rhetorically reënforces the protection of privilege. Though in its essence purely developmental, the series is readily transformed into rigid social classifications, and these interfere with the very process of development that was its reason for being.

To say that hierarchy is inevitable is not to say that any particular hierarchy is inevitable; the crumbling of hierarchies is as true a fact about them as their formation. But to say that the hierarchic principle is indigenous to all well-rounded human thinking, is to state a very important fact about the rhetorical appeal of dialectical symmetry. And it reminds us, on hearing talk of equality, to ask ourselves, without so much as questioning the possibility that things might be otherwise: "Just how does the hierarchic principle work in this particular scheme of equality?"

Though *hierarchy* is exclusive, the *principle* of hierarchy is not; all ranks can "share in it alike." But: It includes also the entelechial tendency, the treatment of the "top" or "culminating" stage as the "image" that best represents the entire "idea." This leads to "mystifications" that cloak the state of division, since the "universal" principle of the hierarchy also happens to be the principle by which the most distinguished rank in the hierarchy enjoys, in the realm of worldly property, its special privileges. Hence, the turn from courtship to ill will, with ironic intermediate grades. At the stage of blunt antithesis, each class would deny, suppress, exorcise the elements it shares with other classes. This attempt leads to the scapegoat (the use of dyslogistic terms for one's own traits as manifested in an "alien" class).

Diderot on "Pantomime"

Let us go back and examine, from the standpoint of our myth, the "enigmatic" quality of Diderot's almost hysterically brilliant dialogue between "Moi" and "Lui" in his *Neveu de Rameau*. Do not the reasons for its puzzling and picturesque perversity forthwith become clear? In his role as a social philosopher, Diderot would not be content to stop at the antitheses of political polemics. While favoring the movement from royalism towards bourgeois liberty, he would be thorough enough to desire such systematic rounding out of a philosophy as the principle of feudal hierarchy in its heyday had provided. Yet he was too enlightened to consider the actual court a fitting exemplar of such a form. Hence, in the deepest sense he would be frustrated. Insofar as the king represented the symmetrical *crowning* of a terminology, Diderot in turning against the king was turning somewhat against *himself*.

There were also complications, of course, in the purely practical realm. He wrote under the threat of imprisonment. In this sense, the mere choice of the dialogue form can be rhetorically motivated. In dividing his thoughts between a "Him" and a "Me," the author could let "Him" voice brightly certain dangerous opinions or attitudes which could be somewhat ploddingly and not too convincingly disapproved by "Me." But there is a profounder working-at-cross-purposes here than can be explained by the mere pragmatic need to outwit a censor. There is the *conflict within,* leading the author at times to say things so perverse and antinomian that they could not possibly serve as alignments for the next phase.

The divisiveness of the dialogue is both implicit and explicit. It is implicit in the sense that the author himself is split into the roles of Lui and Moi, confronting each other in an ambiguously courtly relationship at once frank and estranged, but showing their kinship despite their differences of "position." Next there is the divisiveness within Lui himself, a condition that is carried to the extreme by the picturesque amplifying of his showmanship, as his wide emotional swings are always histrionically exaggerated (the book is further interwoven with a contemporary quarrel over rival theories of opera that, roundabout, had revolutionary implications). The divisiveness is further amplified, as with Lui's account of a certain Bouret, who, having changed his office, made a corresponding change of costume. His dog followed him loyally in his habit as a *fermier général,* but was terrified at the sight of him as *garde des sceaux* (presumably dogs too can sense the "mystery" of class). And the work comes to a rousing finale in an ironic replica of the Carlylean vision. But it uses the *positions of pantomime,* instead of clothes, as the symbol of class.

In his essay on style, De Quincey refers to the pageantry of comedy that enlivened the earlier periods of English society, when all occupational types were very clearly demarcated by their dress. The passage would serve well as a bridge from Carlyle's "Clothes" to Diderot's "positions of pantomime." But though there are signs of the "mystery" everywhere, Diderot manifests them rather like laughter in church. By "pantomime" he means little more than obsequiousness. But the very choice of so gracious a word, however ironic, is in itself a vestige of "courtly" tactics.

The discussion of pantomime comes near the end of the dialogue. Lui has been talking of sensual appetite in general, and of hunger in particular. Next he refers to the postures of indigence; then he talks of viewing from a distance "the different pantomimes of the human race." He launches into one of his brilliant, half-hysterical improvisations, concluding: *"Voilà ma pantomime, à peu près la même que celle des flatteurs, des courtisans, des valets et des gueux."* The author, himself taking over at this point, says: "I see Pantalon in a prelate, a satyr in a president, a pig in a cénobite, an ostrich in a minister, a goose in his chief clerk." (The passage makes an interesting comparison with the one in Rimbaud's *Season in Hell,* where he is describing how his "reasoned derangement of the senses" enables him to translate the literal into the visionary. In Rimbaud the distortion seems more arbitrary, more purely "esthetic." The social reference is far in the background. But in Diderot the social bearing of the "mystery" is systematically obvious.)

Lui says: "In all the realm there is but one man who walks upright. That is the sovereign. The rest take positions." But Moi answers:

> Whoever has need of another is indigent and takes a position. The King takes a position before his mistress and before God; he does

his bit of pantomime. The minister does the steps of the courtier, the flatterer, the valet and the knave before his King. The crowd of the ambitious dances your positions, in a hundred manners each more loathsome than the next, before the minister. . . .

And so on; concluding: *"Ma foi, ce que vous appelez la pantomime des gueux est le grand branle de la terre."*

As Moi talks, Lui dances the part of each type mentioned. There follow some remarks by Moi, on the subject of philosophers like Diogenes, who have dispensed with pantomime. But not so Lui, "who has danced, and will continue to dance, vile pantomime." Lui admits it and turns to tearful memories of his lost wife, who had presumably been his refuge from the world of pantomime, had seemed to him apart from it, *"une espèce de philosophe"* and *"ah! Dieu, quelle croupe!"*

Roundabout, this aspect of Diderot called Lui could even be said to represent the king. For Lui represents the disorder of the hierarchic principle, and so does the king. Perhaps we might even dare to glimpse behind his name a pun on "Louis." In any case, there are Lui's tributes to the gold *louis,* after which Moi starts to speak of being "profoundly penetrated by the value of the *louis,*" but Lui interrupts him: "I understand. We must close our eyes to that."

Lui must also represent a disorder within Diderot himself, since his desire for pyramidal symmetry could not have been gratified unless he had been critically impervious to the conditions about him. Then, however bad things were in actuality, like Coleridge in later life, he could have viewed them idealistically, interpreting Church and State "according to the idea of each." He might have worked out a gladsome vision of the perfect form behind the imperfect image. Such a contrivance would have been Diderot's particular *pas de pantomime,* danced before the king, or the cardinal, or the king's minister, or the king's minister's chief clerk. In doing so, under those conditions, he would have been demoralized in one way. But in refusing to do so, he was demoralized in another, since the refusal required him to frustrate his architectonic imagination as a social philosopher (though his work on the encyclopedia could probably serve as a good substitute for all but such wayward moments as this dialogue).

In sum, the character of Lui was a point of convergence that represented both the "royal" *cause* of the disorder and its demoralizing *effects.* Lui is demoralized, but imaginatively so, and above all, *aristocratically.*

He can represent both a masterly *dévergondage d'intelligence* (according to one editor—a "spilling over" of spirit?) and the wretchedness and even downright physical hunger of an ailing society headed in the king. The confusion attains symbolic unity in an esthetic of crime which is infused, however perversely, with the "mystery" of aristocracy. *"S'il importe d'être sublime en quelque genre,"* Lui says, *"c'est surtout en mal."* Here is talk of the grand crime. And we see the bearing upon class when we recall that, in a monarchic society, the nobility corresponds in the social realm to the sublime in the esthetic. Though Lui represents a side of Diderot, he does not represent bourgeois, antiroyalist "virtue." He represents aristocratic vice, crime that has the appeal of *style*. (Recall Nietzsche on ways in which *class* distinctions become *moral* distinctions.) Variants of the same expression are found in Stendhal's Julien Sorel. But when we turn from Lui and Julien to the esthetic criminals of André Gide, the social reference has retreated behind "pure" demoralization (the change being much like the change we noted, when contrasting the passage in Diderot with the passage in Rimbaud).

Generic, Specific, and Individual Motives in Rochefoucauld

It may be argued that there are other ingredients in the "idea" of one culture than in another. Or it may be argued that all the elements are there always, but in different proportions. Thus, the principles of a society run by barter could be said to overlap upon those of a society run by money, not only because objects of barter are themselves incipient money, or because monetarily rationalized exchange is a roundabout kind of barter, but also because either mode of transaction involves principles prior to both (as numbers are indifferent to trade of any sort, and property, or "mine-own-ness," is grounded not socially, but biologically).

But whatever the ingredients of a culture might be, whatever the exact combination of local and universal motives went to compose it, and however greatly it is determined by relations to the "productive forces," the feeling for the particular combination as a unity would be an idea, or intuition, in its own right, a "new thing." And an artist who exemplified the gist of the entire cultural combination would embody an idea not reducible to certain of the factors, since the "idea" would be the grasp of that precise combination of factors, in precisely that proportion.

Ideology cannot be deduced from economic considerations alone. It also derives from man's nature as a "symbol-using animal." And since the "original economic plant" is the human body, with the divisive centrality of its particular nervous system, the theologian's concerns with Eden and the "fall" come close to the heart of the rhetorical problem. For, behind the theology, there is the perception of generic divisiveness which, being common to all men, is a universal fact about them, prior to any divisiveness caused by social classes. Here is the basis of rhetoric. Out of this emerge the motives for linguistic persuasion. Then, *secondarily,* we get the motives peculiar to particular economic situations.

In parturition begins the centrality of the nervous system. The different nervous systems, through language and the ways of production, erect various communities of interests and insights, social communities varying in nature and scope. And out of the division and the community arises the "universal" rhetorical situation.

Look at La Rochefoucauld's maxims, with this thought in mind. Note his concern with what he calls *intérêt, orgueil, amour-propre.* And with the many kinds of persuasion, frank, amicable, ironic, roundabout, diplomatic, and downright hypocritical, he derives from this divisive source. For his conception is strikingly rhetorical, a "pantomimic" morality ever on the alert for the minutiae of advantage.

Thus La Rochefoucauld speaks of humility as a ruse, a false submissiveness designed to make others submissive, a self-abasement used for self-exaltation, the "first stratagem" of pride. He scrutinizes the rhetoric of weeping, when women grieve over the death of their lovers "not through having loved them, but to show themselves more worthy of being loved." Or he discerns an invidious ingredient in good will, when people publicly deplore the misfortunes of an enemy, not from the goodness of their heart, but because, by giving signs of compassion, they let it be seen that they are superior to the enemy. Or he remarks that people blame themselves only to elicit praise. Or he notes that they confess minor faults in order to persuade (his word) that they have no big ones. Or he derives from *amour-propre* "the absurd persuasions that we have of ourselves." Or he comments variously on the use to which the *appearance* of moral attributes is put, as when he says that "the true mortifications are those which are not known; vanity makes the others easy." And above all, there is the strongly rhetorical ingredient in

La Rochefoucauld's lore on the relations between the sexes, which are discussed almost entirely in terms of coquetry and gallantry, which is to say persuasion and advantage.

Note particularly his statement that our devotion to princes is a second self-love (*la dévotion qu'on donne aux princes est un second amour-propre*).

Here is an aspect of such reversal as Marx sees in "ideology." For if the ways which Rochefoucauld has been describing are strongly affected by the motives of the courtier, then the "self-love" would derive much of its nature from the "devotion paid to princes." That is, the social motive would be "prior" to the individual one, insofar as the court itself is a social institution. But La Rochefoucauld, beginning with self-love as his primary term for the motives of man in society, and scrutinizing it closely enough to discern the element of courtship responsible for its formation, then states the matter the other way round. He says not that the self-love is derived from the courting of princes, but that the courting of princes is a second self-love.

However, we may appear to be contradicting ourselves here. For though we located the rhetorical situation in an individual divisiveness prior to all class cohesion, we are now saying that La Rochefoucauld gets things backwards in deriving a social motive (the honoring of princes) from an individualistic one (self-love). But the self-love La Rochefoucauld describes is not to be confused with man's original biological divisiveness (the "centrality of the nervous system"). Rather, La Rochefoucauld is describing a *courtly* morality—and the "self-love" he is discussing is the individual consciousness that is epitomized in the honoring of princes. Thus, following a Marxist kind of analysis, we would contend that La Rochefoucauld has the two motives "ideologically" reversed. But at the same time, we would interpret the individualist term as justified by an individual divisiveness prior to the social. The irony is that "self-love" is a *social* term for this divisiveness. La Rochefoucauld's maxims are a courtly rhetoric, with the individual defined by his place in an institution.

Perhaps we could break down the process into six distinct moments, thus:

(1) There are the incentives to individual advantage (and its corresponding rhetoric) indigenous to the "centrality of the nervous system," and to the ambiguously divisive and unitary conditions that go with it.

(2) There is implanted in individuals the thinking local to their social class (their place in a community restricted by traditions of property which emerged with the division of labor). (3) Such local thinking is reducible to a principle or idea. In this case it is the idea of courting. It is summed up in the image or topic of "the devotion paid to princes." (4) Then one's own individual identity is conceived in terms of this same principle. (Incidentally, note the pun on "prince" and "principle." It is more than a mere accident. Here again is an instance of what we have called the "entelechial" mode of thought, the feeling that the principle of a genus is represented by its "highest" potentialities. When such a mode of thought is translated into terms of social rank, it makes the prince, or highest rung of the social ladder, represent the general principle of such hierarchic order.) Then, if one conceives his own motives in terms of the devotion paid to princes, it follows that one conceives of oneself rhetorically, in terms of *courting and being courted*. Telescope the two, as the ultimate principle should, and you get self-love. (5) At this point, La Rochefoucauld begins his book. He has reduced the motives of man in society to "self-love" (which equals "pride" and "interest"). And he proceeds to view all passions, sentiments, pretenses and self-deceptions in the light of this term. (6) In the course of scrutinizing his key term, he comes upon the princely principle that lies behind it. But since he has already chosen a "first" term, self-love, he calls this genus of his terminology a "second." Had Rochefoucauld stated this discovery in terms of an Hegelian ideologist, he would probably have given the second self-love some such title as *Ur-Höflichkeit,* to designate an innate, "pre-historic" tendency towards courtship, an "idea" which, in its evolution towards self-consciousness, at one stage of its historical unfolding manifested itself both as a devotion to princes and as *amour-propre*.

But "self" and "king" do not quite round out the design. Where is God, and the ultimate scene, the ground of all possibility? By our interpretation, the term for God should apply to the conditions at the *first* of the six moments into which we divided La Rochefoucauld's maxim. It should deal with the rhetorical motive indigenous to all men, not local to their social position, but characteristic of the human situation universally. Stated theologically, the divisive condition in which all men share is called "original sin." And approaching the problem of God (or ultimate community) in such terms, La Rochefoucauld says that self-love sets up another god, a god that torments, in aggravating the state of division. Thus:

> Dieu a permis, pour punir l'homme du péché originel, qu'il se fît un dieu de son amour-propre, pour en être tourmenté dans toutes les actions de sa vie.

This rounds out the pattern. It comes upon the ultimate division, prior to the community of status (the unity got by common interests, by participation in properties that bring some men together in one estate or class by setting them at odds with other estates or classes).

Pride, interest, self-love, are aristocratically dyslogistic words for motives that the bourgeois vocabulary may transform into such eulogistic forms as "ambition," "private enterprise," perhaps even "dignity of the individual" and "respect for the person." "Honor" was its eulogistic equivalent in the aristocratic scheme. We think of three different routes by which to approach the rhetoric of the judgment contained in the idea of pride:

1. You can think of the term being used as a deterrent to possible encroachments by inferior classes. (There are connotations of the upstart here.) Then this factional use could become universalized, so that the admonition is applied also by members of the nobility to overbearing members of their own class.

2. Or you can think of the term being used as a summing up of age's admonition to youth. And this usage in the universal class war of the generations could then be applied specifically by a ruling class, in praising traits that would perpetuate the *status quo*.

3. Or we could ground the fear of pride in a universal dramatic principle of irony, the purely formal resource of the dramatist, who knows that he gets his best effect by peripety (building up for a let-down, strengthening the confidence, or expectations of a character just prior to the development that will overwhelm him). This formal, ironic grounding, as revealed in the proverb that "pride goes before a fall," would be universally prior to any use for class domination of either social or biological sorts.

De Gourmont on "Dissociation"

Perhaps the most picturesquely radical approach to the subject of identification and division, as they affect the nature of persuasion, is in an essay by Remy de Gourmont, *"La Dissociation des Idées."* (There is an English translation in a volume entitled *Decadence, and Other Essays on the Culture of Ideas.*) De Gourmont, as a literary critic who did much to introduce the French Symbolists, was surely one of the most graceful "ideologists" who ever specialized in that fluctuant realm midway between ideas and images.

Here the great stress is upon *division*. De Gourmont looks upon disassociation as the distinctive mark of his favorite virtue, intelligence. "Divorce," he says, "is the permanent rule in the world of idea, which is the world of free love."

You can accept old associations of ideas, he says, or form new ones— or, if you are rare and expert in the kind of intellectuality he advocates, you can make "original dissociations" (or disassociations). But looking more closely at his essay, we see that its great emphasis upon *division* really serves to sharpen our understanding of *identification*. Indeed, if we were allowed but one text to illustrate how identification operates in language, we would select this essay, which is almost sadistically concerned with the breaking of identifications.

Observing that an idea "is but a worn-out image," he describes the rhetorical commonplaces as associations which resist dissociation because of the part that special interests play in human thinking. Ordinarily, he says, such "truths" are composed of "a fact and an abstraction." He is here using "truth" in the sense of "opinion," associations which people accept without question. If we assume that business enterprise is naturally good, for instance, we automatically combine the "fact" of business institutions with the abstraction, goodness. The goodness would be a "pure" idea; and the commonplace linking it with some conditional matter, some time, place, persons, operations, and the like, would be such a "truth" (in our usage, opinion) as men ordinarily live by.

But the pure cult of ideas is not concerned with pragmatic necessities. It has responsibilities only to the perfection of its craft. Though the world of practical life could not abide by its rules, this problem need not concern the specialist in free inquiry. Maybe the outcome of such inquiry, if carried to its logical conclusion, would mean the end of mankind? That's not the concern of a fine and free intelligence, dissociating ideas for love of the art, and admitting whatever intellectual exercise limbers the mind and fits it for its proper state of "disdainful nobility" (*noblesse dédaigneuse*). His own method of dissociation provided him with a striking stylistic device, a kind of mild schizophrenia, whereby he could talk of dire things blithely. And so he carried the logic of specialization to its ultimate conclusion, in acknowledging only a responsibility to the principles of his profession. Had he been a physicist, and commissioned to make an infernal engine of destruction, he would have striven to make it as efficiently infernal as possible. In the course of his experiments, his "morality of production" would have been Puritanically rigid. He thus gave a sort of operatic gesture to liberal professionalism, as he skeptically and nihilistically broke "truths" apart, to show that their factual side has no logically necessary connection with their abstract, ideal side.

In the course of his essay, he proceeds to "liberate" various commonplaces that men have lived by. That is, he methodically questions the assumption that the conditions in which an abstract ideal is materialized are inherently identified with that abstract ideal. Thus, purely as a specialist in the analysis of ideas, he perfects the critique of idealism. In effect, he discovers that the pattern of the god incarnate lurks in every single commonplace, which links some particular image, or set of worldly conditions, with some abstract principle or idea. (The abstraction is the "purity" or "divinity" that is embodied in whatever empirical condition the given commonplace, or topic, identifies with it. For instance, if the topic identifies a particular kind of economic structure with "freedom," then "freedom" is the god-term, the pure abstraction; and the particular kind of economic structure is the "fact" to which it is topically tied, quite as though it were a pure divinity that came down to earth and took this particular economic structure as its bodily form—for though De Gourmont does not use this theologic analogy, it is what his analysis amounts to.)

Once he has sharpened our perception in such matters, we see that a counter-essay could be written, to show how many "new associations" De Gourmont spontaneously built up, while ostensibly aiming to do nothing but "liberate" old ones. (We have already noted that, as a free thinker, he identified the ideal intellectual enterprise with divorce.) "Freely" improvising cleavage, he smuggles in new linkage. But he himself encourages the kind of scrutiny that enables us to qualify his statements.

As an instance of his method, consider his approach to the idea of justice. Beginning with what Bentham would have called "archetypation," he discerns in the idea of justice the image of scales, of equilibrium. Then, in a free improvisation, he "liberates" the traditional associations linking justice with punishment, tentatively asking whether one might, with much more justice, punish not the swindler but the fool who let himself be swindled. Next, responsible only to his essay, he equates existence with disequilibrium, injustice, on the grounds that each thing exists by robbing other things of their existence. (Is he not here but universalizing the Proudhon proposition that property is theft?) Somewhat in the spirit of La Rochefoucauld, he next points out how the idea of justice is often contaminated with motives of hatred and envy. Bentham at the same place might have said that "justice" can be the "eulogistic covering" for a combination of motives, many of them not socially presentable. Veblen might have called attention to the "invidious" aspects of justice. Marx might have agreed with all of De Gourmont's playful, professional asceticism, provided only it were taken as applying to the conditions of capitalist justice, and De Gourmont's own intellectual nihilism were interpreted as the expression of an acute, late-capitalist stage in culture. And he might have similarly taken De Gourmont's definition of freedom as "an emphatic corruption of the idea of privilege."

Methodologically, we should also note that when De Gourmont treats the *idea* of justice in terms of justice as an *image* (scales in equilibrium), he lays himself open to an error of his own. He is here using his special kind of "archetypation" to disclose how imagery operates unnoticed in our legal and ethical "fictions." Yet even the exposing of an undeclared image can itself be too imagistic, if it is allowed to carry too much weight in the analysis. Such abstract ideas as "justice" will often disclose their meaning more fully if we treat them realistically as *verbs* than if we interpret them nominalistically as *weakened images*.

Realistically inspecting abstractions for their verbal element, we find that "heroism" stands for the way of being a hero, "greenness" for a way of being green, and "justice" for a just way of life. Thus, in the *Grammar,* we pointed out how the Greek word for "justice" does in fact come from a word for "way." And referring to the discussion in *The Republic,* we noted how there were different "justices" in the sense that different social classes had different living conditions, with judgments to match. Methodologically, linguistic realism would correct De Gourmont's overimagistic emphasis. It would call for kinds of analysis more nearly Marxist. For whereas the De Gourmont kind of archetypation might lead one to be content with shuttling between idea and image, a realistic approach to abstraction would lead one to consider it in terms of acts, by agents, in scenes. True, in images there is an attitudinal content. Hence, if you follow them through far enough, you come upon their verbal nature. But this is true only insofar as nominalism is already yielding to realism.

In any case, one should keep in mind the sense in which operational words, like go, run, see, put, bring, etc., are the really "abstract" ones. A thing is here or there, large or small, round or square, etc., but what of a "running" or a "putting"? Or a "may," a "must," a "will," an "ought"? Here are the true universals, capable of representation only by admixture with some incomplete example, such as a particular animal running, etc. Indeed, as regards the archetypal form or idea of "houseness" which Plato would treat as prior to its material embodiment in various particular houses, is he not here seeking for the *verb,* "to-be-a-house," as the universal in which every particular "being-a-house" would participate?

But whatever our reservations on the scope of De Gourmont's analysis, from the standpoint of rhetoric, it is good to make oneself adept at the kind of mental gymnastics in which De Gourmont was so agile. We need not accept the doctrine wholly as stated in his essay. We need not try to persuade ourselves that dissociation is the ultimate in intellectual prowess, since that very argument for dissociation is an association. But we can make out a strong case for it as a method for helping the initiate experimentally to break free of all topical assumptions, and thereby to cease being the victim of his own naïve rhetoric.

De Gourmont here seems to contain the same near-mystical ingredient we saw in Bentham. Accordingly, we should want to place dissociation in a series of stages, as a cleansing transition from old associations that were automatically formed and may enslave by "infancy," to new associations, rationally adopted after "withdrawal" during the period of experimental liberation. Particularly where an association is seen to be moving the world towards a universal calamity, we should try the experiment of dissociating it, not just for love of the art, as De Gourmont might have advised, but for the vision that may come of such ideological manipulations.

Thus there is always the need for the experimental dissociating of patriotism and militarism. (Or, as regards recent conditions, the dissociating of patriotism from a cult of "cold war," since old men are given to talk of a cold war, which younger men are potently prone to translate into talk of a "shooting war.") Return to this suicidal association (or "identification") if you must. But at least put it to the dissociative test, to make sure that your choice has been made after free inquiry, and is not imposed upon you by a dismal rhetoric of warmongering. It is a fallacy to make personal freedom identical with the liberating of all ideas; there is freedom also in associations, if they are the right ones; but no one in the world is free so long as large sections of our population, however inattentively, are being bound by the identifying of patriotism with military boastfulness.

Pascal on "Directing the Intention"

The Pascalian principle of rhetoric is succinctly stated in his seventh *Provincial Letter,* devoted to the analysis, itself vigorously rhetorical, of a corrupt theological rhetoric. We might have used it as a way into our pages on Bentham; but there is also something to be gained by considering it after we have gone from Bentham to Marx and De Gourmont.

Pascal is attacking the casuistry of the Jesuits. Not because it is casuistry, for the application of general principles to particular cases is a necessary act of judgment in law of any sort. But because the Jesuit rhetoric attacked by Pascal was a perversion of casuistry. And though the theological nature of the controversy may lead some to assume that Pascal's analysis has only a historical interest, the linguistic processes he is analyzing are perennial with language, with its shifts between "spiritual" and "material" terms, or between "abstractions" (which are technically "divinities") and words for the "facts" or "material conditions" in which the abstractions are embodied like gods incarnate.

This "Pauline" element at the roots of language (hence at the roots of rhetoric) can be confronted most directly in theological controversy. And where it is perceived with finesse and disclosed with polemic clarity, as in Pascal's seventh letter, you have a device applicable to wholly different linguistic situations. For you can then trace the vestiges of such theology in expressions on their face secular. And whatever the rhetorical powers in theology itself, there is a set of further powers in theology undetected. Marx's attacks upon "ideology" were, of course, aimed at precisely such vestiges, as were Bentham's observations on "eulogistic coverings." But their own concerns were far too secular to disclose the theological principle of language most directly. For that we go to Pascal's piety and De Gourmont's impiety (each in its way concerned with "pure" ideas).

We have said that, casuistry being the application of abstract principles to particular conditions, the relation is essentially like that of mind and body, spirit and matter, God and God's descent into Nature. Or the abstract principle could be considered as the purpose or end, and the material conditions could be considered as the means for embodying the end. But means are necessarily "impure," from the standpoint of any *one* purpose, since they have a nature of their own. This nature allows them to be used for many purposes; but they are "impure" as means to the extent that their intrinsic nature is not wholly formed for any one such purpose. Such "impurity" is not necessarily "bad." It can be a merely technical impurity, due to the fact that its intrinsic nature contains elements irrelevant to the purpose.

But some means are relatively purer than others. Their nature makes them better able than other means to serve the given purpose. Thus, even a blow with a fist might be considered closer to the nature of peace than a blast from a shotgun. (In general, though not in all cases.) A tongue-lashing might be closer to peace than a blow; an argument closer than a tongue-lashing; a plea closer than an argument; a compliment closer than a plea, etc. This being the case, a scrupulous man will never abandon a purpose which he considers absolutely good. But he will choose the purest means available in the given situation. As with the ideal rhetoric in Aristotle, he will consider the entire range of means, and then choose the best that this particular set of circumstances permits.

Here, you will note, the moral question involves the selection of *means*. But such a casuistry readily permits of two caricatures. First, we can choose inferior means, and quiet the conscience by assuring ourselves that they were the best means available. By this device, the doctrine that "the end justifies the means" becomes a mockery (as it always is when not corrected by a methodical concern with a *hierarchy* of means, and an exacting effort to choose the very best means possible to the given situation). For it can be made to justify *any* means, hence can become a mere "eulogistic covering" for means so alien to the nature of the avowed end, and so far below other means actually available, that it amounts to nothing but a blunt perverting of that end.

But this resource prepares the way for another, whereby we can do whatever we like (in accordance with the enlightened Rabelaisian principle, *fais ce que vouldras,* but without the good will by which Rabelais spontaneously limited such liberties). Then having done what we wanted to do, we can *assign* a purpose to our act, selecting some intention socially approved. And we can ask that the act be considered as a means for carrying out this avowed intention.

Pascal's seventh letter is a brilliant attack upon the Jesuits for their use of this rhetorical convenience. True, the Jesuits had faced a bothersome situation. The quality of devotion among great numbers of the faithful had deteriorated alarmingly. The most devout at that time were either turning to Protestant pietism; or, like Pascal, though they remained in the Church, they favored austerities which exposed them to the suspicion of Protestant hankerings. In contrast, there was a large body of easygoing people, people who would not be religiously zealous even in a time of great religious zeal, but whom the Jesuits wanted to retain for the Church, or to reclaim for the Church. They had strayed far from the exacting kind of Christianity preached by St. Paul. In fact, not only did they violate Christian principles (as in the code of dueling, for instance); they didn't even pretend to abide by Christian principles. And the Jesuits, as a propaganda order formed to regain for the Church the ground lost since the Protestant Reformation, had to solve a purely organizational problem: How could they keep these backsliders nominally within the fold? Since these people were living un-Christian lives, yet were not minded to change their ways, how might theology adapt itself to such an embarrassing condition?

In *A Portrait of the Artist as a Young Man,* Joyce's hero ponders how the Jesuits "had earned the name of worldlings at the hands not of the unworldly only but of the worldly also for having pleaded, during all their history, at the bar of God's justice for the souls of the lax and the lukewarm and the prudent." Pascal was ardent. And his letter is a satirical rhetoric pitted against the hypocritical or opportunist rhetoric by which the Jesuits proposed to solve their problem in his day. Their slogan was: "Direct the intention"—so Pascal satirizes *la grande méthode de diriger l'intention.* Since people would not change their ways, and since any severe attempt to make them do so might but lose them for the Church entirely, then let them go on doing exactly the un-Christian things they had been doing. But teach them how to change the intention, by attributing a Christian motive to these same un-Christian acts.

Pascal uses the most effective of all satiric devices, in adopting the role of a somewhat stupid and gullible questioner who is very eager to learn. He consults the Jesuit masters, with plodding earnestness. He struggles hard to understand the depths of their reasoning. He is patient, and very hopeful—and of a sudden he breaks into loud rejoicings, when their formulae have finally enlightened him. These are always the moments, of course, when he is reducing them to absurdity.

As Pascal puts it, supposedly reporting the words of his Jesuit monitor: "If we cannot prevent the act, we at least purify the intention; and thus we correct the viciousness of the means through the purity of the end." (*Quand nous ne pouvons empêcher l'action, nous purifions au moins l'intention; et ainsi nous corrigeons le vice du moyen par la pureté de la fin.*) Or, as Pascal says, in the blunt overzealousness of his delight at this invention for the worldly rescue of the Church: If one is going to a duel, since dueling is forbidden one must instead so "direct the intention" that one is merely going for a walk at the place where the duel is to be held; and when the duel takes place, one directs his intention towards the need of protecting oneself against an enemy who is threatening one's life.

The chapter is hilarious and devastating. But we will say this in favor of the Jesuits: Pascal's most telling blows are struck, not by satirically making up cases which reduce the Jesuit doctrine to absurdity, but by *citation* from Jesuit sources. In carrying out their principle of the directed intention, they had speculated zealously upon all kinds of cases. Hence the Jesuit theorists had thought up the most extreme and embarrassing kinds of cases, to test and illustrate their handy principle with maximum thoroughness. Their professional enterprise gave Pascal his most telling examples. In this respect their role as corruptors of religion compares favorably with many modern spokesmen for the Church, who are content merely to envelop materialist ambitions in an idealistic fog, translating each worldly interest into a spiritual equivalent, thereby doing again the Jesuit trick, but without the theoretical precision which the Jesuits contributed to their own exposure.

In the sphere of international relations, the politicians of one nation may seek to build and subsidize a mighty economic and military alliance against another nation, while "directing the intention" towards peace.

"Administrative" Rhetoric in Machiavelli

Machiavelli's *The Prince* can be treated as a rhetoric insofar as it deals with the *producing of effects upon an audience*. Sometimes the prince's subjects are his audience, sometimes the rulers or inhabitants of foreign states are the audience, sometimes particular factions within the State. If you have a political public in mind, Machiavelli says in effect, here is the sort of thing you must do to move them for your purposes. And he considers such principles of persuasion as these: either treat well or crush; defend weak neighbors and weaken the strong; where you foresee trouble, provoke war; don't make others powerful; be like the prince who appointed a harsh governor to establish order (after this governor had become an object of public hatred in carrying out the prince's wishes, the prince got popular acclaim by putting him to death for his cruelties); do necessary evils at one stroke, pay out benefits little by little; sometimes assure the citizens that the evil days will soon be over, at other times goad them to fear the cruelties of the enemy; be sparing of your own and your subjects' wealth, but be liberal with the wealth of others; be a combination of strength and stealth (lion and fox); *appear* merciful, dependable, humane, devout, upright, but be the opposite in actuality, whenever the circumstances require it; yet always do lip-service to the virtues, since most people judge by appearances; provoke resistance, to make an impression by crushing it; use religion as a pretext for conquest, since it permits of "pious cruelty"; leave "affairs of reproach" to the management of others, but keep those "of grace" in your own hands; be the patron of all talent, proclaim festivals, give spectacles, show deference to local organizations; but always retain the distance of your rank (he could have called this the "mystery" of rule); in order that you may get the advantage of good advice without losing people's respect, give experts permission to speak frankly, but only when asked to speak; have a few intimates who are encouraged to be completely frank, and who are well plied with rewards.

Correspondingly, there are accounts of the human susceptibilities one can play upon, and the resistances one must expect. Thus: new benefits won't make great personages forget old injuries; it is easy to persuade people, but you need force to keep them persuaded; acquisitiveness being natural, those who acquire will be praised, not blamed; the nobles would oppress the people, the people would avoid oppression by the nobles; one can satisfy the people, but not the nobles, by fair dealing; men are bound to you as much by the benefits they give as by the benefits they receive; mercenaries are to be feared for their dastardy, auxiliaries for their valor; the unarmed are despised; often what we call virtue would ruin the State, and what we call vice can save it; cruelty may reconcile and unify; men in general are *ungrateful, fickle, false, cowardly, greedy;* since all men are evil, the prince can always find a good pretext for breaking faith; it is safer to be feared than loved, since people are more likely to offend those they love than those they fear; yet though the prince should be feared, he should not be hated; the worst offense is an offense against property, for a man more quickly forgets the death of his father than the loss of his patrimony; people want to be deceived; if the prince leaves his subjects' property and women untouched, he "has only to contend with the ambitions of a few"; a ruler's best fortress is not to be hated by his own people; any faction within the State can always expect to find allies abroad.

The difference between the two lists is mainly grammatical. For instance, if we use a gerundive, "valor in auxiliaries is to be feared," the statement belongs in the second set. But we can transfer it to the first merely by changing the expression to an imperative: "Fear valor in auxiliaries." Both lists are reducible to "topics" in the Aristotelian sense.

We think of another "Machiavellian" work, written many centuries earlier. It is in praise of "eloquence," the eloquence, it says, that serves in the conquest of the public, of the senate, and of women. But it would concentrate on the third use, for it is Ovid's *Ars Amatoria*. It deals not with political power, but with another order of potency; and where Machiavelli is presumably telling how to get and hold a principality, Ovid is telling how to get and hold a woman.

Grounded in figures of soldiery, of gladiators, of the hunt, of animals enraged or ruttish, it is in form a manual of instructions, like *The Prince*. But it is really a poetic display, an epideictic exercise, the sort of literary ostentation that De Quincey had in mind when selecting Ovid as prime example of rhetoric. For one does not usually read it as he would read instructions for opening a package (though a yearning adolescent might); one reads it rather for the delight he may take in the imagery and ideas themselves, the topics or "places" of love.

But to consider some of the poet's picturesque advice is to see how close it is to the thinking of Machiavelli, except of course for the tonalities, since the Italian is solemn, the Latin playful. Having begun scenically, with a survey of locations where the hunting is good, he proceeds thus:

On deceiving in the name of friendship; feigning just enough drunkenness to be winsome; of feigned passion that may become genuine; on astute use of praise and promises; inducement value of belief in the gods; deceiving deceivers; the utility of tears; the need to guard against the risk that entreaties may merely feed the woman's vanity; inducement value of pallor, which is the proper color of love; advisability of shift in methods, as she who resisted the well-bred may yield to the crude; ways to subdue by yielding; how to be her servant, but as a freeman; risks that gain favor; on operating with the help of the servants; need for caution in gifts; get your slaves to ask her to ask you to be kind to them; the controlled use of compliments; become a habit with her; enjoy others too, but in stealth, and deny if you are found out; rekindle her love by jealousy; make her grieve over you, but not too much, lest she muster enough strength to become angry (as she might, since she always wants to be shut of you); if she has deceived you, let her think you don't know it; give each of her faults the name of the good quality most like it.

And to women he offers advice on dress, cosmetics, the use of pretty faults in speech, gait, poetry, dance, posture, cadence, games, on being seen in public (you may find a husband at the funeral of your husband), deceit to match deceit, on being late at banquets, on table manners, on drinking to excess but only as much as can be deftly controlled.

Machiavelli says of war: "This is the sole art proper to rulers." And similarly Ovid's epideictic manual of love-making is founded on the principle that "love is a kind of war" (*militiae species amor est*). "I can love only when hurt," the poet confesses (*non nisi laesus amo*). And Machiavelli rounds out his politics by saying that it is better to be adventurous than cautious with Fortune, since Fortune is a woman, "and if you wish to keep her subdued, you must beat her and ill-use her."

True, though both books are concerned with the rhetoric of advantage, principles of amative persuasion rely rather on fraud than force. But the point to note for our purposes is that in both cases the rhetoric includes a strongly "administrative" ingredient. The persuasion cannot be confined to the strictly verbal; it is a mixture of symbolism and definite empirical operations. The basic conception in Stendhal's book on love, for instance, is not rhetorical at all. For the rhetoric of love in Stendhal, we should go rather to his *The Red and the Black*. There, as in Ovid, the work is developed on the principle that love is a species of war. But the basic principle underlying Stendhal's *De l'Amour* is that of "crystallization," a concept so purely "internal," so little "addressed," that it belongs completely under the heading of "symbolic" in these volumes, naming but a kind of accretion (both unconsciously and consciously sentimental) that grows about the idea of the beloved, and for all its contagiousness is rather a flowering within the mind of the lover than a ruse shaped for persuasive purposes.

We might put it thus: the nonverbal, or nonsymbolic conditions with which both lover and ruler must operate can themselves be viewed as a kind of symbolism having persuasive effects. For instance, military force can persuade by its sheer "meaning" as well as by its use in actual combat. In this sense, nonverbal acts and material instruments themselves have a symbolic ingredient. The point is particularly necessary when we turn to the rhetoric of bureaucracy, as when a political party bids for favor by passing measures popular with large blocs of voters. In such a case, administrative acts themselves are not merely "scientific" or "operational," but are designed also with an eye for their *appeal*. Popular jokes that refer to policemen's clubs and sex organs as "persuaders" operate on the same principle. For nonverbal conditions or objects can be considered as signs by reason of persuasive ingredients inherent in the "meaning" they have for the audience to which they are "addressed."

It is usual now to treat Machiavelli as a founder of modern political "science," particularly because he uses so naturalistic a terminology of motives, in contrast with notions of justification that go with supernaturalism. But this simple antithesis can prevent accurate placement of *The Prince*. For one thing, as in the case of La Rochefoucauld, you need but adopt the theological device of saying that Machiavelli is dealing with the motives typical of man after the "fall," and there is nothing about his naturalism to put it out of line with supernaturalism. But most of all, the approach to *The Prince* in terms of naturalism *vs.* supernaturalism prevents one from discerning the rhetorical elements that are of its very essence. Here again we come upon the fact that our contemporary views of science are dislocated by the failure to consider it methodically with relation to rhetoric (a failure that leads to a blunt opposing of science to either religion or "magic"). For if the rhetorical motive is not scientific, neither is it in its everyday application religious or magical. The use of symbols to induce action in beings that normally communicate by symbols is essentially realistic in the most practical and pragmatic sense of the term. It is neither "magical" nor "scientific" (neither ritualistic nor informational) for one person to ask help of another. Hence, in approaching the question through a flat antithesis between magic and science, one automatically vows himself to a faulty statement of the case.

Above all, we believe that an approach to the book in terms of rhetoric is necessary if one would give an adequate account of its *form* (and the ability to treat of form is always the major test of a critical method). Thus, though the late Ernst Cassirer gives a very good account of Machiavelli in his *Myth of the State,* his oversimplified treatment in terms of science alone, without the modifications and insights supplied by the principles of rhetoric, completely baffles an attempt to account for the book's structure. Not only does he end by treating the last chapter as a misfit; having likened the earlier chapters to Galileo's writings on the laws of motion, and thereby having offered a description that could not possibly apply to the last chapter, he concludes that the burden of proof rests with those who would consider the last chapter as a fit with the rest. By the rhetorical approach, you can meet his challenge, thus:

The first twenty-four chapters discuss typical situations that have to do with the seizing and wielding of political power. They are analytic accounts of such situations, and of the strategies best suited to the conditions. Thus they are all variants of what, in the *Grammar,* we called the scene-act ratio; and they say, in effect: "Here is the kind of act proper to such-and-such a scene" (the ruler's desire for political mastery being taken as the unchanging purpose that prevails throughout all changes of scene).

However, in the next-to-the-last chapter, Machiavelli modifies his thesis. Whereas he has been pointing out what act of the ruler would, in his opinion, have the most persuasive effect upon the ruled in a given situation, he now observes that people do not always act in accordance with the requirements set them by the scenic conditions. People also act in accordance with their own natures, or temperaments. Thus, a man may act cautiously, not because the scene calls for caution, but merely because he is by nature a cautious man. Conversely, if a man is adventurous by nature, he may act with adventurous boldness, characteristically, even though the situation itself may call for caution. In the *Grammar* we listed such motivations under the heading of the agent-act ratio, since they say, in effect: "Here is the kind of act proper to such-and-such a person."

But there may be fortunate moments in history when both kinds of motives work together, Machiavelli is saying. The scenic conditions require a certain kind of act; and the ruler may happen to have exactly the kind of temperament and character that leads him into this same kind of act. Given such a lucky coincidence, the perfect manifestation of the scene-act ratio is one with the perfect manifestation of the agent-act ratio.

Far from there being any formal break in the book, this concern in the next-to-the-last chapter forms a perfect transition to the final "Exhortation to Liberate Italy from the Barbarians." For this chapter rounds things out in a "Now is the time . . ." manner, by calling for the agent to arise whose acts will simultaneously be in tune with the times and with himself. This man will be the ruler able to redeem Italy from its captivity. And given such a combination, there will be grounds too for the ultimate *identification* of ruler and ruled, since all will benefit, each in his way, by the liberation of their country.

True, in the last chapter there is a certain prayerlike lift not present in the others. Whereas the earlier chapters are a kind of *rhetorica docens,* the peroration becomes a kind of *rhetorica utens.* But that is a standard aspect of rhetorical form, traditional to the wind-up. Far from being added on bluntly, it is very deftly *led into* by the motivational shift in the preceding chapter.

When the ruler happens to be of such a nature that the act characteristic of his nature would also be the act best suited to the situation, we could attribute the happy combination to chance, or fortune. Here again the stress upon science *vs.* magic can somewhat mislead. True, references to a fatal confluence of factors will almost inevitably bring up connotations of "design." Hence, the "fortune" that makes the ruler temperamentally a fit for his times may take on fatelike connotations alien to science. One may find such metaphors of cosmic purpose flitting through Machiavelli's discussion. But they are not the central matter. The central matter is this fortuitous congruity of temperament and external conditions, whereas an "unlucky" combination can prevent the ruler from adopting the proper mode of action (somewhat as Cicero said that the ideal orator should be accomplished in all styles, but human limitations would restrict his range in actuality).

Machiavelli's concern is brought out clearly by La Rochefoucauld, in his comments *Des Modèles de la Nature et de la Fortune.* "It seems," he says, "that Fortune, changing and capricious as she is, renounces change and caprice to act in concert with nature, and that the two concur at times to produce singular and unusual men who become models for posterity. Nature serves to furnish the qualities; Fortune serves to put them into operation." By "nature" he is obviously referring to human nature, capacities of human agents; "fortune" is his word for scenic conditions, which impose themselves independently of human will. He calls the congruence of agent and scene an *"accord de la nature et de la fortune."*

Concerns with the "lucky" or "unlucky" accident that may make a man temperamentally fit or unfit to employ the strategy best suited to the situation may eventually involve one in assumptions about fatal cosmic design along the lines of Carlyle's "mystifications" about heroes in history. And too great a concern with science as antithetical to magic may get one to thinking that the important point lies there. But by treating the book as a manual of "administrative rhetoric," we can place the stress where it belongs: on the problem of the orator's ability to choose the act best suited to the situation, rather than choosing the act best suited to the expression of his own nature.

Likewise, the proper approach to Machiavelli's *choice of vocabulary* is not exclusively in terms of science, but through considerations of rhetoric. (We have in mind his paradoxical distinctions between the virtues of princes and the virtues of private citizens, or his proposal to base political action on the assumption that all men are "ungrateful, fickle, false, cowardly, and greedy.") Is not Machiavelli here but giving a new application to a topic in Aristotle's *Rhetoric?* Aristotle had said in effect that privately we admit to acquisitive motives, but publicly we account for the same act in sacrificial terms. In the Christian terminology that had intervened between Aristotle and Machiavelli, however, the public, sacrificial motives were attributed to the state of *grace,* and the private, acquisitive motives were due to the state of *original sin* after the fall. In the Christian persuasion, the rhetorical distinction noted by Aristotle had thus become written dialectically into the very nature of things. And insofar as a man was genuinely imbued with Christian motives, his *private* virtues would be the traits of character which, if cultivated in the individual, would be most beneficial to mankind *as a whole.*

But Machiavelli is concerned with a different kind of universality. He starts from the principle that men are *universally at odds with one another.* For this is what his stress upon predatory or warlike motives amounts to. He is concerned with motives which will protect *special* interests. *The Prince* is leading towards the period when the interests of a feudal ruler will be *nationalistically* identified, thought to represent one state *as opposed to* other states.

Now, national motives can be placed in a hierarchy of motives, graded from personal and familial, to regional, to national, to international and universal. As so arranged, they might conceivably, in their different orders, complement or perfect one another rather than being in conflict. But where the princes, or the national states identified with them, are conceived antithetically to the interests of other princes and states, or antithetically to factions within the realm, the "virtues" of the ruler could not be the "virtues" which are thought most beneficial to mankind as a whole (in an ideal state of universal cooperation). Similarly, if we carry the Machiavelli pattern down from political to personal relations, the individual may become related to other individuals as ruler to ruled (or at least as would-be ruler to would-not-be ruled)—for here again the divisive motives treated by Machiavelli apply.

Once a national identity is built up, it can be treated as an individual; hence like an individual its condition can be presented in sacrificial terms. Thus, in the case of *The Prince,* the early chapters are stated in acquisitive terms. They have to do with the ways of getting and keeping political power. But the last chapter, looking towards the redemption of Italy as a nation, is presented in sacrificial tonalities; the "virtue of an Italian spirit" is oppressed, enslaved, and scattered, "without head, without order, beaten, despoiled, torn, overrun," and enduring "every kind of desolation." So Italy "entreats God to send some one who shall deliver her from these wrongs and barbarous insolencies." And "she is ready and willing to follow a banner if only some one will raise it." This is the shift in tone that led Ernst Cassirer to treat the last chapter as incongruous with the earlier portions.

In this last chapter, the universal, sacrificial motives are adapted to a competitive end. The Christian vision of mankind's oneness in the suffering Christ becomes the vision of Italians' oneness in the suffering Italy. Since Italy actually is invaded, the analogy is not forced as it is in the vocabulary of imperialist unction. (Contrast it, for instance, with the building of empire under slogans like "the acceptance of grave world responsibility," or "the solemn fulfillment of international commitments," when the support of reactionary regimes was meant.) But whether the nationalist exaltation be for conquest or for uprising against conquerors, in either case there is the possibility of identification between ruler and ruled. Hence the new prince, in bringing about the new order, "would do honor to himself and good to the people of his country." And by such identification of ruler and ruled, Machiavelli offers the ruler precisely the rhetorical opportunity to present privately acquisitive motives publicly in sacrificial terms.

Machiavelli is concerned with political cooperation under conditions which make such cooperation in part a union of conspirators. Where conspiracy is the fact, universality must often be the fiction. The ambiguity in Machiavelli is thus the ambiguity of nationalism itself, which to some extent does fit with the ends of universal cooperation, and to some extent is conspiratorial. The proportions vary, with the Hitlerite State probably containing as high a percentage of the conspiratorial as will be attained in our time, though the conspiratorial motive is now unusually strong in all international dealings. Sovereignty itself is conspiracy. And the pattern is carried into every political or social body, however small. Each office, each fraternal order, each college faculty has its tiny conspiratorial clique. Conspiracy is as natural as breathing. And since the struggles for advantage nearly always have a rhetorical strain, we believe that the systematic contemplation of them forces itself upon the student of rhetoric. Indeed, of all the motives in Machiavelli, is not the most usable for us his attempt to transcend the disorders of his times, not by either total acquiescence or total avoidance, but by seeking to scrutinize them as accurately and calmly as he could?

Dante's De Vulgari Eloquentia

At the point where the rhetoric of "identification" merges with the "unconscious," we might consider Dante's *De Vulgari Eloquentia* for its bearing on this subject. As with Longinus' *On the Sublime,* though the emphasis is upon poetry, the essay operates in the realm where poetic and rhetoric cross. Dante wants a language that will be "illustrious, cardinal, courtly (*aulicum*), and curial." Honor, power, dignity, glory—such are the terms that surround his formula to guide his search for the perfect poetic medium. The "cardinal" we might translate as "central" (like a hinge), while also noting its ecclesiastical connotations. The "illustrious" are those who, themselves illuminated by power (*potestate illuminati*) illuminate others by their justice and charity (*alios et iustitia et caritate illuminant*). Dante is perhaps here following the Ciceronian concern with styles and offices, though he is looking for the important elements that should be combined in one style. But above all we should note, for our purposes, how the four ingredients for the ideal language of poetry all have strongly hierarchic connotations.

Distinguishing between a secondary speech, which is taught, and an earlier kind "which we acquire, without rule, by imitating a nurse (*quam sine omni regula nutricem imitantes accipimus*)," he says that of these two, the popular is the more noble (*"harum quoque duarum nobilior est vulgaris"*). Is that not almost a conceit, equating the "noble" with the "common"? (A conceit with a future.) In any case, just as Longinus was asking what made for tension (the heightened or moving) in language, Dante carried the problem a step farther, in recognizing that such an effect could be got best by using speech that seemed "natural" (his word), through having emerged out of infancy.

As for "infancy" itself, there are, you might say, several "infancies": for besides the speechlessness of the infant, there is the speechlessness of the nonverbal (as the quality of a sensory experience is beyond language, requiring immediate experience); and there is the speechlessness of the "unconscious," as regards complexities vaguely intuited but not yet made verbally explicit (in sum, the symbolically "enigmatic"). Thus, Dante's concern with the "nobility" of the speech learned in infancy would seem to be, within the limits of his terminology, the adumbration of a concern with the motives of the "unconscious" and its kinds of "identification."

In a mixture of positivism and myth, Dante attributes the rise of different languages to the occupational diversity required for building the Tower of Babel. The members of each trade or profession had their own language, the division of labor thus making for the diversity of tongues. And perhaps with theological Latin in mind, he says that the higher the intellectual quality of the specialty, the more barbarous the language.

Dante's search for a "nobler" language learned in childhood, and his discovery of it in the "vulgar" idiom, finds a picturesque parallel (or should we say a caricature?) in the principles of linguistic selection which D. H. Lawrence embodied in *Lady Chatterley's Lover*. For was not Lawrence, too, trying to reclaim, beneath the layers of education, a more primitive, childhood speech? It would have the "nobility" of the "unconscious" (somewhat as Nietzsche's "artistocratic" blonde beast was a markedly "regressive" image, the mythically heroicized replica of a spontaneous child).

True, in both Lawrence and Nietzsche, the search was for a kind of nature's gentleman rather than for the illustrious, cardinal, courtly, and curial. Dante combined the norms of infant-unconscious with the norms of hierarchic splendor (though purely as an ideal; he admitted that he was looking only for such language as would be spoken in Italy's political and legal institutions if they were not in disarray). Lawrence's hierarchy, though essentially "rightist" along Carlylean lines, was identified with no dialectic of vast architectural symmetry. And the cult of sunlight had turned into a cult of darkness.

Yet, matching his project with Dante's, as regards the attempt to refurbish language by drawing upon the appeal of words learned in childhood and outside the areas of *grammatica,* do we not see in Lawrence's "dirty" words for love-making, not a pornographic motive, but a much more pious one? At all intimate moments, Mellors used dialect. As against the "grammatical," learned language of "society," dialect was for Lawrence the truly spontaneous speech of his childhood. It was in this sense "more noble" than the pretentious speech of the culturally decadent, represented by all that Chatterley stood for. And the use of the "dirty" words was an extension of the same principle that he embodied in his use of dialect. The "dirty" words for making love were thus a kind of "baby-talk."

The use of such words as a vocabulary of endearment between the lovers thus drew upon the appeal to the "infancy" of both childhood and the unconscious (the "unconscious" presumably being gratified to the extent that its resistance to taboos could be broken down). There is also the likelihood that the unconscious appeal of "cloacal" ambiguities could figure here too, in the choice of "dirty" words. The privacy of the sexual would thus be regressively linked with the privacy of the fecal, as Freud says the two are mingled in the experiences of the child, in whose fantasies all the private bodily functions and parts may be confused with one another. Lawrence thus aimed at a variant of "vulgarity" that would be more "noble," since it would be more moving as regards the "natural" gratifications of the unconscious.

Rhetoric in the Middle Ages

We do not pretend that our foregoing pages have been a comprehensive survey of works on rhetoric. We have attempted to consider only those writers who, by one device or another, could be brought to "cooperate" in building this particular "philosophy of rhetoric," and whose presence might prevent it from becoming too "idiosyncratic." We want to contemplate the basic principles of the subject, for their bearing both on literary criticism in particular and on human relations in general. But though we have no desire to write a compendium, we should have touched upon all major directions which rhetoric can take. And we should have indicated how they can all be placed with reference to persuasion and/or identification as generating principles. However, since we have mentioned no work appearing in the centuries between Augustine and Pico della Mirandola, to round things out we might refer the reader to two scholarly and authoritative articles by Richard McKeon covering the long stretch which we have perforce neglected.

In his essay on "Rhetoric in the Middle Ages" (published in *Speculum,* January, 1942) McKeon subdivides the era into an earlier period, when rhetoric was treated as "the science of speaking well in civil matters," and a second period with three major strands: (1) rhetoric as a part of logic; (2) as an art of stating truths certified by theology; (3) as an art of words. He also indicates how all these emphases continued to be developed in the Renaissance, despite pretensions to a break with the medieval tradition. And he notes that inquiries so apparently restricted as the study of words led into consideration of the nonverbal things to which words referred, by this route contributing to developments in science and scientific method. ("Symbolic logic, though unconcerned with its past, still repeats the elements of this heritage.")

To give the whole range of rhetoric through the entire era, McKeon sums up thus:

> Rhetoric is at most an unusually clear example among the arts and sciences of a tendency which is possible in the history of rhetoric only because it is universal in intellectual disciplines. In application, the art of rhetoric contributed during the period from the fourth to the fourteenth century not only to the methods of speaking and writing well, of composing letters and petitions, sermons and prayers, legal documents and briefs, poetry and prose, but to the canons of interpreting laws and scripture, to the dialectical devices of discovery and proof, to the establishment of the scholastic method which was to come into universal use in philosophy and theology, and finally to the formulation of scientific inquiry which was to separate philosophy from theology. In manner of application, the art of rhetoric was the source both of doctrines which have long since become the property of other sciences (such as the passions, which were considered in handbooks of rhetoric until Descartes proposed a "scientific" treatment of them different only in details) and of particular devices which have been applied to a variety of subjects (such as to the "common-places," which were sometimes techniques for inventing arguments, sometimes means for dilating statements, sometimes methods for discovering things, or to "definition" or "order" which may be determined entirely by consideration of the verbal conditions of expression, the psychological requirements of persuasion, or the circumstantial probabilities of fact). In theory of application, the art of rhetoric was now identified with, now distinguished from, the whole or part not only of grammar, logic, and dialectic (which were in turn distinguished from or identified with each other), but also of sophistic and science, of "civil philosophy," psychology, law, and literature, and finally of philosophy as such. Yet if rhetoric is defined in terms of a single subject matter—such as style, or literature, or discourse—it has no history during the Middle Ages; the many innovations which are recorded during that period in the arts with which it is related suggest that their histories might profitably be

considered without unique attachment to the field in which their advances are celebrated.

McKeon mentions another aspect of rhetoric, half in the nonsymbolic realm as with the "administrative" devices of Ovid and Machiavelli:

> The crossing lines of rhetoric and medicine are apparent in Eunapius' *Lives of the Philosophers;* cf. particularly his accounts of Zeno of Cyprus, Magnus, Cribasius, and Ionicus.... Magnus made a happy combination of rhetoric and medicine by persuading the patients of other doctors that they had not been cured and then restoring them to health, apparently also by talk and questions; Ionicus was master of philosophy and medicine as well as the arts of rhetoric and poetry. Cf. P. H. and E. A. De Lacy, Philodemus: *On Methods of Inference,* ... where the relations between medicine and rhetoric are discussed in terms of an "empirical" or "conjectural" method.

Applying this statement to our purposes, we could observe that even the medical equipment of a doctor's office is not to be judged purely for its diagnostic usefulness, but also has a function in the *rhetoric* of medicine. Whatever it is as apparatus, it also appeals as imagery; and if a man has been treated to a fulsome series of tappings, scrutinizings, and listenings, with the aid of various scopes, meters, and gauges, he may feel content to have participated as a patient in such histrionic action, though absolutely no material thing has been done for him, whereas he might count himself cheated if he were given a real cure, but without the pageantry. (What McKeon calls "the crossing lines of rhetoric and medicine" would, in our terms, be: "extending the range of rhetoric into medicine." A related *popular* term is "bedside manner," which Aristotle might have classed under topics that appeal by *ethos.*)

A friend said:

"When I was a boy, a companion of mine showed me a device 'for detecting heart trouble.' It was a glass tube with a bulb at each end, and partly filled with a red fluid. He explained: If a person had anything wrong with his heart, when you pressed one of these bulbs against his chest the fluid in the tube would begin to bubble. First he tried the experiment on himself; the fluid remained calm. But when he put one of the bulbs against my heart, I was terrified to see the fluid begin boiling convulsively. As for *enargeia,* the rhetorical appeal to the imagination by the use of images that 'bring a situation before one's very eyes,' that visible, tangible 'medical instrument' certainly did it. I could literally *see* my heart trouble—and from that day to this, I have been 'heart-conscious.'

"Rhetorically amplifying, the boy then handed the contrivance to me. Though it had been quiet while he held it, the moment I took hold of it, it again boiled violently. He even tried pressing one bulb against my shoe—and my heart ailment was shown to be so acute that the fluid boiled even at that remote contact.

"Then, praise God, having got enough delight from my terror, he explained. This device was an instrument used in that most rhetorical of businesses, medical quackery. The fluid in the glass tube was so susceptible to slight changes in temperature, that the warmth of your hand made it boil if you firmly grasped one of the bulbs. But if you wanted the liquid to remain inert, you held the device between two fingers pressed loosely against the tube. In my fright I had not noticed that he held it differently when using it on himself than when using it on me—and when handing it to me, he had held out one of the bulbs, so that I naturally grasped it in a way to make it boil.

"A quack had used it to persuade the ignorant that they had heart trouble. But he assured them that he could guarantee a cure. So, after he had given them a series of 'treatments,' charging all the traffic would bear, he pronounced them well, and sent them on their way rejoicing, filled with an evangelical zeal that brought the quack new customers."

We cite the story to indicate the extra margin of rhetoric in medical apparatus, over and above its purely technical, operative value. Such instruments present diagnosis in terms of the senses, and can thus be so consoling that, even when the apparatus can't restore a man's health, it can help him die well.

Considering together Ovid, Machiavelli, and the rhetorical ingredient in medicine, we could sum up by the proposition that, in all such partly verbal, partly nonverbal kinds of rhetorical devices, the nonverbal element also persuades by reason of its symbolic character. Paper need not *know the meaning* of fire in order to burn. But in the "idea" of fire there is a persuasive ingredient. By this route something of the rhetorical motive comes to lurk in every "meaning," however purely "scientific" its pretensions. Wherever there is persuasion, there is rhetoric. And wherever there is "meaning," there is "persuasion."

Food, eaten and digested, is not rhetorical. But in the *meaning* of food there is much rhetoric, the meaning being persuasive enough for the idea of food to be used, like the ideas of religion, as a rhetorical device of statesmen.

But we were referring to an essay on medieval rhetoric, by Richard McKeon. And we should note that he continues the subject in another, "Poetry and Philosophy in the Twelfth Century, the Renaissance of Rhetoric" (*Modern Philology,* May, 1946). It is particularly notable because the poets and critics of the period did not share the modern tendency to treat didacticism as anthetical to poetry. In their more ample view,

> Moral problems are made poetic by obscuring suggestions of resolution; and poetry may be didactic if its lessons are vague, or metaphysical if it is without commitment to a philosophy, or religious if religion furnishes a restraint to sentiment in the construction of figures.

However, such a latitudinarian view of the didactic might sometimes be closer to modern criteria than the word itself would indicate. For often those today who would exile the "didactic" from poetry could subscribe wholly to the twelfth century position as here formulated. Similarly, they could probably concede the importance of logic in modern art, once they saw that an effect got by *direct violation* of a logical canon belongs as fully under the head of logic as an effect got by obedience to it.

This same latitudinarian usage seems to have prevailed fruitfully in the twelfth century's attitude towards obscurity in art. Recalling Bentham's reference to *tegumen* and *res tegenda* in his remarks on the use of "eulogistic coverings" as *rhetorical* concealments of motives, we may compare it with these comments, scattered through McKeon's essay, on the *poetics* of obscurity: According to Bernard, Virgil "describes under concealment [*sub integumento*] what the human spirit does and suffers, situated temporarily in the human body. . . . Concealment, moreover, is a genus of demonstration which enfolds the understanding of truth under a fabled narration, and therefore it is also called envelopment [*involucrum*]." In Alan of Lille's *De Planctu Naturae,* Alan asks "concerning the nature of Cupid, which various authors have depicted under the concealing envelopment of enigmas (*sub integumentali involucro aenigmatum*)." Hildebert of Lavardin says of wisdom, *"We heard of it in Ephrata,* that is, in a mirror or in a watchtower, that is, hidden in an image, that is, in the manifestation of the New Testament and the obscurity of the Old Testament." Bernard reproaches Abailard "for trying to see all things face to face and for making no use in his philosophy of the device, familiar to poets, of seeing truth in a mirror and enigma."

Here we confront a period when even the image in the mirror could be thought of, not as "clear," but as a kind of "concealment" (*which was in turn a kind of demonstration*). Theological doctrines proclaiming the mysteriousness of God, with history and nature as vague signatures of the divine intention, presumably made critics more willing to accept the puzzles of art. Or rather, the acceptance of obscurity in an artist's symbols was *consistent with* the Pauline view that all images are obscure. With this view we would agree. However, from the standpoint of rhetorical persuasion and identification, we would place the stress upon the *social* implications of the enigmatic, in keeping with Marx on "ideology," Carlyle on "Clothes," and Empson on "Pastoral."

"Infancy," Mystery, and Persuasion

Rhetorically considered, the acceptance of the "enigma" as an element in a symbol's persuasiveness has led us to note the place of "magic" or "mystery" both as a passive reflection of class culture and as an active way of maintaining cultural cohesion. We shall further consider the dialectics of such persuasion in our next section on Order.

The "secret" sometimes concerns privy parts of a strictly economic nature (consider the dislike of having one's income or one's bank account a matter of common knowledge). Yet such secretiveness (possibly involving furtive identifications between monetary and genital treasure) impinges upon many still uncharted realms of "infancy," comprising a "speechlessness" or "unspeakableness" derived at the very least from the technical fact that in all expression there is a convergence of unexpressed elements.

If one feels as an "act," for instance, the generating principle of the logarithmic curve in the spiral of a seashell, to the extent that he cannot reduce it to a mathematical formula he is in a state of "infancy," working with a kind of "intuition" that overlaps upon the realm of the "unconscious" in dreams. On the other hand, if the accurate reduction of the spiral to a mathematical formula implies, however remotely, ideas of the convolvulus that would require, for their expression, imagery of an "enigmatic," poetic nature (of roses, sheaths, fleshy receivings, and the like), then the mathematical expression, however explicit and rigorous, would in its abstractness have its own kind of "infancy." Hence, even in the unformulated appreciation of the purely linguistic principles underlying imagery, there is the mystery of infancy. "Infancy" figures all the more in theories of correspondence whereby empirical objects are treated as symbols of a generating principle itself invisible. And such a theological scheme could have its social equivalent in a "fetishistic" world where all the objects were imbued with "magical" properties by reason of their covert or overt identification as insignia of privilege or signs of deprivation.

Underlying any such social mysteries, there are the natural mysteries, reducible ultimately to the infancy of intuitions (as with the "unspeakable" ingredient in the intuitions of senses and seasons). There is room for argument as to what a poet's image of springtime stands for (what equivalents we would substitute for the medieval concern with allegorical, tropological, and anagogic meanings). But in any case the image derives its resonance from its ability to stand for more than spring as a positivist's "fact."

An "intuition" of spring is not a mere passive perception, a datum of sensory (or even supersensory) *knowledge*. It is an *acting-with,* as our "intuitions" of a phoebe's song in spring are not merely the sensory perception of the air in vibration, nor even a sheerly physical response to the return of spring which the song may signalize, but an acting-with a wider orbit of meanings, some of them not intrinsically "spring-like" at all. The "mystery" here centers in the fact that the articulate tonal *image* stands for a partly inarticulate *act*. The principles of such a contemplative act we may seek to formulate as idea, since in idea there is action, drama. It would thus seem more correct to say that, when intuitively acting-with the bird's song, we respond to the *idea* of spring. And this idea, in its completeness, will probably comprise personal, sexual, social, and universal promises.

Empirically, what theologians discuss as the ultimate Oneness of God is equivalent to the ultimate oneness of the linguistic principle. Rhetoric is thus made from fragments of dialectic. For expression, as persuasion, seeks to escape from infancy by breaking down the oneness of an intuition into several terms, or voices. It defines by partisanship, by de-termination. These terms may bring clarifications that are themselves confusions on another level. For the conversion of dialectical principles into the persuasive topics of rhetoric is somewhat as though one were to call the principle of composition "Loyalty" and the principle of division "Rebellion," and were thereafter to treat of addition and multiplication in arithmetic as "Pure Loyalty," or of subtraction and division as "Absolute Rebellion." (Pythagorean speculations on numbers apparently did something like that. And "Eden" and "the fall" are mythic terms for composition and division. Such terms are *concealments,* so far as their ultimate dialectical reduction is concerned. But they are enigmas of a *revealing* sort, too, insofar as they sum up, or stand for, a complexity of personal, sexual, social, and universal motives. In any case, when their surrounding and modifying imagery is ample, we can begin to see them as a kind of *demonstration,* revealing a complexity of motives that would be *concealed* if reduced to such terms as "composition" and "division" alone.)

All told, may we not glimpse the possibility that "ideological mystification" can be but a "dyslogistic appellative" for an intrinsic property of persuasion itself? Where language is concerned, "spirit" comes before "body" in the sense that the capacity for language must precede its use. In a symbol-using animal, there must be a feeling for the principles of language. The tribe that could spontaneously manipulate a Greek verb was implicitly a tribe of "grammarians." And since the ability to use the grammar of one language argues the ability to use the grammar of other languages, we could say that the feeling for grammar in general is prior to the feeling for this or that particular grammar (quite as the ability to walk is prior to the ability to walk in one particular place, though one learns to walk in general by learning to walk in particular places). And the feeling for dialectic is "spiritual" at least in the sense that the acts of expression and interpretation are not "objects."

Here are steps that might indicate how the "ideological priority of spirit" (and of the "mystifications" derived from it) would be implicit in persuasion itself:

(1) Persuasion is a kind of communication. (2) Communication is between different things. (3) But difference is not felt merely as be-

tween *this* entity and *that* entity. Rather, it is felt realistically, as between *this kind* of entity and *that kind* of entity. (That is, communication between entities becomes communication between *classes* of entities.) (4) A persuasive communication between kinds (that is, persuasion by identification) is the abstract paradigm of *courtship*. Such appeal, or address, would be the technical equivalent of love. (5) But courtship, love, is "mystery." For love is a communion of estranged entities, and strangeness is a condition of mystery. (6) When courtship attains its equivalent in the realm of *group* relations, differences between the sexes has its analogue in the difference between *social* classes. (7) In the respect, reverence, embarrassment, and ironies that go with intercourse between classes, there is the "mystification" of Carlyle's "Clothes," of Diderot's "pantomime," of *genres* like pastoral as treated by Empson, or of such tentative attitudes as Empson calls "comic primness." (Out-and-out hatred is a snapping of the continuity, but it can be socially organized only by the building of a countercontinuity; hence the mystery of persuasion is not categorically abolished, it is transformed.)

(8) Persuasion is "spiritual," in contrast with the producing of change by purely material agencies. For if it is "bodily" to move a man from here to there by pushing him, then by antithesis it is "spiritual" to produce the same movement in pleading, "Come hither." (9) But such "spiritual" communication is abstract. Hence, in it there is the possibility of a *completely* abstract communication (or "courtship") between kinds, or classes. In the *Phaedrus* (as we noted in the *Grammar*) Socrates shows us what the completion of abstract courtship would be. It would be the insemination of *doctrine;* that is to say, it would be *education,* the bringing of the *message.* (10) But there is no message without *science.* And so, out of persuasion, we can even derive pure *information,* which is usually *contrasted* with persuasion.

The tie-ups and cross-references here are endless. But they all start in the proposition that, with a symbol-using animal, the logic of symbols must be "prior" to the effects of any "productive forces" in the socioeconomic meaning of that expression. And one should not forget that the productive forces themselves owe much of their development to linguistic agencies, not merely in the sense that vocabulary is needed for guiding the production of complex instruments and for maintaining the tradition of their use, but also in a more radical sense.

For the distinctive insight in human invention is not the use of tools, since animals use tools; it is in the use of tools for making tools. And this insight-at-one-remove, this reflexive pattern, is much like the insight of language itself, which is not merely speech about things (a dog's barking at a prowler could be called that), but speech about speech. This secondary stage, allowing for "thought of thought," is so integrally connected with the human power to invent tools for making tools, that we might call such power linguistic in essence (as Carlyle did).

Of course, there is always the possibility of "mystification," in the sense that language can be used to deceive. And at least as a kind of rough preparation for finer scrutiny, rhetorical analysis should always be ready to expose mystifications of this simple but ubiquitous sort (mystifications broadly reducible either to "unitary" devices whereby a special group gains unjust advantage from the services of other groups, or to "scapegoat" devices whereby an "enemy abroad" is wholly blamed for untoward conditions due mainly to domestic faults). But we are here asking whether there may be a profounder kind of mystification as well, implicit in the very act of persuasion itself.

As the mystery of courtship is in the act of persuasion intrinsically, so also there is implicit in it the invitation to the mystification of class. We note such motives also in the ambiguously classlike relationships that figure in science, as the material of education involves *classes* of learners hierarchically arranged among themselves. Or there is the class of students as against the class of teachers. And there are classes of teachers, among themselves "invidiously" ranked. Persuasion, thus roundabout, brings a mystery into science, into the very disciplines that are usually taken to be the opposite of mystification.

But also, implicit in persuasion, there is *theology,* since theology is the ultimate reach of communication between *different classes* of beings. The steps here would seem to be: (1) In the courtship of persuasion there are the rudiments of love, respectful pleading. (2) The *ultimate* of this attitude is reverent beseechment, prayer. (3) Prayer has its own invitation to the universalizing of class distinction, the pleader being by nature inferior to the pled-with. (4) The relation attains its utmost thoroughness in the contrast between the mightiest sovereign and the lowliest of his subjects. (We can next note that the pattern may be *brought to earth* in an attenuated form, as social hierarchy.) (5) But in its "pure" form, there is need to find a discussable content, or object. One cannot without an almost suicidal degree of perfection merely pray. One must pray *to something*. (6) Hence, the plunge direct to the *principle* of persuasion, as reduced to its most universal form, leads to the theologian's attempt to establish an *object* of such prayer; namely: God (largely applying to this end terms set by the *social* hierarchy). In sum, we are suggesting: The "theology" that Marx detected in "ideological mystification" is the *last reach of the persuasive principle itself*. And quite as in the social counterpart of such theology, there is likewise a hierarchy implicit in the route from persuasion to science.

If our approach is just, such mystifications cannot be cleared away by a mere debunker's reduction. The high development of magic as a persuasion that promotes cooperation in primitive tribes, and the many reversions to "mystique" in modern policies of right, center, and left, seem to indicate a profounder element here. These manifestations seem to indicate that people are more thorough than they think, and that the *superficial* uses of persuasion (as a mere call that induces action) do have in them the *ultimates* of persuasion, however these may be concealed.

If this were so, if the *ultimate reaches* in the principle of persuasion are implicit in even the *trivial* uses of persuasion, people could not escape the ultimates of language merely by using language trivially (as with some mothers who seem to think that they can make their children "wholesome" merely by keeping them stupid). The choices between war and peace are ultimate choices. Men must make themselves over profoundly, when cooperatively engaged in following such inescapable purposes. And as the acts of persuasion add up in a social texture, they amount to one or the other of those routes—and they are radical, no matter however trivial the errors by which war is permitted to emerge out of peace.

There would then seem to be two kinds of mystification, a special kind and a general kind. You may have no great difficulty in spotting the first kind, though it may be hard to spread the glad tidings of your discovery, since there is usually powerful social organization behind the errors you would clear away, the errors making for the misunderstandings that goad to war. But as for the possibility of a second kind, mystification as the "logical conclusion" of the persuasive principle:

Even if we finally discover that such a development is not *inevitable* to persuasion, there are many reasons to believe that it is a constant *threat,* a constant *tendency* or *temptation* in those who are thorough enough to build a way of thinking in accordance with the implications of persuasion as courtship.

At least, beyond the purely fallacious devices by which our editorial writers build up the notion that the ways of the "Russian East" are "mysterious," surely Stalin in the Kremlin is more "mysterious" as a leader than Truman in the White House, to his own people as well as to ours. Marxism teaches us not to forget the mysteries of class; and Empson shows how they may figure "pastorally" in even a socialist society. And there are also the mysteries of courtship in subtler ways, as we have tried to indicate.

There are also sources of mystery beyond rhetoric. These can be rooted in the secrecy of plans during gestation. Or they are found in fears that arise from the sense of limits (so that one says in effect: "Another perhaps can go beyond that point, but not I"—or "Maybe I can go beyond that point after preparation, but not now"). Or there is mystery in the infancy of the "unconscious," nonverbal, postverbal, and superverbal. By nonverbal we mean the visceral; by postverbal the unutterable complexities to which the implications of words themselves give rise. (Maybe the word should be "coverbal.") And if we go through the verbal to the outer limits of the verbal, the superverbal would comprise whatever might be the jumping-off place. It would be not nature minus speech, but nature as the ground of speech, *hence nature as itself containing the principle of speech*. Such an inclusive nature would be more-than-verbal rather than less-than-verbal.

Part III
ORDER

III

ORDER

Positive, Dialectical, and Ultimate Terms

FIRST, we take it, there are the *positive* terms. They name par excellence the things of experience, the *hic et nunc,* and they are defined *per genus et differentiam,* as with the vocabulary of biological classification. Here are the words for what Bentham called "real entities," in contrast with the "fictitious entities" of the law. ("Tree" is a positive term, but "rights" or "obligations" are legal fictions.) In Kant's alignment, the thing named by a positive term would be a manifold of sensations unified by a concept. Thus, the "sensibility" receives a bundle of "intuitions," intimations of size, shape, texture, color, and the like; and as the "understanding" clamps a unifying term, a "concept," upon the lot, we can say, "This is a house."

The imagery of poetry is positive to the extent that it names things having a visible, tangible existence. We have already observed that there is an important difference between a house as a practically existing object and the image "house" as it appears in a poem. But we are now considering only the respect in which the poetic image, house, can also be defined *per genus et differentiam:* that is, the respect in which, when a poet uses the term, "house," we could get his meaning by consulting Webster's, where we are told that a house is "a structure intended or used as a habitation or shelter for animals of any kind; but especially, a building or edifice for the habitation of man; a dwelling place."

A positive term is most unambiguously itself when it names a visible and tangible thing which can be located in time and place. Hence, the positive ideal is a "physicalist" vocabulary that reduces reference to terms of *motion.* Since the modern mathematics of submicroscopic motion is far indeed from the visible and tangible, the sensory aspect of positive experience can become quite tenuous. But since such manifestations must, in the last analysis, reveal themselves on dials, in measurements and meter readings of one sort or another, the hypothetical entities of electronics can be considered as "positive," insofar as they are capable of empirical recording. A skeptic might offer reasons to believe that such science is less positive than its apologists take it to be. Particularly one might ask himself whether the terms for *relationships* among things are as positive as are the names for the things themselves. But we need not attempt to decide that question here; we need only note that there is a basic terminology of perception grounded on sensation, memory, and "imagination" (in the general, psychological, nonpoetic meaning of the word). And whatever else it may be in its ultimate reaches, such a terminology of perception is "positive" in its everyday, empirical availability. There is nothing "transcendent" about it, for instance.

Bentham's reference to "fictitious entities" of the law indicates another order, comprising terms which we would call "dialectical." These have no such strict location as can be assigned to the objects named in words of the first order. Even insofar as the positive terminology acquires theoretical champions who proclaim the "principles of positivism," we are in the realm of the purely dialectical. "Positivism" itself is not a positive term. For though you may locate the positive referent for the expression "house," you will have a hard time trying to locate a similarly positive referent for the expression, "principles of positivism." Here are words that belong, not in the order of *motion and perception,* but rather in the order of *action and idea.* Here are words for *principles* and *essence* (as we might ask, "Just what is the *essence* of the positivist doctrine?").

Here are "titular" words. Titles like "Elizabethanism" or "capitalism" can have no positive referent, for instance. And though they sum up a vast complexity of conditions which might conceivably be reduced to a near-infinity of positive details, if you succeeded in such a description you would find that your recipe contained many ingredients not peculiar to "Elizabethanism" or "capitalism" at all. In fact, you would find that "Elizabethanism" itself looked different, if matched against, say, "medievalism," than if matched against "Victorianism." And "capitalism" would look different if compared and contrasted with "feudalism" than if dialectically paired with "socialism." Hence terms of this sort are often called "polar."

Bentham said that fictitious entities could not be adequately defined *per genus et differentiam.* He said that they required, rather, definition by *paraphrase,* hence his method of "phraseoplerosis" and "archetypation" for discovering just what people really meant when they used legal fictions. We equate his "fictitious entities" with "dialectical terms" because they refer to *ideas* rather than to *things.* Hence they are more concerned with *action* and *attitude* than with *perception* (they fall under the head of *ethics* and *form* rather than *knowledge* and *information*). You define them by asking how they *behave;* and part of an expression's behavior, as Bentham pointed out, will be revealed by the discovery of the secret modifiers implicit in the expression itself; hence Bentham's project for filling out the expression (phraseoplerosis) and discounting its images (archetypation).

If an expession were complete, such paraphrase would not be necessary. One could then derive all the modifiers explicitly by citation from the expression itself. But particularly in the strife of rhetoric, the expression is left fragmentary. If a poet says, "I love" when he really hates, he will scrupulously proceed, however enigmatically, to round out his statement with the expressions that introduce the necessary modifiers. But when Preen says to Prone, "I want to help you," his statement is incomplete, and may even require interpretation on a purely behavioristic basis. If this "help," as tested behavioristically, amounts to nothing more than what folk rhetoric calls the "run around," then the ultimate test of his meaning is extralinguistic. And much rhetorical statement requires such circumstantial interpretation.

Hypothetically, if our discrimination were keen enough, we could know by the tonalities of Preen's statement, or by the flicker of his eye, just what he meant when he said, "I want to help you." In brief, the expression itself would contain its future implications. But our discrimination is not always keen enough; and besides, the record is usually but a fragment of the expression (as the written word omits all telltale record of gesture and tonality; and not only may our "literacy" keep us from missing the omissions, it may blunt us to the appreciation of tone and gesture, so that even when we witness the full expression, we note only those aspects of it that can be written down).

In public relations, most expressions are as though wigwagged from a great distance, or as uttered behind masks, or as transmitted by hearsay. Hence, one must go to the first frank level of analysis, the extraverbally behavioristic. Next, there are sloganlike utterances by which all men are partially fooled, the orator and his public alike. For this we have Bentham's concern with "archetypation," the images that *improperly* affect our ideas. But here we meet the need for another kind of "filling out," half behavioristic, half imaginal, an ambiguity due to the fact that so much pragmatic behavior itself has symbolic elements.

If, for instance, the church spire actually has been an image of aspirations "towards heaven," and if churchmen pay verbal tribute to the power of the supernatural, and if then on church property they erect business structures soaring far above their church, does not this combination of behavioristic and imaginal tests require us to conclude that their true expression is not in their words, but in the conditions of steel and stone which are weightily there, to dwarf you as the church spire never dwarfed you, and to put you at the bottom of a deep, windswept gulch? Regardless of what they may say in their statements telegraphed world-wide by the news agencies, without gesture, without tonality, have they not, in their mixture of behavior and image, *really* proclaimed that they live by a "post-Christian" order of motives?

If church spires mean anything, they must overtop the buildings that surround them. However, the opposition might point out: There are the catacombs of religion, too. True, there is the *underground*.

In any case, we have again come upon an area where nonverbal things, in their capacity as "meanings," also take on the nature of words, and thus require the extension of dialectic into the realm of the physical. Or, otherwise put, we come to the place where the dialectical realm of ideas is seen to permeate the positive realm of concepts. For if a church spire is a symbolic thing, then the business structure that overtowers it must participate in the same symbolic, however antithetically, as representing an alternate choice of action. Thus the ethical-dramatic-dialectical vocabulary so infuses the empirical-positive world of things that each scientific object becomes available for poetry.

But the distinction between positive and dialectical terms, with the interrelation of the two realms, can deflect attention from a third aspect of vocabulary, which might be called "ultimate." We had thought of calling it "mystical," but that designation too quickly makes readers take sides for or against us. So let us call it "ultimate," and approach this third element of vocabulary thus:

Dialectic in itself may remain on the level of parliamentary conflict, leading to compromise. It being the realm of ideas or principles, if you organize a conflict among spokesmen for competing ideas or principles, you may produce a situation wherein there is no one clear choice. Each of the spokesmen, whose ideas are an extension of special interests, must remain somewhat unconvinced by any solution which does not mean the complete triumph of his partisan interests. Yet he may have to compromise, putting through some portion of his program by making concessions to allies whom, if he could get his wishes absolutely, he would repudiate. Here are standard parliamentary tactics. "Compromise" is perhaps the neutral term, though on the edge of the dyslogistic. "Horse-trading" is clearly a dyslogistic term for the same thing. And a resoundingly dyslogistic term would be "demoralization," justifiable insofar as all "interests" can be translated into terms of "principles," and when they have thus been stylistically ennobled, any yielding on interests becomes a yielding on principles (a stylistic embarrassment upon which our State Department under General Marshall based the rigidity of its dealings with Soviet Russia).

Now, the difference between a merely "dialectical" confronting of parliamentary conflict and an "ultimate" treatment of it would reside in this: The "dialectical" order would leave the competing voices in a jangling relation with one another (a conflict solved *faute de mieux* by "horse-trading"); but the "ultimate" order would place these competing voices themselves in a *hierarchy,* or *sequence,* or *evaluative series,* so that, in some way, we went by a fixed and reasoned progression from one of these to another, the members of the entire group being arranged *developmentally* with relation to one another. The "ultimate" order of terms would thus differ essentially from the "dialectical" (as we use the term *in this particular connection*) in that there would be a "guiding idea" or "unitary principle" behind the diversity of voices. The voices would not confront one another as somewhat disrelated competitors that can work together only by the "mild demoralization" of sheer compromise; rather, they would be like successive positions or moments in a single process.

Thus, confronting the sort of "dialectical" procedure required when "interests" have been translated into a corresponding terminology of "principles," with parliamentary spokesmen aiming to further their interests somewhat by compromising with their principles—we can get a glimpse into a possible alternative, whereby a somewhat formless parliamentary wrangle can, by an "ultimate" vocabulary, be creatively endowed with design. And even though the members of the parliament, being "horse-traders" by nature, may not accept this design, it can have a contemplative effect; it can organize one's attitude towards the struggles of politics, and may suggest reasons why one kind of compromise is, in the long run, to be rated as superior to another.

Consider, for instance, how Plato treats the four kinds of "imperfect government" in *The Republic* (Book VIII and beginning of Book IX). They are presented not merely as one might draw up a list, but *developmentally*. The steps from his ideal government to "timocracy," and thence successively to "oligarchy," "democracy," and "tyranny" are interpreted as the unfolding of a single process. Here, as repeatedly in Platonic dialogues, the interrelationship among the terms for the kinds of government is "ultimate." Indeed, when Socrates celebrates dialectic as the highest kind of knowledge, rising above the separate sciences and mediating among them, he means by dialectic not merely the step from sensory terms to ideas, but also a hierarchic ordering of steps.

"Governments vary as the dispositions of men," Socrates says; and "there must be as many of one as of the other." Whereupon he seeks to define the human dispositions brought to the fore by each of the different political structures. His resulting remarks on the "timocratic man," and on the "oligarchic," "democratic," and "tyrannical man" amount to recipes for what today might be called four different "ideologies." Each of these has its own peculiar idea or summarizing term: "honor" for timocracy, "wealth" for oligarchy, "freedom" for democracy, "protection" for tyranny. And the human dispositions which he describes under these heads could be treated as four different motivational clusters which one must appeal to, when trying to win adherents in an audience typical of each such political state. "As the government, so the citizen," Plato says. Yet he is not content merely to give us four "personality types" (four corresponding types of government, each with its appropriate ideology or kind of consciousness). He is seeking to grade them with reference to their relative distance from a single norm. We are not here arguing for the justice of his grading; we are merely pointing to the principle involved. We are saying that to leave the four kinds merely confronting one another in their diversity would have been "dialectical" in the sense of the parliamentary jangle, but that this attempt to arrange them hierarchically transforms the dialectical into an "ultimate" order.

In an ultimate dialectic, the terms so lead into one another that the completion of each order leads to the next. Thus, a body of positive terms must be brought to a head in a titular term which represents the principle or idea behind the positive terminology as a whole. This summarizing term is in a different order of vocabulary. And if such titles, having been brought into dialectical commerce with one another, are given an order among themselves, there must be a principle of principles involved in such a design—and the step from principles to a principle of principles is likewise both the fulfillment of the previous order and the transcending of it.

We thought of calling the ultimate order "mystical" because the mystic invariably aims to encompass conflicting orders of motivation, not by outlawing any order, however "inferior," but by finding a place for it in a developmental series. Thus at moments when a mystic vocabulary is most accurate, we should not expect to find a flat antithesis between "body" and "spirit." Rather, we should expect "body" (in even its "lowliest" forms) to be treated as a *way into* "spirit." Since antithesis is so strong a verbal instrument in both rhetoric and dialectic, we may often find "short cuts" where the extremes of a developmental series are presented as harshly antithetical. But we should not judge by this alone. Rather, look into the writings of any mystic who has left a record of his methods, and you will find that the entry to ultimate communion is made *through* body, nature, image, systematically treated as a necessary disciplinary step. Indeed, so thoroughly is this the case, that for the most ultimate of his experiences, the mystic will again employ the terms of body, nature, image (on the assumption that, if one has gone through the proper series of steps, one knows how to discount the inadequacies of such language, while the clash of images by oxymoron comes closest to expressing the experience for someone who has not been through it).

Ultimate Elements in the Marxist Persuasion

Once you have placed your terms in a developmental series, you have an arrangement whereby each can be said to participate, within the limitations of its nature, in the ultimate perfection ("finishedness") of the series. Each stage, at its appropriate "moment," represents the movement, the ultimate direction or principle, of the entire series. In this sense, Hegel's "concrete universal" would be "mystical," in that it represents not only itself, in its nature *hic et hunc,* but the universal essence of the development in its entirety (quite as bud, preceding blossom, represents not only its own concrete bud-nature, and its nature as incipient blossom, but also the fruit, the seed, and decline, and the futurity beyond that decline). And since any moment, here and now, would thus represent a developmental principle transcending the concrete particularity of any one moment in the series, here would be a kind of mystical unity, a oneness that both is and is not, as with the paradox of substance discussed in the *Grammar.*

Marx wrote good satire on Hegel's "concrete universal." And in keeping with the same line of thought, he notes in *The German Ideology* how, by the use of an ultimate design for interpreting moments along the path of history, later history can be made to look like the goal of earlier history (as were we to say that America was discovered in order to bring about the French Revolution). Thereby, he says, "history receives its own special aims and becomes 'a person ranking with other persons' (to wit: 'self-consciousness, criticism, the Unique,' etc.), while what is designated with the words 'destiny,' 'goal,' 'germ,' or 'idea' of earlier history is nothing more than an abstraction formed from later history, from the active influence which earlier history exercises on later history."

But can a mode of thought so strongly built upon Hegelian patterns avoid the "mystical" merely by "turning Hegel upside down"? In any case, much of the *rhetorical* strength in the Marxist dialectic comes from the fact that it is "ultimate" in its order. The various classes do not confront one another merely as parliamentary voices that represent conflicting interests. They are arranged hierarchically, each with the disposition, or "consciousness," that matches its peculiar set of circumstances, while the steps from feudal to bourgeois to proletarian are grounded in the very nature of the universe.

Precisely by reason of this ultimate order, a spokesman for the proletariat can think of himself as representing not only the interests of that class alone, but the grand design of the entire historical sequence, its final outcome for all mankind. When gauging the historical situation correctly, when knowing the nature of the moment as part of a universal movement, he finds in the "revolutionary situation" precisely the double nature that permits it to be simultaneously the concrete thing it is, in its own unique combination of conditions, and a participant in the perfection of the total sequence. (To see both the "science" and the "intuition," see Lenin's letters when he had become convinced that the time was ripe in Russia.)

In general, the ultimate hierarchic order of the terminology rises materialistically from the fundamental, unknown particles of the universe, to atoms, to crystals and planetary formations, to the emergence of life, to the evolution of biological forms, to the evolution and revolution of social forms. We cite from the report of a lecture on dialectical materialism by the English physicist, J. D. Bernal, referring to this "natural hierarchy of development in the universe." But from the standpoint of rhetoric, the implanting of an ultimate hierarchy upon social forms is the important thing. Here the hierarchic ordering of the subsocial realms could be considered as an "ideological reflex" or extension of the persuasive principle experienced in the social realm. That is, rhetorically considered, the Marxist hierarchy may go not from a science of nature to a science of society, but from an ultimate dialectic of social development to a corresponding dialectic of natural development. For though there may be a "Marxist physics," Marxism is primarily a *sociology*.

In accord with such thinking as regards current positivist doctrines, one may take a stand that, while neither flatly for nor flatly against, need not be reduced merely to the lame and formless admission that "there is something to be said for both sides." Not only is the positive order of vocabulary "allowable"; we should be reluctant to leave this order. Every question should be reduced to such terms, insofar as the nature of its subject-matter permits. The positivist ideal of language is athletic and exacting. And we should object to it only when dramatic elements are present which cannot legitimately be treated in the positive order alone. The improper migration of positive terms to areas of investigation and contemplation for which they are unfit calls for a flatly antipositivist position, as regards any such cases of terministic impropriety. But from the standpoint of terminology in general, we are not thereby vowed to a doctrine of out-and-out antipositivism, since we can and should accept the positivist order of terms as the proper first stage in a hierarchy of terms.

The same admonition should be introduced with regard to our reservations on technologism, as it is manifested in the cult of manufactured commodities (the doctrine that might be summed up: "It's culture if it's something you can buy"). Man is essentially a "rational" (that is, symbol-using) animal (as stated in the opening words of St. John, *"In the beginning* was the Word," the prior in substance being here expressed as the prior in time). And when we use symbols for things, such symbols are not merely reflections of the things symbolized, or signs for them; they are to a degree a *transcending* of the things symbolized. So, to say that man is a symbol-using animal is by the same token to say that he is a "transcending animal." Thus, there is in language itself a motive force calling man to transcend the "state of nature" (that is, the order of motives that would prevail in a world without language, Logos, "reason"). And in this sense, we can recognize even the cult of commodities (which is an outgrowth of language-guided invention), as a *mode of transcendence*. So we need not be placed in the position of flatly "rejecting" it, a particularly uncomfortable position in view of the fact that the cult of commodities seems able to recruit just about as many devotees as can afford to bear witness (testifying to the sincerity of their faith by money-offerings).

An out-and-out antithetical vocabulary would require you either to live by the cult of commodities, in effect adoring them as household gods, or to reject such a cult quite as a devout believer in the One God would reject idolatry. But by using a graded vocabulary, you can instead recognize the cult of commodities as a mode of transcendence that is genuine, but inferior.

Employing the same hierarchic principle, we note that even a Hitlerite political philosophy, or any such "collusion," would require treatment, not as flatly "antisocial," but rather as a low order of sociality. Such an approach becomes particularly necessary where an inferior order actually prevails, and one is so placed that a flat rejection of the doctrine would be suicidally ineffectual, whereas a grudging minimum acceptance of it might put one in a position to work towards its gradual improvement. But unfortunately, while this way of reasoning is just, it readily lends itself to use unjustly.

Any improvement in social status is a kind of transcendence. And where one is a member of an extremely underprivileged class, as with the Negro in America, an individual attempt at the transcending of inferior status gets increased poignancy from the fact that, atop all the intensity of such effort in itself, there is a working at cross-purposes. The Negro intellectual, Ralph Ellison, says that Booker T. Washington "described the Negro community as a basket of crabs, wherein should one attempt to climb out, the others immediately pull him back." Is there not also an internal compulsion of the same sort, as the individual Negro visits this same judgment upon himself? For he may also take the position of what Mead would call the "generalized other": he may visit upon himself the antagonistic attitude of the whites; or he may feel as "conscience" the judgment of his own class, since he would in a sense be "disloyal" to his class, in transcending the limitations traditionally imposed upon him as a member of that class. Striving for freedom as a human being generically, he must do so as a Negro specifically. But to do so as a Negro is, by the same token, to prevent oneself from doing so in the generic sense; for a Negro could not be free generically except in a situation where the color of the skin had no more social meaning than the color of the eyes.

Recall the lines in *The Merchant of Venice,* where Shakespeare is considering an analogous conflict, as Shylock says:

> I am a Jew. Hath not a Jew eyes? hath not a Jew hands, organs, dimensions, senses, affections, passions? fed with the same food, hurt with the same weapons, subject to the same diseases, healed by the same means, warmed and cooled by the same winter and summer, as a Christian is? If you prick us, do we not bleed? if you tickle us, do we not laugh? if you poison us, do we not die?

Then, following this statement of his identity as a member of mankind generically, Shylock turns to the theme of his specific identity as a Jew in Christian Venice:

> and if you wrong us, shall we not revenge? If we are like you in the rest, we shall resemble you in that. If a Jew wrong a Christian, what is his humility? Revenge. If a Christian wrong a Jew, what should his sufferance be by Christian example? Why, revenge. The villainy you teach me I will execute, and it shall go hard but I will better the instruction.

Note the paradoxical way in which the words "humility" and "sufferance" are used. Revenge as a kind of humble, Christian duty. One might call the notion Shylock's failure to understand Christian doctrine. Or, more justly, one might call it Shylock's very accurate gauging of the way in which Christians themselves characteristically distort Christian sufferance to serve the rhetoric of property. In any case, we see that Shylock would here use the advantages of vengeance itself as a kind of transcendence, a "static" way of lifting himself above his disadvantages as a Jew while in the very same act he reaffirms his status.

Such conflicts are clearly "dialectical." We are beyond the purely positive level of vocabulary; we are in the realm, not of knowledge, but of ideas and action. Hence, unless the terminology becomes ultimate, there is an unresolved, parliamentary jangle, a discordancy of conflicting voices which at best could attain an uneasy compromise, and at worst arrive at the equating of vengeance with humility (which means, in sum, accepting the judgment of the opponent, and merely turning the tables against him). Shylock's "vengeance" is but the most highly generalized statement of such a solution, which in each particular case calls for a joining in a conspiracy against the oppressor, in the hopes that eventually the roles can be reversed. In Richard Wright's *Native Son,* Bigger's criminal protest *as a Negro* is another particularization of the same response. The "humility" of such vengeance is in the acceptance of the opponent's judgment, in finally agreeing to let him set the rules, and then aiming at advantage within the restrictions he has imposed. Purely "racialist" or "nationalist" doctrines of emancipation are a more benign transformation of such "counterconspiracy" (or exclusive league of the excluded). And they may even seem like an ultimate solution, until there develop the wrangles within nationalism, and among rival nationalisms.

Clearly, the rhetorical appeal of the Marxist terminology in such situations is that it can allow for an ultimate order. You may question whether it is the "ultimate-ultimate." You may fear that, as it operates in social textures, it ceases to be the conspiracy-to-end-conspiracy that it claims to be, instead becoming but the condition of a new conspiracy. Maybe yes, maybe no. That is not for us to decide at the moment. It is enough for us to note, as students of rhetoric, that the Marxist terminology is "ultimate" enough to meet at least the primary requirements of this sort. It permits the member of a minority to place his problem in a graded series that keeps transcendence of individual status from seeming like disloyalty to one's group status, and keeps the sufferance of one's group status from assuming some form of mere "vengeance." It allows the member of an underprivileged minority, for instance, to confront the world at once specifically and generically. The Negro does not become equal to the white by a kind of intellectual "passing." He can explicitly recognize that his particular act must be adapted to the nature of his historical situation in which he happens to be placed; yet at the same time, he can view this situation universally (thereby attaining the kind of transcendence at which all men aim, and at which the Negro spiritual had aimed, though there the aim was at the spiritual transcending of a predestined material slavery, whereas the Marxist ultimates allow for a material transcending of inferior status).

True, there is much that no vocabulary can do in these matters. Where there are so many intense conflicts of an extraverbal sort, no merely verbal manipulations can remove them. But verbal manipulations may offer a more orderly approach to them, permitting them to be contemplated with less agitation. And where this is the case, verbal manipulations are the very opposite of the "evasive."

Marxism, considered as an ultimate vocabulary, also owes much of its persuasiveness to the way in which its theory of action fits its theory of order. For if any point, or "moment," in a hierarchic series can be said to represent, in its limited way, the principle or "perfection" of the ultimate design, then each tiny act shares in the absolute meaning of the total act. Thus, the "truth" is not grasped and tested by merely "perceiving" the logic of the entire series. Perception must be grounded in enactment, by participation in some local role, so that the understanding of the total order is reached through this partial involvement. There is perception from without, made possible through nonparticipation. Or there is local participation, which may become so involved in particulars that one never sees beyond them. But there is a third way, the fullest kind of understanding, wherein one gets the immediacy of participation in a local act, yet sees in and through this act an over-all design, sees and *feels* the local act itself as but the partial expression of the the total development. The Marxist persuasion is in the name of this third way. Consider Lenin's *What Is to Be Done?* for instance:

We might first note in the very title a contribution to our previous concern with the relation between rhetoric and opinion. For in his *Book of Fallacies,* Bentham had distinguished between matters of fact (what was done, *quid factum*) and matters of opinion (what is to be done, *quid faciendum*). The future can only be a matter of opinion. Until it has actually come to pass, it must lie outside the orbit of empirically verifiable "scientific fact." So Lenin's question, *What Is to Be Done?* is by such tests clearly in the realm of opinion, and to this extent in the realm of rhetoric. (It is "deliberative.")

The crucial point, as we quoted it in the *Grammar,* revolves about the distinction between trade union activity and the worker's *consciousness* of his role as member of a revolutionary proletariat. Lenin would distinguish between the "spontaneous" response to a situation and the kind of *new act* that arises under a deliberately Marxist interpretation of that situation. And we would interpret the design of Lenin's thinking in this wise: The trade unionist, as such, has no consciousness of the workers' "historical role" in the revolutionary change from capitalism to socialism. Hence, in the mere spontaneity and localism of his responses, he does not transcend the limitations of his class. He acts, and to this extent he has a profounder kind of participation than the purely outside observer. But his act is beclouded by the particulars of his situation, the day-to-day contingencies of earning a livelihood. Now add the Marxist doctrine of universal historical necessity, defining the worker's place in an *ultimate* development. The worker whose understanding becomes infused with this doctrine then sees himself not merely as an individual joining with other individuals to improve his bargaining position with his employer: he sees himself as *member of a class,* the proletariat, which is destined to play *a crucial role in the unfolding of history as a whole.* Thus, while participating with maximum activity in the particular organizational and propagandist problems that mark his local situation, he transcends the limitations of these local conditions and of his "spontaneous" nature as member of the working class. For he sees his role in terms of an *absolute,* an ultimate. In participating *locally,* he is participating in the total dialectic, communicating directly with its universal logic, or ultimate direction. Indeed, we could even say that he now sees himself in *formal* or *ritual* terms, not just as Mr. So-and-so working under such-and-such conditions, but as *"the* Proletarian," with a generic personality calling creatively to ways of action that transcend his limited nature as Mr. So-and-so, and derive their logic from motives of universal scope.

Call it fallacious if you want. That need not concern us here. We are discussing the rhetorical advantages of an ultimate vocabulary as contrasted with a vocabulary left on the level of parliamentary conflict. We are but pointing to a notable formal advantage, got by the union of drama and reason, a wholesome rhetorical procedure in itself, at a time when typical "parliamentary" works like Thurman Arnold's *The Folklore of Capitalism* would ask us rather to unite drama with unreason.

Perhaps the "ultimate" order comes most natural to narrative forms (hence its ease of adaptation to the Hegelian and Marxist "stories" of history). Usually, in narrative, it is so implicit that we may not even discern it. For instance, if the fate of our hero is developed through a succession of encounters, each of these encounters may represent a different "principle," and each of these principles or stages may so lead into the next that the culmination of one lays the ground for the next. In fact, if the work is properly constructed, it will necessarily have such a form. If one breaks down a "dramatic idea" into acts of variously related agents, the successive steps of the plot could be reduced to corresponding developments of the idea; and the agent or scene under the aegis of which a given step was enacted could be said to represent personally the motivational principle of that step. The plot is unnoticeably ultimate, as the reader need not "choose between" different phases of its unfolding, but by going through each becomes prepared for the next. Ultimate vocabularies of motivation aim at the philosophic equivalent of such narrative forms, with a series of steps that need not precede one another in time, but only "in principle," though the formal appeal in the Marxist dialectic of history seems to reside in the fact that, as with narrative, the series in time is also a series "in principle."

"Sociology of Knowledge" vs. Platonic *"Myth"*

Karl Mannheim's project for a "sociology of knowledge," as discussed in his *Ideology and Utopia,* might be described as a methodology that aims at the neutralizing and liberalizing of the Marxist rhetoric. When viewed from the standpoint of the distinction between positive, dialectical, and ultimate terminologies, it seems to go beyond the purely parliamentary kind of dialectic, yet to fall somewhat short of an ultimate order. We might improvise a term, and call it "pro-ultimate." For it would move towards a gradual increase of precision, got by an exact study of the relationship between the positive and dialectical orders.

At least, that is how we would interpret Mannheim's distinction between "relativism" and "relationism." "Relativism" would merely recognize the great variety of ideological perspectives, would describe them in their diversity, and at best would look for workable compromises among them. But "relationism" should be able to build up an exact body of knowledge about ideologies by studying the connection between these ideologies and their ground.

To this end, Mannheim generalizes the Marxist exposure of "mystification" to the point where it becomes the "unmasking" of *any* doctrinal bias. That is, a human terminology of motives is necessarily partial; accordingly, whatever its claims to universal validity, its "principles" favor the interests of some group more than others; and one may look to opposing theorists for discoveries that "unmask" the partisan limitations lurking in speciously "universal" principles.

Any such "unmasking" of an ideology's limitations is itself made from a limited point of view. But each such limited perspective can throw light upon the relation between the universal principles of an ideology and the special interests which they are consciously or unconsciously made to serve. Each point of view could thus reveal something about the relation between an ideology (we might call it a systematized verbal act) and its nonverbal conditions (the scene of that act).

One might thus use rhetorical partisanship for dialectical operations that led towards a body of exact knowledge about the relation between all ideologies and the conditions of living out of which they arise. And by this method, the specialist in such analysis should also be able to discount the partiality of his own position somewhat (a transcending of partiality to which competing specialists might contribute, by unmasking the undetected partiality of their colleagues, thereby making it possible to work steadily towards an increase in the exactitude of ways for discounting bias in views that had seemed to be universally valid). The lore gradually accumulated by such procedures would constitute a "sociology of knowledge."

Only if all the returns were in, could one lay claim to an ultimate order here. But the project for thus systematically utilizing both rhetorical and dialectical elements in the search for an ever closer approximate to absolute knowledge about the nature of "ideologies," would clearly be much nearer to an "ultimate" order than a mere relativistic study of opinions and their background would be. "Relativism" would be hardly more than the first preparatory positivistic research needed to provide the material for the dialectical discipline of "relationism."

In such a project, of course, Marxism would be but one voice among many. And the edges are so knocked off the Marxist definition of ideology that Marxism too becomes analyzable as an ideology. That is, whatever its pretensions to an ultimate vocabulary, as seen from the standpoint of a "sociology of knowledge" it becomes but one step, however important, in the development from the overemphasis and underemphasis of partiality towards a perfectly balanced vocabulary which the systematic use of rhetorical and dialectical operations has wholly discounted for partisanship.

In one sense, "Utopias" are but a special case of ideologies. Specifically, the Utopian bias is progressive, futuristic, whereas the ideological bias is conservative or reactionary, designed to maintain a *status quo* or to reinstate an earlier social order. But Mannheim also seems to employ the term "ideology" in a more general sense, to include both kinds. This shifting of usage is made all the more necessary by the fact that changing historical conditions can change the function of a perspective, so that terms once progressive in their implications can become conservative. However, we would want to add our contention that, if you could analyze a structure of terms fully and closely enough, you should be able to discover by purely internal analysis when such a change in quality occurred, and you would not have to rely simply upon knowledge of the different uses to which the terms had been put in the two different eras.

But there may be another element hidden in the idea of Utopia, as it figures in Mannheim's book. There are good reasons to believe that this "sociology of knowledge" owes some of its appeal, above the general run of sociological works, to a wholly unsociological cause.

It grounds its analysis in the study of chiliastic doctrines, and for all its unwieldiness it never quite loses the resonance of this mythic anecdote. We thus have more the *feel* of an ultimate order than would be the case if the approach were strictly sociological. One can even discern here the elements, broken and reassembled, of a Platonic dialogue.

As written by Plato, the work would probably have proceeded thus: First, the setting up of several voices, each representing a different "ideology," and each aiming rhetorically to unmask the opponents; next, Socrates' dialectical attempt to build a set of generalizations that transcended the bias of the competing rhetorical partisans; next, his vision of the ideal end in such a project; and finally, his rounding out the purely intellectual abstractions by a myth, in this case the chiliastic vision. The myth would be a reduction of the "pure idea" to terms of image and fable. By the nature of the case, it would be very limited in its range and above all, if judged literally, it would be "scientifically" questionable.*

But insofar as the Platonic dialogue lived up to its pretensions, the bias of this concluding myth would be quite different from the bias of the rhetorical partisans with which the discussion began. For the myth should not have emerged until such rhetorical or ideological bias had been dialectically transcended in terms of pure ideas. However, if you disregarded the steps by which the myth had been arrived at, you might find implicit in it much the same partiality and partisanship as was explicitly present in the opening statements of opposing "ideologies." The "myth" might then be said to represent a forward-looking partisanship, in contrast with the backward-looking partisanships of the "ideologies." And you could next scramble the elements of the dialogue, seeking to get a new dialectic by a method that transcended the partiality of both the ideologies and the myth.

There would be this difference lurking at the basis of one's dialectic: In the Platonic dialogue, the step from pure abstract ideas to imaginal myth had been simultaneously a step down and a step up. It was a step down, because it descended from the purity of abstractions to the impurity of images It was a step up, because it here introduced a new level of motivation, motivation *beyond* the ideas, not present in the dialectical reduction to pure ideas.

* In this chapter we are adapting for our purposes the account of Platonist transcendence given in *The Myths of Plato,* by J. A. Stewart.

However, a motivational problem arises, if you treat the mythic motive as on a par with the ideological motives. For you find that, if your method for eliminating all such bias were successful, it would deprive society of its primary motive power. For though bias is false promise, it is promise. Hence, if you eliminate bias (illusion) from men's social motives, where do you find an equally urgent social motive? Such appears to be the nostalgic problem which Mannheim, in the thoroughness of his scrambled "Platonic dialogue," finally confronts. For he explicitly asks himself where the zeal of human effort would come from, if it were not for the false promises of our Utopias. And he asks this, even as he aims by scrupulous method to destroy the zeal of such false promises, or mythic Utopian illusions.

His attempt is all the more justified by the fact that myths are not usually approached through the initiatory discipline of a Platonic dialogue. And insofar as they are taken literally, they do function as ideologies, hence require the kind of discounting provided by a "sociology of knowledge." But if you apply the same sociological methods to eliminate the bias from both ideologies and myth, the success of your method would necessarily transcend a sociological motivation. The mythic motive would differ from the ideological motives only insofar as it could survive the elimination of false ideological motives. But by the method of discounting prescribed for the "sociology of knowledge," it could not survive.

This is not to say that we would find fault with a method of sociological discounting as such. There is a fallacy here only if sociology is expected to provide the ultimate ground of motivation. Thus, the "pro-ultimate" nature of the sociological vocabulary should be interpreted as indigenous to the nature of sociology itself, which cannot figure ultimate motives, and but brings us to the edge of them. At that point, myth may become necessary for figuring motives not sociological at all, hence not grounded in either sociological error or sociological knowledge. And whereas such myths should always be discounted for their biased application, in a formal dialectic their nature as biased translations can be formally recognized at the start.

To review, the steps were, in sum:

1. Mutual exposure of imperfect ideas (ideas bound to the sensory image).

2. Socratic transcending of this partiality.

3. Socratic summarizing vision of the pure idea.

4. Translation of the pure idea into terms of the mythic image.

5. Whereupon enters Mannheim, who proposes to develop a "sociology of knowledge" by treating the first and last steps as though they were of the same nature. Hence, he would perfect a method for discounting the limitations of both ("unmasking" their bias).

6. But:

The step from 3 to 4 had not merely been a translation downward (an incarnation of the "pure idea" into the conditions of the mythic image). For the arrival at the level of pure ideas had been in itself but a *preparation*. It had prepared the understanding to confront a motive which, being *beyond* ideas, would not lend itself to statement in ideas. Only by going from *sensory* images to ideas, then through ideas to the end of ideas, is one free to come upon the *mythic* image. True, such an ultimate motive would not be correctly stated in terms of image. But men have only idea and image to choose from. And the *disciplined arrival at the mythic image through the dialectical transcending of sensory images and the dialectical critique of ideas,* should be a protection against a merely literal interpretation of such a mythic image (as contrasted with the purely empirical or conceptual image that forms the positive ground of dialectical operations).

But though the mythic image had thus figured a motive beyond ideas of reason, in treating the ultimate mythic image as though it were in the same order with the competing ideologies you would find no further motivational element in it than you had found in the ideologies.

Or rather, the original qualitative distinction would now look at most like a distinction between forward-looking (Utopian) and backward-looking ideologies. Hence, insofar as you correct the bias of both ideology and myth (Utopia), you rob yourself of a motive. But of course, if the myth had been interpreted as *figuring a motive beyond the reach of ideology,* the motive of the myth would be felt to *lie beyond the motivational order treated in the competing ideologies.* Its motive would be "ultimate," as the motives of the ideologies were not. True: the fact is that the myths in their heyday *are* taken literally, without the preparatory discipline of Socratic criticism—and to this extent they do lend themselves to admonitory analysis as ideologies. But only a "philosophy of the myth" (and the Platonist dialectic might be called that) could reveal their true nature, in figuring a motive beyond sociological knowledge, a movement from and towards a real and ultimate universal ground.

"Mythic" Ground and "Context of Situation"

You may hold that there is no essential difference between sensory image and mythic image. And both may be treated merely as rhetorical reënforcements of ideas. Hence, all three would be "ideological," in the sense that, where they gain social currency in formal expression, they can be shown to represent the particular perspective of some more or less limited group, to sanction special interests in terms of universal validity. And Mannheim's treatment does seem to proceed on this basis.

However, if you take the Platonic form at face value, analyzing it simply in terms of dialectical structure, you find there an ultimate order whereby ideas would transcend sensory images, and mythic images would in turn transcend ideas. The final stage would be reached through a moral and intellectual development, through processes of discipline and initiation. Such formal preparation would enhance the persuasiveness of the doctrine; hence it requires our attention as a rhetorical device even where we distrust its claims.

In the sense that discursive reason is dialectical, the mythic image may be treated as figuring a motive that transcends reason. It may also make claims to be "religious," since it presumably represents man's relationships to an ultimate ground of motives not available for empirical inspection.

Various possibilities thus present themselves. We can get esthetic myths (in the Hart Crane manner), idealistic and autoerotic. And inasmuch as any "unconscious" motive can be equated with the divine (if only because both are beyond the realm of discursive reason), the "esthetic" myth can become a substitute for the "religious" myth.

We need not try to decide here the extent to which this confusion may be justified. Suffice it to note that, in accordance with many puns about weapons, a "mythic" figure of the "religious gunman" might stand for many ambiguous or "unconscious" sexual motives. Also, a recondite style could itself be simultaneously an "enigmatic" confession of guilt and a symbolic claim of preferment. This preferment would be "spiritual," as compared with hopes for strictly material advantage. And since public acceptance of the stylized and enigmatic confession would be a roundabout exoneration of the poet, there would be ethically motivated courtship here too. It is easy to see why any images thus rich in implications would be felt as transcendentally "mythical" rather than as nakedly sensory.

Thus, often now, with the esthetic myth, image may be taken to so transcend idea that the mere intrusion of idea is resented. Consider how many readers, for instance, have objected to the doctrine of beauty in the last stanza of Keats's "Ode on a Grecian Urn." Or recall the similar disgruntlement with the "moral" that terminates "The Rime of the Ancient Mariner." The resistance is probably due in large part to the fact that idea, rather than mythic image, becomes the final stage in the unfoldment. And other kinds of analysis are needed, to make such an "ultimate" acceptable.

As regards Keats's line, we have an uneasy hunch that it contains an "enigmatic" meaning. And this meaning, if we are right, could best be got by "joycing," that is, by experimentally modifying both "beauty" and "truth" punwise until one found some tonal cognates that made sense, preferably obscene sense, insofar as the divine service to beauty may, with a poet who has profoundly transformed the Christian passion into the romantic passion, be held in an *ecclesia super cloacam*. A combination of pudency and prudence has long prevented us from disclosing how we would translate this Orphic utterance. (However, to give an illustration of the method, we would say that *one* of the meanings we quickly discern in "beauty" is "body," while "truth" could be joyced meaningfully by a metathesis of two letters and the substitution of a cognate for one of the consonantal sounds.)

As for Coleridge's "moral": In his romantic surrender, complicated as it was by identification with his drug, there was a point at which he rescued himself repeatedly, by a purely moralistic effort, or perhaps we should say, more accurately, by a *moralizing* effort. While this was acutely true of him, we trust that it is somewhat true of everyone, though the esthetic conventions of romanticism have usually demanded that the rational recovery from an obsessive imagery must not itself be represented in the work, but must be left to take care of itself outside the work.

But obviously, no matter how "mythic" a reference to the "ultimate" ground may be, it itself arose out of a temporal ground, available to sociological description. In this sense, it may represent such local interests as are disclosed by the Marxist analysis of "ideological mystification." Or we can use the attenuated, neutralized variant of such an approach in Mannheim's perspectivism. Or for a still more generalized form of analysis, on the positive level, we can use the concept of "context of situation," as explained and developed in Bronislaw Malinowski's essay on "The Problem of Meaning in Primitive Languages" (published as a supplement in Ogden and Richards' *Meaning of Meaning*).

Here the relation between the verbal act and its nonverbal scene is stated in a still more generalized form than in the Mannheim book, because Malinowski's anthropological approach lays a greater stress upon the elements of tribal homogeneity as they affect language, whereas Mannheim is concerned rather with a sophisticated technique for transcending strong elements of discord within society. The beginnings of social diversification are visible enough in the tribal culture Malinowski is studying; and its modes of livelihood already have sufficient division of labor, with corresponding social distinctions, to call for the use of magic (mystification) as a rhetorical device for maintaining unity of action in diversity of role. But the stress here is upon the analysis of language in its wholly collective aspect, rather than from the standpoint of the parliamentary agon.

Malinowski is describing a problem he encountered when attempting an English translation of some texts assembled in the course of his research among Polynesian tribes of New Guinea: "magical formulae, items of folk-lore, narratives, fragments of conversation, and statements of my informants." He found that there was no direct dictionary equivalent for much of this material. Hence, instead of translating by "inserting an English word for a native one," he found it necessary to describe the customs, social psychology, and tribal organization that were implicit in a given utterance.

To generalize this requirement, he proposed the expression, "context of situation" which, he says, indicates

> on the one hand that the conception of *context* had to be broadened and on the other that the *situation* in which words are uttered can never be passed over as irrelevant to the linguistic expression.

Malinowski applies the term to living, primitive, spoken languages, in contrast with the written documents of dead classical languages, where the records are "naturally isolated from any context of situation." For he holds that such documents are written "for the express purpose of being self-contained and self-explanatory." But we have already considered both Benthamite and Marxist concerns with such situational elements, even in sophisticated recorded utterance. And in a previously mentioned essay on "Rhetoric in the Middle Ages," Richard McKeon writes:

> When Peter Abailard assembled apparently contradictory texts in his *Sic et Non,* the rules for interpreting them which he set forth in the Prologue are developments of the rules elaborated by a long line of canon lawyers . . . and involve such directions as careful consideration of context, comparison of texts, specification of time, place, and person, determination of original cause of statement, differentiation of general measures from particular. Although this method led to a further step in the dialectical resolution of the contradictions, the method at this stage is rhetorical rather than dialectical.

Such canons of rhetorical discounting are obviously also concerned with extraverbal circumstances, as they figure in even formal and recorded utterance. They are the equivalent in scholastic terms for what Malinowski considers in anthropological terms; and they indicate wherein the principle of "context of situation" may apply to all linguistic expression.

Malinowski's anthropological (or ethnological) treatment of the matter is valuable as a kind of "scientific anecdote" for illustrating in the most general way the relation between verbal act and nonverbal scene. And since he is studying language as used pragmatically in primitive speech "to produce an action and not to describe one," his discussion is particularly useful for pedagogical purposes, to illustrate generally the rhetorical element in speech (as the Ogden and Richards chapter on "The Power of Words" does likewise).

All such rhetorical concerns with the extraverbal circumstances of a verbal act, treated as an aspect of its meaning, are in the positive order of vocabulary, and have their grounding in the conditions of sensory experience (the realm of sensory images and concepts). But they also deal with relations and situations—and since these often require highly rationalized interpretations, we here move towards the dialectical order. The various systematized theories as to just what important relationships and situations there are, particularly in the social and political realm, confront one another as competing orators, hence requiring either dialectical compromise or dialectical resolution by reduction to an ultimate order.

Also, it is worth noting that there is a technical sense in which any ground, not only the mythically ultimate, but even the positivistically sociological, could be treated as "transcending" the verbal act itself. For it is other-than-words—hence even a positivistic reduction of it must contain "mythic" elements to the extent that all verbal accounts are but "suggestive." Add now to this mystery of the unspeakable, the mystery symbolically engendered (when nature is perceived, for instance, through the hierarchic psychosis of the prevailing social order, which causes the things of nature to become emblematic of promises and deprivations not intrinsic to nature but derived secondarily from the relationships of property).

But though such considerations are needed when we begin to ask ourselves in what respects even the most purely pragmatic aspects of technology may be "mythic," we cannot be so exacting for ordinary purposes. Roughly, we could say that the Mannheim project for a sociology of knowledge seems representative of the ways in which modern liberal science would aim at the transcending of "ideology." And for purposes of illustrating the nature of rhetoric, without "invidious" attempt to decide which is better, we can contrast it with the method in a Platonic dialogue (taken as representative of the dialectical progress from rhetorical partisanship to resolution in an ultimate order). A "science" of social relations, to approach positive truth, would note the correlation between ideologies and positive terms designating the nonverbal conditions which the ideologies serve. It would strive thus to advance from opinion (rhetoric) to knowledge (considered as antithetical to rhetoric). And one might afterwards introduce a kind of rhetoric in the sense that vivid, appealing exposition (Cicero's *docere*) could be called rhetorical.

The dialectical method would also be rhetorical in this sense. But we may note its use of other rhetorical elements likewise: First, there is the rhetoric of the dramatic agon, the clash of the partisan rivals, each of whom seeks to overthrow the others; next, there is the rhetorical appeal of the dialectical resolution, the formal satisfaction that comes of transcending such conflicts by systematic means; and finally, there is the rhetoric of *enargeia,* as the New Vision, which transcended imagery, is reduced to terms that "bring it before our very eyes" (though clarity in this sense is not quite the same as the clarity of scientific exposition, since it would involve the use of a "mythic" image for figuring a motive beyond the realm of the empirical, whereas scientific exposition would use imagery but to make empirical knowledge itself more vivid).

For purposes of rhetorical analysis, we need not choose between these methods. We need only note just wherein the difference between them would lie, just how the rhetorical and dialectical ingredients operate in each. Furthermore, one cannot always expect to find the two thus so strictly opposed; any rounded statement of motives will probably have something of both, as we tried to indicate when considering the possible rhetorical function of the chiliastic anecdote in Mannheim's book.

Courtship

By the "principle of courtship" in rhetoric we mean the use of suasive devices for the transcending of social estrangement. There is the "mystery" of courtship when "different kinds of beings" communicate with each other. Thus we look upon any embarrassment or self-imposed constraint as the sign of such "mystery." Quite as Sappho's poem on the acute physical symptoms of love is about the *magic* of love (the beloved is "like a god"), so we interpret any variants, however twisted or attenuated, of embarrassment in social intercourse as sign of a corresponding mystery in communication.

If a woman of higher social standing ("a woman of refinement") were to seek communion by profligate abandonment among the "dregs of society," such yielding in sexual degradation could become in imagination almost mystical (a thought that suggests, from another approach, the strong presence of the Czarist hierarchy in Dostoevski's mysticism of the people). And a writer who gave particularized descriptions of sexual yielding under such conditions might fascinate in a way that mere "pornography" could not. The work might be prosecuted as pornography; but it would really embody (roundabout and in disguise) much the same rhetorical element as shapes the appeal of Shakespeare's *Venus and Adonis* (which treats of a hot-and-cold relation between persons of different classes, here figured as divine and mortal, while the real subject is not primarily sexual lewdness at all, but "social lewdness" mythically expressed in sexual terms).

ORDER

The thought makes one glimpse the possibility of hierarchic motives lurking behind forms of censorship that would supposedly prohibit only *sexual* indecency while permitting the free expression of *political* attitudes. And recalling the Puritan attitude towards the licentious manners of Restoration drama, we can question whether any revolutionary *political* cause can possibly get its full expression unless corresponding variants of it in *sexual* terms are likewise developed.

Ironically, since censorship, if given time enough, invariably defeats its ends, the damming of a revolutionary expression sexually may greatly contribute to the sturdiness of its expression politically. In this respect, for instance, consider Wilhelm Reich's gradual turn from Communist sympathies to ideas of "sexual revolution" that led him to renounce Marxist politics as reactionary. His comparative immunity as a "scientist" permitted him to avoid the laws here as Henry Miller's engaging "pornography" could not, though Miller got the same immunity by publishing in English in France. Both men might be taken as evidence of the ways in which concentration upon "sexual revolution" can weaken the fervor of political revolution. But the political implications of sexual imagery would not stop at this point. For, in a subtler sense, all such terminologies may contribute ultimately to the same broad social and political changes.

But returning to the factor of embarrassment, we could say that any kind of "stage fright" is evidence of social mystery. Thus the coy relations between performer and audience show endless variants of mystification. Consider Thomas Mann's "Death in Venice" or "Mario and the Magician," for instance. And the paradigm perhaps would be the courtship of the *Arabian Nights* sort, where the narrator and author, across their social gulf, have a kind of fascination for each other. (Was there ever a culture where the powers of magic were more clearly associated with social hierarchy than the Arabian?) In "Death in Venice" the artist-audience relation is subtly interwoven with courtship between youth and age as classes; in "Mario and the Magician" the social mystery has strongly political connotations.

A ruler who would put people at their ease would do so at his cost, unless he could still somehow manage to glow in the light of his office, being at once both a "good fellow" and "standoffish." (Falstaff's relations to Prince Henry derive piquancy from the subtle intermingling of these two principles.) And we know of teachers who, assigned to interview students, have not been above exploiting the "mystery" (of the class distinction between teacher and taught) by maintaining an awesome silence, except for brief oracular questions that seem to be probing into the very depths of things, until the disconcerted student strives uneasily to fill every gap in the conversation, and comes away thinking this has been an audience with the Buddha. If one has little to say, by this device he can give the impression of leaving whole volumes unsaid.

"Glamour" is now a term, in the world of publicity, for mystery. And recalling the rigid mysteries of caste that seem essential for infusing free people with rigidly militaristic motives, we glimpsed the scope of the term in one political dopester's assertion that, with General Eisenhower's refusal to run for the presidency, the campaign had lost much of its "glamour." *

On the subject of post-hypnotic suggestion, it is said that people can be hypnotically induced to commit minor offenses after they have awakened (as were the hypnotist to suggest that the hypnotized, after coming out of the hypnotic spell, slap a certain person's face when the phone rings, an injunction that the patient might carry out in obedience to the suggestion, possibly even offering some attempt at a rational explanation for his behavior). But the patient's resistance to such suggestions increases with the gravity of the offense, so that the suggestion to commit highly reprehensible things, such as murder, would not be followed. Now, army discipline must be strong enough in its suggestiveness to produce a kind of "post-hypnotic spell" wherein people will do even the vilest of things, if they have been so commanded. Of course, the sanction of conspiracy helps in this task somewhat. But the conspiracy itself

---

* It is worth dwelling on the meanings of this term, for they clearly indicate an instinctive popular recognition of a hierarchic motive that affects the very nature of perception, endowing objects with a radiance due to their place in the social order. According to Webster's, the word may be a corruption of "gramarye," which means necromancy, magic. (The relation between grammar and magic doubtless goes back to the days when the knowledge of reading and writing was in itself a strong mark of status, because of the cleric's role in civil and religious administration.) The word is also thought to be connected with an Icelandic word for weakness of sight, while Icelandic *glamr* is a name for the moon, and of a ghost. Four meanings for "glamour" are given: a charm affecting the eye, making objects appear different from what they are; witchcraft, magic, a spell; a kind of haze in the air, causing things to appear different from what they really are; any artificial interest in, or association with, an object, through which it appears delusively magnified or glorified.

cannot attain its full magic unless strongly reënforced by the mystery of caste, particularly in the case of a regular army, where the lower ranks have no strong political cause to motivate their actions, but are guided primarily by the *esprit de corps* as manifested in the commands of their superiors.

Thus we doubt whether there is anything but deception in the idealistic hope of having a "democratic" army that would dispense with the offensiveness of military caste. Caste *is* the motive of military discipline as such. Without caste, one might fight for a good cause. But such would not be the motive of the army man as such. The true army man fights when he is told. It is the "glamour" of caste alone that makes him ready to subordinate his will to the will of an institution. Thus, army men will constantly sabotage attempts to "democratize" the army; for an army is in essence not democratic, but Prussian, and they instinctively know it. (We should also recognize the morality of the many purely technical operations here, as with the occupational hierarchy needed for flying a large plane. But though these modes of activity are not essentially military at all, they require a kind of organization that makes them a distressingly perfect fit with the military pattern.)

The Mannheim book we have reviewed seems to pass over the rhetoric of courtship. But can we think of the hierarchic (bureaucratic) structure necessary for teaching scientific method and managing a scientific society, without finding there the conditions for a "rhetorical situation" that requires some "bourgeois," "socialist," or "technocratic" variant of courtliness? Mannheim thinks of intellectuals as a special class whose intellect is their capital. And having ignored the peculiarly Marxist analysis of mystification, Mannheim was not led to ask whether the division of labor, in making for occupational classes, might by the same token create the need for a rhetoric of courtly intercourse between these classes. Mannheim was as eager to overlook such possibilities as Marx was to deny them.

Mannheim seems to assume that a gradually perfected sociology of knowledge would *pari passu* eliminate the mystery of Teufelsdröckh's "Clothes." (We are improvising, since the subject is not discussed.) But at least insofar as the sociological discounting of partisan ideologies fell short of perfection, we assume that there would still be a need for the traditional function of rhetoric. Rhetoric remains the mode of appeal essential for bridging the conditions of estrangement "natural" to society as we know it (be it primitive, feudal, bourgeois, or socialist), with its reliance upon the devices of magic, pantomime, clothes, or pastoral.

Here again, in case you are abolitionist-minded, you can choose to maintain that such rhetoric would end if the "reign of natural science" were fully established. We cannot agree with you, particularly in view of the scientific mystery fiction that is vigorously on the rise. But agreement about the future is not necessary for the analysis of rhetoric as such. It is sufficient for our purposes to note the presence of mystery in works actually written, on the assumption at the very least that there would be a "strong tendency" for such modes of social intercourse to creep undetected into even the ideal "mystery-less" scientific society, unless men exercised a constant antirhetorical vigilance that would likewise call for exactly the same kind of inquiry as we are here undertaking. Believe, if you will, that social classes will be "abolished." Even so, at least grant that there will be a constant "temptation" for them to again arise. And insofar as there are such temptations, there are corresponding "temptations" to the rhetoric of "courtly intercourse" between classes.

"Socioanagogic" Interpretation of Venus and Adonis

For considering characteristic expressions of the courtly motive in literary works, Shakespeare's narrative poem, *Venus and Adonis,* is a good item to examine; for certain oddities in it, as a story of *sexual* courtship, make its implicit *social* identifications more available to our scrutiny.

What are the main elements to which we should reduce this poem of courtship? First, a sexually mature goddess ardently courts a sexually immature human male. He resists, saying that he is interested only in the hunt. However, the alternatives are not so great as they might at first seem. For he says, "I know not love . . . nor will not know it, unless it be a boar, and then I chase it"—and the boar's fatal attack upon him is described in imagery of love, thus:

> He ran upon the boar with his sharp spear,
> Who did not whet this teeth at him again,
> But by a kiss thought to persuade him there;
> And nuzzling in his flank, the loving swine
> Sheath'd unaware the tusk in his soft groin.

If, following the poet's leads, we treat the hunt and its hazards as a form of courting too, we find three major characters in this dramatic narrative, each of them at a different qualitative stage in the hierarchy of motives: a goddess ("sick-thoughted Venus"), a human ("rose-cheek'd Adonis" ... "the tender boy"), and an animal ("this foul, grim, and urchin-snouted boar"). Would it then be excessive to say that each of these major figures in the action is of a different "class"?

There are two subsidiary characters, the "breeding jenny" and Adonis' "trampling courser." At the very least they serve a vital rhetorical function: they amplify the theme of courtship, repeating it by analogy, as Venus' ardor is duplicated in the stallion's. They also provide a dramatic comment, since their relationship contrasts Adonis' real coldness with the mare's coy eagerness (which is described in terms of human coquetry, as "outward strangeness" that only "seems unkind"). Perhaps we already have enough to account for the episode of the "palfrey's" courtship, particularly if we add a matter of mere business, that the loss of his horse makes it more explainable why Adonis, despite his disgruntlement, does not leave while Venus is wearying him with her attentions.

However, there may be more here. For Adonis and his horse may be considered parts of one motivational cluster; and Venus, as the principle of love, must be acting upon the mare, and through the mare, even though her suit of Adonis is frustrate. This amorous horse is an "unback'd breeder"—and a horse's power is not under completely rational control if it has escaped from its human master, and in erotic ardor will not obey him. At the very least we might say that the narrative here acts out a metaphor, is a figure for unbridled passion. Or, assuming still more accuracy in the poem's symbols, we might ask whether Adonis' horse, as proxy for Adonis, can be so zestful precisely because he has escaped from his master (the important clue here being in the stanza where he "breaketh his rein"). Then the moral could be: In the total cluster of motives comprising both Adonis and his horse, there is a heterosexual ardor that is lacking to Adonis alone. And this ardor is present only when the animal appetites alone are active, having escaped from such influences as would characterize the motives of the horse's human ("rational") master.

What, then, might be the motives that deterred Adonis with regard to the goddess, in contrast with the horse's eagerness to join with a mare?

At the sounds indicating that the hunt has begun, Venus in her fear for Adonis' safety runs through the bushes

> Like a milch doe, whose swelling dugs do ache,
> Hasting to feed her fawn hid in some brake.

And previously Venus had said to him,

> I'll be a park, and thou shalt be my deer;
> Feed where thou wilt, on mountain or in dale:
>> Graze on my lips, and if those hills be dry,
>> Stray lower, where the pleasant fountains lie.

Similarly, elsewhere he yields to her caresses "like the froward infant still'd with dandling."

The maternal connotations of these figures, along with the many establishing Adonis as "unripe," give one cause to believe that, so far as concerns the male motives *underlying* the conception of this poem, Venus is to Adonis as mother is to child. Hence, the boy's appetites are centered upon a kind of venery better suited to the "incest tabu." And he acts in accordance with the traditional shifts between the courting of women and the hunting of game. (Consider, for instance, the heart-hart pun near the opening of *Twelfth Night;* or we might note a doctrinal equivalent for this conceit in Rousseau's tract on education, where he advises that Emile's early sexual stirrings be quieted and deflected by the hunt; and in *Sir Gawain and the Green Knight,* to the quest of game and of woman the appetite for food is added, so that, though courtship is spiritualized beyond possibility of sensual fulfillment, there is compensation in the avid pursuit of quarry and the gorgeous banqueting.)

A failure to make the dissociation between the two "kinds" of woman (maternal and erotic) could account for the vaguely homosexual terms that define Adonis' relation to the boar. (The terms are not unmistakably homosexual; for they occur in outcries of Venus, who might properly be expected to take a feminine view of the male's erotic motives.) We have already quoted the most explicit passage of this sort, which might even allow for orgastic connotations of dying (the *Liebestod* ambiguity), as Adonis' groin fatally becomes a sheath for the boar's tusk. If this interpretation is correct, Adonis' death would include, in the one symbol, a guilty yielding and the tragic retribution (such merging of opposites as makes for the most effective kind of symbol), while the death would further serve as tragic dignification of the guilty "cause." Also, we could explain why Adonis' horse, as proxy for Adonis, by lacking some of Adonis' rational or heady motives could be completely heterosexual in his appetites, whereas Adonis was not. The homosexual motive and the problem of the mother would be part of a single moral complex in Adonis; but this complex would not bind the appetites when they have only their riderless, or headless simplicity, as in the horse.

However, our major concern is to discuss the poem in terms of *hierarchy*—and we have considered the mother-son implications merely to get them recognized and cleared away, lest their unformulated presence keep the reader from following another line of explanation. We want now to develop from the observation that goddess, boy, and boar represent three different motivational *classes*.

Recall again Spinoza's seminal formula, *Deus sive Natura*. Here, by a grammatical function, the conjunction "or," Spinoza provides a bridge between two realms of motives. Similarly Carlyle used an image for such a function, his figure of "Clothes," which served to make a communicative bridge between reverence for the divine and reverence for secular highness. Considering the two realms, with or without pontification, we can note these various terminological possibilities: terms in the celestial order alone; terms in the social order alone; terms that avowedly bridge the two realms; terms explicitly celestial but implicitly social; terms explicitly social but implicitly celestial; terms speciously social but actually celestial; terms speciously celestial but actually social. The last five could all be treated as variants of the bridging principle (which is, under another guise, the principle of *identification*).

The "celestial" here need not be a very high order of godhead. Any term for supernatural motivation (be it justified or not) would meet the requirements. Thus we could include under this head even the "preternatural" figures, Peter Quint and Miss Jessel, that symbolize the "spirit" of the motivation in Henry James's ghost story, "The Turn of the Screw." And especially, in accordance with our previous consideration of "mystery" and "mystification," we should be on the lookout for occasions when expressions for motives on their face "divine" are better explained as stylizations of motives belonging to the social hierarchy.

And would not the Venus of Shakespeare's *Venus and Adonis* be better explainable in social terms than theologically? Though she is nominally a goddess courting a mortal, no one would think seriously of reading the poem as he might read a mystic nun's account of courtly intercourse between her and the Celestial Bridegroom, nor as theologians interpret the Canticles. Venus is not a "goddess" in any devout sense. She is a distinguished person compelled to demean herself by begging favors of an inferior. Viewing the poem from this standpoint, judging by its courtly style, and getting stray hints through its imagery, we would take the underlying proportion to be: goddess is to mortal as noblewoman is to commoner. The "divine" attributes here are but those of social preferment. This would be a "fustian" goddess, though she stands somewhat "enigmatically" for an aspect of noble status in general rather than for any particular noblewoman.

We do not intend to plead for a set of perfect correspondences, based on this substitution of social superiority for "divinity." If hard pressed, one could work out such an interpretation. Venus would stand for the upper class, Adonis for the middle class, the boar for the lower classes (as seen through middle-class eyes using courtly spectacles). The horses might represent the potent aspect of the middle class, though ambiguously noble (like all love-making, because of its "divine" elation). The figure of the boar could, roundabout, identify the lower classes with the dregs, with moral evil. In this particular poem the boar (hence the lower classes) could be the evil embodiment of the homosexual offense that seems involved in Adonis' unresponsiveness. Or it could stand for offensiveness generally; and in accordance with the usual workings of the scapegoat mechanism, offensiveness which is situate within is hunted without, so that there is odd intercourse between hunter and hunted. We say so much, to show how a "socioanagogic" interpretation might be filled out, if one were hard pressed.

But we would settle for much less. We would merely contend that one should view this poem in terms of the hierarchic motive, or more specifically, in terms of the *social order,* as befits any inquiry into the rhetoric of *courtship*. Whereupon we should lay much stress upon the notable inversion whereby a superior is depicted begging favors of an inferior. And we would not let the brilliance of the erotic imagery blind us to the underlying pattern here, a pattern in which the erotic enigmatically figures, but which "in principle" is not erotic at all, at least in the narrowly sexual sense of the term. (Our stand would be different if you widened the term to include dialectical motives in general, a realm of ultimate principle, as with the Socratic erotic.)

Looking at the poem "socioanagogically," we would now lay stress upon lines that might otherwise be lost beneath the imagery of ardent wooing. Thus, we note that Adonis is "forc'd to content, but never to obey." Or Venus says,

> What bargains may I make, still to be sealing?
> To sell myself I can be well contented,
> So thou wilt buy and pay and use good dealing.

Or when she forebodingly sees the hounds bleeding from their encounter with the boar,

> Look, how the world's poor people are amaz'd
> At apparitions, signs, and prodigies,
> Whereon with fearful eyes they long have gaz'd,
> Infusing them with dreadful prophecies;
> > So she at these sad sighs draws up her breath,
> > And, sighing it again, exclaims on Death.

Venus is here belittled astronomically, a "goddess" looking at premonitions of Adonis' death like "the world's poor people" staring at the heavens. The passage continues a theme of apotheosis (with Adonis meteorologically exalted) that was introduced at the moment when Adonis finally abandoned her. Coleridge made much of the passage, Richards reminds us, as an instance of "imagination":

> Look, how a bright star shooteth from the sky,
> So glides he in the night from Venus's eye.

Here is signalized a New Order, in which not Venus but Adonis is celestial. The passive superiority he had possessed, in his indifference to her, here blazes into an act. His cult of acquisition (as huntsman) is raised to the very heavens.

To see such developments as dominantly sexual is indeed to be sex-ridden. Rather, one should scrutinize them for certain *principles* of courtship, a *social* manifestation, which by the same token figures a *hierarchic* motive. The vocabularies of social and sexual courtship are so readily interchangeable, not because one is a mere "substitute" for the other, but because sexual courtship is intrinsically fused with the motives of social hierarchy.

Thus, when this poem is viewed "socioanagogically," it will be seen to disclose, in enigmatically roundabout form, a variant of revolutionary challenge. By proxy it demeans the old order, saying remotely, in sexual imagery, what no courtly poet could have wanted to say, or even have thought of saying, in social or political terms. Yet as evidence that the poet had such qualified reversals on his mind, note how the work ends, on Venus' prophecy of a topsy-turvy world where love (among its other turbulent conditions)

> ... shall be sparing and too full of riot,
> Teaching decrepit age to tread the measures;
> The staring ruffian shall it keep in quiet,
> Pluck down the rich, enrich the poor with treasures;
>   It shall be raging mad and silly mild,
>   Make the young old, the old become a child.
>
> It shall be cause of war and dire events,
> And set dissension 'twixt the son and sire;
> Subject and servile to all discontents,
> As dry combustious matter is to fire. ...

Granted: We here come upon paradoxes that lead back into ultimate problems of motives, rooted in situations beyond or prior to social hierarchy. The indeterminately dialectical and natural grounds whereby certain motives readily become convertible (as with relations between love and the hunt, or between sexual appetite and food) seem to be epitomized in the transformations of Venus, as with the antinomian yet intimate relation between love and war. (In the poem the principles are sexualized, as a marriage between Venus and Mars, a love match that is itself a kind of war, as Venus says that Mars was "servile" to her "coy disdain.") We grant that the motivation behind the reversals on which the poem ends could not be exhaustively discussed in terms of social order alone. Yet the ultimate motives, whatever they may be, get poignancy and direction from the social order (that is, from the social hierarchy), so far as the medium of their formal artistic expression is concerned. And we may fittingly note that the poem does not arrive at this prophecy of upheaval until Adonis has died for his affront (an affront which, while involving a principle of social reversal, was stated in terms suited to a pre-Reichian kind of "sexual revolution").

In his *De Vulgari Eloquentia,* Dante selects love, valor, and welfare (*Venus, Virtus, Salus*) as the three themes worthy of heroic verse. Clearly this poem, though somewhat perversely, meets Dante's requirements. Perhaps all three could be reduced to some one recondite ultimate term. But as regards social motives, note that the poem hinges about a question of pride. The jenney (in this poem the paradigm of a woman wooed normally, as judged by courtly standards of those times) is "proud, as females are, to see him woo her." The palfrey, having broken loose, was "proud" in his freedom from the master's constraint. Such pride obviously reflects fluctuant relations of inferiority and superiority (concerns the hierarchic motive, quite as in the myths of the celestial revolt). Thus, subtly, if you grant that her "divinity" is more social than celestial, Venus has been unsexed, that is, outclassed. The class she represents has given up its austere status. Its courtly devices have become suspect. Adonis says to her, "I hate not love, but your device in love."

We do not assume that the poem's concealment of a social allegory in a sexual enigma was consciously contrived. True, scholars who favor the "fustian" theory are tirelessly examining pure poetry for evidence of disguised allusions to prominent contemporary personages. But even where such allusions were deliberately inserted by poets and discerned by readers, such tactics would not argue deliberateness in the sort of expression we are here studying. These identifications can be implicit, and "unconscious."

To get at the sort of thing we are here considering, one must first reject all speculations in keeping with the typical empiricist question: "What do I see when I look at this object?" A poetic observation involves no naked relation between an observed object and the observer's eye. The topics that the poet uses are "charismatic." They glow. You may argue that the medievalist was wrong when he anagogically interpreted the poet's image as a concealment that enigmatically figured the mysteries of the celestial hierarchy. But by combining Marx and Carlyle, with hints from Empson, we should at least see how right the medievalist was in his conviction that the poet's symbols *are* enigmatic, that they stand for a *hidden* realm, a *mystery* (though its "divinity," like that of the Roman Emperor or "Pontifex Maximus" of a secular realm, may be derived from a social hierarchy).

Even the world of natural objects, as they figure in poetry, must have secret "identification" with the judgments of status. (Thus, music and leisure by the sea are profoundly mood-laden, bringing as they do the culminations of social order to confront the abyss of an ultimate order.) The veil of Maya is woven of the strands of hierarchy—and the poet's topics glow through that mist. By "socioanagogic" interpretation we mean the search for such implicit identifications. Though admitting that one can go far wrong in the particular here, we would insist that such analysis is demanded "in principle." The poet's symbol *is* enigmatic, and its enigma *does* derive from its bearing upon "mystery," which in turn is a hierarchic experience, as thinkers in the strongly hierarchized middle ages clearly understood. Marxists today, when under a cloud, call their criticism "sociological," thus fusing it with a modern liberalist science. But what of the relations to an earlier medieval pattern of thought, polemically rediscovered in Marx's theory of "mystification"? "Socioanagogic" interpretation would seem to be the name for the Marxist insight, if one sought a "neutral" approach midway between Marx's rage against "mystification" and Carlyle's adulation of "mystery."

The four medieval kinds of interpretation are defined in the first question, articles eight and nine, of Aquinas' *Summa Theologica,* where Aquinas distinguishes three "spiritual" meanings in addition to the literal meaning. The literal meaning of Scripture is not in the figure, but in that which is figured. For instance, with a metaphor like "God's arm," the literal sense would be "God's operative power." Of the three spiritual senses: Insofar as the Old Law is said by Christians to figure the New Law, the interpretation of the Old Testament becomes "allegorical"; insofar as the acts of Biblical persons are said to provide a model of conduct for all men, the sense is "moral" or "tropological"; and the sense is anagogical insofar as the things of Scripture "signify what relates to eternal glory."

Since we are looking for elements of "social mystery" rather than of "celestial" mystery, hence our term, "socioanagogic." The new equivalent of "moral" or "tropological" criticism would probably be found in a concern with the poem as a ritual that does things for the writer and reader: re-forming, stabilizing, heartening, purifying, socializing, and the like. Any sense in which one order is interpreted as the sign of another would probably be the modern equivalent of the "allegorical." For instance, our psychoanalytic interpretation of Venus as mother; or a flat equating of Venus, Adonis, and the boar with three different social classes. Allegorical and moral senses lead into the socioanagogic insofar as the emphasis is placed upon the hierarchic mystery (the principle of secular divinity, with its range of embarrassment, courtship, modified insult, standoffishness, its possible meteorological dignifications, its scenic embodiment in the worldly equivalent of temples, ritual vestments, rare charismatic vessels, and the like). In brief, the socioanagogic sense notes how the things of books and of the book of Nature "signify what relates to worldly glory."

The scholastics had this jingle for distinguishing the four senses:

> *Littera gesta docet; quid credas allegoria;*
> *Moralis quid agas; quo tendas anagogia.*

The notion of trend, tendency, direction as the distinctive element of the anagogic in itself suggests how the concept of anagoge could be secularized.

The Paradigm of Courtship: Castiglione

Perhaps the best text for our purposes is *The Book of the Courtier,* by Baldassare Castiglione, a contemporary of Machiavelli, and like him concerned with the principles of the Prince. By its gradations, it builds a ladder of courtship dialectically, into a grand design that, in its ultimate stage, would transcend the social mystery, ending Platonically on a mystic, mythic vision of celestial mystery. The work is usually studied as a handbook of manners, or book of etiquette, which had a strong influence on the courtly style of Elizabethan poets. But we would stress rather its nature as a series of formal operations for the dialectical purifying of a rhetorical motive. When viewed thus formally, it is seen to contain a range of persuasiveness usually found but in fragments. And by observing its various kinds of persuasion thus brought together in a unity, we can better detect their significance where they are found only in fragments.

The book tells of four dialogues that supposedly took place on four successive evenings at the Court of the Duke of Urbino, in 1507. The duke being absent, the conversations are held in the presence of the duchess. A dozen members of the court participate in the dialogue. At first they talk of discussing, as a "pastime," the "sweet disdains" that the lover suffers "in the person beloved"; but it is finally decided "to shape in words a good courtier, specifying all such conditions and particular qualities, as of necessity must be in him that deserveth this name."

The first book lists the major endowments which the perfect courtier must have. Here are such items as noble birth, good fortune, skill at arms, good horsemanship, gracefulness, ability to "laugh, dally, jest, and dance," to speak and write well, to play musical instruments (particularly since at court the women's "tender and soft breasts are soon pierced with melody, and filled with sweetness"); the courtier should also be accomplished in drawing and painting (one speaker remarks that in Greece painting had been "received in the first degree of liberal arts, afterwards openly enacted not to be taught to servants and bondmen").

Objections are raised to some of these points. For instance, one speaker having said that the courtier should consider arms the most important thing of all, with "the other good qualities for an ornament thereof," Cardinal Peter Bembo replies that arms and all other gifts should be considered "an ornament of letters," letters being "in dignity so much above arms, as the mind is above the body." Cardinal Bembo's position will come into its own at the end of Book IV. Meanwhile, we need note only that the courtier's endowments are preëminently those of *appeal* (to this extent being rhetorical in essence); and, in keeping, his prime motive is to be "glory," a strongly addressed motive, that seeks to live in the good opinion of others.

The first dialogue closes with "every man taking his leave reverently" of the duchess.

In the second book, the rhetorical motive becomes still more obvious. This chapter deals with the tactics of address, the art of appearing to best advantage. Thus, when the courtier is "at skirmish, or assault, or battle upon the land, or in such other places of enterprise," he should "work the matter wisely in separating himself from the multitude." Whatever "notable and bold feats" he does, he should undertake them "with as little company as he can, and in the sight of noble men that be of most estimation in the camp, and especially in the presence and (if it were possible) before the very eyes of his king or great personage he is in service withal; for indeed it is meet to set forth to the show things well done."

Note that in this way of bearing witness, the courtier's relation to his social superior is as martyr to God, as writer to public, as actor to audience. Much that now goes under the name of "exhibitionism" might thus be placed as a species of the rhetorical motive. We recall a related maxim in La Rochefoucauld: *"Les véritables mortifications sont celles qui ne sont point connues; la vanité rend les autres faciles."* La Rochefoucauld is explicitly contrasting the pure rhetoric of religious appeal with the mere appeal to vanity. Mortifications *must* be witnessed; they are evidence, presented to an invisible divine audience. Martyrdom (bearing witness) is so essentially rhetorical, it even gets its name from the law courts. However, it is vanity when addressed not to the Absolute Witness, but to human onlookers. Martyrdom would be but a severe kind of "epideictic oratory," were it not for the supernatural witness which it postulates (the Christian persuasion being so essentially a rhetoric, that Cicero's thoroughness in rhetoric made him seem essentially Christian).

La Rochefoucauld was discussing a rhetorical situation where the testimony supposedly addressed to a supermundane principle was in actuality addressed to the *haut monde*. But *The Book of the Courtier* is discussing testimony explicitly addressed to a worldly principle. (With regard to the way in which the two realms rhetorically impinge upon each other, making social and religious reverence interchangable, we might recall an editor's reference to an early English book on manners instructing the youth to kneel on one knee before their worldly sovereign, on both knees to God. And when Edmund Burke said that European civilization depended "upon two principles—the spirit of a gentleman and the spirit of religion," his statement suggests the possibility that these "two principles" can be one principle named in two different orders of vocabulary. It is the magical confusion that allows spontaneously for the rhetorical use of religion as an instrument of politics, in keeping with the frank paganism of the old feudal expression, "your Worship.")

We thus confront three kinds of address: bearing witness to God, bearing witness to the sovereign, bearing witness to one's peers under the guise of bearing witness to God. If you bring them all together, and think of "glory" as both heavenly and courtly motive, do you not see the rhetorical ingredient in "conscience" itself, exacting a kind of conduct addressed to the ideal spirit of the community?

Conformism and hypocrisy would also be species of persuasion, but addressed to an audience not conceived in terms sufficiently universalized. And where the criminal seems "unconsciously" willing to be caught, need we assume that a motive of self-punishment, obedience to a self-imposed criterion of justice, leads him to place himself in jeopardy? Such a motive may be present. But can there not also be a more general motive, hence one "logically prior"? For he could be moved mainly by the rhetorical motive *per se,* the desire to bear witness, to address an audience, so that his transgression is an act of "martyrdom," and as such must be seen.

In the crime mysteries of Hollywood, the hierarchic motive (the magic of class relations) is concealed behind the images of private property in general. The cult of property as such (exemplified in reverse by infractions against the code) sometimes obscures the particular nature of property as class insignia. But the shift, by means of money, from low dives to expensive apartments and night clubs, is the basic pattern, along with quarrels over the ownership of "classy dames," while there is much display of the sort Veblen noted, as in the "distinction" of being served obsequiously. Display is felt as action only because it is felt as "mystery."

Under technology the division of labor requires a society of specialists serving one another. The garage man is the dishwasher's servant, and the dishwasher is the garage man's servant, an "invidious" relation made "democratic" by money and by the constant reversal of roles. Recalling the festival of the Roman Saturnalia, where master and servant changed places, we could describe our democracy as a kind of permanent but minute Saturnalia, with constant reversal in the relation between up and down. This is a strongly "irreverent" situation, as regards the mysteries of caste, except in the most generalized sense, as with quantitative, monetary tests of "quality." And the Hollywood crime mystery seems to be an answer to these conditions, giving full expression to the "free" or wayward impulses that go with so fluctuant a hierarchy, while at the same time profoundly reënforcing the hierarchic code at its most essentially capitalist point, the mystery of money as insignia of class distinction.

(We have wandered far from *The Book of the Courtier*. But we introduced Castiglione's work as a paradigm precisely for that purpose. So we should take any opportunity to depart from it. We want to draw the lines of inference from a clear textual example into areas where the same elements, though present, are transformed in keeping with changed conditions. Hence, we look to see what might be the equivalents of the courtly, or hierarchic relation in other modes of expression not usually considered in such terms. We can thus discern the presence of the same rhetorical, courtly motive in many varied transformations that on their face may seem disrelated; yet we need not say that they are all the same, since the very act of bringing them together helps make us aware of their specific differences.)

Returning to the dialogue itself, we should note that at this stage, in Book II, it is concerned mainly with courtly ways of appearing to good advantage. Thus, one speaker questions the propriety of wrestling with men of low social status, for if the man of noble rank wins, his gain is small, "and his loss in being overcome very great." There are warnings against too incessant a display of one's talent, as with those who, if they are good at music, speak as though they were on the verge of breaking into song, or as when you meet a fencer in the market place and he greets you with "a gesture as though he would play at fence." A useful ironic device is suggested for a courtier wearing a mask. Let him disguise himself as someone of inferior rank, such as an uncouth shepherd; then, if he performs superbly on horseback, the show will be doubly effective, since the horseman so greatly outstrips the expectations of the onlookers. The courtier is exhorted "to love and (as it were) to reverence the prince he serveth above all other things, and in his will, manners and fashions, to be altogether pliable to please him." (The transference of this principle from the courtier-sovereign relation to the relation between the courtier and world's judgment generally, is seen in the injunction "to use continually, and especially abroad, the reverence and respect that becometh the servant toward the master.")

The courtier is warned against asking favors for himself directly, lest they either be denied or, what is worse, granted with displeasure. And one eager "to purchase favor at great men's hands" should not "press into the chamber or other secret places where his Lord is withdrawn"; for when great men are alone, they often "love a certain liberty to speak and do what they please," and may resent being surprised. And if the courtier, engaged in important matters for his lord, happens to be "secretly in chamber with him," the courtier "ought to change his coat, and to defer grave matters till an other time and place," watching "that he be not cumbrous to him." The courtier should rather "look to have favor and promotion offered him, than crave it so openly in the face of the world, as many do." He should not be like those who, "if they happen to enter into favor, then passing a mean, they are so drunken on it, that they know not what to do for joy," and "are ready to call company to behold them, and to rejoice with them, as a matter they have not been accustomed withal."* For though a courtier should "esteem favor and promotion," he should not give the impression that he could not live without it, nor "show himself new or strange in it." On the other hand, he should not refuse it "as some, that for very ignorance receive it not, and so make men believe that they acknowledge themselves unworthy of it." The courtier should thus be neither too forward not too retiring but should always:

---

* We are quoting throughout from Sir Thomas Hoby's translation, but have modernized the spelling.

humble himself somewhat under his degree, and not receive favor and promotions so easily as they be offered him, but refuse them modestly, showing he much esteemeth them, and after such a sort, that he may give him an occasion that offereth them, to offer them with a great deal more instance.

The courtier should remember that favors and promotions, when received with modesty, seem to be more deserved—whereupon the speaker gives a Biblical parallel strong in hierarchic thought: "When thou art bid to a marriage, go and sit thee down in the lowest room, that when he cometh that bid thee, he may say, Friend come hither, and so it shall be an honor for thee in the sight of the guests." But we have cited enough to illustrate the "addressed" quality (hence the rhetorical element) in the courtier's ways, as they are treated in this opening section of Book II.

After a series of transitions, warning among other things against both rowdyism and the tendency to tell jokes at one's own expense, the chapter turns to another kind of address, making an almost systematic study of the things "which make men laugh," comic devices valued for their effect upon audiences (though no formal theater was needed since, in the pageantry of their self-absorbed society, the courtiers were audience for one another).

The cult of laughter is suited to the "courtly psychosis" on many counts: first, it is "liberal," befitting a class of freemen (the Rabelaisian motive); it is "humane," since only humans laugh (hence it is probably a function of "rationality," which confronts reality by the roundabout route of symbols). Impropriety can provoke laughter only because at one remove it reaffirms the very propriety it violates; and the explosive laughter of surprise is made possible by the sudden violation of expectancies—hence the "merry jest" could in a free way reaffirm the courtier's code. In displaying his sense of the "right" things to laugh at, the courtier thereby displayed the marks of his class. And in proving himself equal to the tests of merriment, he gave evidence that he was not being outclassed. While superiority to fools and boors draws strongly upon the hierarchic principle, it can readily couple such superiority with a sense of personal misgivings, through subterfuges whereby the laugher subtly identifies himself with the very victim to whom he is superior; for in laughter there can be a transcending of the distinction between laughing-at and laughing-with. Comedy is much more pronouncedly *addressed* than tragedy, as is evident from the ease with which the comedian on the stage can take the audience into his confidence without breaking the frame of the fiction, whereas in tragedy even an aside expressly inserted for the audience's benefit must be spoken rather as though the actor were talking to himself.

The "invidious" element in laughter could deflect into less serious channels all competition for the sovereign's favors. It could thus allow for a kind of solidarity among the courtiers as a professional class. It was like a fraternal meeting of business competitors, a commodity made all the stronger when members of a lower class were chosen as butt of the joke.

The discussion ends on the subject of the "merry prank," which we are told relies on the same "places" as the jest for its effect. Boccaccio's tales being cited as an example, we can thus glimpse behind them an appeal not just as stories, but as a mark of rank. And once the hierarchic relation is firmly established, the mystery can become so subtilized that, as the duchess says, smiling:

> It is not against good manner sometime to use merry pranks with great men also. And I have heard of many that have been played to Duke Frederick, to King Alphonsus of Aragon, to Queen Isabel of Spain, and to many other great Princes, and not only they took it not in ill part, but rewarded very largely them that played them those parts.

Where the irreverence of laughter is thus directed against the very Principle of Courtly Favor itself, it must be so carefully qualified that it signalizes reverence too—whereat the "sacrificial king" need not grow wrathful to restore his dignity, but is grand in exercising with good humor his powers of munificence.

The primary thing to note about *The Book of the Courtier,* from the standpoint of dialectic, is the great change in the quality of motivation that occurs as one turns from the third book to the last. The third book has some inklings of the final transcendence, since it deals with the code of courtly intercourse between men and women. It thus introduces the theme of sexual love which Cardinal Bembo will platonically transform at the ecstatic, sermonlike close of the work. But though there are occasional signs of a new stirring, in general men and women here confront each other as classes, considering questions of advantage, in a war of the sexes reduced to dance steps.

Book III begins with a recipe of traits deemed appealing in women, discusses such related matters as comparative prowess in feats of continence on the part of the two sexes; pathetic sorrow at loss of maidenhood due to forcing; situations that follow from the code of honor, one speaker saying, "in a thousand years I could not repeat all the crafts that men use to frame women to their wills"; and another, who has been complaining that women are cruel to him, is accused of using such complaints "as a certain kind of discretion," to "cloak the favors, contentations and pleasures" he had "received in love," and to assure other women that, if they reward him he will keep the secret. Among other things, the woman's code at court requires that, when invited to dance or play, like the courtier receiving favors, "she ought to be brought to it with suffering her self somewhat to be prayed"—and in innuendo, she should seem to miss the point.

In general, the chapter might have for its device this statement by Lord Cesar Gonzaga:

> Like as no Court, how great soever it be, can have any sightliness or brightness in it, or mirth without women, nor any Courtier can be gracious, pleasant or hardy, nor at any time take any gallant enterprise of Chivalry, unless he be stirred with the conversation and with the love and contentation of women, even so in like case, the Courtier's talk is most unperfect evermore, if the entercourse of women given them not a part of the grace wherewithall they make perfect and deck out their playing the Courtier.

And for the equating of love and war, we are told that "Who so could gather an army of lovers that should fight in the presence of the Ladies they love, should subdue the whole world, unless against it on the contrary part there were an other army likewise in love."

Through these first three books, though the quest of advantage has taken several forms, the motive of "reverence" has been kept within the realm of manners, as related to the sovereign and to the object of courtly sexual love. It has been manifested roundabout, through the perversities of the jest and the merry prank. And much has been said about the properties that make men and women appealing in courtly situations. We now turn to higher orders of persuasion. This fourth book is not less rhetorical than the other three. But the advantages to which it would persuade transcend those of the preceding chapters.

Fittingly, the change in the quality of motives is signalized at the start of the last book by a deathy note. Though the talks were supposedly held on four successive nights, as the author prepares to write out the record of the fourth discourse a "bitter thought" causes him to remember "that not long after these reasonings were had, cruel death bereaved our house of three most rare gentlemen, when in their prosperous age and forwardness of honor they most flourished."

The device is perhaps borrowed from Cicero, who uses it similarly to make the final section of his *De Oratore* more solemn. The justification for it seems greater in this case (in accordance with the puns whereby finality can mean either purpose or demise), since this concluding book is to deal with "the end ... of a perfect Courtier." It is to discuss the ultimate purpose of courtship. So, in introducing it with thoughts of great courtiers who have died, the author reënforces one kind of finality by topics belonging to the other kind (leads into the discussion of end in the philosophic sense through mention of end in the biologic sense). And we might even glimpse a subtler propriety in this opening talk of courtiers' deaths: henceforth the many variants of acquisitive advantage are to be abandoned for efforts more sacrificial.

Above the transitional matter, two themes stand out. The first concerns a rhetoric of *education,* considering the powers of the courtier as *informant* to the prince. In this context the courtier would be winsome for the advancement not of himself personally, but of human relations in general. He would seek ways whereby he can impart even unpalatable truths to his sovereign, "to dissuade him from every ill purpose, and to set him in the way of virtue," in contrast with those who, "to curry favor and to purchase good will," tell their lord only what he would most like to hear ("because among many vices that we see now a days in many of our Princes, the greatest are ignorance and self-liking," yet "there is no treasure that doth so universally hurt, as an ill Prince"). In sum: As the training in "pleasant fashions" is "the flower of Courtliness," so the fruit of it is in "the training and helping forward of the Prince to goodness, and the fearing him from evil."

For our purposes it is not necessary to consider the details of the argument, or even the theory of psychology that goes with it, beyond noting the customary identification of reason with authority: As reason rules over the affections of the body, so it "is chiefly requisite in Princes." The important consideration for our purposes is that this treatise on education grows out of the theories on courtship. Though, according to the hierarchic order in its perfection, the prince would rather be the exemplar for the courtiers, the unsettled nature of the times brought to the fore many princes new to the courtly tradition. Hence, the courtiers, as a special professional class, might find themselves in the role of educators to the prince, initiating him into the mysteries of their code. The situation is not unlike that of scientists today, who are hired to serve the interests of local financial or industrial sovereigns. As hirelings, they should be interested in the tactics of advancement; but as a class of scientific specialists, they represent, with varying degrees of honesty and obsequiousness, a purely professional interest in truth, not identical with the preferences of the "sovereign."

But there is a profounder connection here between courtship and education than derives from the accident of the times. It is an element inborn to the dialectic method itself, as we saw in the *Grammar* when considering the Socratic erotic, "loving" truth, beauty, and goodness pedagogically (a cult that had its variants of courtship, as with Socrates' gallantry when cajoling and enticing young men into the dialectical path of the Absolute).

The imagery of courtship in the Socratic education is to be interpreted mythically. Its primary motives are not positive, but dialectical. And education dialectically approached could not be reduced to sexual terms in the positivist sense. Nor, by the same token, could education dialectically approached be properly reduced to positivist terms of a mere job. It would have a mythic glow, as it would be a form of "pure persuasion," the rhetorical motive dialectically made ultimate. But it would gravitate about the imagery of courtship, since it would be a kind of courtship, as we can see in the *Phaedrus*. And variants of the same motive are seen in Castiglione's fourth book, where we are told that "to become the instructor of a Prince, were the end of a Courtier," quite as Aristotle and Plato "practiced the deeds of Courtiership, and gave themselves to this end, the one with the great Alexander, the other with the kings of Sicilia."

After the pages on the courtier as educator of the prince, by appropriate transitions the work rises to its exhilarating close, the oration by Cardinal Bembo, on Beauty as "an influence of the heavenly bountifulness." By the time the cardinal is finished, we have gone from the image of beauty to the pure idea of beauty (from sense to intellect);

we have united ideal beauty with truth, utility, and goodness; we have heard objections that "the possessing of this beauty which he praiseth so much, without the body, is a dream"; there has been talk of a transcendent insemination (putting the seeds of virtue into a mind, "the right engendering and imprinting of beauty in beauty," though the opposition claims that this should be done by "the engendering of a beautiful child in a beautiful woman"); a penetrating has been advised, but through eye and ear (the least sensual senses), and by the union of mouths, a bond called the "opening of an entry to the souls" (since an ecclesiastical orator is speaking, we may think of the oral as figuring not only the primary gratification of feeding, but also the vocation of prayer); imagination has been praised for its power to fashion "that beauty much more fair than it is in deed," to use perception of one beauty as a stair for climbing to a "universal conceit" for "meddling all beauty together"; then "by reason of the agreement that the fancies have with the body," even this stage must be transcended, until beauty is "seen only with the eyes of the mind," and the soul is turned "to the beholding of her own substance," which is angelic; whereupon the soul is kindled by the desire to partake of the heavenly nature, so that with images of burning, and mounting, and coupling, we end on a prayer to "the father of true pleasures, of grace, peace, lowliness, and good will," and on talk of hopes to "smell those spiritual savors," and of ultimate arrival through bodily death—whereat the cardinal pauses, "ravished and beside himself," having given to the others "a certain sparkle of that godly love that pricked him." It is discovered that the company has talked until dawn. And in contrast with our thoughts of journeys to the end of night, and our tracts foretelling a universal heat-death, "they saw already in the East a fair morning like unto the color of roses, and all stars voided, saving only the sweet Governess of heaven, Venus which keepeth the bounds of the night and day, from which appeared to blow a sweet blast, that filling the air with a biting cold, began to quicken the tunable notes of the pretty birds, among the hushing woods of the hills."

Is it not obvious why we could use this work as a paradigm, when looking for respects in which the rhetoric of persuasion leads dialectically to an ultimate of pure persuasion? The hierarchic principle of courtship sets a pattern of communication between "lower" and "higher" classes (or kinds). This can be universalized in terms of a climbing from body to soul, from senses through reason to understanding, from worldly to the angelic to God, from woman to beauty in general to transcendent desire for Absolute union. Or the communication may be between merely "different" kinds, where the relative grading is not established by general agreement. And, of course, when one analyzes a given case of such "courtship," one can also expect to find ambiguities whereby, even if a set scale is recognized, the roles become reversed, the superior in one respect becomes the inferior in another, or the superior must court the underling.

In making "beauty" both courtly and religious, *The Book of the Courtier* makes religion courtly, thereby "mystically" fusing social and religious "reverence." "Even as in the firmament the sun and the moon and the other stars show to the world (as it were) in a glass, a certain likeness of God: So upon the earth a much more liker image of God are those good Princes that love and worship him, and show unto the people the clear light of his justice." And by being so explicit in its way of advancing from a worldly to a celestial hierarchy, it gives us insight into situations where the "mystery of divinity" inspirits relations that, on their face, call for purely mundane motives.

Such an identification may be present in the man who cannot become a social rebel without becoming an atheist. And conversely, with some the cult of religion can be so grounded in class courtship that explicit instruction in the terms of theological hierarchy implicitly coaches obedience to one particular social hierarchy. Where such motives are formally denied (as with the pragmatic terminologies of technology, finance, and political administration), we are at least admonished to look for persuasive vestiges of them, or perhaps for their emergence in new guises.

For if man, as symbol-using animal, is *homo dialecticus,* and if the use of symbols is a kind of *transcendence,* then such a rounded instance of dialectical transcendence as we find in *The Book of the Courtier* may contain the overt expression of elements that elsewhere exist covertly, and in fragments. The work might thus make precise our understanding of the purely dialectical motives (ultimate verbal motives) behind the rhetorical convertibility between terms for social hierarchy and terms for theologic hierarchy. Here is a source of "mystery" grounded in the very perfection of formal thinking, with worldly and transcendent "reverence" each drawing sustenance from the other (and with all the variants of these, even to the rebel snapping of the continuity).

The Caricature of Courtship: Kafka (The Castle)

With the dialectical symmetry of *The Book of the Courtier* in mind, consider Franz Kafka's grotesque novel, *The Castle*. Thomas Mann calls Kafka "a religious humorist." A good formula, so good that it deserves a fuller explanation than the one its originator gives for it. Mann sees in Kafka the shift between love of the commonplace and desire "to be near to God, to live in God, to live aright and after God's will." And as in Mann's *Tonio Kröger* an unresolved conflict between artistic and bourgeois motives leads to sentiment and humor, so Mann says that the motives responsible for *The Castle* "corresponded in the religious sphere to Tonio Kröger's isolation."

But even in *Tonio Kröger,* as viewed from the standpoint of our concern with the magic of courtship, we should note that there is a pronounced concern with *caste*. Tonio's shy reverence for the bourgeois Ingeborg is but a localization, in sexual terms, of a nostalgic attitude towards the bourgeoisie as a class. True, as the returns have kept coming in, we have begun to see that the artistic "break-away," the bourgeois-turned-Bohemian, was not so antithetical to the motives of his class as he usually felt himself to be. The young Bohemian's wandering is but the first stage of the old Bohemian's homecoming. The Bohemian is "substantially" back before he leaves; but as with the Boyg's instructions to Peer Gynt, he must get there roundabout. Still, however indistinguishable the father and the prodigal son may be as regards their underlying community of motives, they can feel themselves as opposite extremes, as different in *kind*—and Mann's story got much poignancy from the distinction between the practical-bourgeois and the esthetic-bourgeois, treated as alien *classes,* with Tonio vacillating between them, and the two women, Ingeborg and Lizaveta, being courted not merely for themselves alone, but for the contrasting orders of social motives which they represented. They were mysterious vessels, for they were sexual embodiments of two nonsexual principles, two different castes. And the ambiguous courting of them was a roundabout intercourse between the castes.

If you substitute the religious motive for the esthetic motive, you see that Mann is quite correct in noting a motivational analogy between *The Castle* and *Tonio Kröger*. But for our purposes, the significant element of the analogy was omitted from Mann's account of his own story. Add this element, and if you then look at Kafka's novel with the dialectic of *The Courtier* in mind, you will see exactly why and how Mann's formula fits. Kafka is, if you will, "religious" in his concern with the ultimate mystery, the universal ground of human motives. But his account of the religious motive is "humorous" because he never forgets how the terms of the social order incongruously shape our idea of God, inviting men to conceive of communication with God after the analogy of their worldly embarrassments.

The principle of courtship is manifested in Expressionistically grotesque fragments. It is there, because the theme is bureaucracy, communication between higher and lower orders, involving the mysteries of "reverence." And since the ultimate of such courtship would be communion between lowly beings and "the highest," Kafka goes to the very essence of his subject, seeing through social mystery to divine mystery. But he never forgets, or lets us forget, the disproportion between social mystery and divine mystery. Thus, though the social mystery provides an imagery for figuring the divine mystery, this imagery is absurdly incommensurate with the hierarchic principle in its ultimate reaches.

In Kafka's personal case, of course, the social mystery was experienced, and suffered, in the form of anti-Semitism. The Jew in liberal, pre-Hitlerite Austria was never quite blackballed, never quite admitted. Where much liberalism prevailed even while the movement towards Nazism was taking form, the Jew's social status was unsettled. And this extraliterary situation had its analogue in the plot of *The Castle,* notably the uncertainty whether his principal character, "K.," would strengthen or lose his contacts with the Castle. (Similarly, in *The Trial,* there was uncertainty whether K. would be pronounced innocent or guilty by a mysterious court that was nowhere and everywhere; indeed, he could not even learn what the charge against him was.)

To an extent, the condition was like being blackballed, flatly excluded from participation in the mysteries of status. Yet to an extent it was like being hazed. For though hazing is a trial, the "guilty" defendant may hope for eventual admission into the inner sanctum, the holy of holies. The candidate who is being hazed can hope to become an *insider,* even while he undergoes ritual punishments that impress upon him his nature as a partial *outsider.* Or rather, the situation is like that of "exclusive" schools where the upper classmen impose menial duties upon the newcomers; or it is like hierarchic codes for imparting mystery to fraternities and secret orders. No, there is one important difference: usually, where such rituals prevail, they are recognized formally, so that, even while the discomfitures build up as much "reverence" as the dingy institution can command, the candidate knows where he is, knows what acts will finally permit him to become one with the mystic substance. But where there are no such formal fixities, the situation is not recognized for what it is. Though the candidate is being hazed, neither he nor his persecutors recognize what is going on. Hence, nobody is quite sure what the defendant's "guilt" is, or what kind of "trial" he must face, or for what purpose.

Thus, a friend said: "After the financial crash of 1929, you will remember, there was a great rush of liberal intellectuals to join the cause of political radicalism. Of a sudden, radical literary organizations which had been struggling along for years were overwhelmed with new converts. Whereas the old-timers in these organizations had been laboriously attempting to increase the membership, the situation now became reversed. Instead of a welcome for the new men, there was a tendency to prove that they were poor material. And this tendency went so far that often, rather than being propagandists who delighted in the growth of their cause, the old-timers acted like residents of an exclusive neighborhood who resented a new real-estate development near-by.

"Years after, I understood what was wrong. It was not just that the old-timers feared for the loss of their former influence in the organization. It was the careless trampling on the mystery that disturbed them. The new men came in like a troop of boys entering a restaurant. There were no stages, there were no punishments, there was no hazing. At one moment, they weren't there, and at the next moment of a sudden they were. And lacking any formal ritual designed for this situation, the old-timers unbeknownst to themselves worked out a kind of informal hazing process, or tried to, in seeking to freeze out the very persons whom formerly they would have worked like demons to recruit." *

For the Jew Kafka, the hazing that would reaffirm the mystery was not formalized. Indeed, there was not even the assurance that he was being considered. As the novelist says of one ostracized character in *The Castle,* his superiors couldn't forgive him, because they hadn't accused him; and "before he could be forgiven he had to prove his guilt." Still further, there was no clear hint as to where the mystery was, or what it was. The nearest visible, formal signs of it were in the structure of bureaucracy. Giving it maximum resonance, one got to the connotations of "God," hence one was "religious"; but realizing how

---

* When an individual is being received into an alien social group, he may himself feel the need to be "hazed," just as the established members of the group may feel the need to haze him. The conditions of mystery may lead to apprehensions more or less clearly expressed, as the insiders feel that they are being silently judged, or that the newcomer threatens their ways, while he himself has the sense of protruding among the company like what Marcus Aurelius might have called an "abscess." But the embarrassments here go a step farther back, deriving in part from the fact that only a few of the rites necessary to such initiation are formally recognized; and insofar as the rites are uncertain, or are improvised, or are uncompleted, a magic propriety has been violated (the violation being felt on both sides, like an unpaid debt). Then the initiative ceremony is worked out piecemeal, in ways that are unacknowledged, or even unrecognized, except for vague embarrassments, subtle affronts, half-intentional oversights, and the like.

Looking back at Mark Twain's *Pudd'nhead Wilson* in the light of these speculations, we wonder whether some such "savage" or "mystical" level of motives might be found operating there. True, the good people of the community are at first most effusive in their welcome of the two foreigners, Angelo and Luigi ("lovely names; and so grand and foreign"). But it doesn't take a very skilled reader to suspect very early in the story that the author is building up for a letdown. The subsequent harsh treatment of the twins results from misunderstandings caused by the villainous Tom, who puts the foreigners in a bad light in order to conceal his own guilt. But if you drop the explanations, what do you get? The plot then boils down to this: Two foreigners enter a community; despite their exceptional strangeness, they are heartily welcomed; but immediately after, there is a long period when they are subjected to the most severe coolness and suspicion, and undergo painful trials, before they are finally exonerated and admitted. Leaving out the roundabout rationalization, which attributes the villagers' standoffishness to the machinations of a villain, one finds that the newcomers went through a long period of what amounts to informal, improvised hazing. Split the neighbors into two groups, and although both groups treat the strangers badly, the dissociation rationalizes the bad treatment by attributing it to the evil persons alone, thereby concealing its *collective* nature. But omit the rationalization of intent, merely looking at the over-all result, and you find that

inadequate it was as a figuring of the divine, one treated it with grotesque "humor." Thus, the mysterious official whose substance comes not from his intrinsic personality but solely from the dignity of his office here takes on a new dimension. He is a nonentity in the sense that he manifests no *intrinsic properties* fitting him to represent the religious motive; yet the mysteries of rank endow him with "reverence" anyhow. Indeed, his very unfitness as a vicar perversely suggests the dignifying effect of the office itself. (Thus a student wholly impressed with his college as a mystery would manifest this essence not through learning, but through a "college spirit" that would forgo learning. Or a man of means who distributed insults along with his funds, purchasing services solely through his money, beating his dogs with a bone, might more forcefully illustrate the power of money in its "purity" than if he also had appealing traits of character that engaged people's loyalties.) So in *The Castle* the very dinginess of the officialdom as *persons* absurdly suggests the omnipresence of the mystery that infuses their *office*.

Since, according to our view, *The Castle* is a fragmentary caricature of such an order, let us see to what extent the formal elements in Castiglione's dialogue have their grotesque counterpart in Kafka's novel.

The first concern of *The Courtier* is with the qualifications that make one presentable at court, and with the hopes of favor and advancement

---

the citizens, with one notable exception who was himself unjustly in bad repute with the community, had subjected the foreigners to harsh treatment.

Our notion is that, in accordance with the usual workings of the "scapegoat mechanism" as a dramatic device, Twain could break down the motive of hazing into two principles, a "good" and a "bad"—and as a result, the hazing need not be seen as such, even by the author. But its "mystic" or "magical" element, operating beyond or beneath the "rational" explanation (in terms of a dissociation between innocent and villainous neighbors) could be felt by both author and reader, without being explicitly defined.

The thought suggests that we might profitably approach all of Mark Twain's major books in such terms. For instance, we should look for magical and ritualistic motives (strongly infused with the principle of hierarchy), while he uses the figures of children (or of rogues like the king and the duke) to depict such motives realistically. Children and rogues may or not be as thoroughly formalists as he makes them out to be. But even if they aren't, readers can readily accept the novelistic convention that says they are. Hence the element of social "divinity" in the life about us can be lightly and ingratiatingly symbolized, without the reader ever becoming quite aware that his interest is being held by such a motive.

at the hands of the sovereign. This is also the primary concern of the land-surveyor, K. But whereas the courtier is concerned with the procuring of advantage *within* the court, K. is wholly an outsider, with a vast officialdom (the grotesque bureaucratic equivalent of the courtiers) vaguely interposed between him and the mysterious sovereign. K. is at several removes from the source of favor. He is a stranger among the villagers. Though the villagers belong to the castle, there is a gulf between them and the castle. There are messengers (the grotesque counterpart of angels) who live in the village but have access to outer offices in the castle. And there are the officials themselves, who represent the castle in the village, but are so imbued with the mystic standoffishness of hierarchy that throughout the entire novel K. exhausts himself in unsuccessful attempts to get preparatory interviews with them. Where the courtier can consider how one should conduct oneself in the lord's secret chamber, K. must worry how to get beyond the outer vestibule.

Frieda and Amalia are the main translations of the grotesque courtliness into terms of woman. Of Frieda, we are told: "It was her nearness to Klamm" (she had been his mistress before coming to live with K.) "that had made her so irrationally seductive" to K.—and Klamm was the official from the castle whom K. is constantly striving to meet in behalf of his nightmarishly indeterminate cause. Amalia is the girl whose life was ruined when she resented a letter from an official making filthy proposals to her (a letter couched in the language of courtship incongruously reversed). One character quotes a local saying, "Official decisions are as shy as young girls"; the novelist here ingeniously mixes the sexual and bureaucratic orders. And when Kafka is contrasting "the power, merely formal until now, which Klamm exercised over K.'s services" with "the very real power which Klamm possessed in K.'s bedroom," he says: "Never yet had K. seen vocation and life so interlaced as here. . . . One might think that they had exchanged places."

If we recall what we previously said on the relation between mystery and class, this remark seems unusually resonant. Status and division of labor being but two aspects of the same thing, the reference to "vocation" can be read as a roundabout reference to *class*. Indeed, in areas manifesting the cultural tone set by Protestantism, the substantiality of status that arose with the division of labor is likely to be expressed pragmatically, in terms of work. But Protestantism's doctrine of the divinity in secular toil had fused secular and supernatural "mystery" quite as Catholicism's divine sanction for status had done. Hence, in either scheme, there was the convertibility between the two kinds of "reverence," the social and the religious. Consider, thus, Kafka's reference to the interchangeability of "vocation" and "life." He is talking of the way in which Klamm (who represents the mystery of the courtly principle) pervades K.'s sexual relations with Frieda. And he is saying in effect that here the social motives of status ("vocation") become so interwoven with universal motives ("life") that they can exchange places. Recalling the nature of the book, in which the castle fluctuantly represents both the superiority of social caste and the superiority of the godly, do we not see in this passing remark a grotesque way of fusing both kinds of "reverence" (the social and the "divine") in terms of sexual relations?

Since the religious motivation in Kafka is explicitly recognized by both such authorities as Thomas Mann and Kafka's friend, Max Brod, we shall not pause here to establish it. But perhaps the single sentence that most quickly conveys this quality is in the second paragraph of the eighth chapter:

> When K. looked at the Castle, often it seemed to him as if he were observing someone who sat there quietly gazing in front of him, not lost in thought and so oblivious of everything, but free and untroubled, as if he were alone with nobody to observe him, and yet must notice that he was observed, and all the same remained with his calm not even slightly disturbed; and really—one did not know whether it was cause or effect—the gaze of the observer could not remain concentrated there, but slid away.

And in Chapter IX, the discussion of things done "in the name of Klamm," of things "filled by his spirit," or of a person who is but "an instrument in the hand of Klamm," adds a transcendent dimension to the purely bureaucratic mystery. Images of storm and eagle figure here too. Indeed, there is no trouble isolating the traditional theological motive in this work. The problem, rather, as both the Mann and Brod statements in the English translation indicate, is to keep one reminded of the important role played here by the motives of social class.

What of the other two major themes of *The Courtier:* Laughter and education (the themes gorgeously, almost hysterically, brought together in the Rabelaisian rhetoric)? In *The Castle,* the social rhetoric of laughter and education (two forms of "pure persuasion" this side of the religious) is not a subject of discussion, but is rather the essence of the work itself. The laughter, in its grotesque modification, is embedded in the very conception and method of the book, the oddly "humorous" treatment of reverence. The social bid in such expression is perhaps best revealed today in the mixture of grotesqueness and humor that distinguishes the "smartness" of the *New Yorker* sort (the "hierarchic" appeal of which is indicated in turn by the commercial advertisements that accompany it, advertisements obviously addressed to suburban, middle-class "elegance").

At one point, K. is told that the messenger Barnabas had cried when receiving his first commission. As a comment on the mystery, this incident is exceptionally telling. For Barnabas' first commission had been to communicate with K. And previously we had seen the mystery of Barnabas, as he looked to K. This sudden glimpse around the corner, with A mysterious to B and B mysterious to A, all because of their different participation in the mystery of C, does not merely dispel the illusion. For everyone goes on acting *as though* there were a mystery; and since acts are images, the mystery continues to be strong in our imagination. Indeed, once you learn the rules, once you are at home in its grotesque laughter, the very lack of motives for the mystery adds to the sense of mystery.

In a broken, grotesque version of courtship, we are not required to find counterparts for each of the elements in the symmetrical, classical version. Yet there do happen to be analogies for the educational principle. Judged as imagery, K.'s very role as land-surveyor, or rather, his attempt to get himself formally accredited in this role, involves the principle of education. For interpreted symbolically, a land-surveyor is surely one who would specify positions and elevations. And since this half-admitted, half-rejected K. so clearly represents the author, whose account of K.'s quandaries in confronting social hierarchy is itself a precise novelization of the hierarchic motive, it would hardly be exorbitant to say that Kafka here writes as a Jewish "intellectual." (He is "in" to the extent that an intellectual spontaneously considers himself superior to manual workers, as with K.'s attitude towards the peasants and workers of the village; he is "out" to the extent that an unnamed and even unnamable curse is upon him, a curse that keeps him permanently "guilty.") Kafka was "in" insofar as the intellectual spontaneously considers his status superior to that of the laboring classes, though he may "pastorally" court them, a social relation which a Leftist wag (he has since broken with the Party) formulated with suggestive gallantry, thus: "The intelligentsia must penetrate the proletariat." Kafka was "out" insofar as the intellectual class itself is somewhat suspect (though we will say for the Church, Aquinas' angels were pure intellectuals), and because in addition Kafka was Jewish in what was then preparing itself to become a part of Hitler's *Reich*.

Also, there is at least the image of education in the fact that, during much of his uncertainty, K. lives with Frieda in a school where he is supposed to be janitor, and where expressionistically the classroom he uses as living quarters is overrun by the schoolchildren. But the interweaving of education with the theme of childhood involves factors that belong rather under "grammar" and "symbolic." We have elsewhere noted the Grammatical resources that permit logical priority to be stated narratively in terms of temporal priority. By such convertibility, the essence of the hierarchic principle (the castle) can be identified with the conditions of childhood, since an essence is a logical "first," and childhood is a narrative first. Thus, near the beginning of the story, we are told that, at the first sight of the castle, "K. had a fleeting recollection" of the town in which he was born. The peasants are described as children, likewise the childish element in his assistants is commented on several times. When K. tries to phone the castle, the receiver gave out a buzz that "was like the hum of countless children's voices—but yet not a hum, the echo rather of voices singing at an infinite distance." In the schoolroom where he lives with Frieda, their constant invasion of his privacy sets the mark of childhood upon the entire situation.

Again, the German word for castle, *Schloss,* has connotations of internality not present in the English equivalent. For it clearly suggests the idea of enclosure, being related to the verb for closing or locking, *schliessen. Klamm,* as an adjective, means tight or close, related to another word for the act of enclosing, *klemmen.* We might recall the *hortus conclusus* of medieval thought, the ideal "closed garden" that duplicated the protectiveness of the walled town. And in the offing are the words for "advertising" and "calamity," *Reklam, Kalamität.*

So much for the Grammar of "regression." From the standpoint of

"Symbolic" note also that the imagery of childish sexuality is well suited to express the mystery of social courtship in one important respect: since social intercourse is not essentially sexual at all, such courtship is more nearly analogous to the "polymorphous-perverse" nature of infantile sexuality than to mature sexual mating. (See Shirley Jackson's novel, *The Road Through the Wall,* for a subtle and sensitive representation of the ways whereby the unspeakable mysteries of social discrimination become interwoven, in childhood, with the unspeakable mysteries of the sexually unclean.) Since K.'s union with Frieda is but a roundabout approach to Klamm (who represents the mystery of the order headed in the castle), there is a grotesque appropriateness in the fact that K. and Frieda are under the observation of others, even in the most intimate moments of love-making. Here are perhaps the strongest suggestions of the infantile, since children's experiments with sex lack intimacy, privacy, and purpose, quite as with the casual and almost absent-minded sexuality of Frieda and K.

The two major themes that complicate the analysis of *The Castle* in terms of grotesque courtliness are Kafka's illness and his personal conflicts with his father. Recalling Freud's suggestion that children are often figured in dreams as insects, we should probably find the clearest representation of the mysterious, troubled communication between father and son as different "kinds of being" expressed most directly in the story, *Metamorphosis,* about a son who was a monster cockroach. Rhetorically, we may note that, in this very disgrace of the offspring, there is a desperate vengeance against the parent from which it was descended.

Though the references to weariness in *The Castle* show signs of the author's personal illness, it is perhaps figured most clearly in the story of the *Hunger-Artist,* where the wastage of consumption has its analogue in the fantastic account of the performer who starved by profession. Anyone with a feeling for the grotesque might have hit upon the plot of this story as a conceit; but unless a writer were almost prodigiously imaginative, only by actually experiencing tuberculosis could he have developed this fictive counterpart of it with such gruesome thoroughness.

The disease here is also esthetically redeemed, as with much of Mann's work (*Tristan,* for instance) in becoming interwoven with the theme of art. (For a discussion of the story from this point of view, see

R. W. Stallman's essay, "Kafka's Cage," in the Winter 1948 *Accent*.) There are rhetorical implications here, since the problem of being socially received is again considered, with much poignancy. And the rhetorical element that can arise even out of purely physical discomfitures is discernible in the identifications surrounding disease itself, as when Kafka writes: "Illness and weariness give even peasants a look of refinement." Thus such obsessiveness as comes of the castle fits well with the imagery of disease, both physical and mental (or with such literary attenuations of mental disease as reside in the grotesque). For grammatically, disease is "passion," and as such can be a romantic and social analogue of the religious passion.

Kafka's study of law leads directly into rhetorical motives. The paper work, and the strongly hierarchic nature of legal administration could provide much material for the imagery of officialdom that is the basis of the courtlinesss. And behind positive law there always loom the questions of theologic law, as the castle looms above the village.

In his remarks on Kafka, Max Brod writes:

> The connection between the "Castle"—that is Divine Guidance—and the women, this connection half-discovered and half-suspected by K., may appear obscure, and even inexplicable, in the Sortini episode where the official (Heaven) requires the girl to do something obviously immoral and obscene; and here a reference to Kierkegaard's *Fear and Trembling* may be of value—a work which Kafka loved much, read often, and profoundly commented on in many letters. The Sortini episode is literally a parallel to Kierkegaard's book, which starts from the fact that God required of Abraham what was really a crime, the sacrifice of his child; and which uses this paradox to establish triumphantly the conclusion that the categories of morality and religion are by no means identical. The incommensurability of earthly and religious aims; this takes one right into the heart of Kafka's novel.

We might distinguish two important elements in this statement: the problem of the sacrifice (involving the interpretation of a story in Genesis 22) and the problem of the absurd (involving a doctrine of "incommensurability" between religious and social motives). They are so closely interwoven that we cannot discuss one intelligibly without implicating the other. Yet they might be separated for systematic purposes, since a cult of irrationality, or "the absurd," can be derived from many other sources than this chapter in Genesis, and a theory of sacrifice need not lay such stress upon the "kill" as marks Kierkegaard's interpretation of the Biblical story.

A "Dialectical Lyric" (Kierkegaard's Fear and Trembling)

In the department stores of some decades ago, there were little carriages running in tracks between the cashier and the individual sales booths. (You still see them occasionally, but they have mostly been replaced by pneumatic tubes.) They would spurt forth, making quick jerks (like Kierkegaardian leaps) at each right-angled turn—darting in zigzags across the ceiling, and then suddenly disappearing on the way up to some unseen chamber where they would be received, checked, and after appropriate operations would be sent racing back to the counter from which they had come. Their forthright rectangular urgency fascinated—and a pious child, watching them, could feel that they were like messengers bearing communications to Heaven, and returning with prompt answers. Somewhat the same idea crosses the mind now, when we see the capsules being put into pneumatic tubes, or hear them come plumping out again—except that now the communications seem rather to be with a counting house in hell.

Anyhow, we are reminded of those little messengers, communicating between a central terminus and a peripheral terminus, when we think of the Kierkegaardian dialectic, for changing finite species into the currency of the infinite. For the dialectician sends up one thing, something is abstracted from it, and it returns as another thing. However, the change that comes back is not merely something subtracted, or abstracted from the original sum: a notable element has been added as well. This sort of change is a rebirth, a transformation.

What, then, went up, and what came back, as per the "movements" treated in Kierkegaard's "dialectical lyric," *Fear and Trembling?* At first, reducing to sheerly behavioristic terms, we know that Kierkegaard had jilted a girl. When he announced that he had given up his intention of marrying her, she grew importunate. Then (we quote Mr. Walter Lowrie's introduction to the English translation): "In order to liberate Regina from her attachment and to 'set her afloat,' S. K. felt obliged to be cruel enough to make her believe he was a scoundrel who had merely been trifling with her affections." Onlookers might get the same impression. And Kierkegaard seems to have been threatened with doubts himself, at least to the extent that he spent the rest of his highly productive life protesting his innocence in some of the most ingenious dialectical operations known to Protestantism.

Reading *Fear and Trembling,* we see that the species he sent up to be changed comprised this jilting, with his picture of himself as a "scoundrel." After the change, it returned, properly abstracted, as the "knight of infinite resignation." Or was that but an *ad interim* notice that the message was being processed? In any case, after further communications, the jilting was wholly remade, and in its place was the knight of faith, who adores his princess in perpetual repetition. This is the currency of the infinite, but brought down to earth like a god incarnate, a spirit that henceforth infuses all things with its essence, bathes all things in its unitary light, subordinating the disparate facts of the world of contingencies to one transcendent, unitary principle, ironically called the Absurd. This transformation is also called a "leap" across the "incommensurable."

Behind it all should lie the standard Neo-Platonist pattern. That is, we could begin with the world of everyday contingencies (in which there had been a jilting, under slightly suspect conditions). We start this on its Upward Way until it reaches the realm of Oneness in Infinite Being. After it has been thus purified, we start it on its Downward Way, back to the world of business and gossip. When it has thus returned, we find that in its purified form it now requires a totally different vocabulary to chart its motivations. As contrasted with its earlier condition, there has been a momentous "leap." Something "incommensurable" has intervened. And this new step calls forth a new set of dialectical operations so radical, and so spirited, that they apply not only to itself, but can be extended to all things, natural, human, and divine. At the very least, this vocabulary had to be sufficiently transcendent to redeem the relations between Kierkegaard and Regina. But in the course of making it transcendent enough for those purposes, Kierkegaard came upon a principle that could be applied to all finite things; by the natural dialectics of the case it was a principle of "infinity." For once you get a generalization as broad as the "finite," its only proper dialectical partner or counter-term is the "infinite."

So much for the over-all dialectics. There are also fables and images that give the abstract processes body. First, there is the key analogy: Kierkegaard jilting Regina is as Abraham making ready to kill Isaac.

But this story, as told in the Bible, does not quite serve the purpose. For there is nothing in it to parallel the very important point about Kierkegaard's acting "like a scoundrel." The Bible does not say that Abraham lied to Isaac for Isaac's good. However: Kierkegaard, writing in a highly psychologistic century, improvises a "psychology" for Abraham. And *this improvised psychology, not the Biblical story,* is the element that helps him solve the most crucial problem in the redeeming of his conduct. For it is the part that parallels, in Biblical ennoblement, Kierkegaard's depicting of himself as a scoundrel who had trifled with Regina's affections.

Perhaps we should make a distinction here between the "amplifying" and the "psychologizing" of a Biblical story. One would amplify the story if one merely tried to make the reader feel more urgently each principle that the story itself exemplified. Thus, to jog the imagination of the sluggish, one might expatiate on Abraham's love for his son, going to such lengths that nobody could fail to realize this point. A principle already there would thus be rhetorically amplified, but no new principle would be added. In "psychologizing" the narrative, however, Kierkegaard added a new principle of his own—and precisely that is the one he needed to supply transcendent motives for his apparent conduct as a "scoundrel."

We refer, of course, to the ingenious Gidean conceit, which you will certainly not find in the Biblical story:

> He climbed Mount Moriah, but Isaac understood him not. Then for an instant he turned away from him, and when Isaac again saw Abraham's face it was changed, his glance was wild, his form was horror. He seized Isaac by the throat, threw him to the ground, and said, "Stupid boy, dost thou then suppose that I am thy father? I am an idolater. Dost thou suppose that this is God's bidding? No, it is my desire." Then Isaac trembled and cried out in his terror, "O God in Heaven, have compassion upon me. God of Abraham, have compassion upon me. If I have no father upon earth, be Thou my father!" But Abraham in a low voice said to himself, "O Lord in Heaven, I thank Thee. After all it is better for him to believe that I am a monster, rather than that he should lose faith in Thee."

If this addition to the Bible story teaches us anything tropologically, the moral seems to be that religion would sanction lying, even as regards first and last things. But we can pass that up. It is sufficient for us to note that Kierkegaard is here making a purely personal addition to the sacred text. He is not just amplifying principles already there; he is adding a new principle. And if that principle had not been added, the Biblical story would have fallen short of his requirements.

Kierkegaard says in effect: "Here is a Biblical anecdote on which I am basing my theological dialectic." But as regards his actual procedure, what he should have said is: "I would like to present my theological dialectic, in as persuasive a way as possible. Hence, to strike the imagination, I have a picturesque introduction, a privately conceived anecdote, a personal invention of my own. To give it authority, I shall call it Biblical. Then I shall proceed to transform its favorable implications into explications, as an after-dinner speaker might begin his talk with a witty story that illustrates his theme and disposes the audience favorably towards his conclusions."

However, though there is questionableness here on one level, there is extremely revealing honesty on another. For Kierkegaard follows his Biblical psychologizing by a kind of parable. It is meant to reenforce the story, to say the same thing. But might it go deeper into his underlying motives than the official example (Abraham's sacrifice of Isaac)?

> When the child must be weaned, the mother blackens her breast; it would indeed be a shame that the breast should look delicious when the child must not have it. So the child believes that the breast has changed, but the mother is the same, her glance is as loving and tender as ever. Happy the person who had no need of more dreadful expedients for weaning the child!

Though the theme of weaning is repeated several times, the reference to the blackening (which would correspond to the "scoundrelly" ingredient in his act of jilting) drops away. Only such motives as maternal love and sorrow at separation are mentioned. In other words, the very element that the story was supposedly introduced to supply drops out. Yet without it, the act he is accounting for is left unexplained.

These other references, where mention of the blackened breast is omitted, are of this sort: "When the child has grown big and must be weaned, the mother virginally hides her breast, so the child has no more a mother.... When the child must be weaned, the mother too is not without sorrow at the thought that she and the child are separated more and more, that the child which first lay at her heart and later reposed upon her breast will be so near to her no more. . . . When the child must be weaned, the mother has stronger food in readiness, lest the child should perish. Happy the person who has stronger food in readiness!" In a subtle way, a "leap" has taken place even here; we begin with explanation for a questionable way of jilting, and we end on mention of a transcendent sustenance, with the apologetic feature having dropped out, while in its place there is an edified and edifying promise.

Is it not possible that with this humble secondary example we can come closer to the motives for Kierkegaard's relations to Regina than with the one he features? The story of Abraham and Isaac (plus its all-important psychologistic improvisations) sets up the case formally. The figure of the weaned child discusses it informally, even confidentially. And since the book is essentially autobiography, written by a genius of introspection, we may assume that the example is not chosen haphazardly, but is an essential and articulate figuring of his motives. At least, in another reference which the editor quotes from the *Journal*, Kierkegaard says: "He who has explained this riddle has explained my life." Here he interweaves the two themes even more thoroughly than in the book itself, concluding

> When the child has to be weaned the mother blackens her breast, but her eyes rest just as lovingly upon the child. The child believes it is the breast that has changed, but that the mother is unchanged. And why does she blacken her breast? Because, she says, it would be a shame that it should seem delicious when the child must not get it.— This collision is easily resolved, for the breast is only a part of the mother herself. Happy is he who has not experienced more dreadful collisions, who did not need to blacken *himself*, who did not need to go to hell in order to see what the devil looks like, so that he might paint himself accordingly and in that way if possible save another person in that person's God-relationship at least. This would be Abraham's collision.

There is nothing unusual in the thought of acting towards others as one has himself been acted upon. Hence, if Kierkegaard *had* experienced great disturbance during the weaning period of infancy, there would be no difficulty in accounting for the reversal whereby the experience of being weaned is reversed in the figure, as he likens himself to the one who did the weaning rather than to the one who suffered it.

You need only make the asumption that, Kierkegaard being a wholly essential and articulate writer, this anecdote is just as central to his thinking as he says it is. And then you need but look to see what there is in it, assuming that he selected an image of weaning rather than some other image, because this image of weaning came closer to summing up the nature of his basic motives than a different image might have done. And we assume that it came closer because the experience of weaning itself had been of similar outstanding importance.

However, we do not propose to derive the pattern of Kierkegaard's mind from an experience of weaning. A psychologist could point to many relevant connections here. Since the mouth is used for both taking in food and putting forth words, nutrient distress might conceivably be transformed, by a Kierkegaardian leap, into orational zeal. Such a reversal is not hard to think of. But one could with as much justice apply the opposite causal sequence here, noting that many are weaned but few are Kierkegaards. Hence, the child may have already possessed the susceptibilities that would make weaning a matter of such moment. If he were a born word-slinger, he might thereby be even more "mouth-conscious" than most children, at the time of weaning. And he could later connect this problem of dissociation with the problem of distinguishing, at adolescence, between maternal and erotic woman. (At least, his reference to the mother's breast as "virginal" is in the same cluster of motives with his "knightly" view of Regina as a "princess." The same kind of fond aloofness is implied in both.)

But we need only note how the verbal motive as such would be enough to account for his conduct towards Regina. For if this "knight of faith" would court in terms of the infinite, it follows that he would court eternally, in perpetual repetition. Here would be the motive of the dialectician, of Socratic erotic (as considered in the *Grammar,* when on the subject of Plato's *Phaedrus*). But if one would court forever, whereas the object of one's courtship is not only willing to yield, but even becomes importunate in yielding, then the goodly dialectician must supply resistances of his own, from within himself, out of his own "inner check," and by setting up a situation, both emotional and practical, that would restore the necessary distance. First, in somewhat of a panic, he would even act like a "scoundrel" if necessary. For he would do anything to retain the purity of his motives, being an individualist of integrity. If his woman wouldn't refuse him, if she was willing to accept him even when he was but lukewarm, then he would have to become frigid. When, affectionately importunate, she made an affront necessary, he affronted her. He became a "scoundrel."

However, once he had got away from her, and she had become married to another, since they were both highly proper he had again the objective situation necessary to his nature: he could now court her in terms of eternity, that is, in perpetual repetition. The dilemma was solved. On firm moral and legalistic grounds, their union was now impossible. Hence, he could safely become her knight again. To gallantly make amends for his affront, he could psychologistically amend the Bible. Everything was now in order—and with her marriage as the "objective correlative" that matched his own subjective "inner check" (this was the great century of the Schellingesque "identification of subject and object"), he could now court her in terms of the infinite, the incommensurable, the absurd, the faith that will somehow bring about the impossible. Kierkegaard had good grounds for his faith in the impossible—for it was the real impossibility of their marriage that again allowed this "knight of faith" to court his "princess." No wonder "Johannes de Silentio" could then say of the knightly "swain" who loves the "princess" as a distance: "He feels a blissful rapture in letting love tingle through every nerve and yet his soul is as solemn as that of the man who has drained the poisoned goblet and feels how the juices permeate every drop of blood—for this instant is life and death."

For the present we want to discuss the results of the false emphasis that came of Kierkegaard's turn from the amplifying of a Biblical text to the psychologizing of it. Here, we submit, was the true Kierkegaardian leap, so far as dialectic is concerned. For it is a dialectical fact that you cannot get more out of a term than you put into it. This is the reason why theologians insist upon Biblical "revelation" as the ground of faith. Technically, by grounding an argument in Biblical texts as "revelation," the dialectician can put in terms having "universal" authority, while his personal or individual function is exclusively that of translating the implications into explications. We need not here decide whether the authority is real. For as we have said, Kierkegaard does not start by merely putting in a Biblical text from which he will draw forth the implications. Rather, he starts by putting in a *strategic addition* to a Biblical text. Needing the story to motivate the leap, *he himself puts the leap into the story,* when he turns from mere amplification of the text to a psychologizing of the text; and thereby he gets a generating principle that is very much like an ingenious Gidean perversion (almost an early statement, in theological terms, of such transvaluations as Nietzsche was later to treat crisply, in his wholly secular paradoxes).

Or you could put the matter thus: If it is true that, having faith in God, one absurdly gets what one renounces, why should not Abraham have been sure that somehow, by virtue of the Existentialist Absurd, God would take care of any apparent breach between religion and morality? Or why couldn't he have faith in God's ability to so bring it about that the father could simultaneously meet the test and keep his son, as was indeed the case? If the anecdote, as amended by Kierkegaard, justifies such expectations on Kierkegaard's part with relation to Regina, why shouldn't it justify similar confidence on Abraham's part, with relation to Isaac? Or do we have another leap now, from the Old Law, to the New Law, to the Absurd Law (not revealed until the flourishing of nineteenth-century individualist psychologism)?

You can't have it both ways: If Kierkegaard is right in knowing that, by virtue of faith in the Absurd, he will regain Regina in the finite (though infused with the infinite), then by the same token, Abraham would know that he would regain his son in the very act of preparing to slay him, on condition that he genuinely intended to make the sacrifice. In this case, Abraham's confidence would remove the apparent discrepancy between morality and religion. If, on the other hand, Abraham's regaining of Isaac came wholly as a surprise to him, then Abraham's willingness to sacrifice Isaac doesn't indicate as powerful a faith as Kierkegaard's willingness to jilt Regina in accordance with his exalted paradox, "By faith I shall get her in virtue of the absurd." And that would seem to be a kind of absurdity that lies outside the Existentialist Absurd.

The only way out of these difficulties seems to be through our dialectical explanation of his dialectic as a metarhetoric (since by perpetual courtship he is forever getting her while forever not getting her, renunciation and advance being fused in the one attitude). Technically, this could be saluted as the presence of the infinite in the finite —for opposites have been reconciled, and that state of affairs is absurd, being "higher than human reason."

We believe, then, that Kierkegaard was essentially correct in saying that both his jilting of Regina and his subsequent lifelong courting of her involved motives in the realm of the "infinite." For "pure persuasion" is an absolute, logically prior to any one persuasive act. It is of the essence of language. And just as the over-all Title of Titles is a "god-term," so persuasion in all purity would transform courtship into prayer, not prayer for an end, but prayer for its own sake, prayer as Adoration, or as the Absolute Compliment. You can account for such motives by a thoroughly secular dialectic, as we have tried to do here. But even so, as regards the Platonist dialectic at least, they would be, technically, on the side of the "divine," since they would be abstract and universalized.

The Kill and the Absurd

With regard to the sacrifice: the statement quoted from Max Brod indicates how readers are led by Kierkegaard to interpret the Biblical story as saying that God required of Abraham the sacrifice of Isaac. Yet according to the Bible, just as Abraham "took the knife to slay his son," an angel stayed his hand, saying: "Lay not thine hand upon the lad, neither do thou any thing unto him; for now I know that thou fearest God, seeing thou hast not withheld thy son, thine only son from me."

In building a theology about a Biblical anecdote, why play down so important a part of it? The story in its entirety is brief. Yet when using it as a base on which to erect his theological doctrines, Kierkegaard here makes it even briefer. Isn't the assurance that the angel stayed Isaac's hand as important a part of the story as Abraham's willingness to sacrifice Isaac? At least, Isaac must have thought so.

As we see it, this chapter tells not of a father who sacrificed his son, but of a father who was *allowed to substitute a purely vicarious victim*. "Abraham lifted up his eyes, and looked, and beheld behind him a ram caught in a thicket by his horns: and Abraham went and took the ram, and offered him up for a burnt offering in the stead of his son."

Is this a story about a God who demands the killing of Isaac, or is it about a God who demands Abraham's *willingness to sacrifice?* The story itself is quite explicit on this point. It says that what God wanted was not a kill, but a sign; and when he got the sign, he ordered the son to be spared. The "categories of morality and religion" here seem to work quite well together. Religion demands of the devout the willingness to sacrifice even the most precious thing. And *in strictest accordance with the tribal morality,* Abraham's only son is chosen, as test case. For according to the tribal morality, the only son is a most precious thing. God's way here was in perfect keeping with the theory of "topics" in Aristotle's *Rhetoric.* He chose the very place which, in the realm of "opinion" then current, would stand most persuasively for the principle of supreme sacrifice. We need not bring in any "teleological suspension of the ethical."

Among the components of happiness, Aristotle lists the parent's delight in his children. And God, not absurdly, but like a good Aristotelian, was working this topic for all it was worth. As a result, so far as the story is concerned, it gets its effect by *ethos,* in employing exactly such a topic of invention as Aristotle would advocate for building up the character of Abraham.

The Kierkegaardian Existentialism, with typical overparticularization at this point, would not sufficiently generalize the anecdote. Hence, it lays too much stress upon the difference between the image, infanticide (which *in itself* would be morally criminal), whereas it should lay more stress upon the idea, supreme sacrifice (which is religiously pious). Also, there seems some perversity in the fact that no attempt is made to discuss all the important motivating elements. The psychologistic distortion is aggravated by at least one major omission: God's own statement of His motives. The product thus got by a combination of distortion and overparticularization is then generalized, with the perversely exciting literary result that the cult of the kill takes on a theological resonance. A story about Abraham's willingness to sacrifice is then cherished by the literati as though it were about the killing of Isaac.

Often the attempt to obey one moral injunction may oblige us to violate another. There is nothing essentially absurd in such a conflict. But it is true that, unless we are to remain undecided, the solution will require a new act of us, a "leap." To take this step, we may have to go from a principle to a principle of principles (from the dialectical order to an ultimate order of terms)—and such "incommensurability" may be called a "leap" from morality to religion.

In Kierkegaard's case, his personal relations to the "princess" who represented for him the hierarchic principle as translated into sexual terms required ultimate dialectical operations (as distinct from the restricted kind we find in parliamentary clashes). And so far as the appeal to the imagination goes, since he picturesquely reduced his dialectic to an anecdote featuring the mythic imagery of the kill, this image may come to stand for the spirit of his dialectic. Hence readers, in their awareness that man's way is through conflict, are invited to think that the cult of the kill is not a lower morality, but a higher one, even a religious one. Ironically, if the image is stressed more than the dialectic, such doctrine leads *towards* the Holocaust rather than *away from* it. For where personal conflict is solved by the kill, what do you have ultimately but the man who is at peace with himself only on the battlefield, in the midst of slaughter?

In another notable respect the Kierkegaardian alignment needs discounting. We refer to the fact that he summed up his dialectic by entitling it the Absurd.

Admittedly, dialectical operations do involve us in contradictions that might be dramatically called "absurd." Yet we would point out that the operations themselves are quite "rational," when approached methodically. Hence the slogan of the Absurd can easily transform a truth into a half-truth. It is somewhat like the pleasantries of those who remark that a man begins dying the day he is born. So he does, since in every change there is a dying; but in every change there is likewise a being-born—and we can safely use the partial statement only insofar as we know how to discount it. In sum, if one begins with "dialectic," one can come upon the Absurd. But if one begins with the Absurd, one is not likely to get a clear look at the dialectic, even though it is so inescapably in the offing that one is continually coming upon it. By approaching it in the Kierkegaardian manner, under a curse, one is in danger of subtly perverting it at every point; and each time he finds a new aspect of that quite "rational" of instruments (the processes of verbal composition and division) he is invited to think instead that he is coming upon new areas of the Absurd.

Consider the Existentialist movement in France, for instance. Rhetorically, it could serve well during the period of Nazi occupation. Where the French intellectual was under constraint, the Existentialist reworking of Kierkegaard allowed for a kind of "pure" freedom. Existentialism could confront the censor as a literary movement indeterminately midway between Resistance and Collaboration. It offered dialectical devices whereby Frenchmen could be "substantially" free while being subject politically. This was the freedom of "suicide," with the motives of attack being turned back upon the self, such purely private and recondite authority being eulogized as godlike. The movement had relevance, as the translation of a political predicament into "cosmological" terms.

But after the fall of the Nazis, the particular social conditions of the occupation no longer prevailed. The proponents of Existentialism then broadened their movement, developing the study of dialectical operations in general and applying them to "universal" drama. In accordance with the Kierkegaardian twist, however, dialectic may then be reduced to suicide, whereas suicide should be treated as a special case of dialectic (in accordance with the opening pages of this volume).

The ultimate sacrifice does involve a dying. And a dying may involve a killing, by another or by the self. Whereupon, one may come to displace the emphasis, until the element of sacrifice retreats behind the element of murder (or its recent Existentialist variant, suicide). By that time, things have become quite reversed; and whereas sacrifice is the very essence of peace, it becomes instead the essence of war, with men piously persuading themselves that they are never so comforted as when contemplating a blood-bath. Admittedly, there are absurdities here. But a cult of the Absurd in effect sanctions them, whereas an attempt to derive them by rational steps, "dialectically" implies the hope of mitigating their rawness.

When men believe in polytheism, there is no problem in accounting for such sacrifices as God the Father's surrender of Christ the Son. If the "one God" is at war with other gods (or, as in Manicheism, with an equally powerful principle of Evil) for the mastery of the universe, then it is quite "rational" that such a God might have to sacrifice his son to the Prince of Evil as ransom for the human race. However, once polytheism has been transformed into monotheism by quite understandable dialectical procedures that sum up all things in an ultimate Term of Terms, new problems arise in trying to account for the sacrifice. If you start here, you will confront a logical "mystery." For, under monotheism, the cosmologizing of sacrifice is far more difficult to rationalize than under polytheism, though any perversion of Christian sacrifice, as with literary cults of the hunt or with the varieties of fascism, simplify the whole problem in purely militarist terms, until "pure" slaying, for sheer love of the art, becomes a kind of spiritual devotion.

Dialectically, one can spin out the various solutions, and the various subsequent embarrassments proper to each solution. There is no essential "irrationality" here. For reason (Logos) is, at the very least, words—and dialectic is the study of verbal resources. And when we consider such resources formally, we can observe how verbal solutions arise, and how these in turn give rise to verbal difficulties.

Another respect in which the paradoxes of the Absurd can be derived dialectically involves the grammatical resource whereby the sacred and the obscene become interchangeable, since each is a kind of "untouchability." The ritual uncleanness of the lowest Hindu class was but the counterpart of the "absolute dignity" possessed by superior classes. And looking too hastily, we may tend to see a mere evidence of "irrationality" in the "ambivalence" whereby the Latins could apply to criminals their word for "sacred" (a relation also involved in the outlaw's right of sanctuary at the altar). When K. asks a schoolteacher about the castle, the teacher in embarrassment calls attention to the fact that there are children present, speaking to him in French (as the language of "social distinction" in which one can also speak of subjects socially forbidden). The incident foreshadows in quality the letter in which the official Sortini makes filthy proposals to Amalia. Such "irrational ambivalence" need not be derived from a source essentially absurd. It can be explained grammatically as the dramatic expression of a normal relation between species and genus. For if both the holy and the obscene are *set apart* from other classes of things or persons, this *exceptional* quality is something they share in common, *generically,* though each manifests its own *specific* variants of this common element.

The forbidden (of either holy or obscene sorts) can become identified with the magic experiences of infancy, the tabus of the excremental, which are established along with the first steps in language, and fade into the prelinguistic stage of experience. Thus, ironically, the very "seat of highest dignity" can become furtively one with the connotations of the human posterior, in a rhetorical identification between high and low, since both can represent the principle of the tabu. A friend said:

"When I was young, I thought that a king's 'royal highness' was his behind, and that his subjects were required to show it great deference. I could not have told you what the principle of hierarchy is, but in this error I showed that I had got to the very foundations of it."

Gulliver's Travels has many episodes which, in Swift's morbidly playful way, exemplify the symbolic connection between the "sacred" tabus of royalty and the "obscene" tabus of the fecal. Most notably the identification figures roundabout, in satiric denial, near the beginning of Chapter VI, in the "Voyage to Brobdingnag." Here Gulliver recounts:

> I desired the Queen's woman to save for me the combings of her Majesty's hair, whereof in time I got a good quantity, and consulting with my friend the cabinet-maker, who had received general orders to do little jobs for me, I directed him to make two chair frames, no larger than those I had in my box, and then to bore little holes with a fine awl round those parts where I designed the backs and seats; through these holes I wove the strongest hairs I could pick out, just after the manner of cane chairs in England. When they were finished, I made a present of them to her Majesty, who kept them in her cabinet, and used to show them for curiosities, as indeed they were the wonder of every one that beheld them. The Queen would have me sit upon one of these chairs, but I absolutely refused to obey her, protesting I would rather die a thousand deaths than place a dishonorable part of my body on those precious hairs that once adorned her Majesty's head.

Immediately after, there is another identification, though of a nature that could be detected only by internal analysis of Swift's vocabulary. Gulliver speaks of his "mechanical genius." And for the overtones of the word "mechanical" in Swiftian satire, the reader is referred to the grotesquely gnarled adumbrations of psychoanalysis in Swift's essay on "The Mechanical Operation of the Spirit," where he attacks idealistic enthusiasm by deriving it from sources connected with the privy parts.

In *The German Ideology,* Marx touches upon similar identifications when, discussing idealistic systems that lead up to "one sacred head," he says:

> This "cranium system" is as old as the Egyptian pyramids, with which it has many similarities, and as new as the Prussian monarchy, in the capital of which it has recently been resurrected, as young as ever. The idealistic Dalai Lamas have this much in common with their real counterpart: they would like to persuade themselves that the world from which they derive their subsistence could not continue without their holy excrement. As soon as this idealistic folly is put into practice, its malevolent nature is apparent: its charlatanry, its pietistic hypocrisy, its unctuous deceit. Miracles are the asses' bridge leading from the kingdom of the idea to practice.

The last sentence suggests another route whereby the same connotations can arise: in the idealist doctrine whereby the material manifestation of spirit is like the externalizing of the internal.

In sum: Either elegant or filthy language can represent the hierarchic principle, just as both "up" or "down" represent the "principle of height." (The point is quite relevant to *Lady Chatterley's Lover*.) In this way, extremes can meet. To call a man very moral or to call him very immoral is at least "the same" in the sense that, in both cases, one is saying, "This man is to be considered exceptional from the standpoint of moral considerations"—and that is one of the purely "grammatical" factors behind "ambivalence" that might otherwise seem merely "irrational."

In a somewhat decadent bourgeois society, perverse and grotesque expressions of the hierarchic principle (variants of "Thersitism"?) would be more suitable than in a court where, for a stretch of years, much amenity had prevailed. In Kafka's case, there was added incentive to burlesque the "reverence," since he personally encountered such "transcendence" in a very low form, anti-Semitism. But though, as an enlightened intellectual, he could doubly contemn it, pragmatically it retained its "magic" nonetheless; as a going concern it actually did set the conditions of preferment.

Also, the greater shiftiness of status in bourgeois society is an invitation to blaspheme. The "shopkeeper" is absurd, from the "magical" point of view, because his store of riches is on display, not "awesomely," but *obsequiously*, in "aiming to please" the customer who is "always right" (though the ultra-fashionable shop contrives to restore the illusion by suggesting that merchant and client are united in a conspiracy to exclude "inferior" customers). The same problem, in a more exalted way, besets wealthy industrialists who have made their fortunes by the sale of products deemed ludicrous. Masefield's sonnet bathetically contrasting ancient poetic cargoes with modern prosaic ones derives its appeal from an "aristocratic" judgment of the bourgeoisie. For this he deserved to be knighted.

A friend said: "When at high school, mooning and moody with love, I was under an unusual puzzlement and constraint several times daily. For the father of the girl whom I revered in distant awe was a manufacturer of water closets. This sound citizen was proud enough of his commodity to have his name glazed in the enamel of the bowl. And since we had one of his excellent products in our bathroom, I had to confront the name of the beloved in ways that compelled its desecration. I fervently wished that the vessel had been given an impersonal trade name, such as Monarch, or Superior, or Little Gem."

Another incentive to the expression of hierarchy *via* the Absurd is found in the fact that the monetary test of "quality" impairs the magic so far as "racial superiority" goes. For some members of the "inferior" race may be financially better off than many of the "superior" race. In a society where monetary norms are as basic to the rationale of motives as they are in capitalism, a "racist" magic would be intact only if all the "superior" race were rich and all the "inferior" races were poor. Similarly the magic of "white supremacy" is impaired in the South, insofar as Negroes show earning capacity equal to the whites'. This is presumably the "rhetorical" motive for upholding the double standard of wages and jobs. (See Richard Wright's autobiography, *Black Boy,* for accounts of the sullenness and thoroughness with which this "order" can be imposed.) The South for magical reasons strives to hold down its wage scale, thereby as a region getting a smaller proportion of the national income, even while complaining of "Northern exploitation." In keeping the Negroes' wages low, it sets a competing lower standard for wages generally, except insofar as "outside union organizers from the North" can exert pressure for higher rates. A deliberate cult of the irrational, the Absurd, would obscure the perception of such conditions, even suggesting that there is a certain bad taste or literary crudeness in the mere mention of them; but a "dialectical" way of deriving these same absurdities can be "rational."

Again, insofar as an economy is beset by "crises," ("judgments") as the capitalist economy is periodically, the rational enlightenment which shows these to be man-made ills rather than "acts of God" redounds to the discredit of the ruling class, so that there are more incentives to "blaspheme" against the order than to treat it "reverently." But "blasphemy" soon invites to "irrational" excesses.

Again, to the extent that dignity is attested by monetary advantage, there seems to be a "magical" need for the higher officials in the typical business corporation to receive an income "awesomely" greater than that of any ordinary worker. It comes to seem dubious whether "authority" could be preserved by any other means. The "pursuit of happiness" is thus transformed into the search for "more magic," a condition of endless persecution besetting the successes and the failures, and the underlings who do not figure greatly in the race, but are prodded by its goading. The motive is not "greed." We could almost wish that it were, for greed might be sated, appeased, or grow weary. But the striving for "more reverence" in the social realm, this unconscious caricature of the quest for the divine, this illusion made "normal," can have no end. To seek for God in godly ways might be striving enough; all the more must the striving be endless, when men are "seeking for God" in terms of a social illusion, a "reverence" that attains its sympathetic, doctrinal counterpart in a cult of the "Absurd."

Order, the Secret, and the Kill

It is hard today to keep theological-esthetic cults of the Absurd and the Kill distinct from psychological-esthetic ones. Psychologically, for instance, one might begin by asking not, "What did God want of Abraham?" but, "Why did Abraham think that he 'ought to' kill his son?" Thus, with the "war of the generations" in mind (father and son as rival classes), one might interpret the religious motivation psychoanalytically as Abraham's mere "rationalization" of his "suppressed desire" to be rid of Isaac. Or giving the psychology an anthropological twist, one might ask, "What permanent antagonism between father and son is expressed in this story of a father who entertained thoughts of killing his son?" God's "command" would thus be interpreted as the disguised expression of a repugnant infanticidal impulse which Abraham, and all the "pious fathers" he stands for, translates into socially acceptable terms.

But here again, we would object to the stress upon the *killing* as primary. It would be another instance of our claim, stated earlier, that psychoanalysis too often reënforces the cult of the hunt, by transforming the by-product of sacrifice into its purpose, thus making a "devotion" of murder, quite as in fascist genocide and the "liberal" murder mystery. But, approached grammatically, through the "paradox of substance," the motivation acquires the other dimensions needed to present it in its true complexity. "Grammatically," we note that insofar as father and son are *consubstantial,* a father's fantasy of "scrupulously" slaying a beloved and only son would contain two elements: by thus "killing himself" vicariously, the father could simultaneously be destroyed and be saved. Thus, a friend said:

"On one occasion I took my son to the tower of a high building in New York, to show him the city below. When looking from a height, I had always had the fantasy of jumping. Many people have it. Even while knowing that they will not jump, they keep thinking, 'What if I jumped?'—and the imagining can sometimes be strong enough even to nauseate them. I often had this same feeling, though not to an alarming degree.

"But as I stood holding my son so that he could see over the parapet, a variant of this fantasy came over me intensely. I was seized with the thought, 'What if I threw him over?' And whereas, when I had had this fantasy with regard to my own descent, it was moderate, in this form it was brutally extreme. I was humiliated, and puzzled. For I thought I greatly loved this child; I thought he meant to me the very logic of my life. Yet here, even as he snuggled trustfully in my arms, I had thoughts of killing him. I took him to the street, in some haste, worried, and ashamed.

"For weeks I puzzled over this loathsome infanticidal motive, which seemed so contrary to the feelings that I consciously felt for my son. I remembered how, as a child, I had been told of the father rabbits eating the heads of the young, unless the mother was able to protect them. 'Am I no better than that?' I wondered. But I finally figured it out thus:

"With this child I identified myself as closely as I could possibly identify myself with someone other than myself. If, then, I threw him from the height, I could have had, simultaneously, both the jumping and the not-jumping. At least, without jumping, by the vicarious sacrifice of my son in my place, I could have had much more intensely the sense of jumping than when the fantasy involved me alone. Hence, the sudden almost overwhelming return of the old fantasy in this new, criminal form."

Of course, in the realm of fantasy, even mere velleities can take the form of killing (as revealed in the expression, "I could have killed him," to describe minor provocations). In this sense, fantasies of killing may at times be no more than a dramatic way of saying, "I wish I were, at the moment, free of this particular person." (André Gide's scrupulous villains transmogrify such irritability to demoniac proportions.) Under such conditions, fantasies of shooting a man dead might not be essentially different from fantasies of kicking him, or biting him in Stavrogin fashion.

Bunyan apparently felt great remorse for the many "protestant" obsessions of this sort that plagued him (the debtor, the victim of social hierarchy, who sought piously to impose upon himself the judgments of the socially superior, and thus was beset by tiny involuntary rebellions like the promptings of devils, until the problems of social reverence could attain their transcendence in terms of Christian's eventual religious preferment, with the hierarchy of the rich and poor transformed into the hierarchy of the saved and the damned, and the very last step into heaven being signalized by one last dispatching of the damned into hell).

Under some conditions, fantasies of killing can be as "unmoral" as the word "kill" itself, which is not even a "dirty" word as thus generalized, but is loathsome only in particular applications. And there is thus always the possibility that fantasy can approach the act of killing thus "impersonally," even when applied to personal cases conscientiously forbidden. This would be not so much an "eruption" of the "unconscious" as the operation of wholly "rational" faculties. For insofar as conscience itself is the *universalizing* of an act (considering it from the most general point of view), the universalizing of a personal element would be by the same token a kind of depersonalization. (This development may explain in part why a theater audience which would readily accept the sacrifice of a divine *dramatis persona* resents it when an "unhappy ending" befalls an ordinary likable character they have come to know.)

Is it not notable that, whereas the "four-letter words" for a few humble bodily functions are "indecent" and "obscene," the four-letter word for the taking of a human life is quite "neutral," though this act is forbidden us by Eternal commandment? God only knows what may be the motives of a peace-loving wretch who, if left to himself, would harm no one in all his life, and would be squeamishly humanitarian in his attitude towards animals, but is drafted by his nation for service as a professional killer. God only knows just what his confusions may be, and by what strange furies they are later to be manifested. But where the killing is "devotional," as in the Hemingway tradition, the relation between the proscriptions against bodily uncleanness and the proscriptions against killing may give us some clue to the motives. For symbolically, killing may be a kind of "anal act" that is "pure," transcending the tabus of the privy parts. (Anal-offal would be deathy, in contrast with life-giving oral-edible.) "Devotional" killing may thus resolve a psychic problem acquired when the infant is being taught control of excretory functions.

The thought incidentally suggests that, if our militarists finally succeed in establishing compulsory military training, they could not hope to transform our citizens into really devoted soldiers unless they strenuously insisted on early and strenuous punishment in the training of children, to instill in them an almost mystic horror of befouling themselves. By the use of excessive punishment to establish such tabus firmly in the stage of infancy, they might get an army of Roman Stoics who would be willing, with profoundest conscientiousness, to fight devoutly, whenever ordered, so that empire-builders could effectively "accept the solemn responsibility" of an "American Century."

The thought may also suggest why so many of our religionists seem so much more zealous today in helping out the movement towards bigger armies than in trying to promote international amity. Symbolically, there may be a "purer" devotion, as regards transcending of the "privy" tabus, in a cult of military discipline than in the more "unclean" ways of peace. For genuine peace today could be got only by such a dialectic as risked "contamination" by the enemy. Or rather, by such a dialectic as sought deliberately to give full expression to the voice of the enemy, not excluding it, but seeking to assign it an active place in an ultimate order. But when confronting the need for "dyings" and new "births" thus dialectically encouraged, men seem to prefer the simple suicide and homicide of militarist devotion, having persuaded themselves that the further dialectical growth of doctrine would be immoral.

Considering the Cult of the Kill from Veblen's angle of vision, we can also get glimpses of its earlier relation to social hierarchy. Only the upper classes could hunt. The lower classes could but poach. Hunting was thus not merely the insignia of privilege; it did reverence to the principle of *order*. (For though we tend to think of "law and order" as a pleonasm, like "house and home" or "day and time," the second word refers not merely to regulation, but to *hierarchy*. A genuine "new order" is a new *social ladder*.)

The "forest king" may have had his origins in a purely "universal" magic. One might get such an interpretation from the *Golden Bough*, at least to the extent that "primitive" psychology in general is being studied there, rather than "primitive class psychology," even though the signs of priestcraft are, on their face, signs of a "higher" class. In any case, even if one would hold that the "forest king" was not related to social privilege in his very origins, at the very least one would concede that the Robin Hood legends show how such reverence of early magic becomes interwoven with the principle of social hierarchy. For Robin Hood was the magical forest deity, Robert des Boix, *politicalized* (a "universal" myth transformed for "invidious" purposes). This benevolent poacher was the legendary hero of Saxon resistance to the Norman invader, resistance to a *ruling* class by a *subject* class.

In sum: On every hand, we find men, in their quarrels over property, preparing themselves for the slaughter, even to the extent of manipulating the profoundest grammatical, rhetorical, and symbolic resources of human thought to this end. Hence, insofar as one can do so without closing his eyes to the realities, it is relevant to attempt analyzing the tricky ways of thought that now work to complete the devotion of killing. Though churchmen may feel much genuine concern for human betterment in general, even the most scrupulous of them are susceptible to two major kinds of deception as regards religious motives: there can be the obscene mistaking of social reverence for religious reverence; and this obscenity is mingled with another, the furtive intermingling of the divine mystery with the "mystery" of the "demonic trinity," the excretory functions of the body.

The first of these is the more easily recognizable. It is unmistakably present insofar as any congregation is "exclusive." To say as much is to realize its ubiquity. The second is more difficult to detect, but attains its ultimate manifestation in "scrupulous" preference for militaristic solutions over peaceful solutions. The two probably merge in the "mystery" of private property, where many kinds of secrecy seem to converge: the secrecy of the holy, of plans in the stage of gestation, of conspiracy, of infancy and dream, of the privy parts and their functions, and of financial treasure. The study of human relations must attempt to make these interrelationships apparent, either in glimpses or when possible by organized critical method.

So we must keep trying anything and everything, improvising, borrowing from others, developing from others, dialectically using one text as comment upon another, schematizing; using the incentive to new wanderings, returning from these excursions to schematize again, being oversubtle where the straining seems to promise some further glimpse, and making amends by reduction to very simple anecdotes.

Order, the Secret, and the Kill. To study the nature of rhetoric, the relation between rhetoric and dialectic, and the application of both to human relations in general, is to circulate about these three motives. The appeal of Kierkegaard, for those who can follow him, may derive from the fact that his Cult of the Absurd (his word for the Secret) so profoundly involves the other two, Order and the Kill. Starting from any one of them, you find a vast network of dialectical possibilities in the offing, whereupon you may tend to see the whole of the dialectic itself in terms of this starting point, thereby being conservatively slavish to Order, morbidly fascinated by the Secret, militantly envenomed for the Kill. We must consider how the fullness of dialectic ("reality") is continually being concealed behind the mists of one or another of these rhetorical overemphases. Here would be the outer reaches of a Rhetoric of Motives.

We have given much thought to the hierarchic (Order, the ladder, cosmologized by the middle ages in what Lovejoy calls "the Great Chain of Being"). We have tried to show how it involves the Secret (though insofar as the "conspiratorical" secret merges into the private secret, it leads to themes that belong under Symbolic). At the moment we are centering our attention upon the Kill. And we are trying to show the important difference between an approach to the Kill through dialectic, and an approach to dialectic through the Kill.

With the evidence of the Crucifixion before us, we cannot deny that consubstantiality *is* established by common involvement in a killing. But one must not isolate the killing itself as the essence of the exaltation. Rather, one can account for the consubstantiality as arising from common participation in a notable, or solemn experience. Thus, we once saw the history of a human society in miniature, grounded in a rhetoric of primitive magic. Some boys, about ten years of age, had been playing in a vacant lot. They stirred up a rattlesnake, which the father of one boy killed with a hoe. Then they had their pictures taken, dangling the dead snake. Immediately after, they organized the Rattlesnake Club. Their members were made consubstantial by the sacrifice of this victim, representing dangers and triumphs they had shared in common. The snake was a sacred offering; by its death it provided the spirit for this magically united band. (We said that the incident was a human society in miniature. We had in mind the fact that there was also an electing of officers and the collecting of dues. The matter of offices and dues promptly gave rise to quarrels and cliques—thus quickly was the solemnizing spirit of the snake god sacrificed a second time, as there emerged the rhetoric of the Scramble, the discordancies of Babel.)

All told, there is the *self-abnegation* of "sacrifice." And sacrifice is the essence of religion. Symbolically, it is a kind of *suicide,* a willed variant of *dying,* dying to this or that particular thing ("mortification"), not because of those things in themselves, but because the yielding of them represents the principle of sacrifice in the absolute. So, the religious injunctions against suicide in the literal sense are matched by the many religious disciplines for attaining transcendence by dying "dialectically." And where there must thus be simultaneously a dying and a not-dying, what is more plausible than for the paradox of substance to figure here, in providing symbolic devices whereby a man can "substantially" slay himself through the sacrifice of another who is consubstantial with him? Indeed, among the psychological appeals of the Christian sacrifice, wherein the ultimate father sacrifices the ultimate son, may be the fact that in this myth there is the perfect paradigm for such simultaneous losing-and-having, since the two persons of father and son are consubstantial, and the ultimate father sacrifices the ultimate son for the sake of human betterment (as the principle of individual sacrifice itself is ultimately motivated by such social objectives, a sacrificial restraining of individual divisiveness in accordance with "virtues" designed for the advantage of mankind in general).

And when our friend, standing with his son in that high place, felt "infanticidal" impulses, perhaps he was but manifesting roundabout the fact that he felt exalted, as though he and his son shared the attributes of the Ultimate Father and the Ultimate Son in heaven. Even though he may not have got to such feelings by true religious reverence, he could have got to them by the temptations of social reverence. For here was the principle of hierarchy materialized, as he stood atop a high building, while that building itself represented nothing less than the straining social hierarchy of the great modern Babylon. "And upon her forehead was a name written, MYSTERY, BABYLON THE GREAT, THE MOTHER OF HARLOTS AND ABOMINATIONS OF THE EARTH." (Revelation 17:5.)

Pure Persuasion

Apparently the farthest one can go, in matters of rhetoric, is to the question of "pure persuasion." But since that would bring us to the borders of metaphysics, or perhaps better "meta-rhetoric," we should try as much as possible to keep particular examples in mind.

Thus, looking back at *Alice in Wonderland* "meta-rhetorically," let us consider how it looks, when judged as "pure persuasion." Psychoanalysis suggests the nature of its "impurity," its ambiguous gallantry as the courting of a girl child not yet nubile by a man advanced in years. The situation provides such obvious material for psychoanalysis that Empson's superb chapter on Alice is continually being deflected from its own best insight. Yet here is a perfect instance where the courtship is not primarily sexual at all, but a communication between classes, the subtle variants of appeal being strongly mixed with the telltale variants of "standoffishness."

Dodgson is not much concerned with the principle of abstract womanhood (as it might be variously represented in virgin-worship, prostitution, promiscuity, or a cult of seduction). But he never forgets the idea of social courtship. The fantasy represents this principle grotesquely, in reverse, by stories about the characters' comical rudeness and crudeness, as contrasted with Alice's mild priggishness.

In engaging the child's attention by puzzles that tease as well as entertain, the book gets its standoffish element. It says in effect: "I am at your mercy. I don't dare to bore you. But let us not forget that I also have a stance of my own. You are for me magic, music, and mystery. But I can magically, musically mystify you, too." Psychoanalysis makes us see too clearly the perverted sexual lover. He is unquestionably there.

But his presence should not conceal the rhetorical exercise, the artistic persuasion, emboding motives not of sexual but of social intercourse.

Perhaps "social" is not quite accurate. For youth and age, as contrasted communicating "kinds," could not be classed exactly as either sexual or social. They are biological, as with the hierarchal relation between weak and strong. However, both age-youth and weak-strong, with their complications and reversibilities, readily become identified with social elements, particularly as regards familial and political symbols of authority.

It would not be exorbitant to put *Alice in Wonderland* in the same bin not only with *The Castle,* but also with D. H. Lawrence's *Lady Chatterley's Lover.* Each in its way represents social reverence, grotesquely, perversely. Each in its way would repay analysis as observed from the standpoint of *The Book of the Courtier.* Each, in its way, is not merely a work that implicitly embodies the principle of courtship: in all three the principle of courtship is explicitly the subject matter.

We hesitate to say this because Lawrence's work is itself so strongly psychoanalytic in perspective, and so "sexual," that we seem to be impairing our own case. Yet we would have the reader see the entire situation the other way round, noting the intense factor of social hierarchy that characterizes relations among Lawrence's characters, and scrutinizing his view of "the unconscious" itself for connotations of upsurge from coal pits (though the translation of such revolt into psychoanalytic terms transcends the political implications, and thereby negates them). The "filthy" words for sex are but the obverse of the hierarchic reverence present in his psychoanalytically romantic ones. And if you had to make a flat choice between a social and a physical origin for the sexuality in his books, you would be much nearer to the truth if you took the social one (even its relation to the excitability of his disease being social insofar as it involves antitheses of weakness and strength, sensitiveness and bluntness, that fall primarily in the category of the "socially invidious").

With talk of "pure persuasion," the factor of degree can readily confuse us. Thus, we may think of social or literary courtship as pure persuasion, when we contrast it with a direct bid for sexual favors, or with commercial advertising. Similarly, education in contrast with debating might be called pure persuasion. And scientific or religious insemination may seem "pure" when compared with the injection of the doctrinal seed through political ideologies. But all these modes of expression are "impure," and seek advantage, as compared with the absolute, and therefore nonexistent, limit we here speak of. Yet, though what we mean by pure persuasion in the absolute sense exists nowhere, it can be present as a motivational ingredient in any rhetoric, no matter how intensely advantage-seeking such rhetoric may be. The point should become clearer as we proceed. At this stage we need only note that the indication of pure persuasion in any activity is in an element of "standoffishness," or perhaps better, *self-interference,* as judged by the tests of acquisition. Thus, while not essentially sacrificial, it *looks* sacrificial when matched against the acquisitive.

Pure persuasion involves the saying of something, not for an extraverbal advantage to be got by the saying, but because of a satisfaction intrinsic to the saying. It summons because it likes the feel of a summons. It would be nonplused if the summons were answered. It attacks because it revels in the sheer syllables of vituperation. It would be horrified if, each time it finds a way of saying, "Be damned," it really did send a soul to rot in hell. It intuitively says, "This is so," purely and simply because this is so.

Or, since it is formal, it can arise out of expressions quite differently motivated, as when a book, having been developed so far, sets up demands of its own, demands conditioned by the parts already written, so that the book becomes to an extent something not foreseen by its author, and requires him to interfere with his original intentions. We here confront an "ultimate" motive (as distinct from an "ulterior" one). Or if you insist that there is only the "illusion" of such a motive, even so, that "illusion" can be strong enough to act as a motive in its own right. It would then be an "illusion of pure persuasion," after the analogy of De Gourmont's formula for the "illusion of liberty."

In such a realm of the absolute, of course, it is not hard to get quickly from "self-interference" to "freedom." We but exemplify in reverse Kant's discovery that the "free" legislating of a universal law would impose restrictions upon the legislator, a dialectical miracle which we again encounter, partially burlesqued, in the Existentialist notion (like the doctrine of the nihilist in Dostoevski's *The Possessed*) that one is "free," hence a god, in suicide. (Since the idea of self-interference would get its ultimate expression in images of suicide, a kind of religious exhilaration could accompany the Existentialist rationale of suicide whereby real loss is transformed into ideal gain.)

What the anthropologist Malinowski called "phatic communion" might seem close to "pure persuasion." He referred to talk at random, purely for the satisfaction of talking together, the use of speech as such for the establishing of a social bond between speaker and spoken-to. Yet "pure persuasion" should be much more intensely purposive than that, though it would be a "pure" purpose, a kind of purpose which, as judged by the rhetoric of advantage, is no purpose at all, or which might often look like sheer frustration of purpose. For its purpose is like that of solving a puzzle, where the puzzle-solver deliberately takes on a burden in order to throw it off, but if he succeeds, so far as the tests of material profit are concerned he is no further ahead than before he began, since he has advanced not relatively, but "in the absolute."

Yet the "self-interference" of "pure" persuasion can derive from many "impure" sources, or become compromised by "entangling alliances." Its utterances may become the vehicle for all sorts of private ambitions, guilts, and vengeances, or the instrument of other men so motivated. Persons who cannot solve their problems by victory in the Scramble can certainly "compensate for frustration" by solving arbitrary puzzles. Even elements of magic (in the sense of bad science) may come to figure here, as the puzzle-solver may furtively promise himself that, by the solving of arbitrarily chosen puzzles, he will "homoeopathically" solve puzzles imposed upon him by conditions beyond his control.

The devout man's relations to his God have a kind of standoffishness. For his sin is rebellion, and he never lets it be forgot that he is always sinning somewhat. Here are the rudiments for a grim kind of coyness.

Perhaps as near an instance of "pure persuasion" as one could find is in the actor's relation to his audience. Yet you could readily see how it might become homosexual in its implications, hardly other than a roundabout way of recruiting lovers who share the same "persuasion," particularly if the actor's talent was originally developed as an appeal to socially "superior" persons of the same sex. An audience, technically a sexless function, can stand furtively for a kind of *alter ego* that is the narcissistic, socially idealized version of the beloved self.

In Dodgson's case, the "meta-rhetorical" motive was unquestionably interwoven with odd sexual quandaries. Yet we may question whether these themselves were the truly "prior" motives, since they could be developed as a response to the awareness of "hierarchy in general." And while such order would be more social than sexual, it is "prior" even to the social, deriving ultimately from the nature of communication *per se*.

In its essence communication involves the use of verbal symbols for purposes of appeal. Thus, it splits formally into the three elements of speaker, speech, and spoken-to, with the speaker so shaping his speech as to "commune with" the spoken-to. This purely technical pattern is the precondition of *all* appeal. And "standoffishness" is necessary to the form, because without it the appeal could not be maintained. For if union is complete, what incentive can there be for appeal? Rhetorically, there can be courtship only insofar as there is division. Hence, only through interference could one court continually, thereby perpetuating genuine "freedom of rhetoric."

We are not offering this concept of "pure" rhetoric as the highest ideal of human conduct. We are simply trying to show how such a rhetorical motive can of itself supply a principle of interference which, whatever its origin, often has a high ethical value, as with the late Irving Babbitt's concept of the "inner check."

Put it this way. Suppose that there were no motives of incest awe to produce sexual tabus. Suppose that there were no higher and lower social classes, to instill "reverence" for the real, personal, or sentimental properties that came to be the insignia of privilege. Suppose there were no boasting, no goad to display superior prowess. Would there still be a source from which might be derived an athleticism of self-denial, as for instance in priestly or courtly cults of chastity, or in vows of poverty?

We are suggesting that there would be, that such an incentive is implicit in the "transcendent" nature of symbolism itself. And out of this could arise a *symbolically grounded* distrust of acquisitiveness, a feeling that one should not just "take things," but should court them, show gratitude for them, or apologize for killing them (as with the "natural courtesy" that some savages show to the game they have caught, a practice rationalistically explained as the savage's way of thanking the victim for participating so handsomely in the success of the hunt, but basically the incentive of courtliness). Another variant is perhaps discernible in the neurotic artist, suffering wretchedly from his neurosis, yet so slavish in his devotion to symbols that he is hesitant to be cured, lest he impair the persuasiveness of his art.

The "enlightened" absence of this motive (in the modern pragmatism of natural science, where the only acknowledged resistances to the acquisition of power must come from the nature of the physical conditions themselves) could make for more crudeness than it does, if it really prevailed as much as the "enlightened" think it does.

True, even if you granted that such a motive exists, derivable directly from the nature of language rather than indirectly from the social structure, there would be no reason why, in a complex society, with its many hierarchally ordered institutions and their corresponding properties and proprieties, such a motive should not often show rather as its opposite: in a tough cult of acquisition, born of impatience with such exactions. This should be particularly the case when, given the conditions of the Scramble, if one did not first grab, he would not have much chance not to grab. The "emancipated" would like nothing better than a society so burdened with "self-interference" that it could be scooped up easily, in one big fish net.

At the very least, even without intense competitive pressure, any sheer cult of self-denial would be enough, in its austerity, to build up resistances which the body and the mind found gratification in breaking down again. Hence, just as self-denial could come of persuasion, so an acquisitive "negating of the negation" could come from the same source. And for our part, rather than treating the fantastic acquisitiveness of imperialists as a mere "mental replica" of biological desires, we would explain it thus roundabout, as *the dialectical transformation of self-denial into its opposite*.

The mere fact that a withholding, or an interposing of distance, is worked into a system (as it is in the athleticism of the ascetic), makes for an intellectual fullness which may then be transformed into an instrument having new possibilities of gain. Such is apparently the way in which priestcraft comes to the aid of political and economic advantage (particularly when the priests are literate, since clericalism serves so well for tax-gathering, and in general for expansion of a ruler's realm, while also of course helping to ally the ruler with the "divine"). And if you look closely enough at capitalist motives, as the secularization of priestly symbolism, you can glimpse a similar roundabout development (signalized in the doctrine that profit on capital investment is justified as a reward for "postponed consumption"). It is the difference between the finance capitalist's amassing of monetary *symbols* and the earlier stage of "primitive accumulation" (though even in most "primitive accumulation," wealth is not sought for itself alone, but for its "transcendent" value as insignia).

Once we saw a performance by the Chinese ritual dancer, Mei Lanfang. We were vastly impressed by his ceremony of reaching: the slow movements of hand, wrist, and arm whereby he first gradually worked back the long sleeve that covered his fingers—and then, after this patient preparation, the tentative approaching of the freed hand to the object, and finally, the cautious grasping and lifting. The next day we happened to attend an American movie. At one point in the story the phone rang—and the heroine swung around abruptly, to snatch up the receiver like a tigress leaping on a lamb. Ordinarily the incident would have been unnoticeable. This time we jumped.

Let's not deceive ourselves. There's a thoroughly "class" motive that goes far towards explaining such ritual. Where acquisition is assured to a class by the nature of the property structure itself, the class need not snatch. Accordingly, the esthetic spokesmen that represent its values need not snatch. We might also note how, by rites that teach others not to snatch, it might help to perpetuate its privileges. (We recall that, along with such pudency of acquisition, there was a sword dance in which symbolic heads were severed with dispatch.)

Yet note another element here: the ritual. This was a symbolic getting, not a real one. Hence, it could exist only by prolonging or delaying the act, or in the case of the sword dance, by "pure purpose" (Kant's purposiveness without purpose). This element is so intrinsic to the ritual act that, even without the class motive, you could derive it. All purely ritual getting is also a not-getting. After our many remarks on "mystification," we would be the last to deny the importance of the class motive. We only plead to recognize that there can be a factor even prior to that, in that a ritual acquisition is no acquisition, hence is intrinsically an interference with the ways of acquisition (though we would not deny that such rituals of the nonacquisitive might themselves, in bringing the performer prestige and other rewards, serve to his advantage in the most directly acquisitive sense).

We are not making a moralistic statement here. We are not saying that there "should be" pure persuasion, or more of it. Or that "human frailty" is forever making persuasion "impure." We are saying that, as the ultimate of all persuasion, its form or archetype, there *is* pure persuasion. If you want, we are even willing, for the sake of the argument, to take the opposite moralistic position, and say that there "should not be" pure persuasion, or that there "should be less of it." The important consideration is that, in any device, the ultimate form (paradigm or idea) of that device is present, and is acting. And this form would be the "purity."

Since the ultimate form of persuasion is composed of three elements (speaker, speech, and spoken-to), as regards the act of persuasion alone obviously you could not maintain this form except insofar as the plea remained unanswered. When the plea is answered, you have gone from persuasion to something else. Where you had previously been trying to get in, you may now have to try getting out, as we saw in the case of Kierkegaard. This is what we mean by the technical or formal need of "self-interference" as a motive in persuasion. This is why we say that the ultimate cult of persuasion would transcend the use of persuasion for local advantage, as the fourth book of *The Courtier* transcended the preceding three. If you were winsomely persuasive, you could keep on persuading only by yourself supplying the interferences which you overcome in your audiences, like lovers who "quarrel to make up," or as with "virtuous" women who develop a Carlylean cult of Clothes "in all its nakedness," as a mode of "pure persuasion" that ambiguously combines the pudencies of property with the pruriencies of propriety (a "rhetorical" motive that now forms the basis of a major industry).

Where an anthropologist or sociologist might derive sexual tabus from institutional sources, we would not deny his evidence. We would only say that, over and above all such derivations, there is, *implicit in language itself,* the act of persuasion; and *implicit in the perpetuating of persuasion* (in persuasion made universal, pure, hence paradigmatic or formal) *there is the need of "interference."* For a persuasion that succeeds, dies. To go on eternally (as a form does) it could not be directed merely towards attainable advantages. And insofar as the advantages are obtainable, *that* particular object of persuasion could be maintained as such only by interference. Here, we are suggesting, would be the ultimate rhetorical grounds for the tabus of courtship, the conditions of "standoffishness."

The frenzied human cult of advantage, the quest of many things that cannot bring real advantage yet are obtainable, would likewise seem ultimately to require such a "meta-rhetorical" explanation. (At least, this would account for its *origins*. Institutional factors would account for its *intensity*.) Insofar as a society rejects interference "from within" as a device for perpetuating the persuasive act, men can still get the same result by a cult of "new needs" (with the continual shifting of objectives to which men are goaded by the nature of our economic system). By such temporizings, the form of persuasion is permanently maintained. For in proportion as men, threatened with the loss of persuasion through attaining its object, turn to court other objects, such constant shifting of purposes in effect supplies (as it seems, "from without") the principle of self-interference which the perpetuating of the persuasive act demands. To make the attaining of A but the condition for the need of B, and the attaining of B but the condition for the need of C, etc., adds up to the same "form" as if one merely went on forever courting A at a distance. A single need, forever courted, as on Keats's Grecian Urn, would be made possible by self-interference. Drop self-interference, plunge "extravertedly" into the "rat race" of new needs forever changing, and you get the equivalent. (The permanent form would be got in one case by excessive fixity of attention, in the other by excessive distraction; but the distraction can have its kind of continuity too, insofar as all the "new needs" are rationalized by the "unitary" symbolism of money.)

We are not moralistic about our thoughts on pure persuasion, because we cannot see it as either "good" or "bad" in the moralistic, political, institutional sense. We can only surmise that it comes quite close to the origins of the Human Comedy, which gets its costumes from the changing conditions of history, but the form of which, like laughter, derives from the nature of language itself, the "rationality" of *homo dialecticus,* of man as a symbol-using animal whose symbols simultaneously reflect and transcend the "reality" of the nonsymbolic.

Biologically, it is of the essence of man to desire. But by the same token, biologically it is of the essence of man to be sated. Only the motives of "mystery" (making for development towards ever "higher" degrees of ordination) are infinite in their range, as a child learns for himself when he first thinks of counting "to the highest number."

The dialectical transcending of reality through symbols is at the roots of this mystery, at least so far as naturalistic motives are concerned. It culminates in pure persuasion, absolute communication, beseechment for itself alone, praise and blame so universalized as to have no assignable physical object (hence it is led to postulate the Principles of Goodness and Evil in general, as the only "audience" possible for an address so generalized).

Here reverence, God, hierarchy are found to be the ultimates of the dialectical process. Call them the "basic errors" of the dialectic if you want. That need not concern us. We are here talking about ultimate dialectical tendencies, having "god," or a "god-term," as the completion of the linguistic process. If you want to conclude, "so much the worse for the linguistic process," that is your affair. We have enough areas of agreement for our study of rhetoric if you but concede that, language being essentially a means of transcending brute objects, there is implicit in it the "temptation" to come upon an idea of "God" as the *ultimate* transcendence.

Primitive peoples may have deities that are explainable wholly as "nature gods." We doubt it, but we are willing for argument's sake to give an opponent the benefit of the doubt. What we are saying is that, even if there are gods conceived wholly as replicas of natural powers, you would miss the whole point of "mystification" unless at the very least you allowed also for a "dialectic god" ("logos") which could perhaps merge with the "nature god" (somewhat as the God of the New Testament merged with the God of the Old). This title of titles would be the ultimate of what Kant would call the "transcendental dialectic," the all-summarizing Idea.

Our point is: Here, in this conclusion of dialectic, one should look for the ultimate rhetorical motive of *homo dialecticus*. Human effort would thus be grounded not in the search for "advantage," and in the mere "sublimating" of that search by "rationalizations" and "moralizations." Rather, it would be grounded in a *form,* in the persuasiveness of the hierarchic order itself. And considered dialectically, prayer, as pure beseechment, would be addressed not to an *object* (which might "answer" the prayer by providing booty) but to the *hierarchic principle itself,* where the answer is implicit in the address. There is a fallacy of overformal interpretation, which so stresses "pure" motives that the factor of advantage is slighted. But there is also the fallacy of overly materialist interpretations which would slight dialectic as a factor. The fact that tabus get their character from the conditions of a particular property structure does not eliminate their further grounding in tendencies inborn to *oratio.*

We are not discovering "God" here, in the theologian's sense. God, in the theologian's sense, must be much more than an "Idea" dialectically arrived at. Judged from the standpoint of orthodox doctrine, we believe that a pure "dialectic god" would be as unsatisfactory in one way as a mere "nature god" would be in another. But going by the verbal route, from words for positive things to titles, thence to an order among titles, and finally to the title of titles, we come as far as rhetoric-and-dialectic can take us, which is as far as this book contracts to take us.

Yet, perhaps we here overstate the case. A god unites generalization with personification. And whereas a "dialectic god" might seem to lack the second of these elements, it clearly possesses the first. In this sense, "pure persuasion" could qualify as one member of a pantheon. It would be an equivalent for the "Goddess Peitho" at that point where Greek religion and Greek science overlapped (since the Greek equated science with *generalized* knowledge). Yet the principle of personality would be there too, though indirectly. For ideas are personal.

They are personal because only persons can have them. They are an aspect of something so essentially personal as symbol-using ("human rationality"). An idea can seem impersonal because many men, or all men, may share in its personality (or partake of its substance, quite like communicants ritualistically eating the blood and body of their god).

Indeed, once you linger on this question of personality, you find it bristling with dialectical paradoxes whereby the personal and the impersonal subtly change places (paradoxes that furtively invest humans with "divine" attributes, hence adding to the "mystifications" so important in rhetorical prodding). When a figure becomes the personification of some impersonal motive, the result is a *depersonalization*. The person becomes the charismatic vessel of some "absolute" substance. And when thus magically endowed, the person transcends his nature as an individual, becoming instead the image of the idea he stands for. He is then the representative not of himself but of the family or class substance with which he is identified. In this respect he becomes "divine" (and his distinctive marks, such as his clothing, embody the same spirit).

Thus, when the principle of social reverence attains its summing up in the person of a beloved, she is loved not merely "for herself," but for what she "represents," as charismatic vessel of a social motive which the lover, or communicant, would court roundabout. Indeed, marriage as a sacrament so binds social and religious reverence together that you could not tell where "careerism" ends and "God" begins.

Whether the beloved be thought of as "superior," "inferior," or "equal" in social status, she can represent the hierarchic principle, and is to this extent a mystery, a purchasable miracle. She is "ordained" with the properties of an absolute order. Her glow, an almost visible aura, is rhetorical. But the persuasiveness of this rhetoric derives from the perfection or thoroughness of the lover's dialectical enterprise. He loves her for the ordination that she stands for. He can then dream fondly even of her death. For in her ordination she is divine, in her divinity she is immortal, and the idea of immortality must be approached humanly through the imagery of dying, while furthermore, in their dying together, jointly godlike, there would also be symbolically a coitus (all told, a dialectic alchemy whereby acquisition is readily transformed into relinquishment—and the dialectic being verbal, "intellectual," we glimpse a purely dialectical reason why Aquinas' angels, or messengers, should be "intellectuals," as also with the kind of courtship permissible to ordination in priestly celibacy).

But we have digressed, since we saw an opportunity to approach rhetorical "mystery" from another angle. We were telling how we arrived at a "dialectic god" of "pure persuasion." Next we should reverse our direction. Going from "pure hierarchy" of the dialectical form down to its embodiment in particular kinds of effort, we note first such manifestations as in the "reverent" tributes to the earthly hierarchy. We note the equivalents of this, either in a "pastoral" rapport between high and low, or (when the bond is snapped) in such "mystic" hatred as spokesmen for the "toiling masses" sometimes feel for the very idea of the "ruling class," or as spokesmen for the ruling class feel for the leaders of revolt, or even of reform. So, we look for all the attenuations of mystery. For as students of rhetoric, we concede the great persuasive power of mystery (indeed, even to the extent of wondering whether those journalistic apologists of capitalism may be most ironically defeating their own purposes when they attempt to build up the notion that the motives of the Kremlin are "enigmatic," and "inscrutable," that the ancient mysteries of the "East" are threatening to sweep across the enlightened "West"—for the current cult of the mystery story seems indication enough that the people are more than ready to be raped by a mystery).

However, when we hold that there is a hierarchic incentive (with its "mystery") embedded in the very nature of language, when we insist that one would deceive himself who derived "mystery" purely from institutional sources, we are not arguing for or against any particular set of institutions. The relative value of institutions depends pragmatically, Darwinistically, on their fitness to cope with the problems of production, distribution, and consumption that go with conditions peculiar to time and place. Thus, one particular order (or property structure), with its brands of "mystery," may be better suited than another for the prevailing circumstances. Hence, to say that hierarchy is inevitable is not to argue categorically against a new order on the grounds that it would but replace under one label what had been removed under another. It is merely to say that, in any order, there will be the mysteries of hierarchy, since such a principle is grounded in the very nature of language, and reënforced by the resultant diversity of occupational classes. That claim is the important thing, as regards the ultimate reaches of rhetoric. The intensities, morbidities, or particularities of mystery come from institutional sources, but the *aptitude* comes from the nature of man, generically, as a *symbol-using animal*.

Similarly, noting how the Prussian officer had his cultural counterpart in the academic drillmaster whose teaching was like an imperial threat, we might want to deduce all scholastic discrimination from social discrimination. But such a view would slight the principle of ordination essential to the educational process, which inevitably requires a ladder of grading and instruction. The purely "dialectical" motive is real enough here, though forever being burlesqued in the academic "positions of pantomime."

As exclusively institutional explanations mislead us in one respect, so exclusively psychoanalytic explanations can mislead in another. First a dialectical motive implicit in the nature of language is treated psychoanalytically as a mere derivative of psychological motives. Hence, the principle of "self-interference" would be explained wholly as a "sublimation" of psychological drives, whereas these themselves are strongly affected by a purely "formal" situation, the fact that language makes for transcendence, and transcendence imposes distance (a generally dialectical consideration, rather than an exclusively psychological one). Second, psychoanalysis too often conceals the nature of social relations behind the terms for sexual relations. On the first point, what we have said about the way in which institutional explanations ignore the "priority" of the formal element could be applied *mutatis mutandis* to psychoanalytic theories. So let us turn now to the second point, noting how psychoanalysis, unless properly discounted, can lead us even farther afield, by concealing the nature of exclusive social relations behind inclusive terms for sexual relations.

The sheer dialectics of "justice" strongly invites this error. For justice is the *universalization* of a standard. Hence, if one is made neurotic by *social* discriminations (by the hierarchy of class), translation of the disorders into terms of the universally sexual and the universally familial may, by such speciously universal terms, appeal by speaking in the accents of "truth" and "justice." Instead of saying, "*My class* is the victim of a *social* problem," one can say, in terms of the universalizing required by justice, "We are *all* victims of a *sexual* problem." Since the social problem will have its counterpart in sexual disorders, much "evidence" will be found for such deflection. And the deflected universalization has a "charity" that would be lacking in the social version.

The error is not rectified by a stress upon individualistic aggression, compensation, inferiority, and the like. For individualism acts as strongly as universalism to conceal the "mysteries" of class. Similarly, while a theory of "psychological types" in a sense restores a stress upon class, such classes so fall on the bias across the motives of social hierarchy that they are little more than concealments of it. All such interpretation of hierarchic motives in terms of sexual motives seems to continue, under a new guise, the earlier functions of idealistic mystification.

Or we may at once express and conceal the social origins of a neurosis by attributing it to a "birth trauma." The *exclusive* traumatic accident of being born into the quandaries of a particular social situation is thus seen as the *inclusive* misfortune of having been born at all. A malaise which gets its neurotic intensity from the social structure is thus thought to be explainable obstetrically. The specific, *familial* connotations of *class* are interpreted as the generic, *universally physiological* fact of *birth*.

Thus, in literature, a cryptic style, developed by a person with a social "shame" or "secret" of some sort, might be used as a badge of distinction, yet might also symbolize the "guilt," as were the writer to have suffered or feared some form of social discrimination or judgment, an obsession that would manifest itself furtively in the hermetic confession that was simultaneously a boast. But though this bid for distinction arose from a sense of social stigma, and so requires a rhetorical explanation, the fact that it involves ideas of one's "substance" as member of a questioned "family" or "kind" might then lead the analyst instead to look for purely *medical* explanations, as were he to derive it from the shock of birth.

There *is* a "universal" lesson here. But it is in the fact that we confront a "hierarchic psychosis," prevailing in all nations, but particularly sinister in nations which are largely ruled by the "dead hand" of institutions developed from past situations and unsuited to the present. In one form or another, it affects every rung of the social ladder, however imperceptible or roundabout its workings may be. "Psychogenic illness" is now perhaps the usual symptom of such "social diseases"—and here again we confront the difficulty in a "universal" term that conceals its genesis. It is no accident that psychoanalysis grew under the shadow of the ailing Hapsburg bureaucracy.

An adolescent, let us say, goes to an exclusive secondary school. It is beyond his parents' financial reach. They strain every resource to send him there. For they have their son's good at heart. And what is their son's "good"? They are thinking, doubtless, of "connections." What they are not thinking of is the fact that, at a time when he is "normally" beset by sexual quandaries, they expose him to a further bewildering set of social quandaries. There are the morbidities of his questionable status, with its pretensions and guilt, that make him oversensitive, either too obsequious or too aggressive, and secretly in doubt where he really "belongs." So they send him to a psychologist, who discovers that all the misgivings derive from infantile relations to his family. Now, unquestionably, such factors are involved, along with the time he got chicken pox, and the time he got caught stealing fruit from a neighbor's garden, and the time some relative in some way startled or disappointed him. In being "born into" a new hierarchy, with all its unutterable magic, in attempting to acquire the suggestive insignia that will make him a new self, he is affected in every particle of his past. But the greater the stress upon such "universal" or "individual" elements, the greater the deflection from the main source of the mystery. You can take it as an axiom: Where the mystery is, there is the neurosis. Indeed, the entire stress upon early childhood experiences, valuable as it is in itself, can deflect by leading one to place in terms of *familial* substance motives that require placement more broadly in terms of *social* substance.

Popular reference to the "inferiority complex" is another instance where a motive which is really of a *class* nature has the deceptive appearances of individuality (and its dialectical counterpart, universality).

An "inferiority complex" is a sense that one's *kind of* being is inferior to another *kind of* being (or is endangered by that other *kind*). It is not merely an implied comparison between the self and another; it is a comparison between what I think I stand for and what I think the other stands for, in the terms of some *social* judgment. No individual could give another individual an "inferiority complex." Without the notion of an audience, an outside observer, to judge of the relation, the most one would feel would be the awareness of a literal inferiority. But there is a wide discrepancy between inferiority and an "inferiority complex." The first is merely a "fact" (a fact about everybody, by one test or another); the second is an *accusation,* in which one passes a social judgment upon oneself, condemning oneself from the standpoint of some real or imagined court of conscience (another variant of the "courtship" theme).

For this reason, persons who have broken away from their class or "race" (as Negro intellectuals, liberal Jews, or Gentiles who have notably altered their social position for better or worse) have more of an "inferiority complex" than persons who remain wholly within the traditions of their community. Those who remain unchanged feel the reënforcement that comes of being one with their kind, in the quite realistic sense, rather than suffering from a partial sense of isolation, through being, in their nature as the "break-away type," somewhat in a kind all by themselves, *sui generis,* except insofar as they meet cronies who, being similarly derived, are somewhat like fellow conspirators. (Recall the many variants in the Bohemian-expatriate literary movement, with the social mystery often taking the rhetorical form of the hermetic, its nature indicated in the formula, *épater le bourgeois,* a perverse way of courtship not fundamentally different from Dodgson's devices for puzzling little Alices.)

The psychoanalytic emphasis seems to be groping for an important distinction which it is not able to make. We have said that man, as a symbol-using animal, experiences a difference between *this* being and *that* being as a difference between *this kind of* being and *that kind of* being. Here is a *purely dialectical* factor at the very center of realism. Here, implicit in our attitudes toward things, is a principle of *classification.* And classification in this linguistic, or formal sense is all-inclusive, "prior" to classification in the exclusively social sense. The "invidious" aspects of class arise from the nature of man not as a "class animal," but as a "classifying animal."

We recall, for instance, a parlor game in which people were classified according to two antithetical groups of nonsense syllables. Say, for instance, they were distinguished not as "progressive and conservative," "extravert and introvert," or "bourgeois and Bohemian," but as "Vizzles and Vozzles," or "Sliffs and Smooves." Then various members of the party took turns in making up lists of the traits that characterized each such "class." Finally you would get confirmed Vizzelites who were fanatically set against Vozzlians, and Sliffists that were almost exalted in their detestation of Smoovies.

Unquestionably, even while burlesquing the "hierarchic psychosis" to which people are prone, the game was one more indication of "rage for order." That is, even the playful use of nonsense syllables derived piquancy from the animus of "invidious" social situations that really did form the background of the game. But the initial workability of mere nonsense syllables indicates a purely *formal* ground, implicit in the rationality of *homo dialecticus,* a generic aptitude for classification wherein social classification would be a special case.

When psychologists seek to derive human institutions from the nature of man, rather than deriving the nature of man from his institutions, they are apparently moved by the feeling that, as with the instance of the nonsense game, the pressure of institutions alone could not account for the entire expression. But when they looked for "priority," they sought it in the "unconscious-irrational," a psychological source, rather than in the *dialectical,* a formal source. And their rich contribution to the study of symbolism can thus mislead, if it causes us to treat formal logic as merely derivative from psycho-logic.

In our projected *Symbolic of Motives,* we hope to show, by analysis of Freud's work, how many logical and dialectical principles are, by his own account, involved in the operations of the dream. These elements are "prior" to dream life insofar as they are the basis of all "rational" thinking as well. But while psychologistic accounts of human motives seem, in their important stress upon symbolism, closer to the origins of *homo dialecticus* than institutionalist explanations are, we must discount Freud's own vocabulary somewhat; otherwise we cannot appreciate his great prowess as a dialectician, or note how well his analysis of the child's early experiences within the family reveal the operations of the hierarchic motive.

Go through the fantastic list of erotic aberrations in Krafft-Ebing's *Psychopathia Sexualis*. Examine his case histories of those many perverse sufferers with whom (as the translator and editor, Victor Robinson, puts it) "the ability to enjoy or perform the sexual act, in the normal manner, appeared to be the most difficult of the arts." Look there for evidence of the hierarchic motive. And does it not show immediately, in that vast thesaurus of dominance and submission, with the many intermediate variants? Note the odd identifications whereby one seeks to get, roundabout and at a distance, what he would not take simply and directly. Note the recondite "nobility" in the cult of vile things. Consider how abandonment to forms of sexual expression that society deems degrading could be at once a rebellion and a self-accusation, a morbidly tense acceptance of the very judgments by which one refuses to be bound. Consider the twisted beseechments, as with "stuff-fetichists dominated by a shoe or a handkerchief," or "lovers of fur and velvet," or "pageists," entranced by "the idea of being a page to a beautiful girl." Stories of lynchings make clear to us the hierarchic motive in fantasies and acts of sexual violence—and could we not see the same in "sadists who hurt their partners, masochists who thrilled at the sight of a whip," or in *"frotteurs* and *voyeurs, renifleurs* and *stercoraires,"* while a gloomy groveling, as were one to tell oneself meaner things about oneself than an enemy could think of, would surely beset the "slaves of scatology, defilers of statues, despoilers of women and children." Necrophiliacs, paedophiliacs, gerontophiliacs, satyromaniacs, nymphomaniacs—for whatever degree of physical eros there may be in the motives of such, must there not be very many degrees of the hierarchal? Here one finds all sorts of unnatural things, being sought in unnatural ways. Why, then, should they be treated as deriving primarily from natural appetite?

All these are such antics as Diderot would call "positions of pantomime." They are grotesque forms of social courtship. And you'd come closer to the truth if you called them remote variants of pure persuasion (like virgin-worship, or like poems proclaiming the frigidity, cruelty, aloofness, or infidelity of mistresses) than if you confined your explanation to a purely sexual source.

Both psychoanalytic and institutional accounts indicate important sources of pressure for the *animus* behind a given expression. Resources of classification, of abstraction, of comparison and contrast, of merger and division, of derivation, and the like, may characterize the thinking of man *generically,* over and above the nature of his social or personal problems. But his social and personal problems provide the incentive for the particular emphases of his expressions. You are not finished when you have analyzed the formal or dialectical devices implicit, say, in a doctrine of "white supremacy." The "pure persuasion" of the form is frail indeed, as compared with its localized rhetorical application. Psychoanalytic and institutional criticism is needed, to reveal the doctrine's nature as a "scapegoat mechanism" for flattering a sick psyche by proclaiming the categorical superiority of one's "kind," and by organizing modes of injustice that are morbidly considered advantageous to the conspirators as a class.

Our point is, however, that the urgency of such explanations must not be allowed to conceal the full scope of the motivational recipe. Otherwise, rather than being the analysis of rhetorical partisanship, the explanation itself is rhetorical (whereas in its completeness it would be dialectical). But by systematically retreating to the realm of "pure persuasion," we attain a degree of generalization which permits us to include as elements of rhetoric both psychological and institutional motivations (that is, motives in agent and scene respectively). And insofar as "God" is the Term of Terms in dialectic, one also thereby has easy access to the use of theological motives in rhetorical utterance (including the rhetorical use of naturalistic words for the ultimate scene).

For this very reason, you can expect "pure persuasion" always to be on the verge of being lost, even as it is on the verge of being found. And so, to talk about it by citing particular examples of rhetoric is always to find it embodied in the "impurities" of advantage-seeking. For even though the ultimate form is but that of speech relating speaker and spoken-to, this persuasive relation is in essence "courtly," hence involves communication between hierarchally related orders. True, the relation between the two orders need not remain fixed. Thus, as regards monetary tests, the artist who relies upon smartness as a mark of "urbanity" may be "socially inferior" to the "ideal public" he is courting. Yet he is "professionally superior," and courts as an "ideal public" many persons whom he would unquestionably despise in the particular. Yet again, as soon as you thus set him up, you must recall (as with the Arabian Nights relation) that the artist-entertainer is the servant of the very despot-audience he seeks to fascinate (as the spellbinder can tyrannize over his audience only by letting the audience tyrannize over him, in rigidly circumscribing the range and nature of his remarks).

Our mention of an "ideal audience" itself indicates how the simultaneous gain and loss of pure persuasion complicates a Rhetoric of Motives. Symbolically, the "pure exercise" of art for art's sake can become furtively and suicidally allied with motives ranging anywhere from castration to impotence, masturbation perhaps being the golden mean between them. An artist's courting is not just an address to others. His communicative act is subtly infused with motives of ordination that need not arise from without. A particular audience may be but a pretext, itself the symbol of a transcendence within himself (or, more accurately, a transcendence deriving from the nature of symbols as such). Even the artist who "writes down" for big money is thus motivated "ideally," in that the money represents for him the principle of ordination. It has often been said that a large amount of leisure is necessary for the high development of a culture. The statement is usually interpreted in a quantitative sense; for obviously, the society's ability to produce necessities must be great enough to permit a high expenditure of "man hours" on other than biologically or economically necessary work. Yet the analysis of "mystery" as a motive in ambition suggests that the element of "quality" has been a greater incentive. The quantity of extra productivity provides the physical conditions that allow for much concentration on economically unnecessary work. But whatever might be the incentives to "pure" creation in a truly equalitarian society (or rather, in a truly equal society, for equalitarianism is but an idealistic denial of actual inequality), the goad to ambition emanating from the idea of leisure as a privileged, "godlike" attribute has in the past come from the hierarchic structure of society (leisure being the condition antithetical to slavery).

Often artists are called childlike, "regressive." But there is also something childlike in the role of audience as tyrant—and a child-audience is perhaps the most tyrannical of all. (Thus, a teacher of children once told us of a recurring nightmare: She dreamed that, while she was talking to her class, they rose in a body and left the room.) In Dodgson's case ("the child as swain," according to Empson's formula), the entertainer could playfully punish the tyrannic child-audience in the very act of amusing her: his provoking social "mysteries" could serve this double purpose. As courtship, his communication was too essentially "standoffish" to be sexual; that element derived in part from its nature as social (intercourse between youth and age seen in terms of intercourse between "quality" and the vulgar, though this in turn was expressed grotesquely in reverse, the politeness being implied in the rudeness). But the *purely* rhetorical motive was in appeal for appeal's sake, in the "absolute summons" that would not know what to do with an audience who responded to the summons on any but the symbolic level.

Transferring the child-audience-tyrant relation to the realm of practical relations, we can see how the liberal child cult can work in connection with a sense of "substantial" inequality (through whatever form of discrimination, actual or feared, it may arise). The relation between the parents (as members of the "lower" or "subject" class) and their child (as "free") makes the child simultaneously one with them, yet a vessel of the major attribute identified with the "superior" class. The parents' courtship of the child, in allowing the child to be a "tyrant" in the home, is thus roundabout an ideal manifestation of the very hierarchic principle under which the parents suffer. The child, in being at once theirs and courted, simultaneously represents both ends of the hierarchic ladder.

The magic of virtue may also lurk about the edges of such public order made intimate. (By the magic of virtue we have in mind such motives as are expressed in Milton's "Comus," in the passages on the power of chastity to subdue wild beasts, a power that may be metaphorically true at least in one sense: If wildness in beasts stands for tempestuous erotic zeal in men, and if chastity in women stands for sexual frigidity, then truly "chastity" might dampen the ardor of "wildness.") The implied magical equivalent lurking beneath the "liberal" treatment of the child would derive from the fact that the parents, in establishing a pattern of mild courtship, "deserved" the same for themselves (though the sheer *imitation* of a way, the observing of it through sheer "esthetic consistency," is "prior" to its magical "use"). In any case, one has "ambivalence": the child, as their flesh and blood, represents their "inferiority," while at the same time it gets the deference they must show to their "superiors."

Recall Carlyle's equating of tools and symbols. He had much more than a metaphor to justify him. The high development of invented instruments was impossible without a corresponding development of language. And more formally, the kind of thinking that uses tools to make tools depends upon a peculiarly human "rationality" two removes from the nonsymbolic. This is the capacity for words about words ("thought of thought"), the "reflexive" function that modern idealists treat as the critical step from "consciousness" to "self-consciousness."

One might with some justice consider an animal's sounds and postures as "words about things," or about situations. One might say that such mimesis has the elements of grammar, rhetoric, and symbolic. They would be symbolic in their expressiveness as statements of attitude, rhetorical in their nature as threats and calls. And as for grammar, they "substantially" translate their past and future tenses into the behavioristic present, like a dancer. Thus, the dog dances "I will eat" by salivating now, and "I have eaten" by curling around three times now and settling himself to sleep. But (and we are obviously boasting) the dog cannot discourse about his discourse, cannot talk about his grammar, rhetoric, and symbolic. Similarly, all animals use tools in the primary sense. But only humans are tool-using in the secondary sense (as when external agencies are used to produce other external agencies). Thus, technology depends upon kinds of intuition and tradition that are impossible without the dialectic of "rationality."

Word-using is prior to tool-using even in the obscenely punning sense (and that too is always something to be considered, when discussing human motives). The emergence from infancy into word-using precedes by many years the emergence into sexual potency (hence the "polymorphous perverse" nature of infantile sexuality becomes interwoven with the power of symbols long before clear and direct sexual purpose has developed; and when it does develop, it must accommodate itself not to the "glandular situation" alone, but to the many years of symbolic practice that preceded it).

So, all told, though there are respects in which words and mechanical inventions may be classed together, as instruments ("weapons"), there are also important respects in which they must be distinguished. Attempts to divide people into "artisans" and "priests" have their ground in this distinction. It is at the basis of the distinction between the practical and the esthetic (bourgeois and Bohemian). Thus, *homo faber* (tool-using) would seem to come from different sources than *homo dialecticus* (word-using). But by the time you get to complex civilized conduct, the distinction becomes quite obscured. Priestcraft is often a very practical business, as also its secular variants in politics, journalism, and finance. Conversely, there is always a wide range of symbolic elements motivating conduct on its face practical.

And these considerations allow for a distinction between verbal productive forces (the nature of "rationality" or "human consciousness") and the "forces of production" in the economic sense (tools invented by operations of the human brain and transmitted with the help of vocabulary).

"Man" arises out of an extrahuman ground. His source is, as you prefer, "natural," or "divine," or (with Spinoza) both. In any case, the scene out of which he emerges is *ultimate*. And in this respect it must be "super-personal," quite as it must be "super-verbal." For it contains the principle of personality, quite as it contains the principle of verbalizing. The distinction between personal and impersonal, like that between verbal and nonverbal, is scientific, pragmatic, and thus is justified when our concerns are pragmatic. But from the standpoint of ultimate speculation, there must be an *order* here: First, there is "nature" in the less-than-personal sense; next, there is the "personal" distinguished from such "impersonal" nature as an idea of something is distinguished from the thing. But ultimately there must be nature in the "over-all" sense; and nature in this sense must be "superpersonal," since it embraces both "personality" and "impersonality."

Now, though invention of instruments is impossible unless the laws of nature in the less-than-personal sense are obeyed, it is likewise impossible, if attributed to scenic conditions alone, in the restricted meaning of scene (the "less than human," or the kind of nature that exists when the human, or personal, is deducted from it). The element of personality or humanity (agent and his acts) is the new secondary condition that necessarily interposes itself between the natural scene and the invented agency. No one expects our machines to go on inventing themselves after the human race is extinct, even though in the meantime they are doing much (as a mode of transcendence) to remake us, for better or worse. This necessary interposition of the human agent between scene and agency is what we have in mind when we say that "words" are prior to "tools," that *homo dialecticus* is more fundamental than *homo faber,* though the inventions of *homo faber* provide so overwhelmingly the distinctions of property and class that give animus to man's dialectical operations.

A Grammar of Substance was needed, at the very basis of human thinking, to shape traditions of living and thinking whereby a man can be induced to identify himself with the cause of some figure whom he has experienced only by hearsay, through the daily word-slinging of the news. But when thus "grammatically" and "symbolically" considering himself consubstantial with such a figure (a figure that is for him but a purely verbal creation but supposedly represents his interests) he gets the zeal of such identification from conditions of property and social status that were shaped by the economic forces of production. This more recondite development (from words, to tools, to words for social "substance" arising out of tools as property) is responsible for the animus in the logomachy ("cold war," an expression commending itself to the frigidity of old men, but unfortunately, with younger men, suggesting ideas of "warm" and "hot" war, and then finally, in accordance with the intermingling of Mars and Venus, a "shooting" war).

If you insist, we'll abandon, for argument's sake, the notion that nature is "super-personal." The argument is based on the assumption that there is such a thing as "personality" in the human realm. And when you get through dissolving personality into the stream of consciousness, or into dissociated subpersonalities, or into "conditioned reflexes," or into appearances of substance that derive purely from such extrinsic factors as status and role, there may not seem to be any intrinsic core left. So we'll retreat to our more easily defendable position: that nature must be more-than-verbal. For in its totality it encompasses verbal and nonverbal both; and its "nonverbal" ground must have contained the "potentiality" of the verbal, otherwise the verbal could not have emerged from it.

Arguments about nature as "more than personal" could then be protectively reframed and still claim enough for our purposes: We could say simply that, since such a view of nature as "super-personal" is a "natural conclusion" of dialectic, then it is an important ultimate trend of thought which must figure as a "lure" in rhetoric. An ultimate "error" is as important in rhetorical appeal as an ultimate "truth." So in either case we should consider the "dialectical proof of a super-personal ground of all action," because of the relation between rhetoric and dialectic. For no expression can be more profoundly appealing than a rhetoric which follows in the direction of a perfect dialectical symmetry. Suasion is thus "freest," most "edifying," when it embodies "the symmetrical necessity for the existence of God," though some lovers of such symmetry may insist that their god be named Atheos.

However, though our discussion of "pure persuasion" has brought us to the rhetoric of theology, we must again emphasize that "pure persuasion" in itself is not to be equated with "religious" persuasion. Pure persuasion is disembodied and wraithlike; but the benedictions and anathemata of religious persuasion are tremendously sanguine, even bloody. Consider the urgency of the Apocalypse. No bull fight was ever more gory, no Inquisition more eager to terrorize. "In righteousness he doth judge and make war." And punishments are heaped upon punishments for those serving the whore of Babylon, who "glorified herself" and "lived deliciously," until the "merchants of the earth" had "waxed rich through the abundance of her delicacies."

Does not the whole of Revelation swing about the resonant eighteenth chapter, where the voice cries, "Babylon the great is fallen"? And is there not a lovely tone of lamentation here, commingled with the gloating of vengeance? "Alas, alas, that great city Babylon, that mighty city!" Read it carefully, the eighteenth chapter. The prophet is condemning to the "second death" a city that looks surprisingly much like New York at its best. If there were less stench and more fragrance, less noise and more music, you'd have not New York but Babylon the Mysterious, as described in this chapter commemorating its destruction.

Surely the saint is visiting these horrors upon persons no more loathsome, say, than a would-be poet, or ex-poet, now working for an advertising agency, or for some publisher of commercial magazines. (All that is left of his early literary promise is a collection of first and rare editions. Preferably they are books with uncut pages. For here would be a remote variant of virgin-worship, a few secular traces of adolescent religiosity. We should also note, however, a mild renewal of religious interest in him, both for esthetic reasons and as a matter of good business, a neat combining of the "sacrificial" with the "acquisitive," as the collecting of firsts had been too, since he piously got for himself the vessels of the forbidden-virginal.)

Apparently the sin of Babylon was but in being a typical great metropolis. It was moved by the pleasant spirit of parties in a penthouse, drinks served expensively in a high place, to the accompaniment of dance music over the radio, with a girl arranging unobtrusively to spend the night after the guests had departed, for the delight of a man deemed potent in office. The mystery was reduced to sexual terms, there being perhaps more dramatic incentives for such translation in those days of sacred prostitution than now, when men are given uneasily to love-among-the-machines. Then "fornication" had much richer connotations, being recognized as not merely the satisfying of a sexual appetite, but as pious devotion to a rival god. The theme had been introduced early, in the references to "that woman Jezebel" who had cajoled members of the church in Thyatira "to commit fornication, and to eat things sacrificed unto idols." Thus, devotion to Babylon as a whore was devotion to Babylon as a god, an ultimate step in a rival order of motives. It was "reverence" expressed in sexual terms, and reverence among peoples who habitually made social reverence and religious reverence identical, in calling their emperors divine.

Yet as the recital of torments for the damned accumulates, we begin to wonder. The sinner we have spoken of, the well-to-do advertising man, the flower of metropolitan clericalism, would devoutly repent at the first faint rumble of the divine thunder. But the evildoers of the Apocalypse are almost magnificent in their refusal of heaven. Despite the mounting series of horrors and terrors to which they are subjected, one by one, with skilled husbandry on the part of the avenger, and with superb dramatic spacing on the part of the visionary (note, for instance, how, having established our expectation of seven calamities at the breaking of the seven seals, and having quickly run through six, the author interposes a whole chapter of delay between the breaking of the sixth seal and the breaking of the seventh), despite their total inability, in their human frailness, to strike back against the awesome tortures which an all-powerful Lord of All Creation is visiting upon them, they persist in their blasphemies.

Rhetorically, their perverseness offers some justification for continuing the torture. Had they begged to be forgiven, we with our limited understanding of cosmic justice might have been tempted to wish that the Lord would make peace with them. But by continuing to blaspheme even as they cook, they seem more to deserve the cookery. Symbolically, the saint also reads into them his own powers of resistance. He knows what sufferings he would undergo, as testimony to his God; and with unconscious generosity he imparts to the enemy a similar magnificence of motive, assuming that the ad-writer or newscaster of Babylon would testify by actions and passions of the same ferocious zeal.

Yet there is another point to note here. In these eschatological questions of reward and punishment, and of praise to a God of Wrath (the most O.T. spot in the N.T.) we realize that the representatives of Babylon are members of an alien and menacing order. Chapter 18 makes us see that, however frail they might be, as compared with the God of heavenly reverence, their claim upon men's social reverence had been as great as that of all our industrialists and financiers combined. Hence, the city was a menace, not by reason of the individuals in it, but through its *ordination*. And in seeing the mild Babylonian enterprisers as members of that rival ordination, the earnest saint thought of them as persisting to the last in their blasphemies. For in a sense they would persist, vowed to their order until Babylon had fallen, and the New Jerusalem had risen in its place.

We have talked of the hierarchic principle being represented in terms of the head. But particularly in a myth revealing the nature of first and last things, it can also be represented "pastorally" by the least. Or the most efficient reduction of all would be an image containing both ideas: the sacrificial king who is, in one figure, the bleeding, victimized lamb and the victor to whom all do obeisance. Here, the same ordination is represented by bringing the highest and lowest rungs together.

Looking at examples of religious expression, you unquestionably find the lineaments of "pure persuasion" there, as with St. Augustine's use of the epideictic virtuosity cultivated during the "second sophistic" of pagan decadence. Or, considered as an object of pure persuasion, Dante's Beatrice would be not woman idealized, but rather the absolute audience realized. And likewise a prayer might be pure courtship, homage in general, the ultimate idea of an audience, without thought of advantage, but sheerly through love of the exercise.

Yet no material world could be run on such a motive, not even a world genuinely supernatural in its theory of motives. "Pure persuasion" is as biologically unfeasible as that moment when the irresistible force meets the immovable body. It is what Eliot might call the "dead center" of motives. It is the condition of Santayana's transcendental skepticism, where the pendulum is at rest, not hanging, but poised exactly above the fulcrum. It is the change of direction, from systole to diastole, made permanent. Psychologically it is related to a conflict of opposite impulses. Philosophically, it suggests the plight of Buridan's extremely rational ass, starving to death because placed between two exactly equidistant bales of hay. It is the moment of motionlessness, when the axe has been raised to its full height and is just about to fall. It is uncomfortably like suspended animation.

Theologically or politically, it would be the state of intolerable indecision just preceding conversion to a new doctrine. Less exactingly, for our purposes, it is the pause at the window, before descending into the street.*

Rhetorical Radiance of the "Divine"

I. HENRY JAMES ON THE DEITY OF "THINGS"

IN HIS preface to *The Spoils of Poynton* Henry James tells how, one Christmas Eve, before a "table that glowed safe and fair through the brown London night," he heard a remark which he promptly recognized as the "germ" of his plot. It involved a quarrel between a mother and son "over the ownership of the valuable furniture of a fine old house just accruing to the young man by his father's death." He saw this as a "row . . . over their household gods." And he valued the situation, he says, because of

> the sharp light it might project on that most modern of our current passions, the fierce appetite for the upholsterer's and joiner's and brazier's work, the chairs and tables, the cabinets and presses, the material odds and ends, of the more labouring ages. A lively mark

* The closing sentences were originally intended as transition into our section on The War of Words. But that must await publication in a separate volume.

of our manners indeed, the diffusion of this curiosity and this avidity, and full of suggestion, clearly, as to their possible influence on other passions and other relations. On the face of it the "things" themselves would form the very centre of such a crisis; these grouped objects, all conscious of their eminence and their price, would enjoy, in any picture of a conflict, the heroic importance.

Later he resumes:

> The real centre, as I say, the citadel of the interest, with the fight waged round it, would have been the felt beauty and value of the prize of battle, the Things, always the splendid Things, placed in the middle light, figured and constituted, with each identity made vivid, each character discriminated, and their common consciousness of their great dramatic part established.

We dwell on these passages because we consider them a key not only to this particular book, but to James's motivation as a whole. Glancing over some of the tenser expressions scattered through his preface, we find:

> Vital particle . . . grain of gold . . . subtle secrets . . . madness . . . zeal . . . mysteries . . . tiny nugget . . . the table that glowed safe and fair . . . the *whole* of the virus . . . in a flash . . . glimmered . . . builds and piles high . . . blocks quarried in the deeps of his imagination . . . household gods . . . eminence . . . heroic . . . great array . . . exquisite protection . . . the felt beauty and value of the prize of battle . . . placed in the middle light, figured and constituted . . . their great dramatic part . . . the general glittering presence . . . the gleam of brazen idols and precious metals and inserted gems in the tempered light of some arching place of worship . . . romancingly . . . wondrous . . . in fine . . .

We should have the aura of these terms in mind as we read later:

> Yes, it is a story of cabinets and chairs and tables; they formed the bone of contention, but what would merely "become" of them, magnificently passive, seemed to represent a comparatively vulgar issue. The passions, the faculties, the forces their beauty would, like that of antique Helen of Troy, set in motion, was what, as a painter, one had really wanted of them, was the power in them that one had from the first appreciated.

This word, "appreciated," leads into his next development. Thus, on discussing how he might introduce human characters into this drama of Things, he comes upon a typical Jamesian solution, his recipe for the character of Fleda Vetch. One must "lodge somewhere at the heart of one's complexity an irrepressible appreciation," he says, and "from beginning to end ... appreciation, even to that of the very whole, lives in Fleda. ... The 'things' are radiant, shedding afar, with a merciless monotony, all their light, exerting their ravage without remorse; and Fleda almost demonically both sees and feels, while the others but feel without seeing." She is likewise said to be endowed with "the free spirit," which is "always much tormented," and by no means always triumphant, and is "heroic, ironic, pathetic."

We could not say that his references to "mysteries," "household gods," "place of worship," and the like are merely opportunistic and negligible. Nor should we, on the other hand, treat the material "Things" as though he meant them to be endowed with true divinity, like sacred objects on the altar of an Almighty God. The second interpretation would seem by inference to accuse James of blasphemy. The first would make of us esthetic blasphemers, in failing to give the novelist credit for his artistic scruples. Yet clearly these household Things are also Spirits; or they are charismatic vessels of some sort. And Fleda is a rare character who can feel the magic of their presence. The quarrel over heirlooms, desired as a testimony of status, attains a higher dimension, as James finds in the objects a glow that can place them in some realm or order transcending the quarrel as such. Hence, though the preface does not tell us just what mysterious, radiant power they do possess, can we not "socioanagogically" see here an "enigmatic" signature of the hierarchic motive?

2. "SOCIAL RATINGS" OF IMAGES IN JAMES

In James's preface to *The Spoils of Poynton* we find the ground for the statement of policy regarding "socioanagogic" criticism in general. Yet we still do not have an exact procedure for disclosing the hierarchic value of particulars.

We can show how this further step might be contrived, by examining and reapplying some passages from Austin Warren's exceptional essay on Henry James in his book, *Rage for Order*. The entire book, by the way, is much to our purposes, since it is predominantly concerned with hierarchy, both religious and secular. On nearly every page Mr. Warren makes some observation which we could profitably borrow here. His remarks on the theme of bureaucracy in Kafka, for instance; or his suggestion that the appeal of astrology for Yeats "lay in the honorific connection astrology establishes between man and nature and in its imprecise determinism of the individual and the state"; or his analysis of Pope's writings on society as a "wonder"; or his reference to "the characterology (or perhaps hagiography) of James's youth."

The discussion of James's late novels leads to exactly the kind of pontificating device we require. And to make our point, we shall combine portions from several passages:

> The Jamesian equivalent of myth lies ... in the metaphors which ... reach their high richness in *The Bowl* and *The Ivory Tower*. ... Recollected images become metaphor. For years James had traveled diligently in France and Italy, written conscientious commentaries on cathedrals, chateaux, and galleries. Now people remind him of art, his heroines, almost without exception, are thus translated. ... Some embarrassment prevents similar translation of the heroes into paintings or statutes; but the Prince (who is bought, after all, as a work of art and appraised by his father-in-law with the same taste which appraised a Luini) can scarcely be described except out of art history: by way of representing the superior utility and weight of the male, James renders him in architecture. ... The obvious errand of these analogies is honorific; they belong to the high and hallowed world of "culture. ..." Unlike his Prince, who "never saw ... below a certain social plane," James had looked observantly, in his days of "notation," at zoos and aquariums and circuses; and he remembered the crowded perceptions of "A Small Boy" in a remote America. ... Mrs. Newsome is massive because she has no imagination. She rests, sits, *is*—a fact without resilience. Others, the imaginative, must adjust, accommodate. ... If Philistines are to be "imaged" as inflexibly massive, metallic (unimaginative), the children of light owe their erect posture, their equilibrium, to their flexibility. They summon up recollection of ballet dancers, show people, brave ritualists who perform, upon exhibition, feats of persistence and agility. ... In *The Sense of the Past,* the most "imaged" relation is between Ralph Pendrel, American introspective, and the blunt, massive, extraverted Perry Midmore, his contrary. ... Perry has the advantage of not being "cultured": he trusts, animal-like, to his instincts, scents the presence of the clever and alien "as some creature of the woods might scent the bait of the trapper," etc.

Through many pages, Mr. Warren refers to the particular images by which James places each of his characters for the reader. Then, looking through this list, we see that, for our purposes, *we need but reverse the direction.* Where James has used an image to build up a character whose social and moral status is clearly defined in the book, turning things around we can interpret this known status as a hierarchal placement of the image. We thus have the bridging device (or "pontification") that will unite moral and social hierarchies with the natural and artificial objects that James treats as their equivalents. Hence we can unambiguously and methodically disclose the hierarchal judgment implicit for James in a given image.

We might thus perfect a method for disclosing the "hierarchic content" of objects, showing the difference between their perception in art (with the peculiar vibrancy that accompanies it) and the purely empiricist or psychological kinds of perception.

3. RHETORICAL NAMES FOR GOD

But what of those persons who believe that, under some conditions, men may establish a truly mystical communication with an ultimate ground of existence, behind or beyond the beautifying mists of social status? Would there still be room for a belief that natural objects are signatures of a celestial hierarchy too, infused with its motives and deriving their glow from it?

It is conceivable that, through the "infancy" (or speechlessness) of body and mind, there might be communication with elements that are, directly or indirectly, communicant with the ultimate speechless ground of things. Yet even if we grant the possibility of such mystic "revelations," we should ask ourselves how much of "divinity" can be explained neurologically, how much linguistically, and how much "socioanagogically." We should account for as much as possible by these three routes. Then God, genuinely transcendent, would be sought in the direction of whatever was still unaccounted for. The enigma of creation; the immensity of infinite and infinitesimal; love, patience, delight—here could be sufficient signs, perhaps, for most of us. But they are not enough for mystics who are content with nothing less than the conviction that they are God, that they have actually been one with God.

However, even if we grant them their claim, it still remains a fact that we should seek to account for as much of the mystical experience as possible in naturalistic terms. For the mystics have bodies; and other bodies, housing tenants who have not been officially recognized as *bona fide* mystical persons, manifest some natural symptoms like those of the "true" mystics. The area of overlap, then, is presumably not the area of the true revelation. Hence, even one who believed in the true revelation should be willing to look for as many naturalistic explanations as possible, since these would be the basis for a proper *distinction* between natural and supernatural motives.

But there is a consideration still more relevant to our purposes. Even if you grant the distinction between natural and supernatural motives, there is still the drastic fact that the power of rhetoric may arise rather from the *confusion* between the two orders. In his *Art of Rhetoric,* Aristotle noted how we may build up a character by imputing to him the virtues that most nearly resemble his vices, as when we call the foolhardy courageous and the cowardly cautious. And the rhetorical use of religion as an instrument of politics depends upon this very ambiguity. For the priest identifies some questionable secular faction or cause with a transcendent order held to be beyond question. Or consider the radio hack who, in a journalistic idiom that would be an insult even to the devil, praises the most bluntly imperialist of our ambitions as "spiritual," and presents world-wide expansion for bigger profits in terms of a holy war between the valiant armies of God and the vile hordes of Evil. The vulgarity of every word he says proves him to be about as spiritual as the machine out of which his voice is being projected. He is but a function of that machine, and he does the job he is hired for. Those to whom religion means mainly hate are not very exacting as regards the provocations to which they will respond.

But, because of the many "god-terms" that dot men's thinking constantly, most of such rhetoric is profoundly genuine. Dionysius the Areopagite wrote *On the Divine Names.* And a companion treatise, *in usum rhetoricae,* might consider the many declared and undeclared synonyms for God, or rather, for the extension of "God" into the area of "god-terms," generally. Thus, somewhat at random, we offer this list:

GOD: The ground of all possibility; substance; nature; history; society; necessity; mind; consciousness; self-consciousness; truth; *genius loci;* efficient cause. Title of titles; over-all motivation (hence, ultimate generalization, reduction, abstraction); principle of language or dialectic (logos); idea; center, circumference, apex, base (preferably all at once); unclassified, unfiled, miscellaneous, "All." Principle of hierarchy; any person, thing, or situation infused with the hierarchic motive (hence monarch, nobility, or people, as variously summing up or standing for the hierarchic order); hence, authority or resistance to authority; reason; object or source of reverence ("Your Worship"), fear, love, desire, justice; principle of property, privilege, status, Parent or principle of parenthood; principle of familial or social cohesion ("consubstantiality" and "communication"); authority; counterauthority; nation; "race supremacy"; the city. Vocation; calling; hence, science, art, technology, business; hence, laboratory, studio, real estate, counting house, money, the expedient. (The Protestant stress upon the religious motive in secular work is a notable bridging of the two orders.) Principle of action; hence "personality" (grounded in a "super-person"); ideal, plan, purpose; final cause; soul; freedom (hence, free market); conscience; duty; ought; good; grounds for doing what one wants to do; the opposite of what one wants to do; fulfillment (hence, "wish-fulfillment," hence wish, hence striving, hence absence of fulfillment, hence compensatory name for frustration); rest, end of action; beauty; the universal gerundive (maximum generalization of the to-be-done, a meaning closely related to role, hence to hierarchy). Death (in such good words as salvation and immortality); an act's "perfection" would be its "dying," its "finishedness," hence death relates to action insofar as a thing's end is its perfection. (See Pico on *teleutein,* as finish, die.) Unconscious; sleep; the implicit; the unexpressed; the to-be-expressed; the inarticulate; infancy; intuition; "imagination"; beyond-the-rational; insanity; neurotic compulsion experienced as mystic devotion (piety either in yielding or in inability to yield); natural motives (the nonverbal, hence "irrational," nutrient, sexual, excremental, seminal); any natural forms (including states of mind to match), as fire, thunder, power, calamities, mountains, plains, sea. A function of prayer (object of appeal of last resort); generalized principle of the audience; pure persuasion. Principle of rebirth; hence, principle of change or of substratum beneath change. "Evil" in disguise. An honorific name for oneself. A slogan of the Extreme Right. "Nothing" (with this reservation: Symbolically, "nothing" will equal something, though the referent may be dialectical rather than positive). Clash of opposites; resolution of opposites; synthesis of various motives felt but not clearly differentiated (Christ as divine pontification, as god-man, allows for range whereby God can be identified both with victim and victor).

The Romans knew that you could get a god merely by taking an adjective and transforming it into an abstract noun. (One should add, perhaps, that the noun would have in it the implications of an iterative verb.) And particularly, they would detach some attribute from another god, and set it up as a separate divine abstraction. Fides, Libertas, Victoria, Virtus, Felicitas are "instances of close connexion of abstract deities and adjectival cognomina." (*Encyclopaedia of Religion and Ethics.* Article on "Personification.") Thales: "The world is full of gods." Kafka, *The Castle:* "Does not the least degree of authority contain the whole?"

A poet's images, then, might be "enigmatically" infused with the spirit of either hierarchy. Or like the god-man of the Christian myth, or Carlyle's Clothes, or Keats's Grecian Urn, they could be "pontifications," for bridging the two orders.

4. THE "RANGE OF MOUNTINGS"

Aquinas says that the object of faith can be considered in two ways (*dupliciter*): (1) from the side of the thing believed (*ex parte ipsius rei creditae*); here the object of faith is simple (*aliquid incomplexum*); (2) from the side of the believer (*ex parte credentis*); here the object of faith is complex (*aliquid complexum*). Applying this pattern of thought to the symbols of poetry, we note that the symbol, while in itself "uncomplex" (the simple symbol), may readily be broken into various motivational strands, if approached *ex parte critici.*

The many ramifications of this subject could be studied better under the head of Symbolic than here. But because of our special stress upon the "hierarchic motive" in rhetorical identification, we might here consider a possible thesaurus of meanings in the symbol of mounting, either the act, or its corresponding image (for a mountain would be a kind of static mounting, the act congealed into a set design).

First, there is the purely "kinesthetic" appeal: the meaning of height (and depth) as experienced by a kind of being to whom climbing is both an effort and an exhilaration. Here too would be "empathic" responses as Coleridge noted (*Anima Poetae*), in considering how the eye was contented by running along the lines of a ridge:

> One travels along with the lines of a mountain. Years ago I wanted to make Wordsworth sensible of this. How fine is Keswick vale! Would I repose, my soul lies and is quiet upon the broad level vale. Would it act? it darts up into the mountain-top like a kite, and like a chamois-goat runs along the ridge—or like a boy that makes a sport on the road of running along a wall or narrow fence!

This is a jotting of the same Coleridge who wrote:

> The sot, rolling on his sofa, stretching and yawning, exclaimed, "*Utinam hoc esset laborare.*"

"Would that this were work!" Putting the two passages together, do we not glimpse precisely the elation in the purely imaginary act he is noting? By the paradox of substance, such ideal identification with the mountainous mass gives us in one "moment" both an imaginary idea of huge effort and the effortlessness of sheer indolence.

Coleridge's cult of the "impulse," as aggravated by his yielding to the euphoria of opiates, would make him particularly susceptible to such an appeal, where there is no physical strain, but the massiveness and weightiness of the scene envisioned are like a great burden borne with infinite ease.

Close to this purely kinesthetic appeal, yet obviously involving other motives as well, is the climbing of the Alpinist. We here have to do with "Faustian" kinds of fascination. While involving physical dangers and exertions, they seem to contain symbolic ingredients that themselves require "anagogic" or "socioanagogic" explanation. We have read descriptions of mountain-climbing which seem almost mystical, perhaps because the act itself sums up, in a physical operation and its corresponding states of mind, the various orders we are here listing as ingredients in a hypothetically full symbol of mounting, as it might figure in a "compleat poem." Mountain-climbing, as a symbolic act, is done in answer to a call. While carrying out an "attitude" in the most literal way possible (as were you to "do a poem" on murder by actually murdering someone), its motives are wholly "esthetic" (the opposite of the utilitarian or practical) as with a Gidean criminal.

Psychoanalysis, and popular speech, remind us that there is also a sexual mounting. Its most monumental form is perhaps in the notion of the Venusberg. (Translated literally into Latin, "Venusberg" would be *"mons* Veneris.") Since dreams of rising and flight frequently signalize the climactic approach to the sexual orgasm, by the same token in "The Love Song of J. Alfred Prufrock" we find the timid courtier *hesitating* on the stairs. And the theme returns in "Portrait of a Lady," wryly:

> Except for a slight sensation of being ill at ease
> I mount the stairs and turn the handle of the door
> And feel as if I had mounted on my hands and knees.

Even where a fuller range of motivations is involved, traces of the sexual order seem present. Thus, as Virgil explains to Dante in the fourth canto of the *Purgatorio,* the Mount of Purgatory is such that the higher one rises, the easier becomes the ascent, until it is like going downstream in a boat (*come a seconda giuso andar per nave*). The figure incidentally suggests where we might place those magically dream-driven boats of Shelley's (as in "Alastor"), that seem to stand for the poet's state of mind, and idealistically *begin* with starry-eyed motivations that Dante led into realistically, through a long ladder of asperities.

In the English edition of *Fear and Trembling,* Walter Lowrie quotes a related passage from Kierkegaard's *Journal,* describing his condition while at work on his "dialectical lyric." He had been "indolently" pumping up a shower-bath, he says, and "now I have pulled the cord, and the ideas stream down upon me" (though the full value of the figure is lost, in our era of "modern conveniences" when it never occurs to us that a shower-bath should be earned by prior effort, and we take it for granted that one should begin, not with the pumping up, but with the pouring down). "Indolently" does not seem quite the proper word here, except insofar as it suggests a lack of engrossment which does not come until the stage of fullness and release.

Disturbingly interwoven with the motives of erotic mounting, there is the theme of the maternal mountain: the mountain as the parental source, quite as with Mother Earth. Hawthorne's "Great Stone Face" suggests that it may also take on paternal aspects of parenthood. The image could arise from a child's early experience of being carried by adults.

Baudelaire's sonnet, "La Géante," is the grandest instance of incestuous ambiguities in the mountain symbol. The conceit that the poet is living with a "giantess" makes him both lover and child. Looking up at her "like a voluptuous cat at the feet of a queen," peering "into the damp fogs of her eyes" to see if her heart is somberly aflame, he runs "at leisure along her magnificent curves." And as she lies lassitudinously stretched across the countryside, he crawls on the slope of her enormous knees, and sleeps in the shadow of her breasts, "like a peaceful hamlet at the foot of a mountain."

The thought suggests that the Venusberg is likely to contain the same ambiguities, as would certainly be the case were it identified with the Venus we saw in Shakespeare's poem.

Popular usage also suggests connotations of material advantage, or social betterment, as with the term, "climber." Here are the cruel popular distinctions between those "on the way up" and those "on the skids." Or recall how, during the administration of F. D. Roosevelt, an ingenious variant became popular, as officials were said to be "kicked upstairs" when, though dismissed from their active functions, they were rewarded for their loyalty to the Chief by being given some nominally higher job with good pay but no authority.

Jimmy Durante once rang a good variation on the theme of the social climb, thus: He was in the role of an unsuccessful actor waiting in the outer office of a casting bureau; a successful actor, whom he knew, passed him with some disdain; whereupon Durante told him: "You'd better be nice to those you pass on the way up; for you might pass them again on the way down."

We can glimpse how the motive takes on richness when we consider the many-faceted careerism of Stendhal's Julien Sorel (in *The Red and the Black*). Despising his own father, taking Napoleon as alternative ideal father, he seduces the woman who befriends him as a mother. Here he acts "conscientiously," in line of duty, like a soldier (for he conceives of command in sexual and social matters after the analogy of military power). All the hypocrisy in his scheming for position and wealth seems to him a kind of higher honesty, loyalty to a purpose that transcends mere utilitarian profit. And to this extent his attitude is justified: Behind his rhetoric of advantage lies a poetic of incestuous guilt, with relation to women generally. And in response to this motive (presumably implicit in Sorel because it was basic to his creator) the hero and the author share the disdainful conviction that Julien's careerism is essentially different from the ordinary varieties all about him.

Veblen's *Theory of the Leisure Class* indicates how standards of goodness, truth, and beauty might be infused with hierarchal promises of the sort that go with the social climb. Racine's prefaces to his tragedies well reveal the motives of social pageantry in the esthetic of dignity, aloofness, and stylistic exclusion motivating his art. And even in one's choice of questions, there can be a social claim. For among the wide range of questions which men may seek to answer, in philosophy, science, and criticism, the intrinsic value of these questions does not correspond with their rating in a given hierarchy. And though the emphasis is usually placed on the quest for *answers*, "socioanagogic" considerations suggest that much of the urgency comes rather from the hierarchic rating implicit in the *questions*. Questions are infused with social magic quite as are James's "household gods" or natural objects ("the world's body"). And thus, with different schools of literary criticism (which in turn imply different political and social alignments) an answer can seem wholly radiant only with those for whom the question itself has radiance.

Even in naturalism or imagism, regardless of what the writer thinks he is getting, he is really recording the fullness of a world hierarchally endowed. The motive comes clearer to recognition in symbolism and surrealism, though their aims are usually stated in terms of technique or psychology.

In sum: Insofar as things and situations are identified with various stages of social privilege, both "practical" and "esthetic" objects are infused with the spirit of government and business, taxes and price, through identification with the bureaucratic judgments that go with such order.

In his essay on "The Dissociation of Ideas," De Gourmont makes an observation that gives us a further insight into the "magical" view, as regards persons who are charismatic vessels of the hierarchic principle. He is discussing the savage's idea of death, noting that the savage looks upon death, not as accidental or necessary, but as caused by the design of occult forces. (He is here dealing with the attitude that the sociologist Levy-Bruhl labeled "mystic participation.") As evidence that the same attitude still survives, he notes how the death of a prominent personage nearly always starts rumors of foul play. He also mentions Stendhal's preference for explanations that attribute the death of historical figures to poisoning or similar undisclosed plots.

Is it not the principle of social "divinity" that leads the people, or a hierarchy-minded writer like Stendhal, to thus account for these deaths "mysteriously"? The thought suggests that many apparently "factual" statements about the mysterious assassination of kings and emperors might have arisen purely in response to the principle of "mystification" implicit in hierarchy.

Similarly, at the time when the demagogue Huey Long was killed, despite the clear public evidence as to the identity of the slayer a rumor spread among the people that he had been shot by bullets from a different gun the bearer of which was not known. In his death he was thus translated to the "divine" regions of "mystery," as befitted his quasi-imperial role.

Describing how he felt when put in control of the government's policies, Churchill writes:

> At last I had the authority to give directions over the whole scene. I felt as if I were walking with Destiny, and all my past life had been a preparation for this hour and this trial.

"Destiny" here is a word of maximum generalization. Thus, in the technical sense, as an over-all word for human motives, it is a "god-term."

So much for it as regards its place at the apex of a dialectical pyramid. What of it, as regards "context of situation"? The Tory statesman is here discussing his state of mind on being made the head of a social hierarchy. He is in a position to act, but the acts typical of his role will use the entire social structure as their instrument. Primitive action related to the "centrality of the nervous system" will be at a minimum. The characteristic acts of his office will be indirect, hierarchic.

Even the very word "hierarchy," with its original meaning of "priest-rule" (while in English one also hears "higher") has connotations of celestial mystery. And, as we have said, where the principle of hierarchy is involved, the "mystery" need not be confined to any one position in the scheme. A ruler, seeing himself "from within," might be expected to know that he is not "divine"; yet he may feel the motives of "reverence" as strongly as a lowly peasant witnessing, at a respectful distance, a royal pageant. For inasmuch as his typical acts of rule depend upon his place in the dialectical pyramid of the social structure, they are "his" acts only insofar as he identifies himself with the very *principle of order* to which he owes his power. Their sensory reference is just about nil—they are all "spirit."

The result is a "mystic participation." The feeling that one is "walking with Destiny" would then be the "celestialized" or idealistic counterpart to the quite realistic experience of "walking with hierarchy."

However, though ethical, esthetic, philosophic, and scientific norms are greatly affected by the norms of social advantage, there is also a purely moral motive here too, an ethical ascent, a morality of production, a motive of betterment so "autonomous" that it may often be sacrificial in quality, as when a craftsman who works for money refuses to stultify his work for more.

Dante's *Purgatorio* is a sustained symbolization of ethical mounting. The Mount of Purgatory is under the guardianship of Cato, the type of the moral virtues; and the immediate aim is to regain the Earthly Paradise. As the editor of the *Temple* edition puts it: "Physically and spiritually, man must climb back to the 'uplifted garden.'"

The attempt to make oneself generally appealing should, within the terms of this book, be treated as an *ethical* variant of pure persuasion. But our current success literature more often reverses the order of motives here, looking upon the cultivation of a glad and winsome personality purely as an instrument in the quest for advantage.

The doctrine of technological progress (the "higher standard of living") inextricably merges the ethical ascent with the narrower advantage-seeking of the "climber." Sometimes it even seems to be the direct descendant of earlier religious doctrines that looked upon the human body as vile and depraved. For when cherishing as a categorical improvement each new mechanical device that removes men a step further from the natural ways of life, it reaffirms the same mind-body dualism, with the equivalent of "mind" now being the corpus of mechanical inventions (born of intellect).

When discussing the "dialectics of pure practical reason," Kant writes:

> Morality is not properly the doctrine how we should *make* ourselves happy, but how we should become *worthy* of happiness. It is only when religion is added that there also comes in the hope of participating some day in happiness in proportions as we have endeavoured to be not unworthy of it.

Note that an attempt to make oneself "not unworthy of happiness" can become transformed into a symbolic act designed really to *bring about* the happiness. Insofar as "virtue" is used to coerce events (as with the belief that virtue can command the elements), we move towards the areas of magic (in the sense of bad science: the attempt ritually to influence the natural order, or "acts of God"). And exhilaration can sometimes come, unquestionably, from the conviction that somehow an operation of this sort is succeeding. In his *Ethics* Spinoza proposes a doctrine whereby the spiritual goods, of which one would make oneself worthy by virtue, could be said to have been attained already in the beatitude of the virtuous state itself.

The ethical mounting (*"Excelsior! Excelsior!"*) takes so many forms that, in a "Dramatist" analysis of motives, some fragment of it must appear on every page, since ethics is the field of action and drama is the imitation of an action. So we can slight the category here, and turn to the other two not yet considered.

Sometimes the design of the mountain may have fecal meanings. Thus, the Egyptians, who held the dung-beetle sacred, might be said to have buried their kings in pyramidal tombs that were mighty stylized replicas of the dung-pile (the lowly connotations being, in the enigmatic symbol, simultaneously expressed and concealed, affirmed and transcended). Economically, the motivation may have received impetus from the fact that the fields were each year fertilized by the deposits of the Nile, an alluvial soil easily equated with manure. But once the culture had developed its intricate hierarchic structure, then the priestly transcending of corruption, as with mummification and all the magic lore that went with it, could in its own right perfect a kind of "fecal idealism" to express eulogistically the motives that Marx and Swift, in references previously quoted, characterized dyslogistically. Here scatology and eschatology overlap.

Where an expression is thorough, radical, "fundamental," one might well expect the motive of "catharsis" to figure. And the question is:

Just how literally should we interpret this term of Aristotle's, particularly in view of the fact that Aristotelians praise his vocabulary for its "literalness," in contrast with Platonist "analogizing." It is our conviction that a transcendence is not complete until the fecal motive has in some way been expressed and "redeemed." Psychologists have pointed out that the feces are the child's first production. Hence such moral motives as duty and work can have fecal connotations. And esthetic production is often conceived of in fecal terms, either jocularly or in roundabout disguise.

We consider the golden bird of Yeats's Byzantium poem such a disguise, "immortality" itself being here conceived in terms of esthetic output, the ambiguities being more clearly revealed in Brancusi's sculpture of the Golden Bird. And we believe that there is a similar enigma in Hopkins' lines:

> I am soft sift
> In an hourglass—at the wall
> Fast, but mined with a motion, a drift
> And it crowds and it combs to the fall.

A gracious example that has been brought to our attention is in the second *cancion* of the *Cantico Espiritual,* by St. John of the Cross:

> Pastores, los que fuéredes
> allá por las majadas al otero,
> si por ventura viéredes
> aquel que yo más quiero
> decidle que adolezco, peno y muero,

which has been translated thus:

> Shepherds, who go
> up by the sheepcotes to the top of the hill,
> if you should happen to see
> the one I most desire,
> tell him I sicken, suffer and die.

The word *majadas* means "sheepcote, sheepfold" or "dung." It is related to *majadal* (good pasture ground for sheep; land improved by the manure of a flock), and to *majadear* (to take shelter in the night, said of sheep; to manure).

According to St. John, the desires, loves, and sighs are called "shepherds," since they instruct (the word also means "graze") the soul in spiritual goods. And the sheepcotes stand for "the hierarchies and choirs of the angels, through whom, from choir to choir, our signs and prayers go to God, who is here called hill, as he is the ultimate height, and because in him, as on the hill, you see all things, sheepcotes both high and low."

We might also glimpse the dim outlines of a pun here, that would introduce maternal connotations. The word for hill, *otero,* is very close to the word for womb, *utero.* And the Spanish words which are here translated "on the hill" are literally "in the hill." However, the similarity is greatly lessened by the fact that *utero* is accented on the first syllable, *otero* on the second.

Sometimes the transcendence may be got by purely tonal transformations. Notably by umlaut, ablaut, augmentation, diminution metathesis, substitution of cognate consonants, and by portmanteau formations. For instance, if "soteme" were a fecal word, and "seeteme" and "siteme" were words of neutral or honorific meaning, the first might be lurking in a usage of these other two. (Such concealments would involve umlaut and ablaut respectively.) A structure like "stome" would be a diminution; "sozeteme" would be an augmentation. "Metos" would be metathesis. "Sodebe" would be a substitution of cognates, *d* for *t* and *b* for *m*. Portmanteau words would be likely to occur only in dreams, or perhaps in some arbitrarily assigned proper name (except of course in writing like Joyce's). There could also be disguised expressions combining two or more of these resources, as "stobe" would be a diminution plus a replacing of *m* by its cognate *b*. If all these arbitrary syllables are assumed to be meaningful in some one language system, then it is our notion that they could perform this added poetic function, along with their strictly lexicological role, as defined in a dictionary. Thus we knew a man who had kidney trouble, and who jocularly signed his letters "yourn," without meaning to suggest the pun, "urine"—while a serious use of "urn" may, on some occasions, encompass the same ambiguity. Such usages would reduce, sometimes to a single letter or syllable, the process of catharsis, or ritual purging, that is developed at length in tragedy, with its elaborate rites of purification got through the offering of a victim hierarchally infused.*

* We have proposed as a term for critical method the verb "to joyce." By "joycing" we mean the deliberate and systematic coaching of such transformations for heuristic purposes. They can't often prove anything, but they may lead to critical hunches (or help one to discount hunches that one may himself have

In the quotation we previously made from Marx, likening the "cranium system" of German idealism to the fecal motivations of the Egyptian and Tibetan priesthoods, there are suggestions that the entire hierarchic pyramid of dialectical symmetry may be infused with such a spirit. But the form is, of course, likewise derivable from the nature of the symbolic medium in itself, the possibility of terms arranged in ever-mounting orders of generalization, until they reach their culmination in a title of titles which, in its absolute "being," has as its dialectical ground only an equally absolute "nothing."

Here are the resources of the Upward Way, by the *via negativa*, with the possible reversal of direction, a returning to the flatlands in a Downward Way. (On the return the system will contain a principle of transcendent unity which was reached at the culmination of the way up, and henceforth pervades all the world's disparate particulars, causing them to partake of a common universal substance.) This ultimate dialectical resource, while itself aiming beyond all imagery or local conditions, may lead to identification with some local figure, institution, or the like, or with the corresponding imagery. Hence, though it be but the pure form of the principle of hierarchy in general (the suasive principle of ultimate dialectical symmetry), it makes for a susceptibility to particular hierarchic embodiments. Thus it can be consciously used for speculative liberation from a given social order—or both consciously and unconsciously, it can be used for fixing men's loyalty to a given social order.

This would perhaps be an aspect of climactic form in general, the building up of an intensity and its subsidence, as in drama. Usually however, the pyramidal form is implicit, rather than being explicitly figured in terms of higher stages. Likewise, here, we might include those moments of transcendence when a work takes on a new dimension of insight, as with the speech of Shylock which does not merely exploit Christian prejudices against the Jew but suddenly lifts the

---

wrongly developed from such unconscious punning). However, the use of such a device extends far beyond the disclosing of "forbidden" words lurking behind socially acceptable disguises. A critic of twenty years ago, for instance, who had experimentally "joyced" Eliot's "Prufrock," to see what motives might be implicit there, would not have gone far amiss had he discerned, as enigmatic symbolizing of its future, "prove-rock" and "pure-frock." This matter requires further discussion in the *Symbolic*. It has also been treated somewhat in *The Philosophy of Literary Form,* notably pages 51-66, 258-271, 369-378.

situation to terms of universal mankind. (Is it not true that, with the comparing of the body politic to the physical body in *Coriolanus,* the playwright is aiming to establish such a moment of transcendence *at the very outset,* to lift the play but a few lines after it has begun, proclaiming the hierarchic principle as the very essence of its motivation, a motive that Coriolanus proclaimed to be not only his, but everyone's?)

An interesting variant of the ultimate dialectical mounting, where a questionable kind of exaltation is involved, is mentioned in an article by Eric Kahler, "The Secularization of the Devil," reviewing Thomas Mann's *Doctor Faustus* (*Commentary,* April, 1949). Mr. Kahler here speaks of modern "Faustian" man as being "in a diabolical plight, in the state of alienation, of the Fall—the Fall by rising, by ironic transcendence."

As most obvious indication of the way in which dialectical mounting makes for transcendence, imagine this hypothetical instance of "justice":

Imagine a moral code, decreed by yourself, and so narrow in its notion of advantage that every injunction was framed purely for your particular convenience. Thus, if each entry were exactly phrased it would have this form: *"Thou* shalt not do evil to *me."* Even so, you need but generalize this code completely, and the "thou" applies likewise to the propounder of the code, while the "me" stands for "everyman." Whereupon, by carrying out the dialectical process to its ultimate conclusion, you have transcended the original limitations of the code. However narrow its original quest of advantage, by sheer universalization it has moved into the areas of the sacrificial.

Or otherwise put: We need but universalize the idea of a right or privilege, and we have advanced from the acquisitive to the ethical. On the other hand, motives such as doctrines of race supremacy, that do not permit us to think of justice in universal terms, are essentially frustrating. The frustration is not of the sort that the term now usually suggests: the inability to procure some desired convenience or preferment. Rather, it derives from the inability to allow oneself the "expansive" hope for the maximum generalizing of "justice."

As we saw when considering Empson, such self-frustrations on the part of a "superior" class are frequently expressed in a cult of irony, which would thus in itself signalize the class status. Though such an ironist may, if he is a man of imagination, also extend the ironic principle in ways that transcend its local motivation, Marx might question universalizing of this sort as ideological mystification. For as regards its counterpart in the social texture, the more richly universal such irony becomes, the more thoroughly may it be in effect the "universalizing of inequity" (a subtle variant of the original injustice, with those who propound "race supremacy" as a "universal" doctrine).

However, though there is also this dubious transcendence, which allows for a certain range of ironic exaltation, the dialectical form in itself strains ever towards the universalization of justice, even as its counterpart in human institutions makes for hierarchic stratification. And the release through dialectical mounting seems to prevail in proportion as, truly or falsely, we can feel ourselves to be motivated by the universal principle infusing all stages of a hierarchy rather than by aims local to one stage. The two contrary motives are brought into unity by doctrines that proclaim the universal good to be derived from factional strife. Marxism, Adam Smith, and orthodox religions all have their variants of this pattern.

Might we look upon this entire "range of mountings" as a kind of ideal paradigm? Might we conclude that a writer's work would have the maximum vibrancy if all of these ascensions were somehow contained by the same symbol, in exhilarating harmony? And as the early philosophers used to say that maxims and proverbs were fragmentary survivals of an ancient wisdom originally as ample and architectonic as a great cathedral, so might we examine individual expressions for evidence that some portions of a "total mounting" are working within them? Thus whereas the mystic exaltation is in itself ineffable, might its analogue in language reside precisely in the happy simultaneity of all such motives? Similarly, might the mystic accidie set in precisely at the moment when the happy combination is somehow broken, and the motives that were thus being transcended are left like ashes after a bright fire?

5. ELATION AND ACCIDIE IN HOPKINS

Considering the poetry of Gerard Manley Hopkins, we might note these steps:

1. A precocious gift for almost lushly sensuous imagery. Consider the prize poem he wrote at college, for instance, almost an orgy of sensations, in his descriptions of light, flowers, gems, colors. "Spikes of light / Spear'd open lustrous gashes, crimson-white" ... "an orb'd rose ... by hot pantings blown / Apart" ... "With coral, shells, thick-pearlèd cords, whate'er / The abysmal Ocean hoards of strange and rare" ... "the dainty onyx-coronals deflowers, / A glorious wanton" ... "the scarce troubled sea / Gurgled where they had sunk, melodiously" ... "Slumber'd at last in one sweet, deep, heart-broken close."

2. When he joined the Jesuit order, he renounced his verse. He treated it as antithetical to his calling. He here made a choice the opposite to Stephen's in *The Portrait of the Artist as a Young Man*. And the turn from so sensory a medium would seem to be a fitting act of priestly mortification.

3. But a new motive entered when a superior suggested that a poem should be written in commemoration of the nuns who had lost their lives in the wreck of the *Deutschland*. Here, of a sudden, was a way whereby he could welcome the very gift he had rejected.

As regards mystical exaltation, and its analogue in poetry, we believe that this third step is the important one. A motive, when genuinely transcended, is not dropped, but transformed. It is redeemed not by subtraction, but by inclusion in a new fellowship. It is thus *not repressed,* but *expressed,* yet expressed with a difference: for its "nature" has been "graced."

Hopkins could now fill his notebooks with minute observations of natural objects. For if he saw in them, or thought he saw in them, an essence derivable from God, the more accurate his study in the empirical and positivist sense, the more devotional he could be in his conviction that these objects were signatures of the divine presence. Nature could serve as a kind of Christly pontification between the observer and God. If he, in a Schellingesque identification of subject and object, could identify himself as agent with particulars of the natural scene, and if (in his somewhat idealistic interpretation of Scotist *haecceitas*) he could identify the particularity of natural objects with the divine, when all was going well he would have a happy communion of self, nature, and God.

Thus by the same token, the whole range of sensuous imagery was again open to him, and he used it fervently. For what he had previously denied himself, as a way of mortification, he could now use with profusion, *ad majorem Dei gloriam.*

Very complex possibilities present themselves with such a change of motives. Thus, in writing of the shipwreck in which the five nuns perished, he could include passages that refer ambiguously to another kind of shipwreck, his own moral lapses. Then, as the poem shifts to the literal wreck, itself treated as a harvesting for God, there is the implication that roundabout his guilt has been ennobled. That is, there are three kinds of shipwreck here: the literal one, his own depravity, and the gathering of the heroic nuns to God. And in the general exaltation, he has confessed, but the oblique account of his carnal passions has been merged into the glorification of the nuns' religious passion.

Perhaps "The Windhover" is the poem where the exaltation is purest. There are signs of the burdensome motives (notably the reference to "sheer plod" of "plough down sillion," and to "blue-bleak embers" that are said to "fall, gall themselves, and gash gold-vermilion"). But the elation is so great that its spirit saturates the whole, and the down-turning moments are rather like something dropped in an elevator going up. Similarly, in terms like "dappled" and "pied beauty," he seems to have hit upon a signature that brings white and black motives together, not in dualistic conflict, but in a happy merger that redeems the black ones. The theme even flashes through the ecstatic account of the windhover's flight, since the bird, though likened to Christ, is called a "dappled-dawn-drawn Falcon."

Universalize the idea of purpose (as when the mark of God is seen in each creature). Then identify the individual with this universal design. The result is invigorating. But let anything go wrong with the identification, and all that is left is a sorely protruding ego, a very self-sick self. Hence, though the sense of mounting is kept vibrant while things are going well, when the witherings of accidie set in, the exalted identification of the self with a nature itself identified with God is disrupted, and there is left the self alone: "I am gall, I am heartburn" ... "God's most deep decree / Bitter would have me taste; my taste was me" ... "Selfyeast of spirit a dull dough sours" ... "self, self ... poor Jackself."*

---

* I am here giving the gist of an unpublished thesis, "Nature of the Transcendence in the Poetry of Gerard Manley Hopkins," by Judith Bailey, who did

"So will I turn her virtues into pitch," Iago says. What are we to make of the fact that Hopkins, who gave great thought to the overtones of words, uses this very word, "pitch," to name the concrete distinctness of a thing, its selfhood? He can also use it as a verb: man's self was said to be "more highly pitched" than that of other creatures. And in one of the last poems, written in the time of despair, we find: "pitched past pitch of grief." Clearly, the word had ambiguous markings from the start. It lurkingly signified the discomfitures of selfhood at those times when the moment of exaltation would vanish.

6. YEATS: "BYZANTIUM" AND THE LAST POEMS

"Mirror on mirror mirrored is all the show," Yeats wrote in the grim period of his own Last Poems. Or having asked himself out of what "masterful images" his earlier work had grown "in pure mind," he answered in terms of offal, thus:

> A mound of refuse or the sweepings of the street,
> Old kettles, old bottles, and a broken can,
> Old iron, old bones, old rags, that raving slut
> Who keeps the till. Now that my ladder's gone,
> I must lie down where all the ladders start,
> In the foul rag-and-bone shop of the heart.

The "ladder," in the happy days, had been the ascent of the "tower," the "winding stair." But here, indeed, Yeats is talking very explicitly of these hierarchic matters, and of what motives, in the unredeemed fecal order, threaten to proclaim themselves when several of the peaks in the "range of mountings" have ceased to figure, and the "mound of refuse" predominates in its starkness.

Earlier, he had written about the eggs of Leda, from one of which Helen had been born, from the other Castor and Pollux. He had written ecstatically on Leda and the Swan: the heroic history of the Iliad was prophesied as having been conceived at the moment of their union. Helen for love, Castor and Pollux for war; the two heroic themes of ancient Greece. But now, after the descent down the ladder, he finds their equivalence in states without radiance: he writes of "lust and rage."

---

work on Hopkins in conferences with me some years ago. The thesis, an exceptionally competent performance for an undergraduate student, is on file at the Bennington College Library.

In the two Byzantium poems, he had confronted death tragically, but with the full glow. Both poems are under the sign of gold, itself an ambiguous symbol, as psychoanalysts remind us—for in its more dismal fascination, as with the motives of the miser, it is said to have fecal connotations. When he here thinks of himself as gathered "into the artifice of eternity" (a kind of immortality, like that of Keats's Urn,* conceived in esthetic terms, and so possibly having the ambiguities of such output), the gold is transcendent, transformed into an ecstasy of gold, as the word springs forth in nervous, resonant repetition:

> Once out of nature I shall never take
> My bodily form from any natural thing,
> But such a form as Grecian goldsmiths make
> Of hammered gold and gold enamelling
> To keep a drowsy Emperor awake;
> Or set up a golden bough to sing
> To lords and ladies of Byzantium
> Of what is past, or passing, or to come.

Here the corruption of death is translated into its euphemistic equivalent: immortality. In English, too, "gold" has the added resonance of "God" in the offing. And similarly, at the close of the other Byzantium poem, when the poet writes of "that dolphin-torn, that gong-tormented sea," heuristically joycing here, dare we detect in these sounds a strange heresy, poetically disguised, by the enigma of the pun? Might we hear instead: "that devil-torn, that God-tormented sea"?

We would not consider the work of either Hopkins or Yeats prime instances of mystical poetry. But at least there is a trace of mysticism here, in the particular elated moments we have been considering. And in both cases, the indications are that "nature" becomes tyrannously burdensome, once the poet, having made himself at home in "grace," finds that it has been withdrawn.

---

*Since death, disease, the passions, or bodily "corruption" generally (as with religious horror of the body) may be variants of the fecal, their transcending may involve a corresponding translation of the fecal. See (in the *Grammar of Motives*) our analysis of the Keats Ode, as an indication of such transcendence, by the splitting of a distraught state into active and passive, so that the evil element (the suffering) can be abstracted and eliminated, while only purified spiritual activity remains.

7. ELIOT: EARLY POEMS AND "QUARTETS"

In the case of Eliot, we might note a reverse direction, not to any great extent, but enough to be observed and discussed. That is, the poet later uses with fuller connotations images that were at first used somewhat sparsely, as regards the "range of mountings" that seems to be contained in them. To illustrate, let us begin with a formula for the early poems, such as "The Love Song of J. Alfred Prufrock" and "Portrait of a Lady":

A down-turning mood. A subdued, and even smart kind of lamentation (a gesture first developed in Jules Laforgue, who had this way of being genuinely sad and desolate, in accents of literary elegance). Contrast such cautiousness with the full-throated outpourings of Biblical lamentation. The modern style involves social etiquette and literary tact. Here is fragility.

A crabbedness is suggested. Thus, when Prufrock says, "I should have been a pair of ragged claws / Scuttling across the floors of silent seas," he is in dramatic language defining an essential motivation within himself. Later, in the fluently moody "Rhapsody on a Windy Night," the theme is varied ingeniously: "And a crab one afternoon in a pool, / An old crab with barnacles on his back, / Gripped the end of a stick which I held him," the act itself thus standing for a kind of crabbed communication.

One should note also a strongly spectator attitude, a view of the city's dramas impersonally, almost statistically, as in the second Prelude: "One thinks of all the hands / That are raising dingy shades / In a thousand furnished rooms." This is city poetry, not nature poetry. The point is worth noting, for it has bearing upon the more sophisticatedly dialectical nature of the transcendence with which the poet will later be concerned.

A contemplative poet in a great metropolis must necessarily have a somewhat impersonal attitude towards most of the citizenry. This may be expressed through hail-fellow-well-met, idealistic gestures of the Whitman sort, embracing mankind generically, as a broad statement of policy. Or at the other extreme it may involve a kind of tight-lipped aloofness. But no poet is tight-lipped—so the distrust of superficial fraternization leads instead to a modified aloofness, the "statistical" attitude as in turn modified by the mood of fragile lamentation. And there is a strong suggestion of unfulfilled possibilities, even in cases where people do meet as personal acquaintances, in standoffish intimacy, in relations of vaguely frustrate courtship. Hence such elegiac references as

> ... time yet for a hundred indecisions,
> And for a hundred visions and revisions,
> Before the taking of a toast and tea,

then, after an interruption

> And indeed there will be time
> To wonder, "Do I dare?" and, "Do I dare?"
> Time to turn back and descend the stair, ...

With relation to this tentative mood, there arise two notable antitheses: One, the theme of Apeneck Sweeney, a crudely potent male so unrefined that he could shave while a woman on a bed near-by has an epileptic seizure; Sweeney who, in the bath, "shifts from ham to ham." There is a set of such gruff, low organisms, acting directly in response to animal appetites.

The other kind of antithesis is figured in images of faint distant music, or of submerged music, or of faint distant submerged music sung by mermaids, images that seem to match the tentative, unfulfilled possibilities by suggestions of an alternative actuality, with sweetly sexual connotations.

The down-turning mood reaches proportions close to accidie, or mystic drought, in "The Waste Land." Fertility here is under dismal auspices indeed, as in the third section, ironically called The Fire Sermon, where "Tiresias, throbbing between two lives," "old man with wrinkled female breasts," witnesses a crude love affair between "the typist home at tea-time" and the "small house agent's clerk." In this, and other episodes, witnessed from a distance, with deep disgruntlement, we have the poet's documents of social drought. Another kind of antithesis enters here, as mean expressions from contemporary scenes are contrasted with lines cited from contexts that went with earlier, gracious ways.

In the last episode, What the Thunder Said, the themes of social drought are finally summed up in a purely natural imagery of drought. This call for the fertilizing waters is followed by a stanza that prompts us to risk a somewhat foolhardy venture. For the poet gives one explanation of it in his notes. Everyone will agree that he ought to know. Yet we would offer another (our excuse being that this explanation does not contradict his, but supplements it).

The stanza is:

> Who is the third who walks always beside you?
> When I count, there are only you and I together
> But when I look ahead up the white road
> There is always another one walking beside you
> Gliding wrapt in a brown mantle, hooded
> I do not know whether a man or a woman
> —But who is that on the other side of you?

The notes comment thus: "The following lines were stimulated by the account of one of the Antarctic expeditions (I forget which, but I think one of Shackleton's): it was related that the party of explorers, at the extremity of their strength, had the constant delusion that there was *one more member* than could actually be counted."

Our gloss upon this gloss would be based on considerations of this sort: A friend once told us of a time when, after a notable change in his life, he found himself with a group of people whom he had known intimately before his change, but whom he had not, for a considerable time, seen thus together in one company. Despite all that had intervened, on this occasion something of the old relationship was reëstablished—except that a mild fantasy kept recurring. He found himself, again and again, counting the number of those present. No matter how many were in the room, he repeatedly caught himself thinking there must be one more. Afterwards, he explained the fantasy to himself thus: There *was* an extra person in the room. For he himself was of a divided mind, combining in one legal person both an earlier identity and a later one, so far as his attitudes toward these people were concerned. There were two of him, and in his fantasy he had kept saying so.

Is that not relevant to our present case? Here is the transitional poem *par excellence*. Here is the parched call for a new motive. The new motive is figured somewhat intellectualistically at the end of the poem; it is more of a resolve than an actual attainment; but it is present incipiently. And why, precisely, where the new motive is emerging, should it not show as a division within the poet himself? And why should not this division be symbolized in fantasies suggesting that this inward feeling had an outward counterpart (what Eliot the critic might have called an "objective correlative")?

The explanation is not essential to our case, however. For our purposes, one need grant only that the poem is transitional, midway between the early manner and the *Quartets*. The "peace" that it attains at the end is purely formal, like a conventional valediction. Though we are told that "shantih" means "the peace which passeth understanding," the expression as inserted here is several removes from a welling-forth in release. As regards the tests of mystic beatitude, it is little better than a slogan.

Since, even with the soundest of newly acquired positions, one might expect some backsliding, we need not be surprised that, three years later, with "The Hollow Men," the imagery of drought and impotence is even more extreme. However, the borrowing from the Upanishads is now replaced by stuttering, fragmentary abstractions from the Lord's Prayer. (The talk of the world's end, we take it, is a statement of *essential* motivation, hence also roundabout a figuring of the poet's motives.)

"Ash Wednesday" represents the new climb: "at the first turning of the second stair . . . at the second turning of the second stair . . . at the first turning of the third stair . . ." finally

> Fading, fading; strength beyond hope and despair
> Climbing the third stair.

Manifestly, there are still problems here. These stairs are arduous, lowly. In Dante, we are told that the higher one mounts, the easier becomes the climb. Saint Teresa, talking of a similar development, uses her figure of the watered garden, to name the mounting stages of prayer in the progress to mystic communion: first, the way that cannot be done without much labor, as with drawing water out of a well; next, by using a wheel with buckets; third, by letting a small stream run through the garden; and fourth, "By a good shower of rain falling; for then our Lord himself waters the garden, without any labor on our part; and this is by far the best method of all." In each stage, the procuring of the benefit is easier until in the fourth the downpour comes unbidden, somewhat as with the spontaneous rush Hopkins describes in his metaphor of the fruit bursting in the mouth:

> How a lush-kept plush-capped sloe
> Will, mouthed to flesh-burst,
> Gush!—flush the man, the being with it, sour or sweet,
> Brim, in a flash, full!

Admittedly, we here come upon ambiguities of the sort the psychoanalyst would make much of, when evaluating the mystic experience. We leave them unsettled. For our purposes, it is enough to note that, in mystic poetry, such ambiguities will be there, however you choose to interpret them (whether in terms of "nature," or of "grace").

Assuming that a wholly edifying symbol of the mount would contain all the elements we listed, and looking now for portions of the totality, we should first note that, in the Eliot poem, the mounting of the stairs remains arduous. There is no easing. Hence, on this score the imagery would not fully meet the requirements. But there is one notable transformation. For the image *has* taken on a much richer ethical content than it had in the passage we quoted from "Prufrock"; and it similarly transcends the wry reference to diffident courtship in "Portrait of a Lady":

> Except for a slight sensation of being ill at ease
> I mount the stairs and turn the handle of the door
> And feel as if I had mounted on my hands and knees.

In the *Quartets*, we find many such transformations. The rock of the parched desert in "The Waste Land" can become the rock of religious fortitude. The early laments about unfulfilled possibilities as regards one man's indecisions can give way to universal ponderings on human tentativeness. Talk of a rose garden can now stand ambiguously for: (1) purely secular delights; (2) vague adumbrations of exalted delights; (3) the final mystic unfolding and enfoldment. Fire can be of so double a nature that paradoxes are in order:

> The only hope, or else despair
> Lies in the choice of pyre or pyre
> To be redeemed from fire by fire.

Many related kinds of dialectical manipulation can be used. Since reduction to terms of highest generalization allows for permanent or "timeless" principles, and since "eternity" as so couched equals pure being (which in its transcending of conditions is indistinguishable from nothing) there are now even the possibilities of a good meaning for drought, as presented in terms of mortification and the *via negativa*:

> Internal darkness, deprivation
> And destitution of all property,
> Desiccation of the world of sense,
> Evacuation of the world of fancy,
> Inoperancy of the world of spirit.

The objectives of a movement are motionless. If you travel north, the direction itself does not move. And the structure of music just *is*, whether the music is heard or not. Dialectically, "everything moves but the abstraction of motion" (Marx). There are these opportunities for paradoxes.

A world of contingencies can now be placed antithetically to the unconditioned realm. The motivations here would be purely temporal, the unilluminated domain of the Apeneck Sweeneys, its time-mindedness viewed statistically, the early aloofness now having become contemplation *sub specie aeternitatis*.

Also, there can be the temporal as infused with the eternal. This is a variant of the Downward Way after the purifications of the Upward Way.

A moment in history being needed to make the mortal's glimpse of eternity possible, this moment can then become formative even of one's past, which is now envisaged transcendently, in the light of the indeterminate moment when consciousness as an eternal possibility and consciousness as a passing occasion in history come together (or, dialectically, where a term for the individual agent is taken as bridging the gap between terms for particulars and terms for universals). Here are the purely technical resources that allow for transformations whereby the earlier unfulfilled possibilities can become "footfalls" that "echo in the memory." And because they are now fused with the spirit of the formative moment, they have a double nature. The early, humbler possibilities can now be seen as vague adumbrations of the later, higher possibilities. The rose of the early rose garden (a choice not taken, but felt as beckoning) can imply the ultimate mystic rose (celebrated at the close of the fourth Quartet):

> When the tongues of flame are in-folded
> Into the crowned knot of fire
> And the fire and the rose are one.

In sum, we feel that, to approach the *Quartets* in terms of symbolic action, we should first ask ourselves what primary dialectical resources there are here, for exploitation. For, so far as verbal method is concerned, it is apparently the pyramid of dialectical mounting (the resources of Heraclitus) that this poet relies upon mainly, as the means that can endow the earlier down-turning images with new motives, by placing them in the upward-turning configuration that dialectical reduction readily makes possible. There are the terms for change and the terms for the universal, the unchanging; and the agent's mind or consciousness can be the term that mediates between the two orders—and thereby the poet can take us from a down-turning proposition to an up-turning one. Thus, the opening words of "East Coker" are: "In my beginning is my end"—and the last are: "In my end is my beginning." The first can sum up the world of contingent particulars, each leading by mechanical necessity to the next; the reversal of the proposition sums up the possibility of a shift to the realm of universal terms.

All told, the kinds of dialectical resources likely to be encountered here would be these:

> terms for the eternal;
> terms for the temporal;
> terms for the point of intersection between these two realms;
> terms for the temporal as infused with the eternal;
> terms that, in summing up the temporal, transcend it somewhat;
> terms that paradoxically glimpse the eternal in the momentary.

We might expect to find such resources embodied in varying kinds of imagery—and we might "call the plays" at any given point in the text by noting which of such resources is being utilized, and in what sort of images it is embodied.

8. PRINCIPLE OF THE OXYMORON

There is a ground, in both agent and scene, beyond the verbal. Yet as students of literature we should seek to disclose what purely verbal resources are being drawn upon, when the poet is talking of first and last things, or is using images that do not appeal merely to the senses, but derive radiance and vibrancy from their "anagogic" and/or "socio-anagogic" nature. And since the mystic communicates ultimately in terms of the oxymoron (the figure that combines contradictory elements within a single expression), we would see in the packing of an image or idea with divergent motives a more or less remote instance of "literary mysticism."

In a sense, of course, literary mysticism is a contradiction in terms. For as James points out, the mystic's experience is "ineffable." But poetry being expressive, mystic poetry would thus have to "express the ineffable" —and to do that it would have to be what Kant might have called a *Seiendes Unding*.

For practical purposes, however, no such embarrassments need beset us. We might experimentally acknowledge the existence of "mysticism proper" (as the term is applied to mystics like Saint John of the Cross and Saint Teresa, whom the Church has officially recognized). Next, noting the distinctive quality of their writings, we might, in the purely technical sense, apply the term mystical to other writers whose work possesses all or some of these same distinctive qualities. In some cases the likeness would be great; in other cases there would be but fragmentary resemblances. Even a trivial oxymoron might thus be related to the great mystic oxymorons. *But here one would be careful to note that he was dealing with a mere fragment of the mystical motive,* too tiny to be taken as an instance of "revelation," and at best indicating in "natural" terms a remote desire for the saint's "gracious" experience. (We would get such an analogue in turning from the theologian's "sanctifying grace" to its poetic counterparts in secular felicities of style.)

Thus Coleridge, looking at sea, sky, and mountain in a mood of entrancement, calling the scene "an awful omneity in unity," goes on to discuss it as a "perfect union of the sublime with the beautiful, so that they should be felt, that is, at the same minute, though by different faculties, and yet each faculty be predisposed, by itself, to receive the specific modifications from the other." (We are again citing from *Anima Poetae*.) By "beauty" he meant the appeal to the eye, "in shape and color." By the "sublime" he meant appeal "to the mind," through the scene's "immensity."

The passage well illustrates an explicit concern with what we might call the meeting of the empirically esthetic and the hierarchal. For although, in Coleridge's distinction, the beautiful would concern the purely sensory modes of appeal, his idea of the sublime would seem to involve the principle of hierarchy. The sublime resides in moral and intellectual "immensities." And even when the sublimities are represented by physical objects, like plains, sea, sky, and mountains, they are "moral" because the contrast between us and their might and proportion is forcefully hierarchic. Next, insofar as sensory order and social order affect each other, awed and delighted identification with physical power can call forth a transcendent feeling of personal *freedom*. That is, by the paradox of substance, one can imaginatively identify oneself with the mountain's massive assertiveness while at the same time thinking of one's own comparative futility. The identification thus gives a sense of freedom, since it transcends our limitations (though the effect is made possible only by our awareness of these limitations). The logical contradiction (of being simultaneously oppressed *and* free) is felt quasi-temporally, as a kind of fixed progression, or congealed sequence (as a change *from* oppression *to* freedom). The experience is thus "uplifting."* The hierarchic judgments that infuse tragic sublimity are exemplified in reverse by the devices of the ridiculous.

Identification in itself is a kind of transcendence. For instance, since the individual is to some extent distinct from his group, an identifying of him with the group is by the same token a transcending of his distinctness. Hence, just as persuasion terminates in the "meta-rhetoric" of pure persuasion, so identification attains its ultimate expression in mysticism, the identification of the infinitesimally frail with the infinitely powerful. Modes of identification with the "sublime" in nature would then be analyzable as large "fragments" of the mystical motive. And we could then discern faint traces in identifications and oxymorons still farther removed from the perfect paradigm.

Thus a novelist, ending on the death of his heroine, might picture the hero walking silently in the rain. No weeping here. Rather stark "understatement." Or look again, and do you not find that the very heavens are weeping in his behalf? As recall how Lear's brain-storm gets amplification, or Wagnerian scenic duplication, in the raging of the elements. (Act III, Scene IV, the thesaurus of madness: the fool, Edgar, Lear, and the storm, with Lear rounding out the pattern by his reference to "the tempest in my mind.") Or recall Verlaine's similar meteorological attitudinizing: *"Il pleure dans mon coeur comme il pleut sur la ville."*

Rain, then, as a symbol of weeping. There is even a certain covert apotheosis of the emotion here, making it "heavenly" thus roundabout. But note that rain may also be a symbol of fertility. It may figure the vernally emergent. To water with one's tears can thus also ambiguously be to prepare for the next phase. Thus, the idea of weeping can be translated into its imaginal equivalent, as rain. But the image of rain

---

* Do we not here follow much the same course as guided our ideas on "pure persuasion"? There we noted how, in the absolute, the three elements of persuasion (speaker, speech, and spoken-to) coexist in triune simultaneity, as a "timeless" form; and how some kind of interference becomes necessary if the pattern of persuasion is to be perpetuated in temporal terms. Here we see an exaltation or "uplift" got by identification with an eminence. And such a "tendency" is also a *fixity,* an attitudinal incipience, as of a person who retains the expectancy of setting out on a journey by continuing to stay just where he is.

in its own right contains also the idea of rebirth. (The sociologist Thomas D. Elliot has noted what he calls a "ritual of riddance," whereby the very rites that serve to honor the departed also serve as a device for cutting the bonds between the mourner and the deceased.)

We speak of this plot as hypothetical. But might not the recipe apply to the ending of Hemingway's *A Farewell to Arms?* Add the fact that the hero is there returning in the rain to his hotel. Does not such a destination stand for the potentiality of new intimacies?

Or again: If fire can stand for the burnings of carnal appetite, or for transcendent radiance (as with the flames of the *Paradiso*), or for the avenging tortures of hell, or for purification (as with the cleansing fire of the *Purgatorio*), it would not need to stand for these various motives one at a time, but might combine them in a single moment.

Thus we recall a dismal story, conceived by a sex-hungry adolescent, of a man trapped in a burning building with a woman. She had fainted in terror—and as his last act on earth he was about to violate her, when the floor collapsed, so that the two bodies were hurled together into the flames. Here the very situation which first introduced the intent of transgression and then forestalled it, finally made it possible on a "transcendent" level, in the image of the couple's fall into flames that consumed them jointly.

Attention has frequently been called to the scene in Dante's *Inferno,* acting out the metaphor that is in such expressions as "the winds of passion" or "gusts of passion." Since in this canto carnal sinners are pictured as being perpetually blown about by turbulent winds in hell, the image of their passions on earth becomes the image of their suffering (another kind of *pati*) in hell. But is there not a further ambiguity here? After listing several damned lovers, such as Semiramis, Cleopatra, Helen, Achilles, Paris, Tristan, each of whom is alone, Dante tells of Paolo and Francesca, who are being swirled about together. When he would talk with them, they come "as doves called by desire." And after Francesca has told sadly of the occasion when she and her lover had fallen into sin, Dante says: "I fainted with pity, as if I had been dying; and fell, as a dead body falls."

When we recall that Dante proclaimed himself born under the sign of Venus, might we not see in his fall an imagistic counterpart of the same transgression, though his identification with the sinning lovers is here translated into a form moralistically correct? At the very least, the fainting indicates his special susceptibility here. (After all, he is still in hell, and his progress through the three realms also figures a moral and intellectual growth for him personally.) But we would go a step further, asserting that in the particular sympathetic form which the expression of susceptibility takes, the image can also "transcendently" represent the same "fall."

In the mystery of Christ as sacrificial king, the principle of the oxymoron is obvious, in Christ's double role as victimized and victorious. And identification with the tragic scapegoat ranges from the remotely fragmentary to the immediate and total. When criminals were sentenced to death in Athens, instead of being executed at the time, they might be kept imprisoned for some occasion when the gods had to be honored or propitiated by a public sacrifice. Such a prisoner was called a *katharma,* a name for the ritually unclean, and of the same root as the word for purgation, in both its medical meanings and its application by Aristotle to the cathartic effects of tragedy. The ambiguities whereby the object of such a public offering is at once sacred and loathsome are paralleled most startlingly in Luther's radical conception of Christ as the bearer of the world's sinfulness. "All the prophets saw," he says in his comments on the Epistle to the Galatians, "that Christ would be the greatest brigand of all, the greatest adulterer, thief, profaner of temples, blasphemer, and so on, that there would never be a greater in all the world." Again: "God sent his only begotten Son into the world, and laid all sins upon him, saying: 'You are to be Peter the denier, Paul the persecutor, blasphemer, and wild beast, David the adulterer, you are to be the sinner who ate the apple in the Garden of Eden, you are to be the crucified thief, you are to be the person who commits all the sins in the world." (We translate the citations from *Kierkegaard et la philosophie existentielle,* by Léon Chestov.) With drastic logicality, Luther here deduced that the God-man must become immeasurably the worst criminal of all, in taking upon himself the full guilt of humankind. And you begin to wonder whether he threw his inkwell at the Devil, or at this scrupulously morbid vision of Christ as universal *katharma.*

9. ULTIMATE IDENTIFICATION

In his *Varieties of Religious Experience,* in the chapter on Mysticism, William James quotes many excerpts from a wide range of witnesses who testified that they had been mystically exalted at certain rare moments, and who attempted to describe the mystic state. For our closing text, let us make excerpts from these excerpts, and assemble the cullings into one consecutive, dithyrambic but rambling account, which should give a composite portrait of the experience, mystic state, though it does justice to no single person's testimony:

Feeling as if one were "grasped and held by a superior power" ... "prophetic speech, automatic writing, or the mediumistic trance" ... as if one were "born anew," as if one "had the door of paradise thrown wide open" ... "a mighty fascination" ... "transport" ... "the strangely moving power" ... "eternal inner message" ... the sense of having "been there before" ... a state wherein individuality seems "to dissolve and fade away into boundless being" ... a state where "death was an almost laughable impossibility" ... "an innate feeling that everything I see has a meaning" ... "indescribable awe" ... "a gradual but swiftly progressive obliteration of space, time, sensation, and the multitudinous factors of experience" ... insight as to how "the present is pushed on by the past, and sucked forward by the vacuity of the future" ... "the 'now' keeps exfoliating out of itself" ... " 'You could kiss your own lips, and have all the fun to yourself,' it says, if you only knew the trick" ... "the Anaesthetic Revelation is the Initiation of Man into the Immemorial Mystery of the Open Secret of Being, revealed as the Inevitable Vortex of Continuity" ... "I know—as having known—the meaning of Existence: the sane centre of the universe—at once the wonder and assurance of the soul—for which the speech of reason has as yet no name but the Anaesthetic Revelation" ... the sense of having felt "the undemonstrable but irrefragable certainty of God" ... "oneness with this Infinite Power, and this Spirit of Infinite Peace" ... "the disappearance, in these rapturous experiences, of the motor adjustments which habitually intermediate between the constant background of consciousness (which is the Self) and the object in the foreground" ... "grand and spacious, immortal, cosmogonic reveries ... moments divine, ecstatic hours; in which our thought flies from world to world, pierces the great enigma, breathes with a respiration broad, tranquil, and deep as the respiration of the ocean, serene and limitless as the blue firmament" ... "instants of irresistible intuition" ... "such a transparent summer evening. Swiftly arose and spread around me the peace and knowledge that pass all the argument of the earth" ... "a soul-sight of that divine clue and unseen thread which holds the whole congeries of things, all history and time, and all events, however trivial, however momentous, like a leashed dog in the hand of the hunter" ... "an inward state of peace and joy and assurance indescribably intense, accompanied with a sense of being bathed in a warm glow of light" ... "a feeling of having passed beyond the body, though the scene around me stood out more clearly and as if nearer to me than before, by reason of the illumination in the midst of which I seemed to be placed" ... "immersed in the infinite ocean of God" ... "I knew that the fire was within myself" ... "a sense of exultation, of immense joyousness accompanied or immediately followed by an intellectual illumination impossible to describe" ... "experimental union of the individual with the divine" ... "illumined by the light which proceeds from the prophetic source" ... "total absorption in God" ... "as if placed in a vast and profound solitude, to which no created thing has access, in an immense and boundless desert, desert the more delicious the more solitary it is. There, in this abyss of wisdom, the soul grows by what it drinks in from the well-springs of the comprehension of love" ... "*raptus* or ravishment" ... "stupefaction" ... "the habit of ecstasy" ... the soul is "adorned with virtues and adorned with supernatural gifts" ... "intoxicating consolations" ... "Invested with an invincible courage, filled with an impassioned desire to suffer for its God, the soul then is seized with a strange torment—that of not being allowed to suffer enough" ... "this sublime summit" ... "as from a smallness into a vastness ... as from an unrest to a rest" ... James on Dionysius: "It is *super*-lucent, *super*-splendent, *super*-essential, *super*-sublime, *super everything* than can be named" ...

Even if you attributed the mystic state to supernatural sources, you could properly expect it to have its bodily counterpart. Thus, we are told that, under ordinary conditions, the nervous system in action is somewhat like a bureaucratic structure where the carrying-out of one master aim requires great subordination of functions. The expressing of some impulses is contrived by the repression of others, as a child learns to walk by controlling, among various possibilities, its impulse to kick. If this is so (as neurologists like Sherrington tell us it is), then even on the bodily level there is an "infringement of freedom" within us, a sheerly physiological state of "inner contradiction." Discord would have become the norm. However if, going beyond it, the nervous system could fall into a state of radical passivity whereby all nervous impulses "attitudinally glowed" at once (remaining in a halfway stage of incipience, the *status nascendi* of the pursuit figured on Keats's Grecian Urn) there could be total "activation" without the overt acts that require repressive processes. Hence "contradictory" moments could exist simultaneously.

Since our ordinary knowledge reaches us through the senses, any such unusual sensory condition would likewise be felt as knowledge. The mystic would thus have a strong conviction that his experience was "noetic," telling him of a "truth" beyond the realm of logical contradictions, and accordingly best expressed in terms of the oxymoron. And indeed, why would it not be "knowledge"? For if the taste of a new fruit is knowledge, then certainly the experiencing of a rare and felicitous physical condition would be knowledge too, a report of something from outside the mind, communication with an ultimate, unitary ground.

When considering mysticism and its "fragments," we should attempt to account for as much as possible in purely naturalistic terms. These would seem to involve neurological, linguistic, and "socioanagogic" explanations. Even if convinced that some mystics have established genuine union not merely with a pantheistic ground but with an eminent super-natural, super-personal Creator, we should be willing to look for as many sheerly natural elements here as speculation and method can indicate. For if "sanctifying grace" works through "nature," as the theologians say it does, then the more exactly one discriminates in his locating of the purely natural motives, the sounder should be his arguments for the further element of "divine revelation." And in particular, when considering the mystic motive in literary works, we should make every effort to discount for language, the nervous system, and the "eminences" of social hierarchy.

However, recalling James's list, even if you believe in the validity of certain mystic revelations, you must agree that, besides mysticism and its "fragments," there are substitutes for mysticism, *Ersatzmystiken*, as with drugs, insanity, crime, and the many fantastic appetites by which men are goaded, as by demons.

Technically, in fact, the votaries of these cults *are* in communication with demons. For when means become ends, and are sought to the exclusion of all else, then the man for whom they are thus transformed does indeed identify himself with a universal purpose, an over-all unitary design, quite as with mystical communion. He has a god, and he can lose himself in its godhead. He is engrossed, enrapt, entranced.

And the test of such substitute mysticisms, we have said, is the transforming of means into ends. Thus, the votary of speed will seek speed for itself alone, for the sheer ecstatic agony of speed, as with Lawrence of Arabia when, home from the wars, he raced along country roads on his motorcycle—and in the attempt to avoid killing a pedestrian, he killed himself. His entrancement would be a mysticism of speed. And whatever frustrations and contradictions were riding him, he in the moments of his free expression was riding them, or riding with them.

There are many such *Ersatzmystiken*. There is a mysticism of sex, a cult wherein sex is sought as one's overwhelming aim, about which all other motives subordinately cluster. There are mysticisms of money, crime, drugs—and many other such goadings that transform some instrumentality of living into a demonic purpose.

Thus, too, there is the mysticism of war. There are those for whom war is a vocation, to whom the thought of the universal holocaust is soothing, who are torn by internal strife unless, in their profession as killers, they can commune with carnage. The imagery of slaughter is for them the way of mortification. As leaders, they are not mere "careerists," looking for a chance to let their friends in on government contracts at a high figure. They are mystic soldiers, devout—and killing is their calling. What of them?

They find solace in the thought of the great holocaust; and they love the sheer hierarchal pageantry, the Stoicism of the disciplinary drill, the sense of unity in the communal act of all the different military orders marching in step, or the pious contemplation of the parade made static and "eternal," in the design of a military burial grounds, with its motionlessly advancing rank and file of graves.

What of *these* votaries, when their motives are hierarchally amplified, and empowered, with the great new weapons? And what of the fragments of such dedication, among the petty officials and journalistic hacks who know nothing of this quiet, deep-lying terror, but would do their lowly bit towards its unleashing, in daily pronouncements and bureaucratic finaglings that add steadily to the general ill will throughout the world?

Mysticism is no rare thing. True, the attaining of it in its pure state is rare. And its secular analogues, in grand or gracious symbolism, are rare. But the need for it, the itch, is everywhere. And by hierarchy it is intensified.

In hierarchy it can exist under many guises. Nature, society, language, and the division of labor—out of all or any of these the hierarchic motive inevitably develops. Anagogically, if you will, but at least "socio-anagogically," in hierarchy reside the conditions of the "divine," the goadings of "mystery."

But since, for better or worse, the mystery of the hierarchic is forever with us, let us, as students of rhetoric, scrutinize its range of entrancements, both with dismay and in delight. And finally let us observe, all about us, forever goading us, though it be in fragments, the motive that attains its ultimate identification in the thought, not of the universal holocaust, but of the universal order—as with the rhetorical and dialectic symmetry of the Aristotelian metaphysics, whereby all classes of beings are hierarchally arranged in a chain or ladder or pyramid of mounting worth, each kind striving towards the *perfection* of its kind, and so towards the kind next above it, while the strivings of the entire series head in God as the beloved cynosure and sinecure, the end of all desire.

INDEX

A

Abailard, Peter, 174, 206
Abraham, 245-248, 251, 252
   Kierkegaard's psychology for, 246-247
   willingness to sacrifice, 252-253
Absurd, the, 254-256, 265
   cult of, 255, 259-260
   paradox of, 256
Adamitism, 121
Adams, Henry, 11
Address, rhetoric of, 37-39
Advancement of Learning, The, 80
Advantage, 60-61
   cult of, 274-275
Aeschines, 59, 69
Agonistic stress, 52-53
Alan of Lille, 173
Alcuin, 101
Alice in Wonderland, 267-268
Amplification, 69
Anima Poetae, 302, 325
Antidosis, 51
Anti-Semitism, 258
   as social mystery, 234-237
Apartment in Athens, 28
Appeal, formal, 65-69
Aquinas, Thomas, 220, 241, 278
Archetypes, 91
Areopagitica, 4
Aristotle, 25, 36, 49, 51, 52, 62, 77, 164, 230, 253, 299
   appeal to audiences, 38
   entelechy of, 14
   kinds of rhetoric, 70-71
   on audiences, 63-64
   on imagination, 78, 80, 81
   on opinion, 56-57
   on rhetorical form, 68-69
   on virtue, 55, 92
Arnold, Matthew, 12, 15, 17
   imagery of, 9-10
   self-immolation in poetry of, 7-10
Arnold, Thurman, 197
Ars Amatoria, 159-160
"Art of Cheating," 51
Art of Controversy, The, 91
Art of Rhetoric, The (Aristotle), 38, 49, 51, 56, 74, 93, 299
Art of Rhetoric, The (Wilson), 85
As You Like It, 58
"Ash Wednesday," 321
Attitudes Towards History, 12
Audiences, 63-64

Autonomous, the, 27-31
Autonomous principles, importance of, 28-29
Avicenna, 80

B

Babylon, 291-293
Back to Methuselah, 133
Bacon, Francis, 80, 82, 83, 133, 134
Bailey, Judith, 315
Barnabas, 240
Baudelaire, 304
Beatrice, 293
Beauty, 230-232
Bembo, Cardinal, 222, 227, 230
Bentham, Jeremy, 88, 98-99, 108, 151, 153, 154, 173, 196
   entities, 183-185
   on archetypes, 91
   on motives, 99-100
   recognition of interests, 102
   rhetorical analysis in, 90-95
Benthamite project, 93-95
Bentham's Theory of Fictions, 91
Bernal, J. D., 191
Bernard, 173, 174
Black Boy, 259
Blake, William, 82
Boccaccio, 227
Book of Fallacies, 91-92, 94, 100, 102
Book of the Courtier, 221-233, 234, 237, 239, 268
Bowl, The, 297
Brod, Max, 239, 243, 252
Bunyan, John, 262
Bureaucracy, 118
Burke, Edmund, 84, 223
Byzantium, 316

C

Cantico Espiritual, 309
Caplan, Harry, 80
Carlyle, Thomas, 90, 143, 164, 215, 219, 288
   doctrine of clothes, 122
   on mystery, 114-127
Cassiodorus, 101
Cassirer, Ernst, 41, 162, 166
Caste, 211
Castiglione, Baldassare, 221
Castle, The, 233-244, 268, 301
Censorship, 209
Chestov, Léon, 328
Christ, as sacrifice, 328
Churchill, Winston, 51, 113, 306

INDEX

Cicero, 53, 62, 63, 64, 70, 76-77, 98, 207, 222, 229
  list of devices, 66-67, 68
  on epideictic, 70-71
  on persuasion, 49-51
  on universality of rhetoric, 59-60
  styles of rhetoric, 72-74
Civilization, principles of, 223
Climb, social, 304-305
Clothes, 119-122, 215
Coleridge, Samuel Taylor, 10, 17, 68, 70, 78, 80, 82, 91, 144, 216
  cult of the impulse, 302
  moral of, 204
  on beauty and the sublime, 325
Commodities, cult of, 192
Communication, 176-177
Composition, 176
Compromise, 187
"Comus," 132, 287
Concealment, 173-174
Concrete universal, 190
Constitution of the Church and State, According to the Idea of Each, 91
Consubstantiality, 21
Context of situation, 203-212
Corneille, 132
Counterfeiters, The, 135
Courtier, perfect, 221-222, 224-226, 229
Courtship, 208-212
  abstract, 177
  caricature of, 233
  imagery of, 230
  paradigm of, 221-233
  principle of, 208, 234
  rhetoric of, 114
  social, 267-268
Covering, eulogistic, 100, 109
Crane, Hart, 203
Crassus, 49, 70
Crime and Punishment, 117
Croce, Benedetto, 66, 68
Cromwell, Oliver, 112-113
Crucifixion, 265-266

D

Dante, 218, 293, 303, 307, 327-328
  on language, 167-168
De Doctrina Christiana, 50, 53, 66, 74
De Gaulle, 100
De Lacy, E. A., 171
De Lacy, P. H., 171
De l'Amour, 161
De Oratore, 49, 53, 59, 66, 68, 74, 76, 229
De Planctu Naturae, 173
De Quincey, 49, 126, 143
De Vulgari Eloquentia, 167-169, 219
Death and Transfiguration, 14
"Death in Venice," 209
Decadence, and Other Essays on the Culture of Ideas, 150

Demosthenes, 36, 65, 68, 126
Demetrius, 58, 59
Des Modèles de la Nature et de la Fortune, 164
Deus sive Natura, 215
Devices, of speech, 78
  rhetorical, 65-67
Dewey, John, 133
Dialectic, 60
Dialogue, Platonic, 200-201
Diderot, 142 ff., 284
Dionysius the Areopagite, 118, 299
Dissociation de Idées, La, 150, 305
Divine, rhetorical radiance of, 294 ff.
Division, 45-46
  de Gourmont on, 150
  terms for, 176
Doctor Faustus, 312
Dodgson, C. L., 267
Dostoevsky, 117-118, 208, 269
Durante, Jimmy, 304

E

"East Coker," 324
Education, rhetoric of, 229
  in Kafka, 240-241
Education of Henry Adams, The, 11
Eisenhower, General, 210
Elation, 312-316
Elegy in a Country Churchyard, 124
Eliot, T. S., 12, 294, 311, 318-324
  down-turning mood in poetry of, 318-319
Elizabethan and Metaphysical Imagery, 72
Elliot, Thomas D., 327
Ellison, Ralph, 193
Émile, 31
"Empedocles on Etna," 7, 8
Empson, William, 123, 124, 126, 177, 219, 312
Encyclopedia of Religion and Ethics, 301
Encyclopedia of the Social Sciences, 24
English Pastoral Poetry, 123
Entelechy, Aristotelian, 14
Entities, 183-185
Epideictic, 70-72
Essays on the Principles of Human Action, 83-84
Essence, terms for, 13-14
Ethics (Aristotle), 92
Ethics (Spinoza), 308
Eunapius, 171
Evolution, Darwinian, 133, 137
  myth of, 137-140
Existentialism, 269
  in France, 254-255
  Kierkegaardian, 253-254

F

Falstaff, 209
Farewell to Arms, A, 327
Fear and Trembling, 243-252, 303

INDEX

Federation of American Scientists, 33
Finite species, 244-245
Flaubert, Gustave, 59
Folklore of Capitalism, 197
Form, rhetorical, 68-69
Freedom, personal, 325-326
Freud, Sigmund, 38, 135, 136, 242

G

Galileo, 162
Géante, La, 304
Genealogy of Morals, 31, 93
Genesis, 243
Genesis of Plato's Thought, 28
Genocide, 13, 32
German Ideology, The, 103, 104, 107, 109, 110, 115, 190
Gidé, Andre, 37, 135, 145, 262
Glamour, 210
God, concepts of, 275-276
　rhetorical names for, 298-301
　search for, 260
Golden Bough, 264
Gonzaga, Cesar, 228
Gorgias, 54
Gourmont, Remy de, 150-154, 269, 305-306
Grammar of Motives, 13, 14, 21, 22, 76, 89, 152, 162, 190, 196, 317
Gray, Thomas, 124
Great Chain of Being, 265
"Great Stone Face, The," 304
Gromyko, 33
Gulliver's Travels, 69, 257

H

Hawthorne, Nathaniel, 303
Hazing, an affirmation of mystery, 234-236
Hazlitt, William, 83-84
Hegel, 89, 104, 107
　concrete universal, 190
Hemingway, Ernest, 263, 327
Heraclitus, 323
Heroes and Hero-worship, 121
Hierarchy, metaphorical view of, 137-141
　mystery of, 306
Hildebart of Lavardin, 173
Hitler, Adolf, 23
Hitlerism, 30
Hobbes, Thomas, 87
Hoby, Thomas, 225
"Hollow Men, The," 321
Hollywood, 223, 224
Homosexuality, 115-116, 214
Hopkins, Gerard Manly, 309, 312-316, 321
　steps in the poetry of, 314
Hunger-Artist, The, 242

I

Iago, 36, 316
Idea, 84-86
　priority of, 133-137
　ruling, 105-106
　universal, 106-107
Identification, 19-27, 25, 27-31, 45-46, 55-59
　cunning, 35-37
　of autonomous activities, 27-29
　pastoral, 123-126
　ultimate, 35-37
Ideology, as rhetoric, 103
　definition of, 88
　meanings of, 104
Ideology and Utopia, 197-199
Idols of the Cave, 133-134
Image, 84-90
Imagery, at face value, 17-19
　effects of, 17-18
　of Matthew Arnold, 9-10
Images, kinds of, 10
　range of, 12
　social rating of, 296-298
Imagination, 78-84
Imagism, 88
Imitation, 131-132
Individual and His Society, The, 39
Infancy, 167-168, 174-175
Inferiority complex, 282
Inferno, 327
Inquiry, socioanagogic, 219-220
Institutio Oratoria, 49, 52, 59, 74
Intention, direction of, 154-158
Interpretation, medieval kinds of, 220
Invidious, the, 127-130, 131
Isaac, 245-246
Isidore, 101
Isocrates, 49, 51
Ivory Tower, The, 297

J

Jackson, Shirley, 242
James, Henry, 116, 215
　on the deity of things, 294-298
James, William, 328-331
Jesuits, 154, 156-157
Joseph, Sister Miriam, 66
Joyce, James, 156, 310
Joycing, 310
Julius Caesar, 94-95
Justice, 151-152, 280

K

Kierkegaard, 243-252, 265, 275, 303
　existentialism of, 253-255
　faith in the Absurd, 251
　psychology of, 246-247
　theme of weaning, 247-249
Kierkegaard et la philosophie existentielle, 328
Kill, cult of the, 260-267
Killing, fantasies of, 262-263
　motives in terms of, 19-20
King Lear, 326
Kluckhohn, C., 40, 43, 45

INDEX

Knowledge, sociology of, 198-203
Krafft-Ebing, 284

L

La Rochefoucauld, 61, 114, 164, 222
   motives in, 145-149
Lady Chatterley's Lover, 168, 258, 268
Laforgue, Jules, 318
Language, persuasive use of, 43-44
Laughter, cult of, 226-227
   in *The Castle,* 240
Law of the acceleration of history, 11-12
Lawrence, D. H., 168-169, 268
Lawrence of Arabia, 332
Leibnitz, 87
Lenin, 191, 195, 196
Levy-Bruhl, 305
Lives of the Philosophers, 171
Loeb Classical Library, 68
Long, Huey, 306
Longinus, 57-58, 65, 66, 74, 75, 83
   on imagination, 79
"Love Song of J. Alfred Prufrock," 303, 311, 318-319
Lovejoy, Arthur, 265
Lowrie, Walter, 244, 303
Luther, Martin, 328

M

Macbeth, 40
Machiavelli, 158-166, 171, 221
Magic, primitive, 40-42, 44
Magic Mountain, 15
Malinowsky, Bronislas, 43, 65, 269
   context of situation, 205-206
Man under communism, 109
Mann, Thomas, 15, 209, 239, 242
   on Kafka, 233-234
Mannheim, Karl, 197-198, 200-202, 205, 207, 211
Marcus Aurelius, 236
"Mario and the Magician," 209
Mark Antony, 94-95
Mark Twain, 236
Marshall, General, 187
Marx, Karl, 36, 118, 123, 136, 137, 211, 219, 308, 311, 313
   on Hegel, 190
   on mystification, 101-114, 220
   theory of a ruling class, 105
Marxism, 24, 103-104
   analysis of rhetoric, 102-104
   as a vocabulary, 195-197
   as an ideology, 103-104, 199
   persuasion in, 189-197
   terminology of, 101, 194-195
Masefield, John, 259
Maya, 219
Mazzoni, 79
McKeon, Richard, 101, 169, 171, 173, 206
Mead, George Herbert, 90, 193

Meaning of Meaning, The, 65, 205
Means, selection of, 155
"Mechanical Operation of the Spirit, The," 257
Mei Lan-fang, 273
Mein Kampf, 104
Merchant of Venice, 193-194
Metamorphosis, 242
Military training, 263
Miller, Henry, 209
Milton, John, 3-6, 10, 15, 17, 287
Molière, 36
Montesquieu, 119
Motive, courtly, 212
   covering, 99-101
   hierarchic, 284
   Machiavelli's concern with, 165-166
   national, 165
   pecuniary, 127-129
   sacrificial, 164-166
   suicide as, 5-6
Motivation, Christian totality of, 75-76
Mountain design, fecal meanings of, 308
Mountain-climbing, 302-303
Mountings, range of, 301-313
Murder in the Cathedral, 12
Mystery, 114-127
   natural, 175
   of social relations, 125-126, 175, 234
   sources of, 180
Mystic state, composite portrait of, 329-330
Mysticism, 331-332
Mystification, as deception, 178-180
   Carlyle on, 114-127
   Karl Marx on, 101-114
Myth, esthetic, 203-204
   Utopian, 200-202
Myth of the State, 41, 162
Mythic ground, 203
Myths of Plato, The, 200

N

National Socialist militarism, rationale of, 32
Native Son, 117, 194
"Navaho Witchcraft," 40
Negro in America, 193-195
Neo-Platonist pattern, 245
Neurosis, social origins of, 280-282
Neutralization, 96-97
Neveu de Rameau, 142
New Yorker, 63, 240
Nietzsche, 31, 93, 145, 168

O

"Ode on a Grecian Urn," 204
Offices, rhetorical, 73-78
Ogden, C. K., 91
On Methods of Inference, 171
On Style, 58
On the Imagination, 80

INDEX

On the Sublime, 74
Opinion, 53-54
    Aristotle on, 56-57
Oratory, styles of, 73
Order, 265
Ovid, 126, 159, 160, 161, 171
Ownership, 33
    roots of, 130
Oxymoron, principle of, 324-328

P

Pantomime, 143-144
    positions of, 284
Paradiso, 327
Pareto, 104
Pascal, 154-158
Pater, Walter, 10, 17
Peer Gynt, 233
Peitho, 51-52, 277
Personality types, terms for, 15-16
Persuasion, 176-179
    competitive and public ingredient in, 54
    Marxist, 189-197
    pure, 267 ff.
    religious, 291-294
    ultimate form of, 274
Phaedrus, 177, 230
Philodemus, 171
Philosophy of History, 89
Philosophy of Literary Form, The, 311
Pico Della Mirandola, 80, 83, 169
Plato, 153, 188, 200, 230
Platonic dialogue, 200-201
"Poetry and Philosophy in the Twelfth Century, the Renaissance of Rhetoric," 173
Polytheism, 255
Portrait of the Artist as a Young Man, A, 156, 314
Possessed, The, 269
Pride, 149
Prince, The, 158, 159, 161-162, 165
Property, identifying nature of, 23-24
    mystery of, 264-265
    private, 107-108
Proudhon, 152
Provincial Letters, 154
Psychology (Aristotle), 80
Psychopathia Sexualis, 284
Psychosis, hierarchic, 281-283
Pudd'nhead Wilson, 236
Purgatorio, 303, 307, 327

Q

Quartets, 321-323
Quintilian, 51, 53, 59, 62, 70, 85
    classification of rhetoric, 72-73
    on persuasion, 49

R

Rabelais, 156
Rackham, H., 68

Rage for Order, 296
Rain, 326
Realms of Being, 82
Red and the Black, 161, 304
Redemption, 31-32
Regina, 245, 248, 249, 251
Reich, Wilhelm, 208
Relativism, 198-199
Religion, essence of, 266
"Religious Musings," 10
Republic, The, 152, 188
Res tegenda, 99, 173
Rhabanus Maurus, 101
Rhetoric, 22-23
    administrative, 158-166
    basic function of, 41
    classification of, 73-74
    devices of, 66-67
    epideictic, 70-72
    in the Middle Ages, 169-174
    magic in, 40-42
    Marxist analysis of, 102-104
    nature of as addressed, 38-39, **45-46**
    realistic function of, 43-46
    traditional kinds of, 70
    traditional principles of, 89-90
"Rhetoric in the Middle Ages," **169, 206**
Rhetoric (Aristotle), 70, 253
Richards, I. A., 90, 216
Rimbaud, Arthur, 143, 145
"Rime of the Ancient Mariner," **204**
Ritual, 273
Road Through the Wall, The, 242
Robin Hood, 264
Robinson, Victor, 284
Roosevelt, Franklin D., 62, 304
Rousseau, 31, 214

S

Sacrifice, as essence of religion, 266
    willingness to, 251-253
Saint Augustine, 52, 53, 66, 81, 101, 169, **293**
    on persuasion, 50
    rhetoric of, 74-77
Saint John of the Cross, 309, 325
Saint Paul, 75, 76-77
Saint Teresa, 321, 325
Samson Agonistes, 3-6, 17, 28
    suicidal motive in, 5
Santayana, George, 82, 294
Sappho, 208
Sartor Resartus, 90, 114-115, **118-121**
Saturnalia, Roman, 224
Schopenhauer, 91
Science, autonomy of, 28-30
    possibilities of, 32-35
    redemption in, 31-32
Season in Hell, 143
"Secularization of the Devil, The," 312
Self-deception, 35-37

Self-denial, 271-272
Self-immolation, 7-10
Self-interference, 269-270, 279
Self-love, 147, 149
Sense of the Past, 297
Seven Types of Ambiguity, The, 126
Sex relations, mystery of, 115-117
Shakespeare, William, 36, 116, 193, 212
Shakespeare's Use of the Arts of Language, 66
Shaw, George Bernard, 133
Shelley, P. B., 136
Shylock, 193-194, 311
Sic et Non, 206
Sir Gawain and the Green Knight, 214
Situation, context of, 203-212
Smith, Adam, 313
Social relations, mystery of, 125-126, 234
Socrates, 55, 56, 177, 188, 230
Sohrab and Rustum, 7-9
Some Versions of Pastoral, 123
Sophists, 51, 60
Sorel, Julian, 36, 145, 304-305
Soul of Man Under Socialism, 116
Speech, effective devices of, 79
Spinoza, 78, 87, 215, 289, 308
Spirit, 82
Spoils of Poynton, The, 294-298
Stendahl, 36, 37, 145, 161, 304
Stewart, J. A., 200
Stoics, 51, 60
Strauss, Richard, 14
Stress, agonistic, 52-53
Suadere, 52
Substance, ambiguities of, 21
Suggestion, post-hypnotic, 210
Suicide, as motive, 5-6
    Existentialist notion of, 268
Sullivan, Sister Therese, 66
Summa Theologica, 220
Surrealism, 88
Swift, Jonathan, 257, 308
Symbol, as enigma, 120
Symbolic, 22-23
    identities of, 27-28
Symbolism, 88

T

Table of the Springs of Action, 91, 99
Tanala of Madagascar, 39
Tartuffe, 36
Tegumen, 99, 173
Terminology, Marxist, 61, 194-195
    neutral, 96-97
Terms, dialectical, 184-187
    positive, 183-184
    ultimate, 188-189
Teufelsdröckh, 118
Thales, 301

Theology, 170-171
Theory of the Leisure Class, 127-131, 134, 305
Things, deity of, 294-296
Titles, 86
Tonalities, 98
Tonio Kröger, 233, 234
Topics, 56-57, 62-63
Tractatus Theologico-Politicus, 78
Transformation, imaging of, 10-13
    tonal, 310
Trial, The, 234
Tristan, 15, 242
Truman, Harry S., 25
Truth, 76-77
Turn of the Screw, 116-117, 215
Tuve, Rosemond, 72, 79
Twelfth Night, 214

U

Unconscious, The, 167-169
Upanishads, 321
Urbino, Duke of, 221
Utopias, as ideologies, 199-202

V

Varieties of Religious Experience, 328
Veblen, Thorstein, 24, 36, 127-132, 224, 263, 305
Venus and Adonis, 208, 212-221
    explained in social terms, 215-220
    homosexual implications in, 214
Venusberg, 303, 304
Verlaine, 326
Vetch, Fleda, 295-296
Virtue, components of, 55

W

Wallace, Henry, 25
Warren, Austin, 296-297
Washington, Booker T., 193
Waste, 128
"Waste Land, The," 319-320, 322
Weaning, 247-249
Weeping, 326
Westcott, Glenway, 28
What Is to Be Done? 195, 196
Wilde, Oscar, 10, 17, 116
Will, 80-81
Wilson, Thomas, 85
Winspear, David, 28
Wit and Its Relation to the Unconscious, 38
Witchcraft, Navaho, 40, 45
    rhetoric of, 45
Wright, Richard, 117, 194, 259

Y

Yeats, William Butler, 296, 309, 316-317